THE OCCULT IN NATIONAL SOCIALISM

"Much ink has been spilled on the topic of occult Nazism, but this book goes wider and deeper than most previous literature on this subject. It aims, as the author writes, 'to bring the question of Nazi occultism into sharper focus with a more refined lens of understanding.' One of the great merits of the book is that Flowers examines not only the question of the actual nature and extent of occult elements in the Nazi movement and its antecedents but also the huge amount of myth and hype that has grown up around the subject since the end of the Second World War. A central theme of the book is the power of myths, including those that 'lead to misery and destruction,' as in the case of the Third Reich. This searching book sheds new light on a troubled subject."

CHRISTOPHER MCINTOSH, AUTHOR OF *OCCULT RUSSIA: PAGAN, ESOTERIC, AND MYSTICAL TRADITIONS*

"Going way beyond the typical sensationalistic tabloid press approach toward the occult undercurrents of National Socialism, as adopted invariably by most authors on the subject for far too many decades, this book is equally a highly welcome counterweight to Nicholas Goodricke-Clarke's pioneering scholarly study. Himself a well-acknowledged and established occult practitioner as well as an academic scholar, Stephen Flowers deploys the entire arsenal of his critical tradecraft, both emic and etic (in-depth research, shrewd analysis, informed interpretation, historical contextualization, etc.), to present us with a sweeping detailed overview of the contemporary occult and political scene and its eventual culmination in the horrors of World War II and the Holocaust: a sober—and sobering—depiction that is certain to set new standards for coming research well into the foreseeable future."

FRATER U.˙.D.˙., AUTHOR OF *PRACTICAL SIGIL MAGIC, HIGH MAGIC*, AND *LIVING MAGIC*

"Although nothing is 'easy' about this book—not its argument, subtleties, or beneath-the-floorboards history—Stephen E. Flowers's study of Nazism and the occult resounds with vitality and depth; this work must be encountered and reckoned with by anyone who hopes to make a serious consideration of its subject."

MITCH HOROWITZ PEN AWARD–WINNING AUTHOR OF
OCCULT AMERICA AND *UNCERTAIN PLACES*

"In *The Occult in National Socialism,* Stephen Flowers approaches this murky and phantasmal historical grotto with a bright lantern of illumination, an undistorted analytical lens, and a keen, unflinching eye. His exploration dispels propaganda from all sides, including that of the Nazis themselves as well as from the Catholic and Protestant churches; overturns cartloads of dubious claims; and punctures a host of untethered hot-air balloons fueled by vaporous theorizing. But this is more than just a debunker's manual. Flowers is equally adept at cataloging and elucidating the hidden (or even 'occult') influences, shadowy organizations, and mysterious personalities that *did* exist in the pre-Nazi period and the Third Reich. Likewise groundbreaking is the final part of the book: a methodical survey of the postwar era of mythologizing, in which the smoldering ashes of a defeated criminal aggressor-state became a quaggy garden for the cultivation of bizarre tales and pseudo-history. Overall, this volume is a complex study of competing spiritual and ideological forces in a period when the obscured truth often turns out to be more unsettling than the overblown fictions that replaced it."

MICHAEL MOYNIHAN, PH.D., COAUTHOR OF *LORDS OF CHAOS*
AND COEDITOR AND TRANSLATOR OF *THE RUNE POEMS:*
A REAWAKENED TRADITION

"Stephen Flowers rises to the unenviable task of sorting fact from fiction in one of the most notorious questions of the 20th century: To what extent was the Third Reich influenced by and reliant on occult ideas in its quest for world domination? The further we are removed in time from these earth-shattering events, the more the facts about the Nazis' supposed occult interests will be lost in neo-mythology; we need someone like Flowers to put this history in its proper context and to give a sober assessment of what actually lay behind the few genuine occult interests at work within the Third Reich. Flowers skillfully examines the influences on the intellectual and spiritual life of Germany in the early 20th century, while avoiding the typical sensationalist narrative that takes every insinuation of sinister influence at face value. The bar is now considerably higher with the publication of this long-awaited expert analysis."

TOBY CHAPPELL, GRAND MASTER OF THE ORDER OF THE TRAPEZOID
AND AUTHOR OF *INFERNAL GEOMETRY AND THE LEFT HAND PATH*

THE OCCULT IN NATIONAL SOCIALISM

THE SYMBOLIC, SCIENTIFIC, AND MAGICAL INFLUENCES ON THE THIRD REICH

STEPHEN E. FLOWERS, PH.D.

Inner Traditions
Rochester, Vermont

Inner Traditions
One Park Street
Rochester, Vermont 05767
www.InnerTraditions.com

Text stock is SFI certified

Cataloging-in-Publication Data for this title is available from the Library of Congress

ISBN 978-1-64411-574-9 (print)
ISBN 978-1-64411-575-6 (ebook)

Printed and bound in the United States by Lake Book Manufacturing, Inc. The text stock is SFI certified. The Sustainable Forestry Initiative® program promotes sustainable forest management.

10 9 8 7 6 5 4 3 2 1

Text design and layout by Debbie Glogover
This book was typeset in Garamond Premier Pro with Gill Sans MT Pro and VTC Horoscope used as display typefaces

To send correspondence to the author of this book, mail a first-class letter to the author c/o Inner Traditions • Bear & Company, One Park Street, Rochester, VT 05767, and we will forward the communication, or contact the author directly at **www.seekthemysteries.com**.

ACKNOWLEDGMENTS

I especially wish to thank Michael Moynihan for his erudite help in many aspects of this project. Others who were of significant help in one way or another include Michael A. Aquino, Joshua Buckley, Larry Camp, Robert Zoller, Paul Newell, Seth Tyrssen, Mitch Horowitz, Dr. Ulrich Hunger, Stephen Wehmeyer, Timothy Ryback, and Cort Williams.

All errors of fact, or heresies of interpretation are, of course, entirely my own, for which I take complete responsibility.

✳ ✳ ✳

NOTE TO THE READER

The author of this book is not a National Socialist, nor is he a promoter of Nazi ideology, which he finds reprehensible on many counts. At the same time this is not an anti-Nazi propaganda work. As a scholar, the author simply seeks to understand the hidden dimensions of German history that led to the Nazi period as well as the myths and legends that followed in its wake. Just because the author does not deploy pejorative adjectives at every opportunity (an apparent shielding technique used by many) does not mean he agrees with an idea. As an act of political disclosure, the author is a libertarian and proponent of tribal (not nationalistic) organization of society. He is also a Ph.D. (1984) scholar trained in Germanic philology and comparative mythology.

CONTENTS

Abbreviations

ADG *Arbeitsgemeinschaft Deutscher Glaubensbewegung* (Alliance of the German Faith Movement)

BfG *Bund für [Deutsche] Gotterkenntnis* (League for the [German] Knowledge of God)

DAP *Deutsche Arbeiterpartei* (German Workers' Party)

FS *Fraternitas Saturni* (Brotherhood of Saturn)

Ger. German

GGG *Germanische Glaubens-Gemeinschaft* (Germanic Faith Community)

HJ *Hitler-Jugend* (Hitler Youth)

NS National Socialist

NSDAP *Nationalsozialistische Deutsche Arbeiterpartei* (National Socialist German Workers' Party)

OBR Order of the Black Ram

ONT *Ordo Novi Templi* (Order of the New Templars)

OTO *Ordo Templi Orientis* (Order of Oriental Templars)

RSHA *Reichssicherheitshauptamt* (Reich Main Security Office)

RuSHA *Rasse- und Siedlungshauptamt* (Race and Settlement Main Office)

SA *Sturmabteilung* (Storm Division)

SS *Schutzstaffel* (Protection Division)

TS Theosophical Society

UFK *Unabhängige Freikirche* (Independent Free Church)

WO Werewolf Order

PREFACE

It has been more than seventy-five years since the fall of the Third Reich, yet it continues to fascinate the minds of the world—both the rational and irrational. This strange fascination is only likely to increase over the course of the twenty-first century and beyond. Hitler and National Socialism have been inexorably linked—rightly or wrongly—to the whole topic of genetics, genetic engineering, and eugenics. As the future will bring us an accelerating use of genetic technologies, it is also likely that the myths and realities of the Third Reich will be used, positively and negatively, in the coming debates over such issues. But this is only part of the reason why an examination of the dark corners of National Socialist ideology is warranted. In placing these ideas into a general and objective context—certainly without extolling them as virtuous, but at the same time not condemning them as the ultimate evil—perhaps a more rational basis of thought and discussion can be established.

I first encountered the idea of "Nazi occultism" when I read Trevor Ravenscroft's *The Spear of Destiny* in the springtime of 1973. This reading was soon followed by *The Morning of the Magicians* by Louis Pauwels and Jacques Bergier. As fascinating as these sorts of books were, I had questions about their validity. Many of my suspicions were confirmed just a few months later when I began to collect and read the works of Guido von List. List was described by Ravenscroft as a drug fiend and sex maniac who was driven out of Vienna by the good burghers of that city. At the time I was an undergraduate student majoring in German, but it did not take me more than a few hours of firsthand research to dispel all this as sensationalistic and propagandistic nonsense. It soon became clear to me just how much of the *mythology* of Nazi occultism was driven by wartime and postwar anti-German propaganda. This subject is the focus of part 4 of this book.

The present work is a departure from previous books on the general subject of the Nazis and the occult. Contrary to most of what has been published in this genre, it is intended to be an objective study in the history of ideas rather than a series of vague, innuendo-laden biographical studies of admittedly eccentric figures or a monomaniacal diatribe dedicated to a particular sectarian interpretation of history—such as one focused on the mystical power of the "Spear of Destiny" or the idea that the Nazis were inheritors of the Grail and the Cathar legacy. Even otherwise admirable scholarly efforts, such as that of Nicholas Goodrick-Clarke, make use of a limited or imprecise definition of what is actually meant by "the occult."

When contemporary observers look back on the filmic records of National Socialist Germany, or read the ideas of its theoreticians, there can be no doubt that there was *something* occurring there that was extraordinary in the annals of the history of tyrannical states. But just because something was going on, it does not follow that everything imaginable was present. The discovery of the astounding truth requires a sober approach.

Clearly, one of the long-term aims of those who wish to imply that the Nazis were indeed "pagans" or "in league with the devil" is to misdirect the current observer from the truth: the orthodox Christian churches (both Catholic and Lutheran) were in large measure culpable in the crimes of the Nazis. When Pope Benedict XVI was named as head of the Roman Catholic Church, and the fact then came out that he had been a member of the Hitler Youth as a boy, I remember one commentator on a major news network made a remark to the effect that he, Ratzinger, should be forgiven for this because "Nazism was a pagan thing anyway, and had nothing to do with Christianity." For me, at *that* moment, the purpose of the continued postwar demonizing of the Nazis became clear: it was a sophisticated attempt to blame a straw man for crimes committed in the name of a "leading citizen of the world"—the Christian Church. The myth of Nazi occultism was not just a sensationalistic way for crackpot authors to make a few dollars, it was a very useful tool in directing culpability for the crimes of the Nazis away from their Christian coconspirators by placing the entire blame on relatively unimportant, and often virtually nonexistent, "occult forces" and "pagan movements." So, in a manner of speaking, this book is also in small measure an attempt to reopen the file on what some have considered a closed case of mass murder. The true criminal may be a charming pillar of society, while the "usual suspect" is a relatively powerless and unpopular minority. We are accustomed to seeing this sad story play itself out in small-town America, but not on the stage of world history.

Another general tendency in this book is to supply the reader with more historical background and cultural context than is usually the case in such books. This is necessary since the educational system in the United States has progressively diminished the quantity and quality of objective historical instruction provided to the broad mass of the general public in government schools since the mid-1980s. The low level of popular education brought about by this trend allows politicians, teachers, and self-appointed cultural critics to rewrite the past in various ways to make the electorate and/or "customer base" more malleable. (This is a technique that was pioneered by both Bolshevik and National Socialist cultural manipulators.)

Finally, since I began doing research for this study as many as forty years ago, the whole folkloristic aspect of what the word *Nazi* even means has changed drastically. Over these years, Nazism has gone from being a term for an extreme political ideology belonging to a (defeated) enemy state to an abstract symbol for absolute, yet ill-defined, cosmic and perpetual evil. No small role in this process was played by the "Nazi occult" literature we will examine in chapter 13. It is hoped that this study will bring more logical and rational control to the topic.

STEPHEN E. FLOWERS

WOODHARROW

BEGUN: NOVEMBER 11, 2000 (20:00)

FINISHED: JULY 20, 2020 (12:00)

ESSENTIAL QUESTIONS THAT MUST BE ANSWERED

"Nazi occultism" is a much-abused topic in the history of ideas. One is tempted on all points to associate the term with the genre of literature that began in the 1960s and early 1970s with popular books like *The Morning of the Magicians* or *The Spear of Destiny*. But, in fact, the genre had started much earlier, during the course of the Second World War itself, with books such as Lewis Spence's *The Occult Causes of the Present War*. This kind of literature will be more fully explored and analyzed in the fourth part of this book, which is a study of the postwar mythology of Nazi occultism.

Another kind of study, which has unfortunately been much rarer, has used rational models and more careful scholarly research methods and has yielded some interesting results. Nicholas Goodrick-Clarke's *The Occult Roots of Nazism* is a classic study of this sort and could be profitably read in conjunction with this book. The only weakness of Goodrick-Clarke's study is that in his zeal to demonize the German nationalist and paganist strain of occult thought, he omits any real treatment of Christian, scientific, or even conventional forms of occultism (such as astrology and psychic phenomena).

But all of this recent body of literature is flawed by two tendencies. The first tendency is the sensationalistic approach of most authors. Moreover, this is usually marked by an anti-Nazi motivation, although in some cases subtly pro-Nazi leanings can be detected. It is very often the case that literature written about the Nazis and the occult contains some all-encompassing single theory for explaining Nazism in terms of a "cosmic evil." The second tendency is not much different from the first, except that the metanarrative used to criticize National Socialism is more in the contemporary intellectual mainstream. James Webb, for example, sees the kind of occultism exemplified by the Nazis as a "flight from reason," while Goodrick-Clarke, utilizing a subtle Marxist template, sees the *völkisch* nationalists as irrational *reactionaries* to the modern socioeconomic progress being evidenced in the nineteenth and early twentieth centuries.

It is my intention here to present an objective study of the history of ideas. This book does not contain an all-encompassing theory about the role of "the occult" or any other subcultural set of ideas to explain Nazism, nor do I seek to vilify the Nazis as the epitome of cosmic evil. I do not do this because it seems to me to be intellectually dishonest and inaccurate. It is my hypothesis that the use of pejorative adjectives to modify any noun that indicates a person or thing connected with National Socialism is simply a formula used by contemporary academic intellectuals to protect themselves from suspicion among their colleagues and to give their work an aura of moral superiority.

The major thesis of this book is that there were a variety of subcultural and countercultural impulses feeding into the world of Central Europe around the turn of the twentieth century. Many could be called occult, whether they belonged to the Romantic symbolic traditions of the völkisch movement, or to the (pseudo-)scientific realm of the Monists and eugenicists, or to the more usual areas of the "secret sciences." These three streams of ideas, the symbolic, the scientific, and the occult proper, account for the majority of traits found in National Socialism. An overarching element that often binds them all together is a culturally pervasive völkisch ideology. The völkisch idea can present in all three of these streams of thought in late nineteenth- and early twentieth-century Mitteleuropa. Ultimately, even this tripartite approach under the umbrella of the völkisch ideology will not exhaustively treat every possible element that might be considered an "occult" trait in the doctrines and practices of National Socialism, but it will perhaps give a broader overview, through a more objective lens, than has been offered heretofore by other authors.

Whether we look at the occult sciences, the symbolic traditions, or even the natural scientific theories of the period in question (which we can define as 1845–1945), a certain völkisch element can often be discerned. This is not to say that all of these areas of culture were entirely dominated by the völkisch idea, only that what we will call here "volkism" (folkism) was able to infuse itself to one small degree or another into all three of these areas of intellectual life over the approximately hundred-year span of time under discussion.

In his 1964 book *The Crisis of German Ideology,* George Mosse discusses the idea of volkism as follows:

> The set of ideas with which we are concerned in this work has been termed "Volkish"—that is, pertaining to the "Volk." "Volk" is one of those perplexing German terms which connotes far more than its specific meaning. "Volk" is a much more comprehensive term than "people" for to German thinkers ever since the birth of German romanticism in the late eighteenth century "Volk" signified the union of a group of people with a transcendental "essence." This "essence" might be called "nature" or "cosmos" or "mythos," but in each instance it was fused to man's innermost nature, and represented the source of his creativity, his depth of feeling, his individuality, and his unity with other members of the Volk. (Mosse 1964, 4)

Birken (1995, 27) questions Mosse's implication that this concept is somehow unique to the Germans, but for our purposes it is quite enough to understand that such a völkisch movement did exist and did develop an overriding importance within the political right in German-speaking areas of Europe. The völkisch idea elevates the nation,* the race, to a level of transcendental importance; it, and what

---

*The term *völkisch* is greatly misunderstood. It has come to mean "racial" and, more confusingly, "pagan." It is really a native German term for what we call "nationalistic." The Latin word *natio* refers to "birth." A nation is, in the ancient way of thinking, a people bound by common birth; that is, they are naturally (another word derived from the same Latin root), "biologically," or genetically linked. It is upon this genetic link that the idea of a nation was originally formed. This was an ideal in ancient times, and an ideal

is good for it, becomes the *summum bonum* of cultural life. The *Volk* [pron. "folk"] is made up of individuals inexorably bound together by a common race, language, and culture and who were born and raised in a certain landscape. Hence the phrase *Blut und Boden* (blood and soil) used to describe the volkist sentiment.

This idea is of paramount importance to our topic because for a huge segment of Middle Europeans its tenets permeate all elements of intellectual culture as a deep-structure myth. Because the idea of volkism appears to be in and of itself a mystical or mythical idea, it is only natural that it should have quickly developed in those areas of culture interested in the occult and symbolic traditions. It may seem more difficult to understand how it could have found so much hospitality among the natural sciences. However, in science the nineteenth and early twentieth centuries were dominated by concerns over evolution (Lamarck in 1809, Darwin in 1859, and Haeckel in 1866) and the biological, or organic, metaphor was for the nineteenth century what the astrophysical, or mechanical, metaphor had been in the seventeenth and eighteenth centuries. Whereas the Deistic followers of Newton's theories saw the world (and man) as a "great clockwork," the Romantics, and later the readers of Darwin, began to see the world (and man) in organic, and hence evolutionary, terms. These ideas easily lent themselves to occult interpretations and reinforced the longed-for revival of ancient symbolic traditions of a particular *Volk*.

Because of the frequent references to "Nazi occultism," a precise understanding of the meaning of this terminology is fundamental. In the latter half of the twentieth century, the occult has become such an overexposed aspect of popular culture that it has almost become too bourgeois and clichéd to be taken seriously. This should not, however, be allowed to color our views of the ways the occult was received in times past. Studies have focused on the occult origins of everything

---

(*cont. from p. 3*) supported by mythology. Nations were said to be descended from a common ancestor, for example. Only a minority of Germans saw in this model an argument for a return to pagan, pre-Christian religion or culture. Before more recent times, the term *völkisch* could denote a nationalistic understanding of Christianity, and for the most part this is how most Germans in the early twentieth century thought of the term.

from modern science* to modern psychoanalysis.† None of this should surprise us, as the occult literally refers to the "hidden," or something which is "closed off,"‡ and when intellectual explorers and adventurers set out to uncover new methods and truth, it seems inevitable that they must cross the line between the known and the unknown. It also stands to reason that these mind-voyagers should at some point or another be inspired by tales of earlier attempts to reach similar terrae incognit*ae* as they themselves sought. As often as not these earlier explorers, or less "qualified" contemporaries, undertook their travels in obscure or occult fields.

The idea of the occult in the context of the present study can be defined as *ideas or theories, and practices connected with these paradigms, which have either been rejected by, or which have not yet been accepted by, the established intellectual model of a given culture.*

A more elaborate and critical definition of the occult—or more precisely—the esoteric, has been forwarded by Antoine Faivre (1994, xiii; xv–xx) and employed by Rosenthal (1997, 2–5) in the context of a study of the occult in Russian and Soviet culture. According to this

---

*During the Enlightenment, many pioneers of the new scientific methods were steeped in the occult ideology of the Renaissance, rooted as it was in the Hermetic and Neoplatonic traditions of antiquity. For this reason, many of their operating assumptions originated there. This is not to say they were incorrect, but merely to point out that even modern science has occult roots. Many scholarly works have been devoted to this topic. One of the most recent is John Henry, *Religion, Magic, and the Origins of Science in Early Modern England* (London: Routledge, 2018).

†As the "science" of psychology is linked to the very kinds of things that involve the occult world, it is only natural that the roots of this relatively recent modern scientific pursuit of the mysteries of the human mind should be steeped in esoteric ideas. A foundational look at this question was offered by Nandor Fodor, *Freud, Jung, and Occultism* (Secaucus, N.J.: University Books, 1971), and Richard Noll (1994; 1997) explores the roots of the Jungian system in not only its magical roots but also in its background in the völkisch ideology of the early twentieth-century German-speaking world.

‡The word *occult* is of Latin origin and something that was *occultum* was a secret or hidden thing, something that was willfully hidden or concealed. The word evolves into something more akin to the idea of the *esoteric* over time. It should be noted that there is a distinction between that which is hidden from our awareness because another human being has taken steps to hide it and those things that are hidden because of their ineffable and innately mysterious nature.

definition, occultism has four component elements: (1) correspondences, (2) living nature, (3) imagination and mediation, and (4) transmutation.

The idea of correspondences holds that there is an essential link between concrete phenomena in this world and corresponding transcendental forms in a hidden (occult) higher reality. In conjunction with this the occultist posits a living nature; in other words, the idea that all of existence is permeated with a primal substance or energy (= anima mundi). The elements of imagination and mediation imply that a seer can know occult secrets and transmit this knowledge to others. This idea of the transmission of knowledge from master to disciple according to a set of traditions is also a typical sub-element in occult culture. The aim of the occult sometimes appears to be the transmutation of the student—the passage of a person from one level of being to another, higher, and previously unknown (occult) level. Additionally, occult teachings tend to be syncretic; that is, they attempt to reach a concordance of various traditions and find some common essential thread that connects them as one. Occultism is contrasted with mysticism in that the latter seeks union with God, whereas the former seeks increased self-knowledge and even self-transformation.

Theories provide frameworks for doing things. The two main sorts of things that can be done are developmental and manipulative. In the first instance, the developmental approach, we are talking about growing a thing in such a way that it can become something more than it was previously, something better, and so forth. This is perhaps done under the guidance of an outside model. In the second case, that of manipulation, a thing is caused to behave in a certain way as determined by an outside agent.

Accepted modes of development go under names such as "education" or "social progress." Accepted forms of manipulation of substances include chemistry or engineering. However, if development or manipulation takes place under the guidance of an (as yet) unaccepted theory, or even a previously accepted but now rejected theory, it is likely to be called "occult."

The occultist attempts to go below, or rise above, material (or conscious) reality for an explanation of some greater paradigm. There is also a practical dimension in that it is thought that such knowledge can be used to control phenomena in mundane, consensus, reality. This is the promise of power, which the occult holds out for the seeker.

This promise of power is one of the key ingredients that relates to why the concept of the occult is essential to our exploration of factors in National Socialist ideology and policy that may, on the surface, seem well outside the mainstream of contemporaneous political thought. Of course, there is nothing new or even unusual about occult ideas influencing political revolutions—from the time of Alexander the Great to the revolutions of 1776 and 1789 and beyond.* It is of paramount importance to keep all elements of the precise definition of the occult in mind as various occult features of National Socialist beliefs and traditions are discussed.

Ultimately, the threefold division of the dimensions of this study can be analyzed with the traditional German categories of *Geisteswissenschaft, Naturwissenschaft,* and *Geheimwissenschaft*— "Intellectual or Symbolic Science," "Natural Science," and "Secret Science." To each of these there is an occult dimension as well.

SYMBOLIC TRADITIONS

Since the time of the ancient Greeks, the study of the world has been divided into a spiritual (or symbolic) side, the object of which is the *psychē* (or soul), and a natural side, the object of which is *physis* (or nature). Among the German intellectuals of the eighteenth and nineteenth centuries, this division was reflected in the aforementioned terms of *Geisteswissenschaft* and *Naturwissenschaft,* respectively. In

---

*The study of the role of occult ideas in politics and in political movements is a vast field of great interest from all sides, especially as the culture has moved in a direction in which politics and the media have assumed the role of a higher reality in many people's minds. It is well known that Alexander was supposedly taught certain esoteric things by Aristotle and that his mother instilled in him the idea that he was the son of an (Egyptian) god—she was a bit of a New Ager before her time. Both the American and French Revolutions were steeped in esoteric Freemasonic ideals, and the French even attempted to overthrow religion altogether in favor of a Cult of Reason.

recent times the validity of this venerable dichotomy has been increasingly called into question (Shore 1996, 3–71). In the course of this study, there will be a number of places where it will seem impossible to extract the symbolic component from the natural one.

The term *symbolic* classically refers to signs that convey some kind of meaning. Most of what we usually interpret as culture is symbolic in character. This includes religious ritual, motifs of folk art, ways of organizing a group politically, and hundreds of other features that vary more or less from one cultural group to another. This is the most fertile ground in which occult ideas may flourish. It is mainly in the field of symbolic culture that we find the manifestations of völkisch ideas—and this has been the field in which almost all previous studies of Nazi occultism have focused. That the Nazis used runes, or sought the Holy Grail, or were crypto-Cathars, or were some sort of Satanic cult (!)—all of these assertions speak to the level of symbolic culture. Claims of this sort are clearly linked to the idea of volkism and are usually rooted in the traditions of the past.

MYTHOLOGY

At various times, I will have recourse to the use of the term *myth* when discussing ideas in this book. This is certainly a much-misunderstood word and one that requires some definition. I will return to the topic more extensively in the context of the growth of mythic studies in the nineteenth century. At this juncture, suffice it to say that a myth is *not* something that is "untrue." To the contrary, it is something that is so deeply true that it can serve as the motivator of all human actions, and hence of all historical events. A myth, whether or not consciously recognized, is an underlying operating principle or metanarrative of all life and action. To be sure, there are good myths (which lead to better more integrated human life) and bad myths (which lead to misery and destruction). When the word *myth* is used in this text it never means "untruth," but rather it refers to a hyper-truth that motivates action and shapes thought. Myths can be held by whole nations and by individuals as well.

SCIENCE

In contrast to the symbolic aspects, there are the natural scientific or biological ideas that informed the ideology of the Third Reich. These were not concepts thought to be rooted in the past but rather futuristic ideas founded on what were considered to be the most advanced current understandings of the natural world, the "organic," and the "inorganic." These are usually the concepts that are most easily overlooked by those who study the idea of Nazi occultism. The theories of scientists like Ernst Haeckel (1834–1919) and Hans Hörbiger (1860–1931) shaped National Socialist ideology as much as the line-up of usual suspects in the world of symbolic culture, which includes men such as Guido von List and Lanz von Liebenfels. The ideas of Haeckel and Hörbiger, although they are couched in strictly scientific terms, nevertheless harbor deep patterns of that which has been characterized as occult thought.* Haeckel's followers founded the Monist League and tried to establish a new religion, called Monism, based on his interpretation of the natural world and the supposed laws of evolution. However, the Nazi attachment to these ideas was, on the surface, due to the fact that these scientists had been able to crack the code of nature itself. This would facilitate the National Socialism's ability to harness natural laws and processes in a scientific and material way to further their revolutionary aims.

OCCULTISM

For the purposes of this study, we will separate the esoteric from the occult, although in general usage these terms are often almost

---

*Haeckel and Hörbiger came from very different worlds. Haeckel was a fully qualified biologist working in that field in an academic setting. Despite this, in retrospect, many of his ideas have been thought to border on the occult, although they cannot be dismissed easily. Haeckel remains a respected figure in the history of science in the nineteenth century. His forays into religion and politics in the twentieth century make the direction of his thought clear, however. Hörbiger, on the other hand, is typical of the phenomenon of the occult scientific thinker. He is qualified and accomplished in one area (engineering) but tries to make his mark on the scientific world in a field unrelated to his qualifications: cosmology.

interchangeable. The esoteric is made up of symbolic traditions about cosmology, anthropology, and the history of humankind and the world. Its chief aim is initiation, or the transformation of man both individually and collectively. Occultism, on the other hand, is a set of techniques and practices, often connected with esoteric teachings, that enable the practitioner to control the minds of others (e.g., hypnosis), to read the future (e.g., clairvoyance, divination, and astrology), to read the destiny or character of another person, to read the past clairvoyantly, to communicate with the dead (e.g., spiritualism), and so on. Following these definitions, the practice of magic acts as a bridge between the esoteric and the occult. Essential to the definition of "the occult" in the present study is that it is a feature that has been rejected by, or is not (yet) explicable within, the prevailing cultural and intellectual norms of a given society.

MAGIC

Another level of the occult is commonly referred to as "magic." In most instances, it might be better called "sorcery." Contemporary mythology surrounding the Nazis widely attributes the practice of magic to them. This idea can lead the student down a deceptive road of misunderstanding if the concept of magic is allowed to go undefined or if we proceed from a loose and vague layman's definition. In current scientific thought, magic is defined as a system of operative meta-communication. Through communication using symbols and symbolic actions, various structures of the human psyche can interact with one another, or indeed with the natural or phenomenal world, to create effects and changes according to the will and design of the communicator. In other words, magic is the art of translating symbols (verbal, graphic, etc.) into phenomena, events, occurrences, or thoughts and feelings in a target object. The Nazis initiated this communication loop using the media of publications, speeches, rallies, broadcasts, and the display of symbols and signs—all of which carried a specific and targeted message designed to arouse the will of the masses to identify with the will of the program of the NSDAP (Nationalsozialistische Deutsche Arbeiterpartei) in sufficient numbers and to thereby tip the balance of political power in Germany in 1933. Clearly, the National Socialists did practice a kind of magic, but it was performed in a new and more expansive matrix than ever seen before.

NATIONAL SOCIALISM

Since the end of the Second World War, the word *Nazi* has been used as an imprecise pejorative against opinions and personas not in step with liberal-democratic ideas and policies or, increasingly, as a catchall term used to indicate any opponent with whom one might vehemently disagree. The word has been reduced to the level of an ideological label akin to "double-plus-ungood" in the Newspeak jargon of George Orwell's dystopian novel *Nineteen Eighty-Four.* It is for this reason that a more precise definition of National Socialism needs to be established here. The epithet *Nazi* was not much used by the National Socialists themselves. Its etymology is simply based on the pronunciation of the word *Nationalist* in German [*NAH-tzee*-ohn-ahlist], with the word shorted in colloquial reference to Nazi, pronounced [NAH-tzee]. The term *Nazi* had been in use in the nineteenth century, decades before the foundation of the NSDAP. It generally carried the connotation "ruffian."* What we must establish here is an exact definition of National Socialism, free of prejudice. This definition will then be part of the lens through which the occult elements of the ideology can be observed with greater precision.

One of the major difficulties in developing a simple, precise, and comprehensive definition of National Socialism is that it was not a very unified or ideologically centralized philosophy. The National Socialism of Hitler differed substantially in parts from that of Himmler, as it did from that of Rosenberg, or that of the Strasser brothers or Darré. All of these differing views were allowed to flourish to one degree or another during the period of the Third Reich. Therefore, National Socialism must be viewed precisely as a multiplicity rather than as a

---

*For a further discussion of this term, see appendix B: "The Word *Nazi*."

strict unity. This may offend the common belief that Nazism must have been a monolithic reflection of Hitler's personality and an ideology that allowed no deviations from an orthodox standard. This is more what we expect from Bolshevism, which can brook no alternate interpretations of the "party line." Of course, there are a number of general principles to which all National Socialists tended to adhere. To elucidate these principles, it seems most reasonable to refer to a document outlining basic National Socialist doctrine: the Party Program of the NSDAP.*

THE PROGRAM OF THE NSDAP

The program of the German Workers' Party is addressed to its era. After the goals of the program have been achieved, the leaders refuse to set new ones for the purpose of artificially increasing the discontent of the masses, merely in order to make possible the continuance of the Party.

1. We demand the union of all Germans on the basis of the right of self-determination of peoples—in a Greater Germany.

2. We demand equality of the German people with all other nations, the abrogation of the peace treaties of Versailles and Saint-Germain.

3. We demand land and soil (colonies) for the nourishment of our people and for the settlement of our excess population.

4. Only he who is a folk comrade (*Volksgenosse*) can be a citizen. Only he who is of German blood, regardless of his church, can be a folk comrade. No Jew, therefore, can be a folk comrade.

5. He who is not a citizen shall live in Germany only as a guest and must be governed by the law for aliens.

6. The right to make decisions about leadership and law belongs only to citizens. We therefore demand that every public office, no matter what kind, whether national, state, or local, be staffed only by citizens.

---

*The Party Program of the Twenty-Five Points was the foundation of the NSDAP, and, despite periodic efforts to convince Hitler to modify the plan, he refused and these points remained the guiding principles of National Socialism throughout the regime.

We oppose the corrupting parliamentary system of filling offices only according to the needs of the party and without regard for character or ability.

7. We demand that the state pledge itself to assure the productivity and livelihood of citizens above all others. If it is not possible to support the entire population, members of foreign nations (noncitizens) are to be expelled.

8. Any further immigration of non-Germans is to be prevented. We demand that all non-Germans who have entered Germany since August 2, 1914, be forced to leave the Reich immediately.

9. All citizens must possess equal rights and duties.

10. It must be the primary duty of every citizen to work mentally or physically. The activities of the individual may not conflict with the interests of the general public but must be carried on within the framework of the whole and for the good of all.

WE THEREFORE DEMAND:

11. Abolition of income unearned by labor or effort.

BREAKING THE BONDAGE OF INTEREST

12. Considering the enormous sacrifices of property and blood which every war demands from a people, personal enrichment because of war had to be seen as a crime against the people. We therefore demand complete confiscation of all war profits.

13. We demand nationalization of all (previously) incorporated companies (trusts).

14. We demand profit sharing in big businesses.

15. We demand a generous extension of old-age insurance.

16. We demand the creation of and maintenance of a sound middle class; immediate communalization of the great department stores and their leasing to small businessmen at low rents; most favorable consideration to small businessmen in all government purchasing and contracting, whether national, state, or local.

17. We demand land reform suited to our national needs, creation of a law providing for expropriation without compensation

of land for common purposes, abolition of taxes on land and prevention of all speculation.

18. We demand a relentless fight against those whose activities harm the common good. Traitors, usurers, profiteers, and so forth, are to be punished with death, regardless of church and race.

19. We demand the substitution of German Common Law for Roman Law. Roman Law serves a materialistic world order.

20. In order to make it possible for every able and industrious German to obtain a higher education, and thereby to achieve a leading position, the state must take charge of a thorough extension of our entire national educational system. The curricula of all schools must be adapted to the demands of practical life. The school must impress an understanding of the state (civics) very early, at the very beginning of rational thought in the child. We demand the education of gifted children of poor parents at the cost of the state, regardless of the parents' status or profession.

21. The state must improve public health through protection of mother and child, prevention of child labor; by imposing a physical fitness program by means of establishing legal obligations in gymnastics and sports, and by supporting all organizations concerned with the physical training of youth.

22. We demand the abolition of mercenary troops and the creation of a popular army.

23. We demand legal measures against the conscious political lie and its propagation through the press. In order to make possible the creation of a German press, we demand that:

   a. all editors and contributors of German language newspapers be folk comrades;

   b. non-German newspapers must have the express permission of the state to appear. They may not be printed in the German language.

   c. every non-German investment in or influence on German newspapers be legally forbidden and be punished by the closing of the publishing house and the immediate expulsion of the non-Germans involved.

Newspapers which conflict with the common good are to be forbidden. We demand legal measures against any tendency in art and literature which has a subversive influence on the life of our people, and the closing down of any meetings or organizations which do not conform to these demands.

24. We demand freedom for all religious denominations within the state as long as they do not endanger the state or violate the ethical and moral feelings of the German race.

    The party as such subscribes to a positive Christianity without binding itself to a specific denomination. It opposes the Jewish materialistic spirit within and around us and is convinced that a lasting recovery of our people can only come about by an effort from within based on the principle:

THE COMMON GOOD BEFORE
THE INDIVIDUAL GOOD.

25. In order to carry out these policies we demand: creation of a strong central authority in the Reich. The central parliament must have unlimited authority over the entire Reich and all its organizations.

    The formation of chambers according to occupation and profession, to carry out in the individual states the basic law enacted by the Reich.

    The leaders of the party pledge that they will relentlessly seek the implementation of these points, if necessary at the cost of their lives. (Lane and Rupp 1978, 41–43)

An analysis of the contents of this program, originally framed by Dietrich Eckhart and accepted by Hitler and subsequently promoted by him, reveals that it contains a half dozen or so inherent major principles. The legitimate citizenry of the state is defined in racial (nationalistic) terms, which pointedly excludes Jews (anti-Semitism). A centralized state authority is empowered to implement socialistic programs to serve the racially defined citizenry of the state. Productive work is mandated for all citizens, as income gained through financial interest is abolished. Economic policies are geared toward the development of the middle class. Ideally, there is to be a reestablishment of German Common Law (as in the Anglo-Saxon tradition) to replace the Roman Law (or the Napoleonic Code). Both education and the media are to be reformed to serve the interests of the common good. The promotion of a "positive Christianity"* is made explicit. It will be remarkable to see just how many of these principles were supported by occult ideological underpinnings.

Since the trials for Nazi crimes against humanity at Nuremberg, it has become popular to assume that the National Socialist regime was essentially criminal in character. If this was so, just what were the criminal aspects of the ideology? An analysis of National Socialist thought reveals two areas of what could be considered criminal offenses against the prevailing trends in Western Civilization: (1) the disenfranchisement of minorities based on race or religion, which led to genocide; and (2) the creation of a self-sustaining economy independent of the global financial establishment. The former is regularly cited, while the latter is rarely mentioned today, although at the time of the Second World War it was the chief source of moral indignation within the Western elite. Again, both of these criminal offenses can be seen to have their roots in the occult.

National Socialism is what the phrase literally says it is: socialism based on race (nation) rather than on economic class. Its eventual genocidal dimension is no different from that of Marxist socialism, except it tends to have a racial rather than economic or ideological rationale. Throughout this book, we will return to these principles as we focus on the possible occult dimensions of National Socialism proper.

The Soviets "liquidated" as many as twenty million victims. The classically enumerated six million victims of the Third Reich may be less in number, but the motive for these murders—that is, the racial characteristics of the victims—is sentimentally thought of as much more rep-

---

*It should be noted that the reference to "positive Christianity" is the only mention of any sort of religious identity in the Party Program. This topic is discussed more fully in chapter 9.

rehensible than the ideological, economic, or class-based motives of the murders committed by the Bolsheviks. Note, too, that no one has ever been brought to justice for the Soviet murders, whereas poor slobs who acted as low-level guards in Nazi concentration camps are still being hunted down. And this is true despite the fact that many of the Soviet murders were actually based on tribal or ethnic differences—for example, the war on the Ukrainians in which the tactics of mass starvation, originally developed by Generals Grant and Sherman in the American War between the States, were used to annihilate as many as seven million Ukrainians between the years 1932 and 1933. These matters are only mentioned to demonstrate that it was not really the level or dimensions of the crimes committed by the Nazis that set them apart, but *something else*. The mystery of what this thing is occupies some of our attention in the present book.

This work is divided into four parts. The first three treat the genesis and history of National Socialist ideology. Part 1 deals with the deep nineteenth-century roots of the ideas that eventually found expression in Nazism. Part 2 focuses on the initial years of the twentieth century prior to the establishment of the NSDAP. It is here that the immediate roots of National Socialist ideology lie, because it was in these years that the leaders and philosophers of the movement came of age. Part 3 is a study of occult manifestations within the time frame of the actual existence of the NSDAP: 1919–1945. Part 4 is a departure from the historical cast of the previous three parts. It is a critical study of the whole idea and myth of Nazi occultism—the belief that the Nazis formed an occult movement and practiced all manner of (usually sinister) rites and rituals. This belief will be seen to have had its origins in wartime propaganda, later fueled by postwar agendas of a political, cultural, or commercial bent.

In the literature of Nazi occult mythology (or mythologizing), we find many examples of conspiratorial thinking. To the gullible, belief in occult conspiracies is attractive, whereas to the skeptical, such things often seem absurd. Yet, when we look at historical phenomena such as the rise and fall of National Socialism in Germany, we have to wonder. It must be said, however, that most of what seems like a grand conspiracy is often better explained simply by realizing that there is great power in a set of unconscious assumptions held by a group of men sharing the same zeitgeist and acting within a fairly homogeneous group, especially when that group is subject to a sense of existential crises.

As opposed to previous efforts at unraveling the riddle of the twentieth century—the National Socialist movement and its meaning to history—I will neither focus on sensationalistic features merely for entertainment value, such as many authors have done in the recent past (e.g., J. H. Brennan and Peter Levenda), nor will I indulge in a sectarian interpretation that ascribes all of the meaning of the movement to one or another motivation. In point of historical fact, the NS movement was a multifaceted and not very centrally organized one, so that any unified or simplistic effort at interpreting it and its meaning to history will inevitably fall far short of accuracy. It is accuracy and objectivity to which we are dedicated in this study.

In each part of this study, we will focus on a fourfold pattern of cultural features responsible for the occult traits of National Socialist ideology. The völkisch idea infuses each of them with their all-encompassing rationale or vitality. The occult as a feature unto itself is most usually a subtle, or extremely well-hidden, aspect of National Socialist belief and practice. Both volkism and the occult find expression in symbolic culture (rituals, myths, symbols, and signs) as well as scientific culture, where these beliefs are seen to shape theories about biology and physics. Here we want to take all four of these factors—volkism, occultism, symbolic culture, and scientific culture—into account in a way that will bring us closer to a total understanding of the true nature and scope of any possible occultism in the Third Reich. This book is not a work of revisionism, nor is it intended in any way as an apology for Nazi Germany. Rather, it is a study in the history of ideas, focused with an objective lens from the perspective of the dawn of the twenty-first century upon the heart of the myth and the riddle of the twentieth century.

PART I

Foundations of the Nineteenth Century

(1800–1900)

INTRODUCTION TO PART I

Historical events of massive proportions have deep and vast root systems. The ideas of National Socialism and its occult dimensions have not only deep roots but often obscure ones as well. The most common error made by those who represent themselves as doing research into these ideas is that they view the data through a distorted lens shaped by popular slogans. They take their direction from propagandistic phrases such as "Nazism was really a pagan movement," or "Hitler was a Satanist." These misdirecting slogans must be put into firm focus and subjected to much more rigorous historical examination.

All of the ideas made manifest in National Socialism have roots in the nineteenth century. The years between 1800 and 1900 were especially eventful and dynamic for the German-speaking Central European states, most of which would be politically forged together into the Second German Reich by the "Iron Chancellor," Otto von Bismarck, in 1871. In the broader Western world, the whole century was filled with remarkable ideas and towering figures who vigorously professed them. In the realms of the understanding and implementation of myth and symbol, figures such as Jacob and Wilhelm Grimm, J. J. Bachofen, Wilhelm Mannhardt, and Max Müller leap from the pages of history. In the scientific world, men such as Carl Friedrich Gauss, Robert Koch, and Alexander von Humboldt left their indelible marks. The occult world of the nineteenth century offers its own foundational figures, such as Franz Anton Mesmer, Éliphas Lévi, Helena Petrovna Blavatsky (née Hahn), and Karl Friedrich Zöllner.

Some of the major ideas that dominated nineteenth-century

thought, and which often cooperated or conflicted with one another, were German idealism, biology, evolutionary theories, nationalism, romanticism, social Darwinism, Marxism, and positivism. It is therefore little wonder that the most radical and impetuous children of that century would establish institutions flowing from a heady brew concocted from these ideas.

To explain the radical events and historical upheavals of the first half of the twentieth century, we have to understand the effects of intellectual movements beginning a century earlier. Although elite thinkers had held many radically divergent thoughts for a long time in Europe, due to limitations in publishing, education, and economic development this radicalism remained contained. This changed in the nineteenth century. Rational idealism, practiced by Kant and Hegel, was turned into a materialistic economic political philosophy by Karl Marx. Traditional Christian theology was subjected to widespread rationalistic attacks by the new biblical criticism. At the same time, there was an influx of exciting and apparently effective religio-philosophical conceptions from the East. Ideas imported from the Buddhistic and Brahmanic religions, especially as embodied in the work of Arthur Schopenhauer, all led to a new way of thinking that was ready to wipe away the old·established philosophies and theologies. One of the most important figures in popularizing the new revolutionary way of thinking was the artist Richard Wagner, followed by his former acolyte, Friedrich Nietzsche. This package of ideas was a potent mix for cultural change.

We will observe that a new symbolic culture grew from the seeds of the volkist ideology that were planted and cultivated throughout the course of the nineteenth century. Scientific theories—many of them later discredited, or shown to have been misapplied to cultural issues—grew abundantly throughout the century as well. Occultism as such was an abiding interest of Romantics of the early 1800s, and over the following decades it became steadily refocused from a center in religious myth into an increasingly "scientific" mode of expression.

To see the development of the nineteenth century in a clear context, a short overview of this period in German history is necessary.

GERMAN-SPEAKING CENTRAL EUROPE
IN THE NINETEENTH CENTURY

Germany had never been a nation-state in the same way France or England had been since the end of the Middle Ages. Nevertheless, there was a nascent collective cultural identity among all German-speaking peoples of Central Europe. These include inhabitants of present-day Germany, Austria, and the northern cantons of Switzerland. Over the course of the nineteenth century, a number of German-speaking political entities—kingdoms, principalities, free cities, and other political corporations in the western part of the German-speaking area—were unified by Bismarck into a state ruled by the Prussian king and now kaiser, Wilhelm I. The century saw Germany go from a collection of independent, almost tribal, kingdoms to a new empire.

At the dawn of the nineteenth century, all of Europe was involved in a cultural debate between Enlightenment thinking couched in Neo-Classical aesthetics and the new approach proposed by the Romantics. Germany was no exception. The Enlightenment valued the rational mind above all else; Enlightenment thinkers questioned received traditions and extolled the virtues of simplicity, precision, and clarity. Enlightenment aesthetics revolved around mechanistic models—the whole world was seen as a great machine or clockwork with the Creator as the great clockmaker. Politically, the Enlightenment favored the development of international institutions and interconnections.

It was in the name of the Enlightenment that Napoleon conquered much of Europe in wars lasting from 1803 to 1815. Romanticism, on the other hand, criticized the arrogant naïveté of the Enlightenment and insisted on the primacy of emotion for human happiness. Romantics turned to the wildness of nature, extolled the "noble savage," and delved into the night side of life, into dreams and myths. In the Romantic introversion, the individual body was revalorized as was the collective organic body known as the nation (or Volk). The energy to throw off Napoleon, the foreign conqueror who had originally been welcomed to Germany as a liberator, came from that Romantic spirit.

German Enlightenment thinkers in particular tended to be conservative and optimistic—accepting the political status quo of the fragmented state of the German people. Romantics yearned for a political reality in which the nation and the state would be integrated into an organic whole. Germany, according to Romantic philosophers such as Hegel and Fichte, should be a state made up of German people who speak the German language. This stance was revolutionary and opposed to the conservative position, which favored retaining all of the various political bodies—some two hundred in number.

Romantic revolutionary fervor boiled over in a variety of states in Europe in the year 1848. (Coincidentally, this was the same year that Karl Marx and Friedrich Engels issued *The Communist Manifesto*.) These uprisings were turned back by the conservative forces of many state authorities. This moment also marked the end of those unified cultural movements in which politics, religion, art, and literature could all be seen as exponents of a single philosophical position. After this time, culture began to become fragmented into the compartmentalized aspects of the now familiar modern world. At this point artists, mystics, poets, and writers tended to go underground to pursue their dreams.

Nevertheless, the next generation saw a steady movement toward the unification of various German states under the leadership of Prussia, the most powerful single German state of the time. Wars with Austria (the Seven Weeks' War of 1866) and the Franco-Prussian War (1870–1871) resulted in the consolidation of Prussian power among the western German states. The Franco-Prussian War ended with the victorious Germans occupying Paris and declaring the establishment of the Second German Empire on January 18, 1871, in the Hall of Mirrors in the palace of Versailles.

Austrian cultural history in the last half of the nineteenth century was marked by increasing demands made by ethnic minorities in the Austrian Empire—especially Hungarians and Czechs—upon the central German-speaking authority in Vienna. This pressure helped to promote ideas of a Großdeutschland, a greater unification between the German-speaking Austrians and the burgeoning German Reich to the west.

The last quarter of the century witnessed the growth of the German

Reich as a world power with the development of advanced technology, overseas colonies, and a modern military.

Additionally, Germany continued to pioneer policies of public welfare, such as health insurance and benefits for disabled and elderly citizens. By the turn of the century, Germany was the most technologically advanced, highly educated, and industrialized country in the world. The expected national ambitions commensurate with these accomplishments in a world that had little room for an upstart major player in geopolitics could only lead to disaster.

Throughout the nineteenth century the symbolic world of volkism, the realm of scientific research, and the occult subculture were fermenting toward the eventual outpouring of an intoxicating brew in the twentieth century. But it must be remembered that all and everything the twentieth century manifested—the entire spectrum of activity— had roots in what went before it in time. There is nothing inevitable or natural about how any of these older ideas were used by later artists, scientists, or politicians. Each remains responsible for his own actions. We shall now explore in more detail the foundations of the folkish, scientific, and occult realms of the nineteenth century.

CHAPTER 1

FOUNDATIONS OF VOLKISM
The Deep Background of What
Became National Socialism

Folkish [Ger. *völkisch*] thought did not come naturally to the Germans of the nineteenth century. In essence there is nothing uniquely German about the idea. All nations with a keen awareness and high estimation of their ethnic culture, language, and history could be seen as being folkish, be they Russian slavophiles, Jewish Zionists, or Black Muslims. All peoples who survived and thrived in the earliest epochs of history were by necessity folkish in their outlook. Volkism simply sees its primary motivator as the preservation and promotion of the interest of one's native people over all others—not necessarily because one's native people is superior to others, but simply because the individual belongs to it and sees himself or herself as a part of its greater whole. Germans in the centuries immediately preceding 1800 were among the least folkish in Europe. Over the course of the nineteenth century, the Germans were educated into volkism, and while National Socialism was one particular historical outcome of this education, it cannot be seen as its inevitable result. Other historical and cultural manifestations were also possible. The concepts of nationalism and myth, coupled with the avenues of scholarship, art, and cultural movements, led the way in this early education of the people.

NATIONALISM

To understand the particular form of German nationalism we see in the nineteenth century, we must understand Romanticism. Culturally, this

25

great movement can be said to have had its most widespread influence between the 1770s (instigated by the writings of the French philosopher Jean-Jacques Rousseau) and the watershed year of 1848. The Romantics turned away from the exclusive focus on Reason, the hallmark of the Enlightenment, and focused instead on a variety of interests, which included nature, the soul, love, the subjective experience of the religious impulse, and nationalism. The Romantics did not abandon Reason, which had been so idealized by the Enlightenment and its intellectual heir, Neoclassicism; they simply saw its limitations in the pursuit of the greater goal, which they shared with Enlightenment thinkers: the perfection of man. As modern thinkers, both Romantics and Neoclassicists hold that man could be perfected through the discovery and application of certain laws. The Neoclassicist saw these laws as being fairly simple and self-evident, whereas the Romantics saw them as being exceedingly complex, obscure, and subtle.

Both the Neoclassical Enlightenment and the Romantics held that man was a perfectible being. The Classicist thought that certain laws or regulations could be discovered rationally in nature and that man could be educated or manipulated along these lines to such an extent that the species of man would be perfected and thus would need no more laws or constraint. The Romantics also believed in the perfectibility of mankind, but they held that this perfection was something innate and that overmuch civilization had submerged this perfect, more primitive state. Both of these theories could be characterized as bordering on the occult, as neither has any verifiable basis for the claim that humanity is any more perfect as a species now than it has been at any point in the past.

The deeper roots of German Romantic nationalism lie in the philosophies of men such as Johann Gottlieb Fichte (1762–1814) and Georg Wilhelm Friedrich Hegel (1770–1831). Hegel emphasized the organic nature of culture and asserted that the differences between and among cultures represented manifestations of a natural order, while Fichte, in his *Reden an die deutsche Nation* (Addresses to the German Nation), actually broached the topic of German nationalism. The German proclivity for a dark form of Romanticism stems from the fact that in Germany the movement had its origins in the brooding precursor phase known as the *Sturm und Drang* (Storm and Stress) period (ca. 1765–1785), in which there was a great deal of interest in the night-side of reality, the occult, and the mysterious.

In the nineteenth century, a more mature form of Romanticism emerged that tried to actualize many of the aesthetic notions of the earlier time. There was an enormous interest in the distant past—yet the Germans tended to lag behind the rest of Europe with regard to solid knowledge about their own antiquities. This was because ancient Germanic material had been neglected for the most part since the Middle Ages and could only be recovered through refined scholarship. It was therefore the Romantics who developed the scientific tools necessary to rediscover this past.

THE BROTHERS GRIMM

Jacob Grimm (1785–1863) and his brother Wilhelm (1786–1859) joined forces to lay a scholarly foundation for the reawakening of Germanic identity and prestige. Together they founded the modern scholarly disciplines of folklore, comparative linguistics, and comparative mythology. Their researches probed into language, myth, heroic literature, legal history, and various kinds of folk traditions. Best known for their collection of "Fairy Tales" (*Kinder- und Hausmärchen;* 1812), their actual deeper motivation for all of their work was the redevelopment and recovery of a sense of Germanic identity to rival that of the Greeks or Romans. The underlying purpose for this was the instilling of a sense of a unified national identity in the politically disjointed German-speaking world.

The Grimms worked in Kassel as librarians and professors before moving to Göttingen to assume more prestigious posts. Their works were always understood by them to be part of an applied cultural endeavor and not simply a scholarly pursuit. In 1837 the Grimm brothers, along with five other professors, refused to pledge personal loyalty to the King of Hannover. These "Göttinger Sieben" (Göttingen Seven) lost their jobs because of their loyalty to the idea of a united German nation. After a short stay back in Kassel, both brothers were invited to assume professorships at the University of Berlin by King Friedrich Wilhelm IV of Prussia. Jacob and Wilhelm continued their work at the university until giving up their formal positions in 1848 and 1852, respectively. In 1848, Jacob Grimm was elected to the Frankfurt National Parliament, where he made speeches that reflected both his deep love of the fatherland and his interests in old Germanic philology. But Grimm was not suited to a political life, so he returned to his scholarly pursuits, which he continued right up until the moment of his death.

The Brothers Grimm issued several joint works, which include *Kinder- und Hausmärchen* (Tales for Children and Household), published in two volumes in editions spanning from 1812 to 1857; *Der arme Heinrich von Hartmann von der Aue* (*Poor Heinrich* by Hartmann von der Aue), 1815, which is an edition with commentary of an important Middle High German epic poem; *Lieder der alten Edda* (Lays from the Old Edda), 1815; and *Deutsche Sagen* (German Legends), 2 volumes, 1816–1818. The brothers also began the great German dictionary (*Deutsches Wörterbuch*) but only finished through most of the letter F by the time of their deaths. The project was not completed until 1960. Jacob completed the following projects on his own: *Deutsche Grammatik* (German Grammar) in 4 volumes, 1819–1837; *Geschichte der deutschen Sprache* (History of the German Language), 2 volumes, 1848; *Deutsche Rechtsaltertümer* (German Legal Antiquities), 1828; and *Deutsche Mythologie* (Teutonic Mythology), 4 volumes, 1835–1853. Wilhelm's major individual efforts were *Altdänische Heldenlieder, Balladen und Märchen* (Old Danish Heroic Lays, Ballads, and Folktales), 1811; *Ueber deutsche Runen* (On Germanic Runes), 1821; and *Die deutsche Heldensage* (The German Heroic Legend), 1829. Together these works laid a firm foundation for the continuing development of the scientific study of old Germanic linguistics, mythology, and culture. In the Grimms' minds, however, the results of these studies were to be applied to broader real-world cultural concerns.

At the conclusion of Jacob Grimm's autobiographical essay, he says:

> Nearly all my labours have been devoted, either directly or indirectly,
> to the investigation of our earlier language, poetry and laws. These

studies may have appeared to many, and may still appear, useless; to me they have always seemed a noble and earnest task, definitely and inseparably connected with our common fatherland, and calculated to foster the love of it. My principle has always been in these investigations to under-value nothing, but to utilize the small for the illustration of the great, the popular tradition for the elucidation of the written monuments. (Quoted in Sweet 1911, 600)

This quote, better than any interpretation, indicates clearly that the significance of the Grimms' works was intended to be a foundation for cultural activism and not merely a disinterested form of academic study.

One of the things that characterized the initial phase of the reawakening of the German national spirit—represented by Herder, Fichte, and the Grimms—was its positive nature. It was relatively unmixed with aggression or hatred toward an "enemy." This aggressive spirit would, however, become an increasing part of the subsequent phase of German nationalism.

VATER JAHN

Approximately contemporaneous with the Grimms was the life of the Prussian patriot Friedrich Ludwig Jahn (1778–1852), the father of the German "gymnastics," or Turner movement. For this reason, he was often referred to as Vater (Father) Jahn. In contrast to Herder's view that all peoples (Völker) were different, yet equal in value in nature's plan, Jahn held that only one Volk was closest to the divine model and was thus destined "to bring salvation and happiness to mankind" (Kohn 1960, 89). For Jahn, this was none other than the German Volk.

Jahn was an educator in a college preparatory school (*Gymnasium*) in Berlin and saw the reeducation of the nation as the key to its transformation into a folkish state. His activities took place in three different realms: he promoted militia groups called the *Freikorps,* who were patriotic military volunteers; he founded gymnastic associations (*Turnerschaften*); and he established student fraternities (*Burschenschaften*) at universities around the country. These latter groups accepted only Christian (i.e., non-Jewish) members and generally tried to promote serious activities and minimize drinking and dueling.

Jahn's first book, which he wrote in 1799 when he was twenty-one years of age, was on Prussian patriotism. His best-known work, *Deutsches Volkstum* (German Folkdom), appeared in 1810. This work is a basic outline of his philosophy and contains sections on the formation and shape of an ideal state, education, the philosophy of the Volk and the state, religion, popular festivals, literature, and householding.

This educator of the Volk transferred his initial ideas of nationalistic Prussian patriotism throughout all of Germany. Jahn's nationalism was fueled by an animosity toward all things foreign. This was developed from his reaction to the invasion of the German states by Napoleon. He was against teaching foreign languages (especially French) and the use of foreign words in the German language. This was generally a response to the fact that in the royal courts of many German states, the language used was often French. Additionally, he wished to instill in the people the idea of a "sacredness of nationality."

For Jahn, Romantic nationalism took a decidedly anti-Semitic as well as anti-foreign turn. Whereas the Grimms developed their national consciousness on the basis of positive spiritual and subtle mythic levels, Jahn was a master of cultural organization and multilevel activism. He saw that a military wing was needed to provide the threat of physical violence, a program of physical fitness to combat what he saw as the over-emphasis in the German character for spiritual or intellectual pursuits, and a network of social organization at the highest level of the intelligentsia. This latter goal was accomplished by creating the Burschenschaften, which would bring young men together in associations that would carry over into networks of loyalty for the rest of their lives.

Jahn did not always have an easy life. He was incarcerated in 1818 as a demagogue whose ideas about German unity were seen as a threat to law and order. During the same year he was incarcerated, his gymnastic associations (*Turnvereine*) were closed by royal decree. He spent six years in prison and remained under police surveillance for the next thirty-three years. However, times did change under his influence. In 1842, King Friedrich Wilhelm IV declared Jahn's gymnastics to be a "necessary and indispensable part of the general education of young men." Jahn, along with Jacob Grimm, was a member of the German parliament of 1848. There Jahn was recognized as a great German patriot and originator of the Burschenschaften.

As a symbol of his movement, Jahn adapted the swastika, or *Hakenkreuz,* which he discovered in archaeological studies of ancient Germanic Iron Age urns. But Jahn used a form of the symbol that consisted of four F-shaped arms. The "four Fs" indicated his formula: *frisch, fromm, froh, frei*—fresh, pious, happy, free (Bronder 1975, 105).

Vater Jahn's ideology essentially combined Romanticism with Prussian patriotism and some of the French revolutionary ideas—all in the service of the concept of the Volk and of German patriotism.

RICHARD WAGNER

No figure towers higher over late-nineteenth-century volkism than that of the musical genius Richard Wagner. The story of his development and his legacy is indicative of the vicissitudes of the folkish movement in Germany in the bridge of time between that century and the following one. Richard Wagner (1813–1883) was a social as well as an artistic revolutionary.

In the early part of his career in Dresden, Wagner was an optimistic political revolutionary. But the events of 1848 convinced him that a more artistic and culturally revolutionary path was necessary. He developed the idea of the "total work of art" (*Gesamtkunstwerk*), which was to bring about a cultural and spiritual rebirth in the German people and thus lead to a whole new civilization. This idea of the total work of art was the never-before consciously attempted unity of sound, word, image, and movement (Kohn 1960, 190). We more ordinarily call these efforts the "operas" of Wagner. Most of these works had themes rooted in early or medieval German myth and legend. The most famous of these are the tetralogy *Der Ring des Nibelungen* (1869–1876) and *Parsifal* (1882).

Wagner was essentially a Romantic artist who saw his art as a revolutionary tool. He thundered "against the nineteenth century bourgeois world, against men without myth, passion and greatness" (Kohn 1960, 190). Essentially, Wagner attempted to synthesize the "spirit of the North" with the philosophy of Arthur Schopenhauer. For the early Wagner, the artist must be, at heart, a revolutionary—bent on the destruction of the state. More important than the state is the folk, "an organic and loving community of free individuals" (Kohn 1960, 198). According to Wagner, all great art can only originate in a true folk-community. Because no such community then existed, Wagner thought that no great art could actually be produced in this modern world.

Politically, Wagner envisioned a coming republican monarchy in which the basic problem of modern society, capitalism or plutocracy, would be vanquished. He saw a future in which a new Germany—free of class and capital—would create colonies around the world and bring a new form of culture to all peoples everywhere.

Although Wagner was a theoretical anti-Semite, he had many Jewish friends, followers, promoters, and collaborators. His anti-Semitism is quite ironic, as it appears that he himself may have been of largely Jewish ancestry (Bronder 1975, 373–74). In spirit and character at least, Wagner's anti-Semitism was rooted in Christianity. In *Die Wibelungen,* a study that preceded his composition of the Ring Cycle, he equates Jesus and Siegfried. Siegfried was a "striking likeness to Christ himself, who died, was mourned, and was avenged . . . as we still take revenge on the Jews of today" (Kohn 1960, 195).

Parallel to Wagner's anti-Semitism is his general racism. From early on, Wagner was a propagandist in Germany for the ideas of the French racial philosopher Arthur de Gobineau (1816–1882), who is sometimes referred to as the "father of modern racism."* Gobineau held that races are unequal in value and that there exists a relative ranking of their qualities. Further, the abilities of a race as a whole depend on the purity of its blood, and so any mixing of civilizations by means of mixing of the races would have an inevitable deleterious effect.

As Wagner became more materially successful, he became more

---

*While Gobineau by no means invented racism, it is his codification of it that remains the dominant sort of thinking among modern or current racists today.

conservative in his views. With the growth of Wagner's conservatism, his anti-Semitism also deepened. At the end of his life, he saw the Jews, capitalism, and democracy as parts of a greater whole. After the master's death, his wife, Cosima, carried on and further developed this aspect of his ideology. She would eventually form an alliance with National Socialism as early as 1924.

It can be seen clearly in the progression of the philosophies from Herder and the Grimms to Jahn, and then on to Wagner, how the folkish idea developed from a positive and benign idea, suited to the development of a people's identity and self-determination, into an instrument of aggression toward a perceived oppressor and even toward a cultural minority. Initially, there is nothing in volkism that necessitates any sort of anti-Semitic corollary. Yet, in the particular history of Central Europe, the coalition between folkish interests and those motivated by anti-Semitism became an ever-increasing reality.

MYTH

Throughout the nineteenth century the word and concept of *myth* grew in stature and importance. The serious pursuit of the deeper meaning of myth was a particularly Germanic one during this time. Most of the thinkers responsible for developing this concept and its understanding were either German or English.* In the earlier part of the century, the Enlightenment definition of *myth* seemed to dominate—that is, that myth was something akin to a fable, an untrue story told by simple and savage minds to explain what they did not understand. This attitude was weakened under the onslaught of Romantic scholarship, such as

---

*Because Classical mythology (that of the Greeks and Romans) had been a part of standard reading and education since the Renaissance and because many texts relating to this mythology were readily available and educated men were traditionally taught to read the Latin and Greek in which they originally appeared, their study seemed to require little in the way of scientific investigation. However, the indigenous mythologies of the Germanic and Celtic peoples were not so readily available, either linguistically or materially (i.e., written texts were rare). This situation was the catalyst and motive for the development of the scientific study of mythology in northern Europe.

that of the Grimms, when it was shown that myth is a powerful and persistent feature of all cultures at all times.

No one definition of *myth* will satisfy all specialists in the field of mythography and be useful for the nonspecialist in a study of the kind we are presenting here. But we can clarify this multifaceted concept and bring it to bear on our topic. Let us begin with a definition offered by the great Mircea Eliade.

> [M]yths describe the various and sometimes dramatic breakthroughs of the sacred . . . into the World. It is this sudden breakthrough of the sacred that really establishes the World and makes it what it is today. (Eliade 1963, 6)

Myth is something that is not necessarily *factually* true but rather describes a higher (i.e., derived from what Eliade calls the "sacred") reality as it is made manifest in the consciousness of humanity. Myths describe an underlying pattern of reality that is often invisible in what we call history, but which nevertheless shapes history. In short, myths are conscious or unconscious metanarratives that explain the unseen reality from which all events unfold. History may be accurate or inaccurate because the data collected may be true or false, but myth is always true on a higher level. Although we think of myth in terms of the great mythologies of the past, in fact, myths are being created or re-created in contemporary life all the time. These "new" myths can usually be interpreted in light of archaic myths, but they often serve slightly different purposes than the ancient myths did.

For example, the myth of Germanic racial purity—the idea that the Germans were somehow more racially pure than their neighbors, a notion that can be traced back to the first century CE and Tacitus's ethnographical work *Germania** is a metanarrative used by adherents

---

*Much has been made in recent years about how dangerous the book *Germania* supposedly is or was. Of course, it is merely a work by a Roman historian and ethnographer. The book itself is a treasure trove of information about the Germanic peoples, but only if read with an awareness of why Tacitus wrote it in the first place. Tacitus's comments must also be weighed in conjunction with corroborating archaeological and comparative

of the völkisch idea to explain why the Germans were a people of destiny with regard to the development of a better form of humanity (a *Herrenvolk,* or "Master Race"). The archaic mythic truth underlying this metanarrative is the fact that many ancient traditional peoples (i.e., tribes) have the unshakable belief that they are special, set apart from others, descended from the gods, and destined to fulfill some great and heroic purpose. As long as the myth remains just that—a myth, in all its power and prestige—it can serve a good purpose. But when, as in the case of the myth of German racial purity, it tries to verify itself scientifically, it runs the risk of being disproved and thus discredited.*

At its core, the myth of volkism is that humanity is naturally segmented into various organic cultural entities, each one with its own integral biological, religious, material, and linguistic history and traditions. Furthermore, it is held that these divisions are good and healthy for the world and that work to ensure the viability of these various "endangered cultural species" is noble.

The concept of myth as a metanarrative will also be called upon to clarify matters in the fourth part of this book when we look at the mythology of Nazi occultism. There we will see that all of the factors that were present for the völkisch myth-makers and discoverers of myth of the nineteenth and twentieth centuries are likewise in evidence when it comes to the postwar search for meaning and power in connection with the history and symbolism of National Socialist Germany.

(*cont.*) literary evidence from subsequent times. The idea that the Germans were more racially pure than their neighbors is clearly absurd. By the time of Tacitus, the Germanic culture had spread over many tribal areas, and with each expansion other tribes or ethnic groups were assimilated. One of the Germanic tribes in the East was even called the Bastarnae, which indicates a mixed heritage: they were probably made up of elements from among Celtic and Sarmatian (Iranian) peoples. In antiquity, they were thought to be Celtic, but they were probably a tribe in linguistic transition from being Celtic speakers to Germanic in language.

*Clearly, one of Tacitus's motives in writing the *Germania* was an attempt to contrast the "pure" Germans with what he thought was a bastardization of the Roman aristocratic tribes. There is no evidence that early Germanic peoples themselves had anything to say about racial purity, but it does seem to have been something the Romans were thinking about and lamenting the loss of their own ethnic identity.

The current idea of myth itself developed from the time of Herder, who in 1767 was concerned about "how we can use mythology for the cultivation of our inventive powers, in order to approach the ancients in spirit rather than through imitation" (Feldman and Richardson 1972, 230). Myth in general was elevated to the level of a quasi-religion, which needed to be first discovered and then emulated to return modern man to a state of dignity and heroic stature. This is what Wagner was lamenting when he said that modern man was "without myth, passion and greatness."

Knowledge of Germanic myth in particular was slowly being developed over the course of the nineteenth century. Jacob Grimm published the first edition of his *Deutsche Mythologie* (Teutonic Mythology) in 1835. This marked the beginning of the general scientific study of Germanic myth. Grimm's work was followed by the less reliable but more popular *Handbuch der deutschen Mythologie* by Karl Simrock (1853–1855). In the last decade of that century several other major works on the subjects of Germanic mythology and religion appeared, such as those by E. H. Meyer (1891), Wolfgang Golther (1895), and Paul Hermann (1898).*

It should be noted, however, that the more sophisticated levels of understanding of the mythology of the ancient Germanic peoples was not developed in time to be assimilated on a popular level during the generation in which the leaders of the National Socialist movement were growing up and being educated. Therefore, little of its true essence was ever actually expressed in the active ideology of Nazism.

Today, when we think of myth per se, we most often think of Greco-Roman mythology, or perhaps the Norse mythology that was preserved in medieval Icelandic literature. However, in Germany especially, there was a clear understanding of a *medieval* mythology as well—a heroic legendary set of narratives that spanned the spectrum from historical figures, such as Emperor Friedrich Barbarossa, to mythic heroes, such as Siegfried and Parzival. The Grimms had also

---

*The definitive history of the investigation of myth is provided by Jan de Vries in his *Forschungsgeschichte der Mythologie* (1961).

done their part in the collection and popularizing of these legends—for example, in their compendium titled *Deutsche Sagen*.* The medieval chivalric world of the German knights as depicted in their own mythic tales provided a suitable set of values for the aims and aspirations of the völkisch enthusiasts. The martial virtues of faith, honor, courage, and loyalty could easily be transferred from the chivalric tales to the field of cultural warfare in modern times. Other equally knightly virtues such as *milde* (kindness) and *mâze* (moderation) were all too often conveniently ignored.

It can be seen that Wagner, in his effort to encode a new mythic structure founded on his ideas, but clothed in the aesthetic of the past, used both ancient Germanic and medieval imagery in this effort.

Although myth had been historically used by cultures of the past to mobilize a collective cultural, political, and military willpower, it had never before been so scientifically studied in preparation for the theories being put to practical use. This conscious effort is itself characteristic perhaps of some sort of modern decadence. But it can also be seen as the only possible way in which modern man can come to understand the power of myth in anything approaching a popularized form. The necessity for myth being put to use in a popular way hinges on the growing effects of democratization. As more people were progressively enfranchised in the political process, and were thus able to affect the political and cultural directions of their nations, thinkers and leaders had to devise more pointed ways of conveying mythic ideas to an ever-broader social spectrum to motivate the masses in great movements. Karl Marx used a modern mythology, while others reached back to the past to try to revive what was perceived to be a lost heroic ethos. Myth, as properly understood and defined, appears to be the most effective means for communicating at this deeper level of cultural reality.

---

*The German word *Sage* is not the same as the Norse-derived term *saga*. In German, a *Sage* is a "legend," a type of material that concerns a historical place or person, about which or about whom mythic tales have developed. Legends are rooted in the landscape of local life and history.

ANTI-SEMITISM

Another symbolic theme of the nineteenth century was the growth of a new form of anti-Semitism. This theme belongs to the symbolic world of völkisch mythology because it developed in that framework in the late nineteenth century. To understand this trend requires some detailed knowledge of both modern and medieval cultural history. Ultimately, it will be seen that the form of anti-Semitism to which National Socialism subscribed was a secular creation of the nineteenth century but the *substance* out of which it was created was entirely rooted in medieval Christianity.

Although current popular culture might seem to insinuate it, the Nazis did not invent anti-Semitism. The term *anti-Semitism* was first coined in 1879 by the German writer Wilhelm Marr, who used it to identify a principle of his cause, which was to combat what he saw as growing Jewish influence in the social and economic life of Central Europe. According to the second edition of the *Oxford English Dictionary,* the term was first used in English in 1881—also in reference to the anti-Jewish cause. It was not used as a pejorative until 1935 in the context of anti-German propaganda.

Regardless of the history and implications of the term *anti-Semitism,* friction between the Jews and other peoples and religions is ancient and widespread. None other than Theodor Herzl, the founder of modern Zionism, said:

> The Jewish question still exists. It would be useless to deny it. . . . The Jewish question exists wherever Jews live in perceptible numbers. Where it does not exist, it is carried by Jews in the course of their migrations. We naturally move to those places where we are not persecuted, and there our presence produces persecution. . . . The unfortunate Jews are now carrying the seeds of Anti-Semitism into England; they have already introduced it into America. (Herzl 1904, 4)

Some of the stereotypical cultural characteristics imputed to the Jews by their enemies go back to pre-Christian observers. The aforementioned Tacitus, a pagan Roman historian, wrote an extensive description of the Jews from his particular perspective (*Histories,* V, 1–13) at the beginning of the second century CE. In these comments, he describes the Jewish religion as being "paradoxical and degraded." He roughly cites the events surrounding the biblical exodus of the Hebrews from Egypt but blames the exiles for bringing disease to Egypt and says that this is the reason why they were driven out of the land. Tacitus generally has nothing but disdain for the Jewish religion, which he, as well as other Romans, saw as tantamount to a superstition devoid of any philosophical sophistication. He depicts the Jews as a singularly immoral people: "Among the Jews all things are profane that we hold sacred; on the other hand, they regard as permissible what seems to us immoral" (Tacitus 1975, 273).* The reason for this special animosity probably stemmed from the perceptions that the Jews "despised the gods" and had "no feelings of patriotism" (Tacitus 1975, 273–74).† They stubbornly would not submit to Roman authority, while holding to beliefs of cosmic superiority. This was a formula destined to aggravate Roman sensibilities.

The comments made by Tacitus may seem surprising as they were written seventeen to eighteen centuries before the advent of secular anti-Semitism. However, they point directly to the ancient and deep-seated nature of the problem. Although systematic aggression toward the Jews is properly ascribed to the practices of the medieval Roman Catholic Church, it should also be remembered that the church felt itself to be the inheritor of the *Roman* Imperium—and perhaps with

---

*Here the depiction of the Jews by Tacitus was perhaps used by pagan Romans against the Christians, who were probably thought of as just another sect of Jews in the early centuries of the existence of Christianity in the Roman Empire. Many traditional Romans from the time of Tacitus and the next several centuries would have thought of Christians as an insurgent sect and a gang of criminals (was their founder not an executed criminal?) intent on overthrowing the empire—which they did.

†This view of the negative political and cultural position of the Jews expressed by Tacitus (1975, 273–74) was later used by church fathers, and nineteenth-century anti-Semites as well, to make propaganda against the Jews. First the Romans and then the Roman Christians sought to exclude the Jews from their body politic. This is the position that the Nazis imitated in the twentieth century.

this inheritance came all the former animosities of that empire. In general, it must be said that virulent and organized anti-Semitism has historically been found exclusively in the religions based on Judaic myth and theology: Christianity and Islam.

So-called church fathers such as Augustine and John Chrysostom actually created a mythology in which the Jews were seen as a specifically evil race. This relegation of other peoples to a status of existential inferiority and odiousness is not foreign to mankind in general; it was popular among the Chinese, Japanese, Egyptians—and most especially among the Jews themselves, whose historicized demonization of Egyptians, Moabites, Canaanites, Philistines, and Babylonians reached mythic proportions. Generally speaking, the historical Indo-Europeans did not demonize "others" because they would, as a rule, intermarry with those whom they conquered. They were for the most part literally and figuratively xenophilic. A notable exception to this can be found among the Aryans of India, who were certainly Indo-Europeans yet famously rejected the indigenous population of the subcontinent—at least in their mythology.*

Ultimately, the roots of ancient and medieval anti-Semitism, or animosity toward the Jews, may be traced back to their stubborn religious separatism and their mythic claims of exclusiveness. First Roman emperors, and later church councils, sought to limit the rights of Jewish citizens and subjects. For centuries, the Jews were generally restricted in the places where they could live and the kinds of professions they could pursue. Medieval papal decrees preventing Christians from lending money and charging interest on loans (usury) or acting as bankers, for example, both opened this line of endeavor to Jews and endeared those same Jews to secular kings, who often needed this loaned capital to finance their state apparatus and military campaigns.

The idea that animosity was properly and piously directed toward the Jews because they were somehow responsible for killing Christ

---

*The rivalry in Iranian mythology between *Ir*an and *Tur*an is, by contrast, a myth of ultimate inclusion and not rejection, as the people of Turan will also eventually come to accept the Truth, and thus become truly "Aryan."

developed later. This idea was perhaps an influence from primitive European (including Germanic) religious conceptions. If Christ is the same as God, and God is "our Father," then someone who murdered him should be subjected to the custom of blood vengeance. Of course, this whole paradigm ignores the supposed theological and soteriological function of Christ's death: his death and resurrection as signs of God's eternal grace and as a prerequisite for universal salvation. As illogical as this motivation for dislike of the Jews might be, it was nevertheless a powerful impetus for anti-Semitism among the masses of European peasants for centuries. In the Middle Ages, Jews were often blamed for calamities such as the Black Death in the fourteenth century and were expelled from areas such as Germany to be relocated in the eastern frontiers. In the medieval mind, God was punishing Christian people with these calamities for not sufficiently avenging Christ's death at the hands of the Jews.

Ancient and medieval forms of anti-Semitism, however, provide a clear background and context for later modern secular anti-Semitism. Without the earlier medieval and church-based context, the phenomenon of modern, nineteenth-century "biological" anti-Semitism would have been utterly impossible. The modern form of anti-Semitism proper is traced directly from the progressive emancipation of the Jews in the eighteenth and early nineteenth centuries. This general emancipation, or lifting of legal restrictions on the Jews, came in the wake of the Enlightenment. Friedrich the Great of Prussia (1740–1786) began to lift such restrictions encouraged by literary works such as *Nathan der Weise* (Nathan the Wise) by Gotthold Ephraim Lessing (1779). The American constitution (1789) provided for full citizenship regardless of religion. In France, the Revolutionary Constitution of 1791 provided for full rights of citizenship for the Jews, but those rights were eroded by the Napoleonic decree of 1808.

The general emancipation of the Jews followed throughout the northern part of Europe after the middle of the nineteenth century—for example, in Holland (1848), Denmark (1849), Britain (1858), Austria (1866), Prussia (1869), Sweden (1870), in united Germany at its inception (1871), Switzerland (1874), and in Norway (1891). This emancipation from legal restrictions on the participation of Jews in the economic and political activities of these countries was concurrent with the socioeconomic effects of the Industrial Revolution (1750–1850). The social upheavals connected to these economic developments, which occurred under the influence of liberalizing political policies (among them the emancipation of the Jews), caused deep-seated resentment and anxiety in more conservative cultural enclaves. It is among those who resisted modern development that the later form of anti-Semitism was inspired, in part, as a reaction to the increasing economic and political role of a people who had traditionally been considered a foreign nation resident within a host nation—be that Germany, England, France, or wherever.

The fact that the Jews were devoted to the development of their intellectual capacities, deeply honored learning, were often trilingual and not seldom highly ambitious once freed from the restrictive laws imposed from the Middle Ages, led to the circumstance of Jews often gaining great success in their host cultures in all fields in which they were allowed to participate. Their overrepresentation in high-level professions would later be used as proof of their conspiratorial nature.

The general intellectual foundations of anti-Semitism were being laid throughout the nineteenth century with racial theories and theories of racial inequality by Gobineau, which advanced the superiority of the Aryan race, and other thinkers and theorists such as Wagner, with his *Judentum in der Musik* (Judaism in Music; 1850 and 1869), and Houston Stewart Chamberlain, whose *Die Grundlagen des 19. Jahrhunderts* (The Foundations of the Nineteenth Century) appeared in 1899. But it was not until after the word *anti-Semitism* was first coined by Wilhelm Marr in his work *Der Sieg des Judentums über das Germanentum* (The Victory of Judaism over Germanism; 1879) that we can begin to speak about the kind of thinking that led directly to the form of anti-Semitism to which, for example, National Socialism subscribed.

Although the roots of anti-Semitism can be traced directly back to the medieval opposition between Judaism and Christianity, in modern times this shifted to an opposition between liberal modernism and conservative tradition. Jews were progressively liberated and brought increasingly into the mainstream of Western European social and economic life by expanding liberal economic and political reforms. Clearly, many modern anti-Semites interpreted the increasing presence of Jews in their society as the *cause* of the unwanted changes, not as an *effect* of those changes. If the principal opposition had remained religious—that is, a rivalry between Judaism and Christianity—then the völkisch movement in Germany would not have been so quick to be involved in anti-Semitism. But, as Hitler points out in *Mein Kampf,* in the mind of the Germanic nationalists, a minority had to be identified and targeted for hate simply as a mechanism to engender fierce nationalistic identity and solidarity among the majority.* Traditional religion had been discredited among many leaders of such movements, perhaps, but the masses were still deeply—even if unconsciously— moved by medieval passions. It was therefore necessary for the nationalists to reorient the nature of the animosity toward the Jews from a religious one to a racial or biological one. But obviously without the Christian medieval background, anti-Semitism would have been an impotent tool in the efforts of nationalistic theorists to galvanize and manipulate the masses.

When people today use the word *Nazi* as a pejorative term, it is interesting to ask them: "What's so bad about the Nazis?" The vast majority of people will have no answer to this, because of the abysmal level of ignorance that pervades contemporary society. However, the very few who do have a cogent answer will perhaps refer to the Nazis' mass murder of the Jews. If we view this crime as a criminologist would, we may ask: What was the motive for the crime? Clearly, the deep cultural and historical motives lie in ancient Roman, Roman Catholic, Lutheran, and general Christian animosity toward the Jews played out over almost two thousand years of history. For purposes of this study, we must acknowledge that the criminal motive is not directly connected to ideas of volkism or the occult. These connections are

---

*Among the Nazis there would be those who were virulent anti-Semites, and for whom the animosity toward the Jews was the dominant factor in their lives, while others viewed the whole matter cynically, as a mere means to a political end. For the former group, a driving motivation was hate; for the latter, it was an unbridled lust for power.

tenuous and indirect at best when compared to the long-established and deep-seated motives of the medieval mind of Europe. It is just as clear that later efforts to create a mythology of occult Nazi evil—with paganism, the occult, weird science, or even Satanism (!) as motivating factors behind Nazi crimes—are actually quasi-organized attempts by the true criminals to misdirect any would-be detectives. Realistically, the sum total of German involvement with the occult and related alternative cultural ideas that are the topic of this book is relatively insignificant when compared with the deeply established and usually quite conscious attitudes that were instilled in the ordinary German of the early twentieth century and that have their roots in the Middle Ages. The degree to which the leadership of National Socialism did employ occult techniques to manipulate the masses is only intelligible when we understand that the object of these manipulations would not have been pagans and occultists but rather the collective unconscious, or "mass mind," of the average and ordinary Central European citizens of the day.

As a side note, I believe that during the time of the Second World War itself, most average Americans or English people, when considering the question "What's so *bad* about the Nazis?" would mainly have been enraged by the Nazis' arrogant attitude about being a Master Race—when it was widely believed that *we* (read: Americans or English) were the real Master Race, after all! We will see that even "fringy" occult-type anti-German propaganda during the war (such as that of Lewis Spence) also tended to imply this attitude.

THE NINETEENTH-CENTURY FOUNDATIONS OF TWENTIETH-CENTURY VOLKISM

The underlying phenomenon that we identify as "volkism" is not limited to Germany nor to the modern world. It is simply the technical term for the manifestation of a mythic understanding of national (biological) heritage projected into the world of symbols and signs. In the Germanic world, a similar phenomenon was seen to manifest itself in Scandinavia in the early modern period when the Swedes thought of

themselves as descendants of Atlantis and to be the "original people."*
In fact, of course, such self-modeling is a feature of most archaic
societies—"volkism" in principle was the rule of the day in ancient
China, Israel, and India among the tribes of the Mediterranean from
the Spartans to the Romans. Nazi Germany was merely the last of the
major modern European nations to actualize these beliefs, and it did so
in such a dramatic and colossal manner that it has come to be almost
exclusively identified with a process of which it is merely the most mem-
orable example, but certainly not its last.[†]

THEOSOPHY

The seeds of volkism had been sown by the myth-makers and myth-
researchers, by the visionaries and national educators of the earlier
part of the nineteenth century, but the water and fertilizer for the true
growth of the völkisch movement was clearly provided by the occult
school of thought known as Theosophy, especially as espoused by its
leading figure, Helena Petrovna Blavatsky.

Theosophy did not enter into an ideological vacuum when it
arrived in German-speaking Central Europe in the 1880s. There
had already begun a general movement toward cultural alternatives

---

*This movement in Scandinavia, and especially in Sweden, is known as *storgöticism,*
"megalo-Gothicism." During the sixteenth to seventeenth centuries, Sweden was counted
as one of the world's great military powers, and it played a decisive role in the direction
of the Thirty Years' War (1618–1649). In this general period, leading Swedish figures—
especially scholars such as Johannes Bureus and Olof Rudbeck—promoted ideas extolling Sweden as the oldest country in the world and the Swedes as a people of special
destiny.

†The idea of "volkism" is likely an outgrowth of the ancient human beliefs about
tribal/ancestral mythologies, which are then artificially expanded into national models
in more recent times. The racial myth is virtually universal in human history, as the
study of more obscure examples tends to prove. One such example is that of the Korean
people, who have their own racial myth. This is the object of study by B. R. Myers,
The Cleanest Race (New York: Mellville, 2010). In the case of the Nazis, there is nothing particularly unique or special about their belief system other than that their efforts
were marked with great style, were well recorded for posterity, and the fact that they
came to serve a useful mythic role in twenty-first-century culture.

there, a movement that goes by the German label *Lebensreform* (Life Reform).* Reforms in many areas of life were envisioned largely by German thinkers: these included the environment, nutrition, health/medicine, sexuality, farming, land-use, education, clothing, theater, art, and human spirituality. The Reform movement is the great-grandfather of the American hippies[†] of the 1960s and must be viewed as a broad and all-inclusive movement beyond the model of partisan politics. The men who made up the Nazi leadership came of age when this movement was in full swing, which perhaps accounts for a great deal of the unorthodox beliefs held by many of these men—for example, why Hitler was a teetotalist, antivivisectionist vegetarian!

The Central European occult revival was just one part of the general Reform movement. The breadth of this movement is perhaps responsible for the depth to which new and unusual beliefs could so quickly penetrate the culture at a mass level. For the most part the ideas of the Reformers were and are good and wholesome ones. But the additional dynamism that these ideas insinuated into the turn-of-the-century culture also accounts for the radicalism that was comfortably practiced by that generation.

Blavatsky and Theosophy

The most important single event in the rise of the occult revival of the late nineteenth century in Europe was the foundation of the theosophical Society coupled with the works of its leading ideologue, Helena Petrovna Blavatsky (1831–1891). The major text of the theosophical movement, *The Secret Doctrine* (1888), is often cited in the literature of occult Nazism as somehow being the basis of Nazi racial doctrine and a host of other things. While the influence of Theosophy should not be underestimated when it comes to the general alternative culture of Europe and Germany in the late nineteenth and early twentieth centuries, a direct transference of theosophical doctrine to National Socialism

---

*The German Lebensreform movement is well documented in the reference work edited by Kerbs and Reulecke, *Handbuch der deutschen Reformbewegungen 1880–1933* (1998). †The origins of the American hippy phenomenon in the earlier German Lebensreform movement is the subject of Gordon Kennedy's 1998 book *Children of the Sun*.

Fig. 1.1. Theosophical seal

proves untenable. Rather, Theosophy provided a modern, eclectic alternative myth with which to oppose mainstream culture. Such alternatives always prove valuable to revolutionaries of any stripe, who seek first to destabilize the status quo and then to insert a new mythology with which to reshape society.

HPB

Helena Blavatsky, whose maiden name was von Hahn, was descended on her father's side from ethnic Germans. Born in 1831 in Ukraine, she had a stimulating childhood with inspiring female role models: her mother wrote feminist novels, and her grandmother was a dilettante in science. Helena was known for her active imagination and ability to spin wild tales. But when she was seventeen she was married off to a man twenty-three years her senior, Nikifor Blavatsky. He took her to Yrivan, Armenia, where he was to be vice governor. Soon thereafter Helena abandoned her husband, taking only his name with her to Constantinople.

The next twenty-five years are shrouded in mystery due to a lack of information. During this time, she supposedly traveled in Europe, the Middle East, and North America. She became involved in spiritualism and led a generally Bohemian lifestyle—she bore as many as two children out of wedlock and indulged in the use of drugs, especially hashish.*

In 1871, Helena Blavatsky founded a spiritualistic society in Cairo: the Societé Spirite. She eventually emigrated to the USA in 1873. The following year she met the journalist and occult enthusiast Henry Steel Olcott. The two became friends and partners in the business of the occult. In 1875 they founded the Theosophical Society (TS). Although Blavatsky was not the sole leader of the group at first, it was her charisma and voluminous writings that attracted and retained most Theosophists.

Not long after founding the society, Blavatsky visited the house of Hiram Carson in Ithaca, New York. The purpose of her visit was to help him make spiritualistic contact with his daughter, who had recently died. Based on the books she found in Carson's library, she began to write her first major work, *Isis Unveiled*. From the title it can be seen that this book traced—as has been usual in "New Age" think-ing since the time of Plato and Alexander the Great—the theosophical spiritual tradition back to ancient Egypt.

During its first few years, the society was not very successful. It seemed to lack any definition or identity outside spiritualism, and in making links to the myth and magic of Egypt and the Middle East it differed little from the mainstream. But Blavatsky began to forge a new identity for the group linked to India and the Aryan world. In 1878, there was a brief official merger between the TS and the Arya Smaj, an Indian cultural and political organization promoting a return to archaic Vedic, Aryan (Indo-European) values and customs. This was the start of a long-running close relationship that the TS would have with Indian society and politics. In 1879 the headquarters of the TS were moved to India. Theosophy became open to ever increasing amounts of Indian and Tibetan teachings.

It is only after the move to India that the Mahatmas (Great-souled

---

*Perhaps the best general introductions to the life and work of Blavatsky are offered by Bruce Campbell (1980) and Nicholas Goodrick-Clarke (2004). Blavatsky expended considerable effort trying to obscure many facts about her life.

Ones), or Masters, became an integral part of theosophical teachings. Blavatsky would later claim that she had been taught by them in Tibet, back in the obscure pre-1873 period of her life. It seems most likely that the Myth of the Mahatmas was created as a sort of sorcerer's trick to gain prestige, power, and charisma so as to give the message of Theosophy greater influence. Blavatsky had repurposed her mediumistic talent for communicating with people's dead relatives into an ability to make contact with "Hidden Masters."

The last five years of her life were devoted to writing her magnum opus, *The Secret Doctrine* (1888). This text is the chief summation of theosophical teachings. The society reached new levels of influence. In 1891, Blavatsky died. But her words and ideas would guide the Society for the foreseeable future.

THEOSOPHY: OCCULT MYTHOLOGY

There is no more important organization to the so-called occult revival of the nineteenth century than the Theosophical Society. It would exert formative influence on many other writers and groups, including the Hermetic Order of the Golden Dawn in England. *The Secret Doctrine* would become a sort of occult bible for countless individuals and organizations, regardless of whether they openly acknowledged the influence.

In fact, *The Secret Doctrine* does not seem to have been a singular text but instead started out as a three-foot-high stack of written pages with little organization, which Blavatsky brought to England from her sojourn in America (Campbell 1980, 60). Nevertheless, Theosophy did emerge as a more or less coherent system with certain major doctrines.

Theosophical Doctrines

Theosophy appealed to the educated minds of the nineteenth century because it successfully incorporated the idea of evolution into a spiritual framework. The ideas of Charles Darwin were certainly controversial, and remain so, yet the educated minds of the day tended to believe in this scientific theory. Evolution was found as a myth underpinning the origin and development of the cosmos (cosmogenesis) and of mankind (anthropogenesis). When it comes to the cosmos, great cycles of time are envisioned, called the Days and Night of Brahma: ages of cosmic expansion and contraction. Seen in the history of the development of humanity, Theosophy teaches an elaborate theory of root races. Of these there will eventually be seven. We are presently at the end of the evolution of the Fifth Root Race (the Aryans). Preceding the Fifth Root Race were the First Root Race (bodiless astral entities), the Second Root Race (boneless etheric entities), the Third Root Race (androgynous Lemurians), and the Fourth Root Race (giant Atlanteans). The Fifth Root Race is now dominated by the Aryans, but two further Root Races will evolve: the Sixth and Seventh Root Races, which will be vastly superior to the sort of mankind that currently exists.

Certainly, when it comes to race and interbreeding of races, Blavatsky cannot be seen as a precursor to Nazi ideology in any technical sense. She says:

> Occult philosophy teaches that even now . . . the new Race and Races are preparing to be formed, and that it is in America that the transformation will take place. . . . Americans of the United States have already become a nation apart, and owing to a strong admixture of various nationalities and inter-marriage, almost a race sui generis. . . . They are . . . the germs of the Sixth sub-race. (Blavatsky 1888, II, 444)

This will eventually evolve into the Sixth Root Race.

Theosophical teachings on the nature or constitution of the individual human being are generally drawn from esoteric Eastern traditions. Blavatsky (1888, II, 596) sees Man to be made up of seven constituent parts:

1. Universal Soul (Atman)
2. Spiritual Soul (Buddhi)
3. Human Soul, Mind

4. Animal Soul
5. Astral Body
6. Life Essence
7. Body

These correspond, of course, to the seven levels of human evolution encoded in the doctrine of the Root Races. The individual human is subject to the laws of reincarnation and karma roughly as defined by Eastern teachings: after death, reincarnation will occur in a higher or lower state, depending on the moral and spiritual nature of the life just lived and according to the actions (karma) of the individual.

Fundamental to theosophical mythology is the idea of the Hidden Masters and the origin of the teachings in Central Asia. The Central Asian origin myth provides a suitably remote and exotic locale to supply prestige, mystery, and a certain kind of plausibility—the world was less well known then and unexplored territories were extremely mystery laden. The Central Asian myth did two things: it removed the center of gravity from Egypt and the Middle East and transferred it to a location in keeping with what was believed at the time about the origins of the Aryans. The Hidden Masters who regularly communicated with Blavatsky provided authority and prestige on a continuous basis for her. The idea of a hidden directorate is an ancient one and is appealing to people in times when history seems to be spinning out of control. The existence of a master plan is reassuring.

THEOSOPHY IN GERMANY

On the one hand, Theosophy as a set of ideas, and the Theosophical Society as an organization, had great success in Germany. On the other hand, however, it was also subjected to radical reforms as offshoot philosophies were quickly and vigorously developed by German and Austrian innovators and syncretists. Ideas that lay dormant or unemphasized in Blavatsky's thought were sometimes brought to the forefront and developed in ways that responded to particularly German-speaking Central European cultural needs. Theosophy must also be seen in the context of the larger Lebensreform movement of Central Europe in the late nineteenth and early twentieth centuries.

The Theosophical Society and the writings of theosophists were introduced into the German-speaking world roughly ten years after their appearance in English. The Germans were thorough and for the most part enthusiastic in their acceptance of these basic ideas, which appealed to many sectors of German society. There was an early Theosophical Society in Germany in 1884 followed by new impulses from Franz Hartmann, Paul Zillmann, and others. The German sector was prolific in the production of multivolume series of published works, which included translations from English as well as original texts. *Die Geheimlehre,* the German translation of *The Secret Doctrine,* appeared between 1897 and 1901. By 1902 the Theosophical Society was well established in Central Europe, with major centers in Berlin and Leipzig, groups in ten other cities, and as many as thirty smaller circles throughout the region. The German branch of Theosophy was much more involved in the scientific, or pseudoscientific, investigation of psychic phenomena than was the parent TS.

In Vienna, Friedrich Eckstein founded a branch in 1887. Rudolf Steiner was a member of this circle. This group was artistic, subjective, sentimental, and made up of cultured individuals devoted to "mystical Christianity" and "personal Gnosticism" (Goodrick-Clarke 1985, 30). After the turn of the century, this group became increasingly anti-Catholic, nationalistic, and interested in mythology and folklore.

Two major figures from Austria, Guido von List and Lanz von Liebenfels, were directly and profoundly indebted to Theosophy for significant parts of their ideologies. As we will see when we study these two individuals and the movement they collaborated on, which Lanz called Ariosophy,* we will recognize many theosophical traits. Certain theosophical ideas were certainly the starting points for the development of Ariosophy, but Theosophy is not identical to Ariosophy, as many Nazi mythologists would like for us to believe.

---

*The term, which was certainly influenced by that of Theosophy (divine wisdom), connotes "Aryan wisdom."

Maximilian Ferdinand Sebaldt von Werth

Perhaps the most important, yet at the same time most obscure, link between Theosophy and Ariosophy is the person of Maximilian Ferdinand Sebaldt von Werth (1859–1916). This prolific writer was a bank director in Berlin, chairman of the theosophical lodge in that city, and a member of the Druiden-Orden (Druidic Order). He wrote several books on what he termed *sexual magic* and eugenics, most of which appeared under various pseudonyms, such as Maximilian Ferdinand and Professor G. Herman. He edited the journal *Die Schönheit,* which extolled nudism and the cult of beauty of the human form. In partnership with Richard Ungewitter, he formed the first nudist organization in Germany in 1906. This was the Wissenschaftliche Nacktloge A.N.N.A. (Scientific Nudist Lodge—Aristocratic–Nude–Nation–Alliance). Shortly before his death, Sebaldt von Werth held a lively meeting of the League for Naturalists (Bund für Naturkenner) on the topic of "The Geosophic Causes of the War"—in this case, of course, the contemporary Great War, which was still raging at the time. At this meeting, Johannes Balzli and Peryt Shou (1873–1953) had a heated argument about the occult geographic and temporal causes for the current war.

Sebaldt von Werth identified himself in his works as a "druid." This, however, did not have the meaning one might suspect. Sebaldt von Werth clearly sees the idea of Druidism as a common Celto-Germanic concept, an idea that goes back to an earlier time when druids, megalithic monuments, and Germanic antiquities were indiscriminately mixed together.* At the end of the nineteenth century, he was active in forming spiritualistic groups in Central Europe called Psychologische Gesellschaften.

An interesting aspect of Sebaldt von Werth's ideology is his belief in an ancient link between the German and Jewish cultures. This stems from the time of Atlantis in his mythic explanation. Because he was himself of partially Jewish ancestry, this particular idea must have

---

*This kind of association between the Germanic and Celtic peoples and their histories goes back into the centuries before Sebaldt von Werth was writing and is exemplified in Wilhelm Reynitzsch's *Über Truhten und Truhtensteine, Barden und Bardenlieder* (On Druids and Druidic Stones, Bards and Bardic Songs [Gotha: Ettinger, 1902]).

appealed to him greatly. He was not alone in having such ideas, however. For example, similar beliefs were held and articulated by the writer and later NSDAP member Hanns Heinz Ewers, who wrote an article titled "Why I am a Philosemite" (1916).

A survey of Sebaldt von Werth's works (most published between 1897 and 1909) demonstrates the clear lines of influence between himself and men such as List and Liebenfels. But at the same time, he was a unique thinker: he embraces Monism and demonstrates an eclectic approach, but often rebukes mainstream Theosophy for its Buddhistic bias, and rejects anti-Semitism.

His major works include *D.I.S.: Die Arische Sexual-Religion* (1897), a voluminous work on "Aryan Sexual Religion" that is reminiscent of the style of Blavatsky's *Secret Doctrine*. This book is made up of three parts: I. Diaphethur (Dis-Vater) Sexual-Mystik der Vergangenheit (Sexual Mysticism of the Past); II. Iggdrasil (Ich-Tracht) Sexual-Moral der Gegenwart ([Ego-Raiment] Sexual Morality of the Present); and III. Saeming (Besamung) Sexual-Magie der Zukunft ([Insemination] Sexual Magic of the Future). Another major contribution was *Genesis: Das Gesetz der Zeugung* (Genesis: The Law of Procreation), published in Leipzig in five volumes between 1898 and 1903. In 1909 he published *"Nackte Wahrheit:" Aktenmässige Darstellung des Verhältnisses zwischen Schönheits-Abenden und Nackt-Logen* ("The Naked Truth": A Documentary Presentation of the Relationship between Evenings of Beauty and Nudist Lodges).

Sebaldt von Werth's use of Germanic names and words and imagery are often much more suggestive than they are substantive. In general, it appears that he was more a part of the world of the Central European *Reformbewegungen** than he was of the strictly Pan-Germanic mystical milieu of men such as List and Liebenfels.

---

*Sebaldt von Werth's work appears to be a synthesis of various religious and mystical beliefs and systems, which he brings to the doorstep of a relationship with Germanic imagery and mythology. The substance seems drawn from Christianity and Theosophy, but the aesthetic and terminology are beginning to engage with Germanic ideology, or at least the icons of the latter. His ideas also seem to express much of what was on the minds of Reform-minded men and women of the German-speaking world in the 1890s.

It is noteworthy that the substance and core of the mysticism extolled by Sebaldt von Werth was rooted more in the popular scientific milieu of turn-of-the-century Central Europe than it was in the symbolic and mythic world of the Norse gods as inspired by Wagner. Clearly, the aims of Sebaldt von Werth were largely eugenic and directed toward the unfolding of something like the next theosophical Root Race. The mysteries are seen as physical and biological realities and not reserved to symbolic and mythic paradigms.

Although Sebaldt von Wirth clothed the aesthetic of his work in a Germanic and Nordic facade, it included elements from Christian, Buddhist, and Hindu ideologies. In other words, it followed in the general line of thinking pioneered by Blavatsky but with a predominantly Celto-Germanic tone.

Sebaldt von Werth widely uses ideas drawn from the biological sciences of his day. It is in this field that we will find many of the now obscure and discredited ideologies that were at the heart of a great number of the major basic assumptions of National Socialism.

THE ROOTS OF POSITIVE CHRISTIANITY

Because later mythology about Nazi occultism has focused so much on ideas of paganism and "weird science," one aspect of the movement that has gone virtually unremarked—although it is the only occult topic that would later be explicitly mentioned in the Party Program of the NSDAP—is "Positive Christianity." At first glance this formula appears to be a general reference to some sort of "affirmative" Christianity. But this is not the case. In this context, the German adjective *positiv* (from the French *positif*) actually refers to the philosophical concept of the application of critical knowledge and reason to the questions of theology and biblical text criticism pioneered by nineteenth-century thinkers such as Emil-Louis Burnouf (1821–1907) and Paul de Lagarde (1827–1891).

For some, the practice of what became known as biblical textual criticism among German philologists in the nineteenth century provided a deep blow to the possibility of believing in the doctrines taught by the church over the previous centuries. Such criticism had begun as early as the late seventeenth century, but it reached a high point among German philologists of the nineteenth century. As the Bible was scientifically (linguistically) demonstrated to be a hodgepodge of texts written at different times by various interests and authors, with little underlying coherence, it became harder for thinking men to believe in the mythology constructed by the churches. This, then, opened the door for elite thinkers to engage not only with a burgeoning atheistic scientism but with various forms of neopaganism as well.

Obviously, people had been thinking about the person of Jesus in a similar critical way for a long time. One is reminded of the third president of the United States, Thomas Jefferson, who created his so-called Jefferson Bible by taking a straight razor to the text and cutting out all references to things he thought to be unreasonable.

The French philologist Emile Burnouf was a professor of several oriental languages and an early (if poor) Indo-Europeanist. He identified the European connection to what he discovered in Sanskrit texts and thought he found the oldest Aryan religion. He spent most of his time still speculating on biblical tales, however. He thought the Hebrew peoples were really two different races: one that worshipped Elohim—who were Semites—and one that worshipped Yahweh. The latter group were centered in the Galilee region and were, in fact, Aryans. In Burnouf's mind, this racial difference explains why Jesus (an Aryan) was rejected by the Semites and accepted by Greek speakers.

Within this new criticism in Germany there continued to develop a strong element of nationalism and anti-Semitism. In the years prior to the establishment of the German Empire (1871), these trends were revolutionary, whereas after that date they became more conservative. The anti-Semitism of these thinkers was just another layer on top of the deep, persistent, and centuries-old anti-Semitic features of the mainstream churches (both Catholic and Protestant).*

---

*The history of anti-Judaic thought, or "anti-Semitism" as it came to be called and understood, is outlined in the monumental four-volume work by Leon Poliakov, *The History of Anti-Semitism* (Philadelphia: University of Pennsylvania Press, 2003).

In Germany, Enlightenment biblical criticism developed an agenda of "de-Judaizing" Christianity in the name of Reason. Johann Semler was a leader in this movement. He advocated for the emancipation of the Jews in civic life but also heavily criticized the Jews and Judaism using medieval stereotypes. The hidden agenda of some intellectuals at this time appears to have been to secularize the Jews and then absorb them en masse into the mainstream of European culture, thus eliminating them from history. Some even see the advent of Reform Judaism as a ploy to convert the Jews to something other than Judaism. To be fair, this intellectual movement toward textual criticism, with adherents such as J. G. Herder and August Schleiermacher, also led to advances in our abilities to interpret and understand texts and symbolic data from ancient sources. Using these methods, scholars have been able to show that the Jesus created by the church was a composite of ancient myth, a body of ethical teachings by a certain contemporary teacher (or tradition of a school of such teachers), and a fictional biography of the Jesus figure. This line of thought did not necessarily lead in anti-Semitic directions, but for many it did.

The grandfather of German Positive Christianity was Paul de Lagarde, a professor of Oriental languages (e.g., Syriac, Aramaic, Coptic, Hebrew, Persian, etc.) at Göttingen. Alongside his philological work, however, he developed an interest in the development of a new religion of the future rooted in a more purely German mind-set. He began writing prolifically on these topics after 1853, and his ideas were influential on both Wagner and Chamberlain. Through the pens of these writers, Jesus was transformed into an *Aryan* hero struggling against the Jews and Judaism. The magical or miraculous aspects of the story of Jesus were minimized (just as Enlightenment thinkers had done). Jesus was seen as a heroic teacher, whose death was a tragic consequence of his struggle—but not the prefigured ultimate sign of God's grace. It was commonly argued that the population of the Galilee region was Indo-Germanic, not Semitic, hence the Aryan pedigree of Jesus. Some suggested from ancient sources, both Christian and Jewish, that he was the biological son of a Roman soldier named

Pant(h)era (= Tiberius Julius Abdes Pantera). In the history of Christianity, a reimagining of Jesus in the image of the believers is not an uncommon occurrence—most strikingly, an example we see today is the "Black Jesus" phenomenon among modern Americans of African descent.

The *occult* dimension of Positive Christianity should be obvious given our previous definition of occultism. These theories were at first academic constructs—contrary to the established and accepted norms of theology—and never became established norms anywhere and continued to be virtual academic secret teachings. The genie was released from the bottle, so to speak, and into the mainstream via the popularity of Wagner and, more specifically, through the agency of Houston Stewart Chamberlain. (To this could also be added the "Antichrist" message of Friedrich Nietzsche.) This whole popularization did little to *establish* these ideas, which remained as esoteric as ever—and today find only vague reflections in what came to be called Christian Identity. Positive Christianity had its foundation in the highest ivory towers of the French and German academies, whereas Christian Identity and British Israelite traditions had far less stellar pedigrees.

In her 1994 article on Christian anti-Semitism, Doris L. Bergen notes the pivotal role played by long-standing Christian sentiments in making the crimes of the Holocaust possible. Without twelve hundred years of organized anti-Semitism on the part of both the Catholic and Protestant Churches, the activities of the twelve years of the Third Reich are quite incomprehensible.

✳ ✳ ✳

The nineteenth century is a time of great breakthroughs in human thought and science, but it is even more important as a preparatory staging ground for greater and more astounding things to come. The German nation-state was finally founded in 1871. The sciences of philology, linguistics, and comparative studies scientifically revealed many truths that had languished for centuries in the doldrums of misguided medieval tradition and superstition. For the formation of the NSDAP, the most important factor was perhaps the establishment of the existence of a distinctive and authentic Germanic culture. The importance of this idea was so great, its power so ground shaking, that the Roman historian Tacitus's treastise on Germania would be later thought of as a "black book of power"! In reality these things are just historical facts, but to a nation long in the dark about its own heritage, these ideas came as lightning bolts to the collective mind.

In the form of Theosophy the groundwork was laid for leading figures of the early twentieth-century völkisch movement, such as Guido von List and Lanz von Liebenfels. In Central Europe, the roots had been deeply struck for the Reformbewegungen movements that would profoundly affect the thoughts and beliefs of a wide spectrum of people living on the Continent. Much of this spirit was involved with a more rational and even scientific approach to life, humanity, health, and well-being on all levels. But as history will show, the rational can quickly be turned to an extreme misreading of reality.

As a final note for emphasis here: the völkisch concept has by now become identified with the virtually neopagan dimension of the alternative culture of the nineteenth- and twentieth-century German-speaking world. This understanding is, however, misguided and incorrect. Volkism is more general and all-encompassing than that. It simply implies that the value system of the person is centered principally upon the national identity—"race" in old-style parlance—of that person. Such people think primarily in terms of ethnic identity—they may be Christians, pagans, or pure materialists, but for them their race comes first.

It is only natural that distinct and highly identifiable groups of people—nations, tribes, and so on—develop myths about their identity and special place in the world. This is merely an extension and collectivization of a mythology in which an individuated person or group comes to believe in a special purpose or destiny for itself. These beliefs were originally bound to nations or tribes and then became artificially extended to cults and religions. The label of "volkism" generally refers to the reversion of people to the older model of having a special category based on actual (biological or symbolic) ethnic identity. In the folkish myth, a person who belongs to a particular folk does not have a choice in the matter; belonging is predetermined by a complex of natural birth, culture, language, and common history. Volkism has been practiced by many races throughout history; it is in Germany that this idea came to be articulated in a very clear form.

CHAPTER 2

FOUNDATIONS OF THE SCIENTIFIC CULTURE
Science and Pseudoscience of the Nineteenth Century at the Root of National Socialism

Myth, science, and occultism have always been closely related throughout history, although they are three distinct avenues of human thought. At the end of the nineteenth century, the English mage Aleister Crowley used the motto "The method of science; the aim of religion." This perfectly expresses the yearning of the nineteenth-century mind. Religion had been largely discredited among intellectuals, and science had exerted its own mythic grip on the imagination of humanity.

Nineteenth-century Germany was a hotbed of scientific activity. Not all of it was entirely orthodox by current standards. Some of these ideas became scientific gospel, whereas others were never accepted by the establishment. There were also ideas that had a momentary day in the sun before being obscured by historical or scientific developments. Occasionally, an idea thought to be crazy at the time might actually come to be accepted later, such as the hypothesis of continental drift first scientifically posited by Alfred Wegener. The image of the German as the mad scientist par excellence is an old one. When Mary Shelley wrote her great novel *Frankenstein,* she made the creator of the monster an ethnic German, and his creation was given life in the old German university town of Ingolstadt. In the nineteenth century Germany was seen by the English (and many Americans) as the land of dreamers, of dark impenetrable forests and of intellectual fanaticism.

The borderland between science and occult has always been a shifting one. Many of today's scientific disciplines started out as what is now considered occult thought; for example, chemistry started as alchemy, and astronomy has its roots in astrology. Of course, in traditional times there was a spiritual or symbolic side to practical observations and manipulations. Modern man sought to disengage these two components, the symbolic and the practical. We will also see how in Central Europe there are other examples of scientific work eventually sliding off into occult applications, such as with the "animal magnetism" of Mesmer or the "odic force" of Reichenbach. All of this only testifies more strongly as to the shifting line between what we call science and what we deem to be the occult.

In a greater sense, the occult, or magic, and science share many essential traits. The aim of magic or the occult is to make routine what is normally miraculous and to exert control over the otherwise uncontrollable. Science aims at similar goals, to make repeatable results from experimentation and to apply the results of these experiments to practical problems, thus controlling nature and the environment in ways about which ancient man could only have dreamed.

All branches of science were subject to either being generated out of the occult or falling into the occult realm if and when they proved impractical, untenable, or simply fell out of fashion intellectually. It is also true that many scientific theories that remain well established can be used as the inspiration for occult speculations without these speculations or theories in any way impinging on the scientific legitimacy of the theory in question. Here Darwinism springs to mind. At this point we will divide the sciences into two main categories: physics and biology. Under physics we discuss all things having to do with the mechanics of the mineral kingdom, while under biology we will look at anything belonging to the vegetable or animal kingdoms. This latter category will, for the purposes of our discussion, include *Homo sapiens.*

PHYSICS

The theories of physics fall into two categories. The first involves the science of the Earth and of the space surrounding it. Theories about these things frequently border on the religious or mystical, because they are often matters of belief for many people. Some still believe the Earth is flat, for example. The second category involves the analysis of more immediate forms of matter and its eventual manipulation in some technical way.

To this latter category belong the efforts of Baron Karl von Reichenbach (1788–1869), who tried to identify a vital physical force in the universe that permeated everything and was conducted by all living things. Reichenbach was a very well-established scientist in Germany and made many extremely practical contributions to chemistry, including the development of a number of valuable hydrocarbon compounds that included creosote, eupione, paraffin, and phenol.

Reichenbach turned away from these industrial pursuits in 1839, however, to pursue the study of the human nervous system and its disorders. Influenced by the ideas of Franz Anton Mesmer (see below), he developed a theory of environmental electromagnetism, which he came to call "od" or the "odic force." In the following passage, in lamenting the fact that he has not been able to create a machine to measure od, Reichenbach both provides the rationale behind the name of the odic force as well as defines it as an energy form which permeates all matter.

And the reason . . . why no odoscope has so far been invented springs from the very nature of od itself, that is to say, from its power of penetrating all matter and space without incurring congestion at any point, without permitting of its densification up to the point of general perceptibility. Heat, electricity, and light have isolators of their own up to a certain point, but I have never been able to discover an isolator for od. I have considered myself called upon to make use of this property of exemption from all obstructibility, in order to form a convenient name for it, pliable enough to adapt itself to the multifarious needs of science. "Va" in Sanskrit means "to move about." "Vado" in Latin and "vada" in Old Norse mean "I go quickly, hurry away, stream forth." Hence "Wodan" in Old Germanic [*sic*] expresses the idea of the "All-Transcending"; in the various idioms it appears as "Wuodan," "Odan," and "Odin," signifying the power penetrating all nature which is ultimately personified as a Germanic deity. "Od" is consequently the word to express a dynamid or force which, with a power that cannot be obstructed, quickly penetrates and courses through everything in the universe. (Reichenbach 1968, 92–93)

Because the odic force could not be measured, isolated, and ultimately manipulated in a scientific manner, it was eventually relegated to the occult, where it informed ideas of the human aura and so forth.

Beginning in the nineteenth century, there developed a scientific set of speculations concerning archaic geography. Myths of Atlantis had fascinated Western man since Plato gave rise to the legend in the fourth century BCE. It had been the object of utopian philosophers from Francis Bacon (*The New Atlantis;* 1627) to the Swedish polymath Olof Rudbeck (*Atland;* 1679–1702). Even Isaac Newton participated with his work *The Chronology of the Ancient Kingdoms Amended* (1728). In the middle of the nineteenth century, the Mesoamerican scholar Charles Etienne Brasseur de Bourbourg speculated extensively on the possible links between the Mayan and Aztec cultures, on the one hand, and that of the ancient Egyptians on the other. This idea persists in popular occult culture of today, even though the pyramids of Egypt predate those of Mesoamerica by as many as ten centuries! The myth of Atlantis really enters the occult world with the works of the American populist politician Ignatius Donnelly, such as *Atlantis: The Antediluvian World* (1882).

As the science of geology developed during the nineteenth century, it seemed that the geological record in many parts of the world corroborated the myth of a worldwide deluge having occurred many thousands of years ago. Christians would point to this evidence as proof of the flood of Noah, which led to his ark coming to rest on Mount Ararat. Scholars dismissed this idea because it was not ancient enough, and because this mountain is not very high when compared to the Himalayas, for example. In the late eighteenth century J. G. Herder pointed out that if there had been a worldwide deluge, the highest lands, such as the Himalayas, might not have been submerged at all and it was there that mankind could have survived and reemerged. This idea was later coupled with the discovery of the linguistic relationship of Sanskrit, the classical language of India, and the European languages (such as German, Greek, and Latin). This then led to the theory that the most ancient civilization of mankind stemmed from the Himalayan region. From these fairly simple and tentative assumptions, a whole set of esoteric doctrines would eventually be developed.* It should be noted that the initial jump to the conclusion of a truly worldwide flood is influenced by biblical narrative and is not supported by scientific data. Certain lower areas of the Earth were at times below water, but at no time was the vast majority of the landmass submerged.

Both the myth of Atlantis and that of the Himalayas as the cradle of civilization are exercises in the importance of the myth of origins in the struggle among cultures for prestige and hence political power.

BIOLOGY

As we have seen, the nineteenth century was characterized by advances in the life sciences, or biology. This interest in the life force and its origins, development, and uses was deeply rooted in the Romantic spirit of northern Europe at this time. Although these interests were generally purely scientific in nature, some of them were thought to have immediate applications in practical matters that aimed at fulfilling the Enlightenment's dream of perfecting mankind, or at least making man's life happier.

---

*For a general discussion of the Indo-Europeans and the history of the discovery of their existence and their connection to the modern world, see J. P. Mallory, *In Search of the Indo-Europeans* (London: Thames & Hudson, 1989). The basic error in trying to draw a biological connection by means of linguistic evidence is that the biological groupings of the human species took place long before the present-day systems of languages developed; so we can study human communities from a biological perspective going back hundreds of thousands of years, but we only have linguistic records for the past few thousand years. Plus, these linguistic records are of various ages and geographical distribution.

The most important figure in the history of German biological sciences in the late nineteenth century is the Jena professor Ernst Haeckel (1834–1919). It was Haeckel who introduced the ideas of Darwin to German science and furthermore popularized them in a quasi-political manner using an organization he founded called the Monist League (Ger. *Monistenbund*). One American historian, Daniel Gasman, made his reputation on two books that traced the roots of National Socialism not to occult organizations or Germanic myth and legend but rather to the prevailing biological science of the day. Gasman's two books are titled *The Scientific Origins of National Socialism* (1971) and *Haeckel's Monism and the Birth of Fascist Ideology* (1998).

There can be no doubt that Haeckel was a bona fide genius and that his ideas made significant contributions to the fields of biology, zoology, and the life sciences in general. He is, for example, credited with coining the terms *anthropogeny, ecology, phylum, phylogeny,* and *stem cell.* In his own lifetime he was generally credited with being a leading scientist. However, some of his ideas have subsequently been rejected (often for political reasons, and sometimes for scientific ones). His wider interest in the philosophical and political implications of his scientific work and the whole theory of evolution can be said to have relegated him to an intellectual gray zone between mainstream science and the occult realm of rejected knowledge.

Three currents of thought were brought together in Haeckel's intellectual vision: (1) Romanticism, as a nationalistic *Naturphilosophie* with its developmental (proto-evolutionary) idea of interconnectedness and distinct natural kinds; (2) materialism, as a positivistic, empirical science opposed to idealism; and (3) Darwinism, wherein the idea of struggle as the basis of the laws of human society is enshrined and seen as the struggle between the higher and lower races of humans.*

---

*In retrospect, despite the scholarship and erudition of Gasman, it would appear that he has made many of the same kind of errors as those who claim that the Nazis held certain pagan or occult views and then make the direct and causal *connection* to others in German culture who held similar views before them. Apparently, the same kind of false connections can be drawn in the scientific world as well.

Far from being a pure scientist, Haeckel was also an activist. He sought ways to popularize his ideas and have them make a difference in the lives of people living today and in the future. To this end he wrote books with a more popular appeal—such as *Natürliche Schöpfungsgeschichte* (A Natural History of Creation; 1868), *Anthropogenie* (1874), and culminating in his most important book, *Welträtsel* (Riddle of the World; 1899)—and formed organizations such as the Deutsche Monistenbund to implement and spread his ideas.

> Through evolution he studied the world and everything in it including man and society as part of an organized and consistent whole. He therefore called his new evolutionary philosophy "Monism," and contrasted it with all of traditional thought, which he rather disdainfully labelled "Dualism," condemning the latter for making distinctions between matter and spirit, and for invidiously separating man from nature. (Gasman 1971, 6–7)

In Gasman's view, it was clearly Haeckel's Monism and evolutionary philosophy, enthusiastically expanded into the realms of philosophy, sociology, religion, and politics, that served as a scientific basis for German ideas on eugenics and the concept of breeding a Master Race as a cosmically heroic act of political will. The Monist was as much an atheist as the Marxist; it was just that the Monist, and the National Socialist after him, would see the blood and biological aspects of life as a god, whereas the Marxist sees monetary value (*Kapital*) as a sort of god. The Nazi seeks to control and manipulate the blood to transform the world, the Marxist-Leninist wants to control and manipulate class, labor, and capital to a similar end.

One important aspect of the study of the influence of the radically new scientific theories of Monism and the ideas of Haeckel is that it flies in the face of the Marxist critique of National Socialism as an irrational reaction to modern scientific social progress. Monism was allied with atheistic "free thought" (*Freidenken*) in Germany and as such was not ideologically that distant from the ideas of the Bolsheviks. In fact, many of the ideas that were incorporated into Bolshevism in Russia had their roots in the ideas of German Monists.

We shall also see that Hitler and the National Socialists were actually shown the way to the implementation of eugenics programs not by the Monist League of Haeckel and his followers but by the unlikely, yet well-documented, source of the American eugenics movement and the ideas of the American industrialist Henry Ford. Despite all the fantastic ideas ascribed to Hitler and to Nazi eugenics (breeding a Master Race with superhuman powers, etc.), for the most part NS eugenics will be seen to be a fairly down-to-earth ideology more at home in a barnyard than a mad scientist's laboratory.

HOMEOPATHY

Homeopathic medicine was first tentatively suggested by a Paracelcean formula: *experientia ac ratio* (experiment and apply reason). But this type of medical therapy was only developed into a modern system with the work of the German physician Samuel Hahnemann (1755–1843). The basic idea behind homeopathy is that remedies for diseases are prepared by making use of substances that cause effects similar to the symptoms of the disease in question. The actual amount of active ingredient is often either negligible or entirely absent by the time the preparation is complete. Obviously, the roots of this theory go back to alchemical concepts, which make use of the law of similars. Homeopathy was a respected alternative form of medicine throughout much of the nineteenth century, especially in the Reform movement in Germany.

But over time, as its remedies and medicines were independently subjected to more rigorous scientific examination and found to be lacking any form of effective therapeutic value, homeopathy quickly began to fade into the alternative subculture, where it continues to find adherents today (homeopathic pharmacies are still widely found in Germany, Austria, and other European countries). By the time Himmler was encouraging homeopathic experimentation in the concentration camps, such things were already considered a pseudoscience by the mainstream Western medical establishment.

In the scientific world, the human cranium and its contents have become the focus of research concerning human development and behaviors. Mental disorders that were once attributed to "unclean spirits" in the Christian etiology of disease are today more often ascribed to physical causes in the brain, such as chemical imbalances or hyper- or hypoactivity in certain areas of the brain. In the nineteenth century scientists were also looking at physical manifestations as indicators of psychological states, human character, and intelligence. Certain scientists meticulously measured the human skull and developed a typology of the skull based on so-called racial types, with the Nordic type being the dolichocephalic (long-headed) kind. This study was referred to as "craniometry," and the classificatory system of measurement developed by the craniometric scientists was taken up by physical anthropology as a convenient system of analysis of various human types, but originally this system also addressed the idea of cranial capacity and linked it to intelligence. Pioneers in this field were the Americans Samuel George Morton (1799–1851), Josiah Nott (1804–1873), and George Gliddon (1809–1857), and the Frenchman Georges Vacher de Lapouge (1854–1936). Their ideas suggested a polygenistic origin of the human races—in other words, that they evolved from different genetic lineages in different regions of the world. This, by the way, was entirely contrary to Darwin's idea of monogenism, that mankind has a single origin and a common ancestor. Darwin's theory has been supported by more recent genetic science. Polygenism is a theory favored by racists for obvious reasons. Josiah Nott contributed a scientific appendix to the first English translation of Arthur de Gobineau's *Essai sur l'inégalité des races humaines,* which appeared under the title *The Moral and Intellectual Diversity of Races* in 1856. Theories of this kind, based on craniometry, were to fall by the wayside and be relegated to the junk pile of science during the twentieth century.*

---

*Many of the crackpot racial theories of history are reviewed by Stephen Jay Gould in his book *The Mismeasure of Man* (New York: Norton, 1981).

One often overlooked aspect of the Nazi embrace of the idea of eugenics is the fact that these ideas and many related practices, such as forced sterilization and the promotion of selective breeding, were advanced and supported most of all by Americans. At first the Nazis mainly imitated and followed the practices and ideas of the British and especially the American pioneers in this field. Few people today are aware of the degree to which many American states actualized eugenics programs in the late nineteenth and early twentieth centuries. These were supported by men such as Theodore Roosevelt and Henry Ford (who was also a strong influence on Hitler's anti-Semitism). The Carnegie Institution and the Rockefeller Foundation both funded eugenics programs, some of them in Nazi Germany itself, and Margaret Sanger (founder of Planned Parenthood) was also active in the American eugenics movement. Post-WWII propaganda, which tried to make it appear that only those crazy and evil Nazis thought of things such as "selective breeding," "forced sterilization," and attempted to create a "perfect race," can in many ways be seen as an effort to deflect truthseekers from discovering and realizing that it was in America that these ideas were first implemented and made practical. The Carnegie Institute even funded a 1911 study that included euthanasia as one of the methods for cleansing society of undesirable genetic traits. The glaring differences are those of scale, scope, and style—the Nazis did it bigger, broader, and with more imagination—rather than philosophical principles.* It certainly seems at this point that the very idea of eugenics has become, if not an occult idea, certainly a taboo one.

* * *

The nineteenth century was one in which science made many theoretical leaps, and technology was beginning to reform human society in

---

*For a general history of eugenics, see Bashford and Levine (2012). The topic remains so loaded with scientific, political, and cultural controversy and conflicting agendas that it is difficult to find a general objective viewpoint. For a history of eugenics in an American context, see Isenberg's politically correct presentation in her fascinating study *White Trash* (2016, 174–205).

profound ways. The ever-increasing educated masses also turned their questioning minds to matters of the mysterious and stange on a scale never before known in human history.

In the next chapter, we will see the extent to which scientists of some repute in the rigorous world of the German *Naturwissenschaften,* or natural sciences, became involved in what are generally thought to be the occult sciences.

CHAPTER 3

FOUNDATIONS OF GERMAN OCCULTISM
The Deep Occult Background of the Age

Germany had for centuries been seen as the land of the occult. When Englishmen or Americans thought of alchemists, sorcerers, and mad scientists they thought first of Germany. This was, of course, in many cases their own primeval homeland, too, and a suitable place to look for origins—both good and evil. When it comes to matters of the occult, Germany delivers on many of these expectations. This runs along a spectrum spanning from the fantastic wizardry and witchcraft contained in the folktales collected by the Brothers Grimm to the ceremonial magic and philosophical approach of Paracelsus, magician, alchemist, and father of modern medicine and pharmacology.

When the founders of the Hermetic Order of the Golden Dawn wanted to conjure up a locale for the mysterious origins of their order, so as to give the latter more prestige, they placed the point of origin in Germany.* The mythic prototype of the dark magician, Faust, was a German. Besides the aforementioned Paracelsus, other occult personalities from Germany include Albertus Magnus (ca. 1200–1280)

---

*Ellic Howe, writing in his sober historical account of the Golden Dawn (1978, 1–25), concludes that the "Cypher Manuscripts" upon which the Golden Dawn was founded are likely to have been forgeries concocted by William Wynn Westcott. These manuscripts supposedly had a German origin, although they were written in English! Clearly, there were several motives for locating the origin of the order in Germany: the exotic locale makes the origins more obscure and less subject to questions; Germany was point of origin for Rosicrucianism, to which the Golden Dawn had a theoretical attachment; and Germany was also seen as a land of dark mystery where all sorts of strange things have their origins.

and Heinrich Cornelius Agrippa von Nettesheim (1486–1535). The whole of the Rosicrucian tradition (1614–ca. 1700) had its origins in German-speaking areas of Europe as well.

The occult revival of the nineteenth century, which would to one degree or another influence ideas held by some of the leaders of the National Socialist movement, had its direct origins in the ideas and writings of Emmanuel Swedenborg (1688–1772) and Franz Anton Mesmer (1734–1815), for it was from these roots in spiritualism and animal magnetism that the American spiritualists such as Andrew Jackson Davis and the Fox Sisters derived their operating assumptions from about 1848 onward. These American pioneers of popular spiritualism quickly gave further impetus to a German movement that was already underway.

Whereas the American spiritualism of the Davis and Fox variety was but thinly veiled carny trickery (confessed as such by the Fox sisters, Kate and Margaret, in 1888), when these ideas took root in Germany they were further tended in the soil of German academia, natural sciences, and medical science.

But the German-speaking world was also an old hotbed of what might be called superstitious beliefs in ghosts, witches, and prophets. The whole of Central Europe was a maelstrom of tales of the magical and uncanny. Famously, the entourage of Lord Byron to which Mary Shelley belonged in the summer of 1816 read from a book titled *Fantasmagoriana, ou Recueil d'Histoires d'Apparitions, de Spectres, Revenants, etc.* (1812), which was a French translation of German stories published in the *Gespensterbuch* (Book of Ghost Stories; 1811–1815). Such stories were thought to be sufficiently German as to lend the name Gothic to the genre.

The volatile mixture of magic and secret organizations, on the one hand, and politics on the other seems to have been a constant feature of German and Austrian culture. The most notorious of these is the Bavarian Illuminati—a favorite bugbear of current American right-wing fantasists. The later demonization of the Illuminati is a strange chapter in conspiracy theory. The Illuminati, founded by Adam Weishaupt in 1776, was organized on a three-man cell structure. The ideology of the

Illuminati was virtually the same as the American Founding Fathers: international brotherhood of man, equality of men (no distinction between "noble" and "common"), freedom of speech and religion, and so forth. Their opponents were the royals, who ruled by divine right. The Bavarian Illuminati was eventually broken up by the Bavarian police as a threat to civic order. The opponents of the Illuminati believed in the power of kings over their subjects and the rigid control of the church over the common individual.

In the earlier part of the nineteenth century, occultism, or the night-side of the soul, was still the purview of Romanticism. This was rooted in the *Naturphilosophie* of Friedrich Schelling, which became current in 1799. Schelling's philosophy, in turn, owed much to the writings of the Viennese physician Franz Anton Mesmer, whose theories on "a mysterious healing force known as animal magnetism" (Treitel 2004, 34) swept Europe in the 1770s. Schelling's ideas hinged on the concept of a "world soul" closely connected to Mesmer's concept of animal magnetism. Groups, schools, and congresses sprang up all over Germany dedicated to experiments in Mesmerism. Mesmer postulated that energy flowed freely through thousands of mysterious channels in the human body. Obstructions of these channels caused illness and mental disturbances. If these obstructions could not be freed in a natural manner, then the techniques he had developed were brought to bear. Mesmer's experiments are considered precursors to the practice of hypnotism.

Writers such as E. T. A. Hoffmann and Clemens Brentano embraced these ideas, as did the philosopher J. G. Fichte. The whole idea of the night-side of the human soul entered academia, with chairs devoted to animal magnetism being established at two German universities (Bonn and Berlin). While much of German academia was beginning to tend toward materialism and reject such notions as the night-life of the soul, one man, Arthur Schopenhauer posited the idea of the will as a transcendental link between the unconscious and practical metaphysics. His ideas would inspire a new generation, including Friedrich Nietzsche.

Occult ideology only really starts to have any widespread appeal and notoriety in the mass culture in the 1890s. In that decade publishing houses, magazines, and organizations began to proliferate.* This time frame is, of course, significant to our present study because most of the leaders of the NSDAP were born approximately during this period. They would have spent their whole lives in an environment shaped by an undercurrent of these ideas.

SPIRITUALISM AND PSYCHIC INVESTIGATIONS

Spiritualism has its roots in the activities of the American charlatans Andrew Jackson Davis and the Fox sisters, Kate and Margaret. But its ideas greatly influenced the imaginations of people outside the limits of spiritualism as such. In many ways spiritualism follows the lead of Mesmer. The distinguished German botanist, zoologist, physician, and natural philosopher Christian Gottfried Daniel Nees von Esenbeck (1776–1858) was a professor at Breslau. He was an investigator into the ideas of Mesmer and then discovered the spiritualistic writings of Andrew Jackson Davis and had these translated into German by Gregor Konstantin Wittig. Wittig then developed a whole series of publications called *Bibliothek des Spiritualismus für Deutschland* (Library of Spiritualism for Germany), which began issuing editions in 1868. Nees von Esenbeck became more seriously involved in political life after the events of 1848. This led to the loss of his professorship, forcing him to live very meagerly until his death. In 1873, Wittig founded a spiritualistic association in Leipzig and published the journal *Psychische Studien* beginning in 1874. This was the leading occult publication in Germany at the time.

In the 1870s in Leipzig there was an academic circle led by a professor of astrophysics, Johann Karl Friedrich Zöllner (1834–1882). This circle included many other leading professors as well (Treitel 2004, 3–4). An American medium of questionable repute named Henry Slade,

---

*Corinna Treitel provides a wonderful resource in her book *A Science for the Soul* (2004, 264–73) on the many publishing houses, magazines, and organizations that arose in the late nineteenth and early twentieth century in German-speaking areas of Central Europe. This data shows the general distribution of interests and gives some idea about the size of the movement in the context of the larger society.

Fig. 3.1. The first issue of the German theosophical journal *Die Sphinx,* 1886

at the time fleeing charges against him in England, arrived on the scene in Leipzig. Zöllner enlisted Slade in experiments revolving around Zöllner's theories concerning the fourth dimension. Zöllner concluded that the phenomena attributed to departed spirits of humans were actually linked to an intersection between our world of three dimensions and one that includes a fourth dimension of time-space. Zöllner postulated a form of transcendental physics: whereas most spiritualists of the day ascribed the supposed phenomena that occurred in séances to the spirits of departed humans, Zöllner left the cause of the phenomena open—they could be entities from the fourth dimension or psychological factors yet unknown. Zöllner's theories led some of his contemporaries to consider him insane.

Other scientific investigators in this area were Gregor Konstantin Wittig and Alexander Aksakow, who put out the monthly journal *Psychische Studien* between 1874 and 1925, while Eduard von Hartmann published *Der Spiritismus* in 1884. Following in the wake of Zöllner were other subsequent quasi-scientific explorations of the unseen world. In 1886, the Psychologische Gesellschaft (Psychological Society) was founded, as was the theosophical journal called *Die Sphinx*. This journal, published by Wilhelm Hübbe-Schleiden, was very influential and featured a wide variety of authors (including Leo Tolstoy and the Social Democrat Kurt Eisner). Articles in *Die Sphinx* covered a wide range of topics including astrology, magic, and other occult sciences. In March 1886 there appeared an article by A. Chiltoff titled "Fernwirkung des Willens" (Long-Distance Effect of the Will). The Psychological Society used scientific methods to investigate the results of mediums in order to discover new things about the human mind.

The late nineteenth-century school of quasi-scientific occultism in Germany is best exemplified by the debate between two leaders of the movement, Albert von Schrenck-Notzing and Carl du Prel. As a philosopher, du Prel was interested in founding a school of "transcendental psychology" as a scientific way of opposing the prevailing materialism of his time. Schrenck-Notzing, on the other hand, was desirous of bringing the "occult sciences" out of the shadows of mysticism and into the light of hard science through the newly developed advances in hypnosis. In 1889 the two went their separate ways, with du Prel founding the Gesellschaft für Experimentalpsychologie while Schrenck-Notzing continued to lead the original organization, out of which emerged the study of parapsychology.

The world of practical magic, even folk magic, was summarized in the 1840s in the monumental twelve-volume work undertaken by Johann Scheible called *Das Kloster* (1845–1849). It contained printed versions of magical grimoires from earlier times, tales of magic and magicians, folk-magic practices, and the like. This popular collection is really a testimony to the widespread interest in such things as early as the middle of the nineteenth century.

In Germany during the late nineteenth century there was a growing popular interest in the history of magic and occultism, but the main new contributions came in the form of a pragmatic and experimental approach to concepts and procedures that had formerly belonged to the shadow world of the occult. Psychic phenomena, spiritualism, and hypnosis increasingly came to be thought of in *scientific* terms. The roots of concepts such as mind-control through long-distance hypnosis lay far back in the folklore of magic, but it seems that the German mind of the late nineteenth century was moving these ideas ever closer to the world of experimental science.

As we have already seen, the theosophical movement in Germany was at first heterogeneous in its origins and organization. Regardless of this, little serious organization took place until the 1890s. The earliest record of theosophical activity in Germany is the foundation of the Loge Isis in Hamburg in 1879. Another group connected with theosophical circles was the Illuminaten-Orden, theoretically founded in 1895 by Theodor Reuss, a singer, journalist, Prussian spy, and sometime activist in socialist causes in England. This organization evolved into the Ordo Templi Orientis (OTO). Some of the men involved in these organizations—Theodor Reuss, Karl Kellner, Leopold Engel, and Heinrich Klein—had some connection with the Hermetic Brotherhood of Light, which preserved the teachings of the American occultist Paschal Beverly Randolph concerning sexual magic. In any event, Reuss especially must have taken advantage of the great conflux of influences that came about in the 1890s in the German-speaking world. The sex-magical ideas of American and English writers, such as Randolph, his student Reuben Swinburne Clymer, and the phallicist Freemason Hargrave Jennings, converged with the growth of the study of, and obsession with, sexual matters in Central Europe beginning especially with the publication of the study *Psychopathia Sexualis* by Richard von Krafft-Ebing in 1886. Sexology was just on the verge of being shaped by thinkers such as Max Hirschfeld and Havelock Ellis. Although this would later become more popularized due to the prolific writings of the English magus Aleister Crowley, the original OTO was a far more secret affair, as it had to be at the time.

A word and concept that would play a part in later mythology surrounding Nazi occultism, *Vril* and *Vril-ya,* had its origins in the consciousness of the West in works published in the late nineteenth century. Edward Bulwer-Lytton wrote a novel called *The Coming Race* in 1871, in which a power called Vril was posited. Just a few years later, in 1873, a French consul in Calcutta named Louis Jacolliot wrote a book titled *Le fils de Dieu* (The Sons of God; 1873) and three years later one called *Les Traditions Indo-européennes et Africaines,* both of which mentioned the existence of a power called Vril. There is a record of a group called the Vril Gesellschaft (Vril Society) founded in 1923.

ASTROLOGY AND POPULAR MAGIC

Reading portents in the stars, a medieval preoccupation, had almost entirely died out of any sort of popular interest in Germany by the nineteenth century. Interest had fared better in England, but in France astrological knowledge was just about as sparse as it was in Germany.

A certain professor of mathematics in Erlangen, Julius Pfaff (1774–1835), published a study titled *Astrologie* in 1816 in Nuremberg. It would be the advent of the Theosophical Society, which would provide the root of renewed popular interest in astrology in Germany during the late nineteenth century (Howe 1984, 78–79). Up to that point, German interest in astrology had been a relatively subcultural phenomenon. Karl Kiesewetter (1854–1895) was the first to write anything about it in German in *Die Sphinx.* Interest in astrology among the Theosophists of Britain as well as Germany would get its start in the nineteenth century, but it would not be until the advent of the new century that this would bear any fruit.

It should also be mentioned that in the nineteenth century there was quite a craze in the German-speaking world for what we would today call stage magic. Practitioners of these arts gained widespread fame and notoriety, especially in Vienna. These included Ludwig Döbler (1801–1864), who pioneered techniques that paved the way for the motion pictures of later times, and Johann Nepomuk Hofzinser (1806–1875), who specialized in card magic. At that time, and well into the twentieth century, such performances remained tinged with the supernatural and paved the way for figures such as Erik Jan Hanussen in Berlin (see chapter 6).

Without these foundational aspects of culture in the areas of nationalistic symbolism, scientific and pseudoscientific theories, and occult beliefs and practices, the concrete basis for the mind-sets of the founders and promoters of what became National Socialism would have been impossible. This is the situation, there can be no doubt, but it would be a mistake to believe that there was something utterly unique about such a concatenation of elements. While the exact mixture of the elements under examination here was unique to late nineteenth-century Germany and German-speaking Central Europe, it can be seen that a similar formula could result in similarly momentous developments in other times and places throughout history. For example, equally complex constellations of specific circumstances would be necessary for the foundation of the Italian Renaissance, the American Revolution, and the Bolshevik Revolution as well. Big events are not the result of spontaneous generation, but rather they spring from the seeds and germs of a fertile ground that provides them a requisite foundation.

It must be emphasized that the cultural phenomena of volkism (with both a pagan and Christian orientation), the unorthodox applications of scientific and pseudoscientific theories and methods, as well as matters of overt occultism itself, all existed within, and were supported by, a more general social atmosphere shaped by the Life-Reform movements (Lebensreformbewegungen) that were interpenetrating all aspects and levels of German-speaking culture from the late nineteenth century forward. These various movements, which had no central authority or unified direction, began in earnest circa 1880, but had deeper roots, of course. By the 1890s and most especially at the inception of the twentieth century, these movements, which strove for radical reforms in all aspects of life, had become a part of German popular culture, affecting even those who professed no special interests in the specific agendas of the Reformers. And for those who were searching as young people for new solutions, the landscape was rich in radical alternatives.

PART II

Before Hitler Came
(1900–1919/1933)

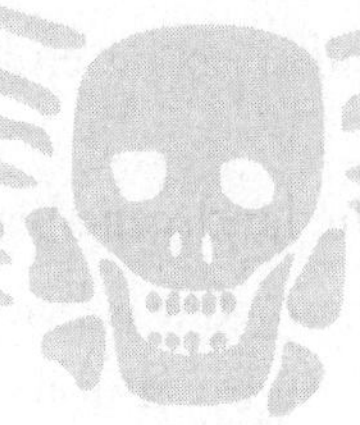

INTRODUCTION TO PART II

The turn of the twentieth century was a time of dramatic and astounding change and breakthroughs in every avenue of human endeavor. The world was ripe for revolutionary change, and there was a variety of men and movements ready and willing to make these leaps into the unknown. Technological revolutions such as the light bulb (1879), the motion-picture camera (1891), powered flight (1903), radar (1904), radio (1906), and the affordable motor car (1908) all served as transformational developments. These technical inventions also fired the imaginations of people on a popular level, and this was mixed with dramatic new ideas in social organization. Marxism was on the march from the 1850s onward; Social Darwinism from the 1880s onward; and in the very year of 1900, Freud published *On the Interpretation of Dreams,* inaugurating a new era of psychology. These new developments were stimulating in a special way in the German-speaking lands of Central Europe, where the ideas of the Reform movement were well-established. The upshot of this was that radical solutions to age-old problems and questions tended to be embraced with a special—even fanatical—enthusiasm.

Without Hitler there would probably have not been a National Socialist movement of the kind that it became. His skills at organizing and motivating an array of highly ambitious, power-hungry, ruthless, and violent men are the material of myth and legend. His first encounter with the rag-tag seed-group that he would shape into the National Socialist German Workers' Party in July 1919 would be a watershed moment in history. One of the men in that original circle, Rudolf von

Sebottendorf (1875–1945), would later write a book titled *Bevor Hitler kam* (1933) about the movement that Hitler shaped. The heading of this section is based on that book's title.

In this section I will discuss things that occurred in the realm of the occult subculture prior to the year 1919 and therefore are not directly linked to the National Socialists. The DAP/NSDAP was first organized in 1919, and that is why this date is of such great importance to the present study. Many of the initiatives that were developed in the first part of the twentieth century, such as the Guido von List Society or the Ordo Novi Templi, and that continued to exist in some form until well after the Nazis took control of the German government (1933) and annexed Austria (1938), more naturally belong in this chapter. Although we cannot speak of actual National Socialism before 1919, its advent into German life can be measured over the fourteen-year period between 1919 and 1933, when the Nazis officially come to power in Germany.

The early twentieth century was a boiling cauldron of historical events. Technology was exploding, science was advancing, economies were booming, and many in the world were filled with unbridled optimism about the future. *Progress* was a myth that was being fulfilled. It was an age of visionaries and men of action—until it all came crashing down in the blood-drenched trenches of France and a hundred other fields of mass slaughter across Europe.

To appreciate fully the occult trends in a given culture, the overall historical and social context of a given region must be addressed. Historically, the most important event during the period we are focusing on here is the so-called Great War, or the "War to End All Wars," later to be dubbed the First World War (July 28, 1914–November 11, 1918). In 1919, the year after the war, and as a response to the political defeat of Germany and Austria, the NSDAP was engendered. It was also the year in which both Guido von List and Ernst Haeckel died, and the Weimar Republic was formed.

At the turn of the twentieth century, Germany had more Ph.D.s per capita than any other country in the world. It was the most educated and most literate of the world's major nations. Germany led the globe in many areas of the arts, sciences, and industry. Industrial areas such as steel, optics, pharmaceuticals, and chemical engineering were dominated by the Germans. Germany was still a young political entity, having become a unified state only in 1871. By contrast, Austria had political roots going back to the days of Charlemagne.

In some ways Austria, or the Austro-Hungarian Empire as it had become by the early twentieth century, was a cultural part of Greater Germany when it came to language and education, but politically it was very different. Both were monarchies, but Germany was largely a homgeneous population, mostly identifying as German and having German as their first language. Austria, on the other hand, was a true empire made up of as many as eleven different nations or major ethno-linguistic groups: Germans, Poles, Czechs, Slovaks, Slovenians, Croatians, Serbians, Ukrainians, Hungarians, Romanians, and Italians. Historically, German had been its official language, and the language of education, but after 1867 the minority languages began to make inroads into the German linguistic hegemony as the different ethno-linguistic groups vied for political power. The tensions between and among the various ethnic groups in the empire was the backdrop of the assassination of the Austrian Archduke Franz Ferdinand on June 28, 1914, which was the spark that set the Great War into motion.

The world of the early twentieth century was a witches' cauldron of contradictions. The modernist belief in unlimited progress based on the rational application of scientific principles was riding high, but skepticism about, and resistance to, the dream of the modern world ran just as deep.

The United States had entered the world stage as a geopolitical player, while the British Empire had not yet begun to show its fatal cracks and flaws. In the East, the collapse of Russia during the war and the consequent Bolshevik Revolution of 1917 meant that there was an aggressive exporter of revolutionary ideology on the eastern edge of Central Europe. The idea of socialism was in the ascendancy across much of Europe.

Soon after the turn of the century, the völkisch movement began in earnest. Men such as Guido von List and Lanz von Liebenfels, with some of their ideological roots in theosophical thought, began to articulate a vision of volkism that went well beyond anything that had been imagined previously. In the case of List, this would be cast largely in a pagan or pre-Christian mold, whereas Liebenfels primarily used medieval Christian imagery. The pagan dimension of Ariosophy has been greatly exaggerated for reasons we will explain more thoroughly in chapter 6. The far more common and mainstream folkish approach was one that understood itself within the framework of Christian imagery and mythology. This ran the gamut from the extreme eccentricities of the ONT to the far more lethal trends found in the ideologies of the mainstream denominations. This last aspect would find expression in what became known as Positive Christianity, with its roots in nineteenth-century theology and its Wagnerian synthesis.

Generally speaking, early twentieth-century German opposition to Christianity and Christian doctrines was not so much rooted in pre-Christian paganism as it was in hypermodernistic materialism and scientism. The hostility to Christianity and to traditional religion that many leading Nazis felt was largely rooted in the same soil as the opposition to these ideas found among Russian Bolsheviks. In both cases their particular political and economic ideologies were envisioned as replacements for the church and religion. A revived form of paganism, as understood based on scholarly evidence of the past, would have been far too difficult to control over time.

John Cornwell (2003, 38–46) presents a survey of German scientific and technological triumphs of the early decades of the twentieth century in which he characterizes Germany as the "Science Mecca." Nobel prizes flowed to her scientists during this period. Academic departments flourished in all fields, and with the ever-practical orientation of German science, these advances were usually almost immediately used in the transformation of scientific experiments into useful and beneficial products in industry and medicine. These advances continued unabated, even through the years of the First World War—a pointless conflagration that later would prove so devastating to the fates of many a European nation.

Occultism as such would also take a great leap forward in its popularity and effect on general society after the turn of the century. Things that had been the purview of highly educated and scientific minds in the previous century became much more of a bourgeois activity and concern as the century developed. Much of this had to do with economic development: the expansion of the middle class and the ever-rising educational level in that economic demographic. A demand developed for readings in the occult, and the publishing industry rushed to fill that market niche. In many ways pre-Nazi Germany and Austria share certain traits with post-WWII America and Britain, where alternative modes of thinking abounded and experimental solutions were considered. It would not be too much of an exaggeration to say that what America went through in the 1960s (an era that, culturally speaking, spans the years 1964–1974) shared certain similarities with what Germany and Austria experienced in the interwar years (more precisely, 1919–1933). The importance of popular culture and its parameters should never be overlooked when considering how culture and the history of ideas develop through time.

CHAPTER 4

SYMBOLIC VOLKISM

*The World of Symbols and Signs into which
the Third Reich Entered*

The dimension of National Socialism that most strongly comes to mind nowadays, when people think of occult ideas, is the aspect of volkism—the idea of the Aryan race, its identification with Nordic Europeans, and its virtual deification in a political organization. As we will see throughout the course of our investigation, this is not the only occult idea held by the Nazis or about the Nazis. But it is the one that has attracted the most attention in more recent years. As we will also see, such attention has perhaps been overemphasized for cultural, political, and commercial reasons.

When we consider symbolic volkism, we are excluding any ideas that refer to biological manipulations (such as eugenics programs), scientific beliefs, or other more classically occult conceptions of magic, and so on. Symbolic volkism concerns the use of ideas, propaganda, mythology, rituals, and the employment of symbols and signs toward the end of instilling in the population of the German people a sense of identity, solidarity, and purpose—all of which were directed toward the program of the NSDAP and its *Führer,* Adolf Hitler. Similar uses of symbolism were implemented by the Bolsheviks in Russia.* Despite Hitler's expressed animosity toward Bolshevism and the Russians (or Slavs in

---

*Most people today do not realize the degree to which Russian Bolshevism was influenced by various symbolic and occult elements throughout its history. This is the subject of my work titled *The Occult Roots of Bolshevism* (2022).

general), the program of the NSDAP was in many respects inspired by the success of the Bolshevik Revolution of 1917. National Socialism was, after all, still a form of *socialism*.

In this chapter, we will consider the roots of symbolic volkism. These were deeply established in the world of German-speaking Central Europe. They profoundly affected the generation that fought in WWI and subsequently shaped the NSDAP and its programs.

Today it seems most people are mainly interested in the supposed pagan—and even Satanic (!)—ideas purportedly lurking in the heart of National Socialism. Clearly, there was a strong pagan undercurrent among a significant minority of Nazis. These were largely generational trends inherited from the Lebensreformbewegungen, the Life-Reform movements. There was no large-scale pagan organization in Germany openly advocating for the revival of the ancient Germanic religion in the early twentieth century, but we can discern these pagan impulses in somewhat subtler symbolic ideologies. We will discuss the major exponents of such ideas in this chapter. Few of these figures approached the archaic past in a theistic or authentically mythic way, however. Most of them were virtually *atheistic* in their attitudes. In this respect they were again similar to the Bolsheviks. The Nazis focused on race and biology as the keys to power; the Bolsheviks on class and economics. It was not Wotan whom most Nazis wished to revive or worship but rather the German Volk that they sought to perfect and empower. Because there was a significant neopagan element in German culture during the early part of the nineteenth century, these tendencies are discussed in some detail. However, one must be on guard not to let such elements overwhelm the narrative. The neopagan groups are important, but not as dominant as later critics would have us believe.

Another important form of symbolic volkism in early twentieth-century Germany—and one that is almost entirely ignored today, for a variety of reasons—was that of Positive Christianity. As we have seen, this was initially popularized as a sort of Wagnerian conception, codified for the masses by Houston Stewart Chamberlain in 1899 in his *Die Grundlagen des Neunzehnten Jahrhunderts,* and cultivated throughout the early years of the twentieth century in the cult of the Grail,* and so on.

Nowadays, most people pass right over the most obvious fact about National Socialism: its occult *Christian* foundation. Although Nicholas Goodrick-Clarke proposed to examine "the occult roots of Nazism," he never addressed the issue of the occult form of Christianity that lies at the basis of Nazism and that is actually explicitly mentioned in the program of the NSDAP as "Positive Christianity."† The connection of Christianity to volkism stems from the fact that in the early twentieth century, Germany had only one significant non-Christian minority: the Jews. For the Nazis, *Christian* meant non-Jewish people of German heritage. *Christian* was the functional equivalent of *Aryan*.

Symbolic volkism was not a monolithic movement. It was a kaleidoscope of writers, mystics, philosophers, and professors who often represented organizations both large and small, each of which had as their driving principle the idea that *Germanentum*—"Germandom" or "German-ness"—should be the basis of national renewal. This broad movement, born out of a dimension of the Life-Reform movements, also almost universally shared an element of anti-Semitism. This element was not necessary for the development of an affirmative vision of pure Germanentum, but its usage as a tool for heightening a sense

---

*With its deep roots in the medieval romance of *Parzivâl,* which was then adapted by Wagner in his operatic work *Parsifal* (1882), the mythos of the Holy Grail had a great influence on German-speaking culture around the beginning of the twentieth century. In his essay "Gralsmotive um die Jahrhundertwende" (Grail Motifs at the Turn of the Century), Jost Hermand (1969, 269–97) outlines a number of groups and individuals of different sorts—ranging from the artistic to the mystical, to the political and racial—who used the Grail as a metaphor for their own brand of quest in life.

†The word *positive* in this phrase is easy to misunderstand. It is associated with the materialistic drift that occurred in the philosophical world of nineteenth-century Europe. It must be understood in the context of the idea that the limits of human knowledge are linked to what can be objectively known and proved by collected data. This meant that what traditional churches had taught about Jesus and Christianity was brought under heavy criticism and largely discounted, to be replaced by more "scientific" assertions—which included ideas of race and history particular to the tastes of the nineteenth century.

of group solidarity by focusing on a common enemy (real or imagined) would be seen as indispensable by the National Socialist movement.

GUIDO VON LIST AND THE ARMANENSCHAFT

For some observers, the most important figure in the question of the "occult roots of Nazism" is the Austrian poet, artist, and mystic Guido von List. Our present study exists in part to correct this misimpression. List is important to the protohistory of National Socialism, there can be no doubt about that. However, the true scope of possible occult influences on this development is far broader than anything that might be encompassed by the works of Guido von List and other so-called Ariosophists.

When reading some of the works that relate to the topic of Nazi occultism, one can often get the impression that there is some sort of direct connection—a straight line—between Guido von List's writings and the ovens at Auschwitz. Principal among such works is *The Occult Roots of Nazism* by Nicholas Goodrick-Clarke (1985). The simple equation of volkism = paganism or occultism is not critically sustainable. There is far more to occult theory than was contained in the völkisch ideology. As regards volkism itself, the influence of Guido von List was an important one, but there again, not entirely dominant. List

Fig 4.1. List's inverted fleur-de-lis

was mainly a popular figure in the world of *esoteric* volkism, a world in which some of the founders of Nazism would have at least dabbled as younger men, while others would have rejected it.

Here I will delve into any actual links between List and National Socialism and at the same time separate his ideas from the supposed Nazi use of them. There are several factors that have led to an increased interest in Guido von List in the English-speaking world. These include Goodrick-Clarke's 1985 presentation; the new biography of List, *Wotan's Awakening,* by Eckehard Lenthe (2018); the appearance of English translations of some of List's works; and esoteric interest in List's peculiar system of runology, the so-called eighteen-rune futhork.

The Life of Guido von List

Guido Anton Karl List was born on October 5, 1848, in Vienna. His father was a moderately successful merchant in the city. Guido was the oldest child, and his father wanted him to follow him into the profession. This was despite the fact that the boy was more interested in art, adventure, and mythology. An episode in the fourteen-year-old Guido's life has been widely known, in which he reports that, during a tour of the catacombs under St. Stephen's Cathedral in central Vienna, he stood before what he took to be an altar to Wotan and swore that when he grew up he would build a temple to Wotan.

Guido received a thorough basic education at the (Jesuit) St. Anne School in Vienna and then went on to a business school to learn to run his father's affairs. He was able to read English and later audited classes at the University of Vienna. In his twenties, from 1868 to 1877, he led a somewhat carefree life, founding a theater company called Valhalla, boating on the Danube, and mountain climbing. In 1877 his father died of tuberculosis, which constantly plagued the city of Vienna. He had already started writing freelance newspaper and journal articles, but now he had to devote himself to business, which he did until 1884, when he transitioned into a full-time career in writing, editing, and publishing. He founded a trade journal called *Die Sport-Industrie,* which related to equestrian activities.

In the 1880s he established himself in the upper-class circles around the Viennese politician Georg von Schönerer and became a celebrated poet, novelist, and playwright. By the 1890s he was a noted figure, famous for his articles and two historical novels, *Carnuntum* (1888) and *Pipara* (1896). He was involved with conservative, Neo-Romantic literary groups such as the one that coalesced around the journal *Iduna* and, later, the Independent German Society for Literature.

Famously, List underwent cataract surgery in 1902 and was virtually blind for almost an entire year. During this time, it is said that he had great revelations concerning the esoteric value of language, myth, and ancient Germanic culture. He would devote the rest of his life to fulfilling that vision. He founded a Guido von List Society to support his work, and between 1908 and 1918 he came out with a whole series of books on esoteric topics. His works were influential to a generation of seekers of secret Germanic lore—and to many well beyond that generation.

List died in Berlin on May 17, 1919, seven months after the armistice ending the Great War. Much controversy surrounds the manuscript of his final work, *Armanismus und Kabbala*. Some say the manuscript was lost, while others claim that it has been secretly safeguarded in a private archive by inner initiates of the Armanen-Orden (Lenthe 2018, 213).

The lives of men such as Guido von List do not end with their physical deaths. List left behind a considerable body of systematic work and an organization to carry on his ideas. As is often the case with such organizations, the work of the master is sometimes altered in some way to respond to the needs of the group in the newer times. In the case of List, the world he left behind was one in a state of volatile turmoil and radical change, with both the empires of Germany and Austria having been shattered in the wake of the Great War.

The Ideology of Guido von List

A more extensive yet succinct introduction to List's ideological world is provided in the introductory material to my translation of *The Secret of the Runes* (1988). The philosophical development of Guido von List can be divided into two major phases: the pre-theosophical and the theosophical. The pre-theosophical phase is perhaps best exemplified in his little book *Der Unbesiegbare* (The Invincible). It was subtitled "An Outline of Germanic Philosophy." This summary of his basic ideas circa 1898 shows a vitalistic, Romantic vision expressing only marginal theosophical influence. It was written as a catechism to be used in Austrian schools. The section of the book called "The Divine Laws," clearly inspired by the Decalogue, gives some insight into the pre-Armanen work of List. His interest in influencing the culture around him is quite evident.

The Divine Laws

1. Acknowledge God and do not disturb others in their faith in God.
2. Fulfill your duties and live in such a way that you gain the love and respect of your fellow man.
3. Maintain the established days of rest and attend divine services with proper devotions on these days.
4. Honor your father and mother and be thankful for the love and care they have given you; happiness and blessedness will then accompany you on the pathways of your life.
5. Preserve your human dignity and do not lower yourself to the level of the predatory beast.
6. Do not lead a degraded life and don't give others a bad example.
7. Do not steal and do not envy others their possessions and property.
8. Observe the law and contracts; do not swear falsely and do not bear false witness.
9. Honor and protect women; keep the family sacred and protect it from hardship and danger.
10. Be true to your folk and fatherland unto death. (List 1996, 24)

For List, significant exposure to Theosophy would have come only after 1887 with the establishment of a theosophical organization in Vienna. List is often characterized as an "Ariosophist." It should be understood that this is technically a word used to refer to the followers of Lanz von Liebenfels and was only later used as a general label for all of the Germanic-oriented Reformers. List consistently called himself an *Armane,* an "Armanist."*

In the years of his youth, List might be regarded as a Neo-Romantic, caught up in the wave of Wagnerian popular culture in the 1860s and 1870s. Because he was well connected with the artistic and bohemian world of Viennese culture, he was also aware of the ideas of Theosophy as soon as they began to be disseminated in Central Europe. He absorbed and synthesized these ideas, and they found full expression in his more esoteric writings after 1908.

List wrote a wide variety of plays, novels, poems, and journalistic articles between the years 1877 and 1900. These were not always explicitly esoteric in the sense his later writings would be. It does appear, however, that in List's own conception his ideas were being synthesized into a more coherent vision during the decade just prior to 1900. The key to his vision lies in the systematic treatment of the sounds of the German language, which are, in turn, eventually keyed to the runes. List's recent biographer, Eckehard Lenthe, makes note of the fact that List began to use a *pentagram* in his signature from 1898 onward. This is taken as an external sign by List that his intentions had become *magical* and that he was dedicating himself to an activist role to alter or change the political and cultural landscape in some way. Clearly, during the decade of the 1890s in Vienna, List was directly exposed to the personalities of men such as the Theosophist Franz Hartmann, Rudolf Steiner, and Karl Kellner. In 1900, List's poem "Wuotans Erwachen" (Wuotan's Awakening) was published in the journal *Der Scherer.* Otherwise, List had for a long time been well connected with conservative military men, politicians, and industrialists, as the later membership rolls in his Guido von List Society amply show.

---

*Guido von List coined the word *Armane* (sg. *Armane,* pl. *Armanen,* with *Armanen-* used to form compounds as well). The word is based ultimately on a Germanic ethnic or tribal name reported by Tacitus in the first century: Herminones, widely reconstructed as Erminones or Irminones, with refernce to the famous *Irminsûl* of the pagan continental Saxons. Roman authors almost universally added an initial *h-* sound to foreign words beginning with a vowel, and just as notoriously dropped an initial *h-* in words of foreign origin. (This linguistic tendency persists in speakers of Romance languages.) List's coinage was meant to bring the term into harmony with the Sanskrit *Arya-.*

The Armanenschaft of Guido von List

As already mentioned, the ideology of Guido von List is often categorized under the heading "Ariosophical." This is technically incorrect,
as rarely, if ever, did he refer to his ideology as "Ariosophy," but rather
more consistently as *Armanentum.* Ariosophy has, however, become the
general term connecting all esoteric völkisch schools of thought of the
twentieth century (Lenthe 2018, 260).

Underlying the post-1904 work of Guido von List are certain
esoteric methodologies. These include clairvoyance (especially focused
on supposed historical or sacred sites of the ancient Armanen), esoteric
linguistics (his idiosyncratic views on language, its development, and
hidden meanings), esoteric symbology (hidden interpretations of symbols and signs from folklore), and numerological analysis, which some
call Kabbalah.

List's intense esoteric output would span from 1908 to the year of
his death, 1919, and beyond, as his works were widely perpetuated and
reprinted by the Guido von List Society well into the Nazi years. All
of the generation of the leadership of the NSDAP with any interest in
things esoteric, Germanic, or runic would probably have been directly
or indirectly familiar with the content of his work. At the time of the
beginning of the popular wave of völkisch literature (1908), the average age of the men who would become the leaders of the NSDAP was
thirteen—they literally came of age during this wave of popularity
between 1908 and 1919.

The first of List's esoteric volumes was one titled *Das Geheimnis
der Runen* (The Secret of the Runes; 1908). This volume contains a
sort of esoteric runology based on a section of the Old Norse poem
"Hávamál."* It is telling to note that List reinterprets some of the runic
meanings in ways that, although not always unique to his vision, were
probably the portal by which these interpretations entered the collective

---

*"Hávamál" is found in a thirteenth-century collection of Old Norse poems, the *Codex
Regius,* also called the *Poetic Edda* or *Elder Edda.* The poems are often much older than
the date of the written manuscript. As a literary man, List was prone to value greatly the
power of the written word, as a sort of scripture as a basis for tradition. Thus, this written document became the bedrock of his tradition.

imagination of the German-speaking world in the pre-WWI period. Table 4.1 shows a summary of List's interpretations of the individual runes in his eighteen-rune futhork.

TABLE 4.1 THE ARMANEN FUTHORK

No.	Shape	Name	Meaning
1.	ᚠ	FA	Fa, feh, feo = fire-generation, fire-borer, livestock, property, to grow, to wander, to destroy, to shred. "Generate your own luck and you will have it."
2.	ᚢ	UR	ur = *Ur* [i.e., "the primordial"], eternity, primal fire, primal light, primal bull (= primal generation), aurochs, resurrection (life after death). "Know yourself, then you will know all!"
3.	ᚦ	THORN	thorr, thurs, thorn = Thorr (thunder, thunderbolt, lightning flash), thorn. Thorn of life and death. "Preserve your ego."
4.	ᚨ	OS	os, as, ask = Ase [i.e., one of the Æsir], mouth, arising, ash, ashes. "Your spiritual force makes you free."
5.	ᚱ	RIT	rit, reith, rath, ruoh, rita, rat [English rede]. Roth [red]. Rad [wheel], rod, rott, Recht [right], etc. "I am my *rod* [right], this *rod* is indestructible, therefore I am myself indestructible, because I am my *rod*."
6.	ᚲ	KA	ka, kaun kuna, kien, kiel, kon, *kühn* [bold], *kein* [none], etc. "Your blood, your highest possession."
7.	ᚼ	HAGAL	hagal = the All-hedge, to enclose, hail, to destroy. "Harbor the All in yourself, and you will control All!"
8.	ᚾ	NOT	nauth, noth [need], Norn, compulsion of fate. "Use your fate, do not strive against it!"
9.	ᛁ	IS	is, ire, iron [*Eisen*]. "Win power over yourself and you will have power over everything in the spiritual and physical worlds that strives against you."

TABLE 4.1 THE ARMANEN FUTHORK (*cont.*)

No.	Shape	Name	Meaning
10.		AR	ar, sun, primal fire, ar-yans, nobles, etc. "Respect the primal fire!"
11.		SIG	sol, sal, sul, sig, sigi, sun, sal-vation, victory [*Sieg*], column [*Säule*], school, etc. "The creative spirit must conquer."
12.		TYR	tyr, tar, tur, animal [*Tier*], etc. Týr, the sun- and sword-god; Tiu, Zio, Ziu, Zeus; tar- = "to generate, to turn, to conceal"; thus *Tarnkappe* [cap or cape of concealment], etc. "Fear not death—it cannot kill you!"
13.		BAR	bar, beork, biork, birt, song, bier, etc. Birth, life, death, rebirth. "Thy life stands in the hands of god, trust it in you."
14.		LAF	laf, lagu, lögr, primal law, sea, life, downfall (defeat). "First learn to steer, then dare the sea-journey!"
15.		MAN	man, mon, moon (*ma* = to mother, to increase; empty or dead). The exoteric and esoteric concept of man. "Be a man."
16.		YR	yr, eur, iris, rain-bow, yew-wood bow, error, anger, etc. Mutability of the feminine essence. "Think about the end!"
17.		EH	eh, marriage [Ger. *Ehe*], law, horse, court, etc. "Marriage is the raw-root of the Aryans!"
18.		GIBOR	ge, gi, gifa, gibor, gift, giver, god, gea, geo, earth, gigur, death, etc. "Man, be One with God!"

Of these runes and their particular interpretations, certain ones had an effect on how runes were thought of in the period of National Socialism. A more complete history of the evolution of runic symbolism is the subject of my book *Revival of the Runes* (Rochester, Vt.: Inner Traditions, 2021). As can be seen, the Armanen-futhork is based on the Younger Futhark used in Scandinavia during the Viking Age. List altered the order of the runes for **l, m,** and **y,** which are traditionally in the order **m–l–y.** It is likely he did so to juxtapose the runes ᛉ and ᛘ, which for him became a pair of runes symbolizing life and death, man and woman, light and dark. The rune ✳ was radically reinterpreted as being related to the modern German *hegen,* "to enclose, protect," from its original meaning, "hail," which connoted disaster. The ᛋ-rune was slightly reinterpreted in that it was firmly associated with the German word *Sieg,* "victory." Its original meaning was simply "sun." The portal for reinterpreting this rune as "victory" likely came from the form of the Old English rune-name, *sigel* [pron. see^y-el] with a palatalized /g/. The Old English spelling was enough to suggest the connection with the German *Sieg.* List also borrowed the form of the ᛢ-rune from medieval manuscript runes. Its normal form is X. (It was not used in the Viking Age runic system at all.) He also supplies it with a peculiar name, *gibor,* and it is associated with the symbol known as the *Hakenkreuz* (i.e., the swastika). It should be noted that the shapes usually associated with the **f-, u-** and **r-**runes in later Armanen tradition (under the influence of S. A. Kummer and K. Spiesberger) are not emphasized by List himself.

A more extensive overview and analysis of the works published by List in the series known as the Guido-von-List-Bücherei (Guido von List

Fig. 4.2. Guido von List, circa 1910
(Photograph by Conrad Schiffer)

Library) during the years between 1908 and 1919 are given in the introduction to *The Secret of the Runes* (1988, 15–17). Lenthe (2018, 165–214) spends a whole chapter on the concept and the fate of the manuscript of *Armanismus und Kabbalah* (Armanism and Kabbalah).

For List, the Armanenschaft was seen as an institution inherited from antiquity and preserved by a secret institution called the Hohe Heimliche Acht (High Secret Institution) made up of Armanen who were creative transformers of their doctrines into forms that could survive in changing times; for example, with the coming of Christianity, which List did not see as a horrible breaking of the old traditions but rather an opportunity for the Armanen to re-encode their wisdom in apparently Christian forms. This process is explained in some detail in List's book *Der Übergang von Wuotanismus zum Christentum* (1911).*

Perhaps the most essential feature of the secret teachings of the Armanen was the discovery and demonstration of the process by which all things continue and perpetuate themselves according to a set of cosmic laws of arising, becoming and passing away to a new beginning. By this process, death is seen as a transitional phase to a new formation based on eternal principles. The maintenance of this secret teaching is the responsibility of the Armanenschaft. Almost everything in List's ideology seems to come back to this cyclical principle in one way or another.

During the time of List's blindness, he apparently had the insight that allowed for his mystical analysis of the origin and history of language. He is purported to have discovered the *Ursprache* of the Aryo-Germanic people. Structurally this *Ursprache,* or "primeval language," is a syllabic system in which the sounds of these syllables provide the links to their esoteric meaning. The system allows words from all languages to be analyzed on esoteric levels, whether Old Norse or modern German. This interpretation of words and of all sorts of art objects (heraldic arms, inscriptions, and even buildings) falls under the Listian concept of *kala,* "mystical interpretation." This constitutes a method of interpretation, or secret key, that reveals the threefold meaning of words

---

*This book appears in a translation as *The Transition from Wuotanism to Christianity* (Bastrop, Tex.: Lodestar, 2022).

and things. A concrete example of how this works is shown in his text *The Secret of the Runes* (1988, 72) where the Old Norse term *Yggdrasill,* the name of the Cosmic Tree, is analyzed on three levels:

I.   *"ig"*   = "I" as shaper, generator, producer, consecration;
        "dra" = turning, generation (trifos), generation of fire.
  "sil" (*sal*)   = sal-vation.

II.   *"ig"*   = (*uig, wig*) struggle (Viking);
        "dra" = to drag, carry.
        "sul" = law, pillar [*Säule*]

III.   *"ig"*   = terror, death.
        "dra" = to destroy (dragon).
  "sil" (*zil*)   = aim, end.

This demonstrates that on an esoteric level, key words could be interpreted on a *generational* level, a level of *life* or *struggle,* and on a *death* or *transition level.* These three interpretive levels correspond to a further insight that List had about the structure of society itself.

List saw that society bore a definite class structure, which was made up of the *Lehrstand–Wehrstand–Nährstand.* The *Lehrstand* (Teacher-Class) was made up of priests, poets, and artists who were responsible for teaching the people about their traditions. Their sponsor was Wuotan. Warriors made up the *Wehrstand* (Defender-Class), which was responsible for defending and expanding the territory of the folk. Finally, the *Nährstand* (Nourisher-Class) was made up of the farmers and other craftsmen necessary to the peasantry. This was a hierarchical system, but each part of it was given high honor. It was said that all men are first and foremost farmers, then they take on other aspects as needed.*

---

*Some might notice that the mythological system discovered by the French philologist Georges Dumézil bears a striking similarity to the system of Guido von List. The Listian system and that of Dumézil are based on a tripartite analysis of both the mythic world and the human society rooted in archaic Indo-European ideology. This appears to have been an example of two different men, from two different intellectual and cultural worlds, discovering similar things at approximately the same time. Dumézil is known to have first become aware of the system in reading ancient Iranian texts.

Listian Origins of Some
National Socialist Terminology

The differences between Listian ideology and that which would become National Socialism are vast. Those who try to draw a direct line between the two do not understand the complexities of this historical period or the vast array of ideas that were vying for supremacy in the first half of the twentieth century. List was no more anti-Semitic than the average Christian of Austria during his lifetime. Some of his later followers even felt compelled to apologize for the master's lack of vehemence against the Jews and Freemasons. Lenthe (2018, 227–38) points out several key words and phrases coined or popularized by List and his followers, which were later used by National Socialists. These include *Ahnenerbe,* "ancestral heritage" (*Die Armanenschaft* I, 29), *Herrenmenschheit,* "master-humanity" (*DieArmanenschaft* II, 83), and others. List's tripartite formula *Werden–Wirken–Vergehen* (Becoming–Being–Passing Away) was even used by Hitler in *Mein Kampf.* The very name and concept "National Socialism" was first coined by Franz Herndl in 1897 or 1898. Herndl was the vice president of the Guido von List Society between 1908 and 1909. List, perhaps more than any other writer, popularized the use of the swastika in völkisch circles.

Although List is often cited as some sort of inspiration for the National Socialist movement, this only makes any sense if we only look at certain leaders (such as Himmler) who were most interested in esoteric matters. For the most part, of course, National Socialists were obsessed with political and economic power. List foresaw that his ideas might be used by partisan politicians and explicitly warned against this on the grounds that political parties are temporal and temporary in their natures, whereas his vision of the Armanenschaft was of a hidden institution that was just the opposite: spiritual and perennial.

With that being said, the work known as *Die Armanenschaft der Ario-Germanen* (Armanendom of the Aryo-Germanic People), volume 2, first published in 1911, contains an extensive section called *"Die Wandlung"* ("Transformation," 51–119) that shows some influences from certain works of Lanz von Liebenfels and that outlines a hierarchical utopian political organization of a state governed by

Armanic principles. Undoubtedly, material of this sort was read and absorbed by a number of those in the generation that would become Nazi leaders several decades later, and it may have inspired them to some degree. There was, however, little to no direct transference of members or ideology from the Armanenschaft of Guido von List to the NSDAP. Lenthe (2018, 400), in his meticulous analysis of the membership rolls of the Guido von List Society and the NSDAP, shows that only fifteen members of the List Society ever became members of the NSDAP. By his reckoning this constituted only 3.4 percent of the membership of List's group. Only one of these, Herman Wirth, was of any great consequence—and he was virtually ousted from his role in the Party for holding heretical views, which included pacifism and feminism! What does this say about the "evil influence" of List on Nazism? It says that it was vague and general and in no way direct or determinative.

List did inaugurate a new wave of what can be called *esoteric* runology in the German-speaking world. Others who followed his lead were Rudolf John Gorsleben, Friedrich Bernhard Marby, Siegfried Adolf Kummer, and E. Tristan Kurtzahn.* As will be seen, those connected with National Socialism who took an interest, both academic and esoteric, in the runes did not strictly adhere to the system outlined by List in his written works. National Socialist runology, such as it was, was more sensitive to the long tradition of academic research than were List and his direct followers. However, as the information we have shown above indicates, List's suggestions and writings may be seen to have had a formative effect on many readers' minds of members of the generation to which the founders of National Socialism belonged, such that they could not help but follow—even if unconsciously—some of his suggestions and interpretations.

Several of the rune esotericists, such as Marby and Kummer, took their work in directions that List never publically wrote about or seemed to have envisioned. Marby and Kummer used runes in an overtly magical way and developed systems of bodily postures that sym-

---

*For a history of the Listian school after List's death, see my books *Rune Might* (2018; published under the pen name Edred Thorsson) and *Revival of the Runes* (2021).

bolically represented the shapes of the runes. This system was called *Runengymnastik* by Marby and *Runen-Yoga* by Kummer. The exercises these teachers developed were designed to engage energies and powers in the environment and guide these forces in willed directions to cause changes in the practitioner or in the world around him. Kummer's system was clearly and directly derived from the system of Guido von List. Marby claimed to have developed his teachings independently but was nevertheless clearly influenced by the works of List.*

More closely allied with the spirit and methods of List was Rudolf John Gorsleben, who was also an organizer of the esoteric folkish group called the Edda Gesellschaft (Edda Society). He published a monumental book titled *Die Hochzeit der Menschheit* (The Zenith of Humanity) in 1930, shortly before his death. This book covered many topics of esoteric lore and was explicitly within the Armanen tradition. It became a highly influential text over the years that followed.

Writers such as Marby, Kummer, and Gorsleben published their works either just on the eve of the assumption of power by the National Socialists, or even in the first couple of years after 1933, before the crackdown on esoteric groups in 1935. Marby overtly expressed sympathies with National Socialism, whereas Kummer soon disappeared from sight. Marby then actually ran afoul of Nazi authorities for his refusal to stop publishing his esoteric work independently. Marby was tried and convicted in 1936, and all of his property was confiscated. He spent the duration of the war incarcerated in various concentration camps. He was liberated from Dachau on April 29, 1945. Due to his early written support of National Socialism, the Allies denied him any compensation for his arrest and detention.

Another rune-esotericist who belongs to this general milieu is Karl Maria Wiligut (1866–1946). But because he is best known as an actual participant in National Socialist symbolism and ideology, he will be discussed in chapter 7.

---

*For a general introduction to the world of early twentieth-century German runic gymnastics, or "yoga," see my *Rune Might* (2018), and for a more academic approach, see Wedemeyer-Kolwe, "Runengymnastik."

Fig 4.3. Templar cross

LANZ VON LIEBENFELS AND
THE ORDO NOVI TEMPLI

Lanz von Liebenfels has gained much notoriety in the realm of the study of Nazi occultism, initially as the result of a 1958 book by Wilfried Daim titled *Der Mann, der Hitler die Ideen gab* (The Man Who Gave Hitler His Ideas). Although this is a well-researched book, and an excellent study of Lanz's work and ideology, it fails to make the case for a direct connection between mainstream National Socialist ideas on race and/or eugenics and the very particular—and even downright peculiar—concepts surrounding these topics as espoused in the works of Lanz von Liebenfels.

It is hard to know whether to consider Liebenfels as part of the pagan or Christian movements of the early twentieth century. He really belongs firmly in both camps. His symbolism is entirely Christian—Templar and Grail oriented—but his ideology is so thoroughly enmeshed in that of Theosophy and other forms of non-Christian occultism that his ideology is quite distant from the concerns of orthodox Christianity.

Like most other occult leaders, Lanz von Liebenfels's talent lay not in his essential originality but rather in the power of his unique synthesis and vivification of elements extant, nascent, or latent in the culture around him. These he mixed and melded, developed and directed—much as a composer would arrange a piece of music. In the particular case of Lanz, this process was probably mostly unconscious, as he felt himself to be actually reviving and continuing what was old rather than introducing genuinely new elements. The ideology professed by Lanz was, in the end, an ad hoc mixture of all the major streams of occult thinking present in Central Europe in the late nineteenth and early twentieth centuries. In retrospect, it is remarkable just how many ideologies and theories were established in Central Europe during the first decade of the twentieth century, such as Houston Stewart Chamberlain, *Foundations of the Nineteenth Century* (1899); Sigmund Freud, *On the Interpretation of Dreams* (1901); Theodor Herzl, *Alt-Neuland* (1903); Albert Einstein, *General Theory of Relativity* (1905); and Guido von List, *Secret of the Runes* (1908).

The complex ideology of Lanz von Liebenfels is an idiosyncratic synthesis of conservative Catholicism, Darwinism, Theosophy, Armanism, and Wagnerism. One of the central facts about the development of his ideas is that it took place over a twelve-year period between 1893 and 1905, when his *Theozoologie* was first published.* Although he added elements to his thought, nothing was essentially changed from that presented in his seminal treatise.

The biography of Lanz von Liebenfels is shrouded in secrecy. He was born Adolf Josef Lanz on July 19, 1874, in Vienna. He regularly provided an "astrological pseudonym" in which his birth data was given as May 1, 1872, in Massina, Italy. He was also known by several variations of this name, including Josef Lanz, Jörg Lanz, and Georg Lancz von Liebenfels or Lancz de Liebenfels.

Lanz's parents were Johann Lanz, a Viennese teacher, and Katharina née Hoffenreich, who were married in Vienna on October 22, 1873, in the church at Reindorf in Vienna. Very little is known of their son's youth. From his own account, it was the obscure 1829 opera *Der Templer und die Jüdin* (The Templar and the Jewess) by Heinrich Marschner

---

*The full original title is *Theozoologie oder die Kunde von den Sodoms-Äfflingen und dem Götter-Elektron: Eine Einführung in die älteste und neuste Weltanschauung und ein Rechtfertigung des Fürstentums und des Adels* (Theozoology, or the Science of the Sodomite Apelings and the Divine Electron: An Introduction to the Most Ancient and Most Modern Philosophy and a Justification of the Monarchy and the Nobility).

that enflamed the boy's enthusiasm for the Knights Templar (Daim 1958, 45).* Here it is interesting to compare the role supposedly played by Wagner's *Rienzi* on the development of the youthful Adolf Hitler.[†] None of this should really be surprising, however, as in the late 1800s opera played a role in popular culture analogous to that which motion pictures do today. His enthusiasm for the Templars led him to read everything he could find about them and to travel extensively to visit supposed old Templar sites.

When Adolf Lanz entered the Heiligenkreuz Abbey situated in the Wienerwald near the Austrian capital in 1893, he took the order name Georg (Daim 1958, 42). Later he would use the Austrian form of the name, Jörg, as his secular Christian name. While in the monastery Lanz discovered a grave slab depicting a knight trampling on a monstrous figure. He interpreted this as a symbol of the victory of the Templars, as representatives of the blond Aryan race, over the lower "mongrel" races.[‡]

Fig. 4.4. Jörg Lanz von Liebenfels in monastic garb, from a 1907 publication

---

*The plot of the opera in question was based partly on Sir Walter Scott's adventure novel *Ivanhoe*.

†Kubizek (2006, 116–18) recounts the story about how the experience of the Wagnerian opera *Rienzi* had a profound effect on the young Adolf Hitler.

‡This event is described by both Daim (1958, 47–52) and Mund (1976, 18–22).

One of his mentors in the monastery was Nivard Schlögl, who according to all sources was a dedicated anti-Semite.* Additionally, he was making some contacts in the Pan-Germanic movement and is supposed to have met the Armanen mystic, Guido von List, as early as 1893 (Goodrick-Clarke 1985, 90). Lanz was ordained to the priesthood on September 12, 1897. The exact circumstances surrounding Lanz's departure from the abbey are unknown. The entry in the Latin-language records of the abbey note that he had been "seized by carnal love" and was apostate (Daim 1958, 53). In the months immediately after his departure from the abbey, his activities clearly show the path he was on. He wrote three anti-Catholic—or at least anti-Roman and anti-Jesuit—books that were published in subsequent years (Goodrick-Clarke 1985, 241). Lanz joined the Pan-Germanic political/esoteric movement—and there is even the suggestion that he converted to Protestantism (Goodrick-Clarke 1985, 92). The gravitation toward Protestantism was common among the generally Catholic "conservative" revolutionaries of Austria as they undertook to alter their cultural environment in a radical way. This was done in a spirit of nationalism, to rid German culture of Roman influence, and was known as the Los-von-Rom! (Away from Rome!) movement. The main basis of Lanz's protest against the church was his belief that it had abandoned its original purpose, which according to him was to serve as an Ariosophical institute for the sacred and heroic cultivation of the race. What Lanz intended to do was to reform this state of affairs by founding his own order of Templars, which would restore the church to its original purpose as an overseer of racial purity.

According to Lanz's own account written in 1942 (Mund 1976, 37) the Ordo Novi Templi (ONT), the "Order of the New Templars," was founded on December 25, 1900, in Vienna. The first objective signs of the existence of the order do not, however, begin to appear before some seven years later when the castle Werfenstein on the Danube near Studen in Austria was purchased and made the headquarters of the ONT and the program of the order was published in the December 1907 issue of the journal *Ostara*. Throughout these years (1899–1907),

---

*This is reported by both Daim (1958, 53) and Mund (1976, 23).

Fig. 4.5. Cover of the *Regularium* (Rule) of the Ordo Novi Templi, 1921

Lanz pursued his political connections with the Pan-Germanic movement, became involved with learned scientific societies, delved into the occult (including most especially H. P. Blavatsky's Theosophy), and continued with his scholarly work in collaboration with prestigious biblical scholars on a multivolume project for publishing old Jewish texts. This series was to be called Monumenta Judaica. This project was never fully realized, but the circumstances surrounding it give us some valuable insights into Lanz's intellectual environment. First, he was apparently well respected among certain leading biblical scholars, as he was chosen to be an editor of the Monumenta Judaica, who was to represent the Catholic viewpoint (Goodrick-Clarke 1985, 99). Also the fact that he worked closely with Jewish scholars indicates that his own view, as well as that of many other Pan-Germanic esotericists before the Great War, was not as blatantly anti-Jewish as later accounts would suggest. In fact, the rabbinical scholar Moritz Altschüler, who worked with Lanz on the project, was even a member of the Guido von List Society himself. But it would be a mistake to conclude from this evidence that Lanz and List were not generally anti-Semitic, in theory at least. The fact that Lanz also wrote for the *Hammer*, published by Theodor Fritsch—an openly anti-Semitic journal—only shows how complex the social and ideological chemistry of fin de siècle Vienna was.

During the ten-year period before the end of the Great War, Lanz was busy consolidating the ideological base of the ONT and participating in the German occult revival. Although Lanz had certainly been familiar with theosophical doctrines for some time, these teachings were not heavily represented in his own work until around the beginning of this period. He became involved not only with Guido von List and his group of theosophically influenced Armanen but also with the theosophical publication *Neue Lotusblüten* (Goodrick-Clarke 1985, 101).

The ONT probably never had more than a hundred initiates at any one time in its history. However, the brothers were quite often influential men of some intellectual or financial status.

From 1921 to 1933, Lanz maintained a growing utopian estate in Marienkamp-St. Balázs. But things abruptly changed in 1933 when Lanz left his priory at Marienkamp and went to Lucerne, Switzerland. It was from there that he began to issue what became known as the "Lucerne Letters" until about 1937. Although Lanz was initially enthusiastic about the rise of National Socialism and Fascism, his enthusiasm waned as the regimes demonstrated that his work, and especially the activities of his order, would not be tolerated. Although it is possible that Lanz and his writings had some vague formative inspirational effect on the young Adolf Hitler in Vienna (1907–1913),* and perhaps because of the apparent relationship between National Socialist ideology and the "electro-theology" of Lanz, the works of Jörg Lanz von Liebenfels and the ONT itself were officially banned in 1938 throughout the Third Reich (which by that time included Germany and Austria). That event essentially marked the end of significant ONT activity. It is clear that Lanz retreated into a more private world throughout the war, which

---

*For a long time it was widely thought that Hitler's references to reading anti-Semitic tracts in Vienna were a reference to the widely available work of Lanz von Liebenfels. This is suggested by both Daim (1958, 18–41) and Jones (1983, 117–18). The only problem is that Lanz's work, once examined, proves to be very little oriented toward anti-Semitism itself.

he spent in politically and militarily neutral Switzerland. He was very perplexed by his feeling that he had been instrumental in founding the movement that had developed into National Socialism and yet had been spurned by that very movement. As our whole study up to this point has shown, ideas much closer to actual National Socialist ideology were quite prevalent and common throughout Europe and in Vienna—ideas that had nothing to do with those of Lanz and that were free of his speculations and fantasies about sodomitic "sex-apes" and the like. His paranoia likely stemmed from other sources: perhaps a combination of his own inner feelings of guilt with a sense of self-importance.

After the war Lanz eventually returned to his native Vienna. It is very likely that Lanz was apprehensive living in postwar Vienna, occupied as it was by the Allied powers. He believed in his influence on the origin of National Socialism and was also aware of the fact that such influence might be considered a crime by the courts and commissions set up by the Allies to denazify Central Europe. Many ONT leaders in Austria were subjected to hearings after the war. Had not Alfred Rosenberg been hanged on October 16, 1946, for largely ideological crimes? It seems, however, that Lanz was never even seriously investigated. It is the supposition of this study that he was amply protected by his connection to the Catholic Church and its apparent symbolism—even if he was unaware of it at the time. It may also be true that any real investigator would see that the ONT ideology was just too eccentric and fantastical to be characterized as politically dangerous. Anyone reading his ideas would see in them something more akin to a scenario from a horror film or science-fiction novel than any serious program of eugenics.

But the degree to which Lanz himself thought of National Socialism as a reflection of his own philosophy is attested to in a postscript to a letter written to Fra Aemilius, dated February 22, 1932. He wrote:

> You [Aemilius] were one of our first followers and Templars! Do you know that Hitler is one of our students? You will yet see that he, and therefore also we, will have victory and will unfold a movement that will make the world tremble. (Daim 1958, 12)

On May 11, 1951, Lanz was visited at his apartment at Grinzinger Strasse 32 in Vienna by the political psychologist Wilfried Daim, who undertook a study of Lanz and his ideas. This was published in 1958 as *Der Mann, der Hitler die Ideen gab* (The Man Who Gave Hitler His Ideas). Daim did not want to cause any trouble for Lanz, so he waited until after his death to publish the work.

Lanz received the last sacraments and died in the morning hours of April 22, 1954. He was given a requiem mass at Heiligenkreuz and his body interred in the Penzinger Cemetery in Vienna with other members of the Lanz family, group 2, row 18, grave 17. He was buried in the vestments of the Cistercians decorated with the Cross of the New Templars (✠). His gravestone reads: "Georgius Lanz 1.V.1872–22.IV.1954" (Daim 1958, 171). This is the wrong date of birth, which Lanz used as an astrological pseudonym.

In his obituary for Lanz, longtime follower Fra Dietrich (Theodor Czepl) characterized him as "one of the greatest Romantics of our time." This seems to sum up the true character of Jörg Lanz von Liebenfels, who took his own subjective vision of the past and future and attempted to project this vision on a broad scale into the objective universe. To be sure, Lanz was in great measure a product of the zeitgeist derived from the worlds of Darwin, Marx, Wagner, and Blavatsky, combined with a radically conservative Roman Catholic worldview. But additionally, Lanz crafted a unique—if in many respects bizarre—vision that he projected with some magical and organizational skill on his environment. The ONT and the movements it influenced became something of a Frankenstein's monster for Lanz. For whatever else might be said of the success of his efforts in the short term, by the end of his life the causes for which he fought were far more lost than at the time he began to champion them.

The Ariosophy of Lanz von Liebenfels

Ariosophy is a word that Lanz himself coined around 1915. It is formed from a synthesis of several cultural and ideological streams swirling around fin de siècle Vienna. Underlying the peculiar philosophy of Lanz was, of course, a particular view of the role and nature of Catholicism, but to this were added the contemporary stream of neo-Germanic ideologies and the all-important occult school of Theosophy. Another element was the still prevalent scientific ideology of Monism, a set of ideas to which Lanz frequently resorted in his writings. Clearly, the term *Ariosophy* is a play on "Theosophy," but probably only after *Anthroposophy* had been coined by Rudolf Steiner, as the Anthroposophical Society was founded in 1912. For Lanz, this term had a very specific meaning outlined in the ideology of the ONT, but the term has taken on a life of its own as a general designation for the folkish-oriented segment of the German occult revival.

Ideology

One of the most common misconceptions about the ideology of Lanz von Liebenfels is that it was anti-Semitic. For him, the test of Aryanism was simply a matter of appearance: if a person was blond with blue eyes and fair skin, he was Aryan and Nordic, the highest form of humanity. All other "darker" characteristics a person might have were seen as signs of human interbreeding with "bestial" creatures. No existing human being was entirely free of simian elements, however. The Christian Fall of Man, Original Sin, and the Sin of Adam were equated with the act of primeval interbreeding that the original "god-men," who possessed the "divine electron," committed with the "sex-apes"—the *pagutus* and *udumus*—resulting in the forms of humanity that now exist.

It was through a radical interpretation of Judeo-Christian mythology—that is, the Old and New Testaments—that Lanz derived the majority of his ideas. The Judaic tradition is easily turned to these ends as it contains a mythic substructure that involves a racial component in the form of a "chosen people" opposed to a variety of foreign peoples or lands, which are demonized in the narrative: the Egyptians, Babylonians, Moabites, Canaanites, Philistines, and the list goes on.

There are certain basic principles, articulated by R. J. Mund, that characterize the Ariosophical ideology of Lanz von Liebenfels:

1. In the beginning there were on the earth living gods who possessed an organ, often called the Third Eye, by which even matter could be transformed.
2. These gods are called Electrozoa by Lanz, and were divided according to a law of polarity into two groups, one practicing white magic and the other black magic.
3. Those Electrozoa that practiced white magic are called Theozoa by Lanz, while those that practiced black magic are called Daemonozoa. The Theozoa attempted to propagate themselves in a pure way among themselves, giving rise to the Aryan race. Whereas the Daemonozoa bred with animal life forms, which developed into the dark races.
4. Lanz identifies the myth of the Fall of Adam in the Bible as the process of racial contamination with bestial forms.
5. Lanz identifies the figure of Jesus Christ as the Electrozoa-man, the pure Aryan come to restore the old laws of racial purity.

(Mund, 1976)

Lanz is often focused on the idea that humans would have sexual relations with "apelings" and that these creatures were actually bred and developed in ancient cities such as Sodom for purposes of providing sexual pleasure and for the breeding of yet further mixed beings. Just how far this fixation could go is illustrated in his interpretation of what the crucifixion of Jesus was really all about.

After Jesus has been tortured in various ways, he was "crucified." In the Acta Johannis it is said that the things which Jesus suffered are not told, and what he did not suffer are told. In Numbers 25:4 primeval men (r'ashe ha-'am) are "nailed to the cross" in honor of Helios (Shemesh, who is Jehovah in this context). Sym. speaks of "burning." It is obvious that "burning" and "crucifying" are the same thing. The Septuagint doesn't have "crucify" but rather "bake in the sun" (Gk. heliazein). (Just as II Kings 21:9, Esther 9:13.) The "crucifixion" consisted of binding wild and unruly Sodomite monsters to poles in order to be able to copulate with them without danger (cf. Job 40:24, Thren. V, 13). On the other hand, however, people were bound to such poles in order to have them Sodomized by lascivious apelings. This was the torture to which early Christians were put (Pastor Hermae III, 2) and that was also the torture of Jesus. (Lanz 1908, 124–25)

In many ways, the ideology of Lanz von Liebenfels is another example of the turn-of-the-century obsession with *sexuality,* which gripped European culture generally and gave rise to the birth of sexology and the psychoanalysis of men such as Sigmund Freud.

Here I will present a lengthy, but slightly abridged, translation of the final section of Lanz's *Theozoology,* called "Telos—The End."* This presentation, better than any secondhand characterization of the man, reveals the nature of his thought.

My Friends, who I, in my body and soul, feel to be the children and sons of the primeval enemies of the apelings, let us hold in the highest regard the most precious heritage of our fathers—our blood, our seed—as something Divine! We do not wish ourselves to be regarded as angels, the blood of each and every one of us is more or less mixed with the water of Sodom. But from this point forward a halt should be called to this mixing. Mankind is unequal, and a deep moat that cannot be overwhelmed surrounds Walhalla—a moat that no apeling must be allowed to jump over. In the struggle against the apes of Sodom each one must begin within himself, especially in the choice of his wife, then he can fight against the apes of Sodom which surround him . . . Victory will be ours—ancient, divine oracles speak in our

---

*In 1989, I privately published a translation of *Theozoology.* This was done in hopes of showing the English-speaking world just how absurd most of the ideas of Lanz von Liebenfels were. He had enjoyed a reputation in folkish circles in the English-speaking world that far exceeded what was due to him. It was my supposition that once the mystery surrounding the work of this individual was lifted, his reputation would wane. I am sure this happened for rational readers, but I was amazed to learn that some people could actually read the words and still be under the spell of the reputation. It was one of my first lessons in the power of faith in weird ideas.

behalf. Among our foes is the ape, in us and for us is God—the all-knowing, all-powerful entity of the original cosmos. It follows from many passages in the Bible that the European white man—in short, the Germanic man—is the Son of Heaven. He is the white stone (Rev. 6:8), the White Rider who conquers the colored people, he is the Logos (Rev. 6; 19). Also in the Koran (7:43) it is said that Paradise is certain for the whites. The original homeland of the white man is Germania—kings and heroes have been coming from there since prehistory. Up to a certain time only ape- and beast-men lived outside Germany. For this reason the Germanic peoples eagerly took up an exalting doctrine, such as the teachings of Jesus. But the Sodomite spirit of Rome and Byzantium could not let the Gothic folk live. That glorious folk of the gods was ripped apart by the ancient *pagutu-* and *udumu*-brood, to the rest of the Germanic peoples a counterfeit Christianity was preached, and their powerful arm of the gods bound by the cord of the "commandment of brotherly love." Rome and Byzantium extirpated the ancient scriptures, for they would have documented our divine origins and their simian descent. For over a thousand years, the "Welsh" [= Romanized French] and the Slavs, along with the rest of the mob of apemen, have been a constant danger to our culture; they are our bitter enemies for whom no act of malice or violence is too terrible for them to use to destroy us! Woe to the brood of Sodom when we settle our accounts with them! They are more dangerous now than ever before. We have ourselves bred them upward. The wheat-fields of mankind have become sallow and overripe. Both "wheat" and "weeds" have grown up (Matt. 13:30). The linen-wick of Sodom is still glimmering, the reed of Sodom is not yet broken. From the chalice, which the adulterous "foreign" wives of our fathers' fathers mixed, from which they slurped the frothing mellow-wine of raging Sodomite lust—from this we must now drink the bitter dregs. The time has come about which the Sibyl (II.154) spoke. . . . Women cannot, or do not want to, bear healthy children! Those women who would have been suited to have been mothers lament their existences as old maids, the whore gets married and rules over our domestic and public life. The whore in the whorehouse is no sin, there she fulfills her purpose. But the whore in the marriage-bed is the downfall of peoples and states. Pleasure-apes burn down the city (Prov. 29:8). We must finally start to "breed humans." . . .

The strictest pure-breeding standards are necessary. We may not cast the pearls before the swine, we have to keep the salt for ourselves (Mark 9:49).

Obviously, the Kingdom of Heaven will be reached through intervention in the sexual life of man. Those of lesser value must be exterminated in a gentle way—by castration and sterilization (Matt. 19:12). Origen interpreted this passage literally and castrated himself. This exegesis, proven in practice, is more authoritative to me than that of the present-day pastors. The Jesuits, too, hold fast to a literal exegesis in their order policies—and history shows what a gigantic force this idea has. Also, the restriction of sexual indulgence is advantageous for spiritual men. To one is given the ability to generate beautiful and good children, to the other to create immortal spiritual works. Women can only make up for the sin of Eve through reasonable love, devoid of its ape-nature (Tim. 2:15). Woman indulged in more Sodomite lust, therefore she must suffer more today—especially at the hands of the sons of the Sodomite lovers of her mothers.

Adultery by wives and their quite strange preference for lusty, satyr-like—so-called "interesting men"—must be obviated as much as possible. "Abstain from lascivious beings" (I Thess. 5:22). . . . Bastards are usually physically and culturally poor. Among the Persians when someone commits a crime an investigation is made as to whether he is a bastard (Her. I,137). He who is of God cannot sin, while he who is of the beast-men must sin (I John 3:8). Juvenile delinquents should be castrated without mercy, or sterilized (by radiation). The invention of a functional sterilization device or agent would be the greatest boon for mankind. I am certainly not against condoms. They should be increasingly distributed. Only noble men alone, men with a heroic way of thinking, who know what it means to raise and support a child, only men who cherish children, only they will then engender children. But those who seek out copulation only for purposes of lascivious enjoyment, the nymphomaniacal baboon she-creatures afraid of birth pains—they will exterminate themselves, will strangle themselves with the rubber. Everywhere and always we must protect the institution of marriage, for it is the secure refuge of the race, the warm nest of the young phoenix and the future God-Man. . . . Marital fidelity must be required of all women in all circumstances, because adultery on the wife's part adulterates the family. But marital fidelity on the husband's part is also necessary. Marital infidelity by the husband is actually not a sin, but is an act of stupidity that is usually severely punished, because a strong man can barely satisfy one woman. Besides, coarse eroticism plays a subordinate role for a racially pure Germanic husband. He only enjoys coitus when his chosen wife meets all aesthetic requirements, and he enjoys it only insofar as he gives his beloved wife the highest enjoyment in this way. With regard to women, these men are uncommonly choosy—a worn-down shoe, a bad accent, or bad personal habits cause many men to be impotent for women who otherwise possess every possible charm. It is just this characteristic of the man of higher race—of his being incapable of immediately servicing any and every woman—that must be further developed and expanded in a systematic way so that husbands will only be potent with their own wives, and with all other women they will be impotent in the literal sense.

For the sake of the "Kingdom of Heaven," we must become eunuchs. As highly as we honor the wife in the family and in the home, we must just as intensely fight against the intrusion of women into public life, because the ultimate outcome of these efforts would be, and to some extent is already, unilateral women's rights, which would make the world into a big brothel in which everything revolves around penises and pussies in a silly and absurd satyrs' orgy and the proper wife, the loyal mother of the house, and the healthy strong troop of children will be mercilessly driven out of the chaste and legitimate home. No one other than those women with their lascivious ape-like natures destroyed the cultures of antiquity and they will bring down our culture as well if men do not stop and think soon.

The adulterous and sensual woman belongs in the whorehouse; the honor of motherhood is withdrawn from her and her name is blotted out of the Book of Life. Likewise criminals, the mentally ill, or those with hereditary diseases should be prevented from reproducing. If we only allow fit persons to reproduce, the hospitals, prisons, and the giant criminal justice system will become superfluous. Pure-breeding is the priority for true disciples of the Logos, who abhor all bastardizing mongrelization as both contrary to law and Godless. . . . Avoid Sodomy and copulation with the hobgoblins of pleasure; rear your own species (Sib. III, 762). Every man should avoid marrying a woman who has whored around a lot if he wants to generate descendants. The male semen has an effect on the woman such that the child, even when it comes from a legitimate father, still inherits characteristics from all those men with whom the wife has had pre-marital or extramarital intercourse. It is for this reason that the old laws favor marriage with virgins . . . and draw a sharp distinction between the sexual rights of women and men. Just as different races of men have unequal rights, so too do men and women have unequal rights. The old custom of law, which allowed the lord of the manor to sleep with every virgin first, proves that the ancients knew that it is the man who is responsible for breeding the race upward.

Dear ladies, tell me honestly, whose wives would you be today if noble men, if godlike Siegfrieds, had not torn you away from the Sodomite monsters, if they had not put you in warm nests, if they had not defended you—sword in hand—throughout thousands and thousands of years against Slavs, Mongols, Moors, and Turks? Choose between us and those sons of Sodom, have yourselves sexually serviced on the mound of corpses made up of your husbands who fell in battle—as so many of your mothers' mothers did! Take them to your husbands' houses, so they can make harem slaves of you, so you can become the mother of a brood of lascivious, blood-thirsty beasts, who know no motherly or wifely love! What woman is today, she has become thanks to the sword and power of man. Man wrestled woman from the apes of Sodom, and for this reason she is his property!

The man must assume leadership for the upbreeding of humanity; the woman must follow him. The man is the head and object of woman; Christ, the future God-man, is the head and object of man (Eph. 5:23; Col. 3:18). Woman still today loves pleasure-apes and makes the effort to breed humanity downward. The so-called modern woman of free love finds herself depressed by melancholy and vague longings. . . . The modern woman . . . is fleeing the Germanic man and would rather make children with Slavs and Mediterraneans. . . .

We will no longer generate men by means of carnal intercourse, but rather perhaps by means of radiation. Jesus came to abolish the work of woman. We will once more become similar to the electrical God-men physically as well—we will again become pure Gods. We must take off the dark pelt of the ape and put on the shining breastplate of the God-man (Rom. 13:12). We come from God and to God we will return, that is the great secret of the transmigration of souls, of the process of becoming man, of the suffering, of the death and of the Resurrection, the return, and of the great Supper (John 6:35) of the Gods. Christ is the original-man of the past and the evolved-man of the future, he is the A and the O, beginning and end. . . . Cold Boreas must again sweep through the withered garden of mankind and Nordic blood extinguish the southern ape-rut. . . .

German men [are to] love the strong, loyal, Nordic woman in whom the divine electron still slumbers. (Lanz 1908, 144–55)

It should be noted that many of the ideas on eugenics and selective breeding expressed by Lanz von Liebenfels were simply ones that were current at that time around the globe—most especially in the USA. That more contemporary researchers may not have seen these now shocking ideas in print before they saw them expressed by Liebenfels may account for the false direct connection between the ideas of Lanz and those of Hitler and the National Socialists. The theoretical matrix into which Liebenfels projected ideas on eugenics were entirely unique to the ONT and probably not sincerely shared even by the majority of people who identified themselves as Ariosophists. Traces of any particular and unique ONT ideology are hard to find in mainstream National Socialist theory. The methods of ONT textual exegesis is akin to those used by men obsessed with eroticism (who see every word or phrase as being somehow related to a sexual act of pleasure or procreation) or with intoxicants (who see in every word a coded reference to the employment of drugs). In Lanz's case, he is obsessed with bestiality, race, and miscegenation. I have spent as much space as I have on the topic of Lanz so as to show that (1) he had neglible influence on the actual ideology of National Socialism, and (2) his ideology is scientifically eccentric in the extreme.

THEODOR FRITSCH AND THE GERMANEN-ORDEN

In contrast to the Armanenschaft and the ONT, with only tenuous and indirect connections to the development of National Socialism, the Germanen-Orden (Germanic Order) and its subsidiary, the Thule-Gesellschaft, have more direct and historically linked relationships to Hitler and the Nazis. Leaders of the Germanen-Orden, founded in 1912, included Philipp Stauff, Prof. Heinrich Kräger, Hermann Pohl, and its mastermind, Theodor Fritsch, author of the *Handbuch der Judenfrage* (Handbook of the Jewish Question).*

Fritsch (1852–1933), born Emil Theodor Fritsche, was instrumental in the formulation of a biologically based anti-Semitism that would appeal to those for whom the age-old religiously based anti-Semitism, with its origins in the medieval church, had lost some of its credibility. He graduated from the Berlin Institute of Technology in 1875 and acquired a publishing firm for technical works. In 1880 he founded the Deutsche Müllerbund (German Millers League). Fritsch was motivated by anti-Semitism to become involved in politics in an effort to unite all of the 190 different anti-Semitic parties and groups in Central Europe. He was unsuccessful in this. In October of 1901 he founded the Hammer-Verlag as an instrument for anti-Semitic activities, which

---

*Fritsch originally published a book by the title *Der antisemitische Katechismus* (The Anti-Semitic Catechism) in 1888. This was revised and expanded into the *Handbuch der Judenfrage* in 1907.

published the periodical *Hammer—Blätter für deutschen Sinn*. In this publishing house both *The Protocols of the Elders of Zion** and *The International Jew* by the American automotive industrialist Henry Ford appeared. In 1912, Fritsch established the Reichshammerbund (Imperial Hammer-League) as an anti-Semitic political organization, and at the same time he founded an esoteric branch of it called the Germanen-Orden. Fritsch was directly involved in politics as a representative of the Deutschvölkische Freiheitspartei (German-völkisch Freedom Party), which acted as a surrogate for the Nazis when they were banned from political participation after the 1923 Putsch attempt in Munich. Fritsch was supportive of Hitler and overtly promoted and aided the NSDAP in seizing power in Germany in 1933. Fritsch did live to see Hitler come to power before his death at home in September of that year.

The Germanen-Orden was essentially a pseudo-Masonic order with ritual based on Wagnerian imagery. Although according to Fritsch's theories the Freemasons were part of the international Jewish conspiracy, the Germanen-Orden was organized along Masonic lines and the ritual was influenced by Masonic principles. This was probably fueled by one of the original members, Hermann Pohl, who was said to be a renegade Mason. Requirements for membership included proof that the prospective member was free of Jewish blood and that he was not married to a Jewish woman. This purity could also be further verified by analyzing photographs or even by using the "platometer" to measure the dimensions of the person's skull.

In 1916, during WWI, the Germanen-Orden split into two groups. The loyalist group was led by Eberhard von Brockhusen, a wealthy patron of Guido von List. The schismatic group was renamed

---

**The Protocols of the Elders of Zion,* also known as *The Protocols of the Meetings of the Learned Elders of Zion,* was a document concocted by monarchist Russian journalists and political officials, first published in Russian in 1903. Its original intent was to create scapegoats out of the Jews for the failings of the Romanov regime. It soon became an international sensation as it was translated into many languages and disseminated widely. Henry Ford had 500,000 copies printed in English. The core of the book describes meetings in which Jewish conspirators discuss plans for worldwide domination. Although it was demonstrated to be a hoax as early as 1921, it remains an intellectual fetish of many groups today.

Germanen-Orden Walvater and led by Hermann Pohl. Pohl's organization seems to have been more involved in the esoteric aspects, whereas the original body appears to have existed to support more overtly political aims. The Germanen-Orden Walvater published the newsletter *Runen* (Runes), in which runic esoterica of the kind made popular by Guido von List regularly appeared.

The Germanen-Orden seems to have disbanded in 1922, perhaps after its mission of establishing a viable political party in the form of the NSDAP had been accomplished.

The outline of the Germanen-Orden initiation ritual survives in the German Federal Archive. It describes how the candidate waits in an adjoining chamber while in the main hall the Master (armed with a spear and wearing a horned helmet), two Knights, a Bard, and the Master of Music (who plays a harmonium) have the members enter. This they do while singing the "Pilgrim's Chorus" from Wagner's *Tannhäuser.* The candidate is led in blindfolded while wearing a pilgrim's garb. He stands before the Master to hear an address in which the distinctions between the Jews (along with other inferior races) and the noble Aryo-Germanic folk are outlined. The Bard lights a fire and the blindfold is removed so that the candidate will be enlightened. The Master thrusts his spear, the spear of Wotan, toward the initiate and the two Knights cross their swords over the spear-shaft, forming the Hagal-rune shape: ✳. Hereupon music from *Lohengrin* is played.

Although the Germanen-Orden had direct links to the foundation of the NSDAP, or perhaps because of this, previous membership in the order excluded the person from ever being a member of the NSDAP itself (Howe 1970).

RUDOLF VON SEBOTTENDORF AND THE THULE GESELLSCHAFT

The Life of Rudolf von Sebottendorf

The shadowy figure of Rudolf von Sebottendorf (1875–1945) hovers around the early history of the NSDAP in ways that invite speculation.

Fig. 4.6. The cover of Sebottendorff's *Bevor Hitler kam* (1933)

The best approach to a wider understanding is contained in my treatment of his practical work in *The Secret Practices of the Sufi Freemasons* (2013). He is also treated at some length by Goodrick-Clarke (1985, 135–52).

The Baron Rudolf von Sebottendorf von der Rose was truly an international man of mystery. A great deal of his life story remains unknown, and perhaps our only real insight is often to be found in the pages of his semi-autobiographical 1925 novel *Der Talisman des Rosenkreuzers* (The Talisman of the Rosicrucian). Generally, it appears that much of the obscurity surrounding his life is a veil of his own manufacture.

To begin with, he was no baron and his name was not Sebottendorf. He obtained the name and title later in life by being adopted by Baron Heinrich von Sebottendorf. He was born Adam Alfred Rudolf Glauer in Hoyerswerda near Dresden on November 9, 1875. His father was a locomotive engineer and veteran of the Prussian army. When his father died in 1893, enough money was left to finance his son's formal education.

At first Glauer trained as a mechanical engineer, but these studies were never completed. He preferred to live a life of adventure in exotic locales and on the high seas. This continued until 1900, when he met a wealthy Turkish landowner, Hussain Pasha. He moved to Turkey and managed Pasha's estate at Bursa. Hussain Pasha was a practitioner of Sufism, and he also introduced Glauer to the Greco-Jewish Termudi family. The patriarch of this family was a student of the Kabbalah and Rosicricianism, and a Freemason. Glauer was initiated into Freemasonry and remained in Turkey, studying Turkish and occultism. In 1910 he founded a mystical lodge in Constantinople—which was really a *tariqat,* or school, of the Bektashi Order of Sufis. The next year he was both legally adopted by a German expatriate named Heinrich von Sebottendorf and became a legal citizen of Turkey. With this adoption he not only obtained a new identity but also became heir to the title of baron (Ger. *Freiherr*). He served in the Red Crescent, the Islamic version of the Red Cross, during the Balkan War (1912–1913), when he was wounded and became a POW. After this he returned to live in Germany and Austria.

As we shall see, in this man we have a genuine link to the early members of the NSDAP and someone who is confirmed to have been involved in occult practices, from secret Sufi spiritual exercises to the practice of astrology. A great deal remains obscure about his life, his motives, and even his death. A good deal of this obscurity was of his own manufacture, to be sure. It is perhaps true that he just acted as a channel for specific ideas to be insinuated into German awareness at the time. In fact, this is something he often appears to want to imply to his readers. It is also possible that his activities in the years just after the Great War were all intimately connected to ideas implicit in one of his occult books: *Die Praxis der alten türkischen Freimauerei: Der Schlüssel zum Verständis der Alchemie* (1924).* Sebottendorf learned these

---

*The English edition, which I have translated and edited, is *The Secret Practices of the Sufi Freemasons* (2013).

exercises in connection with the Bektashi order of dervishes in Istanbul. It seems odd that a proto-Nazi, such as Sebottendorf is often depicted to be in postwar literature, would have resorted to what appears to be a clearly non-Aryan source for a model. It was probably just a matter of his application of what he was already familiar with to the task at hand: that task, as perceived by Sebottendorf and Hitler alike, was the development of solidarity within the German Volk. He had witnessed the solidarity he felt the Turks had and wanted to develop this sort of thing among his fellow Germans as well.

As the winds of war had come to the world and the Great War was raging in 1916, Sebottendorf found himself living in Bad Aibling in Bavaria. At this time he joined the Germanen-Orden Walvater, at first only by correspondence. But in September of that year he personally visited Hermann Pohl, then head of the Germanen-Orden Walvater in Berlin. During the course of the following year, 1917, he became the publisher for the Germanen-Orden and was elected Master of the Bavarian province of the order.

By the closing months of the next year, 1918, the military and political tides had turned against Germany. Emboldened by the Bolshevik Revolution in Russia, communist insurgents were vying for political power in Bavaria. It was the self-appointed mission of the Germanen-Orden to stem this red uprising. The name "Thule-Gesellschaft" (Thule Society) was adopted by the Germanen-Orden as a cover identity to operate in this atmosphere of violence and chaos.* Rented space at the Hotel Vierjahreszeiten (Four Seasons) in Munich became the venue for weekly meetings held by the Thule group. Although the political dimension was always present, to some extent the Thule Society also began to operate independently in the area of occult lectures delivered at their meetings by the baron.

---

*Bavaria had an especially violent political atmosphere in the aftermath of WWI. Kurt Eisner declared Bavaria to be a free state in November of 1918 and in February of the following year was assassinated, leading to the outbreak of Communist revolt, in which Bavaria was turned into a Socialist, or Soviet Republic (*Räterepublik*) in April 1919. This was, however, quickly crushed by elements of the Freikorps and the army in just the next month. This was the atmosphere in which the Thule Society was active.

Sebottendorf was the leader of this Thule Society for a short time only, from April 1918 to July 1919. But it was during this short period that he accomplished three important things:

1. He formed an armed militia to fight the Communists.
2. He was instrumental in the foundation of the political group called the German Workers' Party.
3. He bought a newspaper, the *Münchener Beobachter* (Munich Observer).

In April 1919, Communist revolutionaries seized power in the state of Bavaria. In this process, they took seven members of the Thule Society hostage and subsequently executed them. This atrocity, which occurred on April 30,* became a rallying point for the various right-wing militias. In the end the militias succeeded in defeating the Bolshevik Revolution in Bavaria. Shortly after this, the German Workers' Party was joined and subsequently reformed by a new charismatic leader—Adolf Hitler. The party was renamed the National Socialist German Workers' Party (National-Sozialistische Deutsche Arbeiterpartei—NSDAP). The newspaper that Sebottendorf owned was sold to Dietrich Eckhart, representing the Party, and it became the official organ of the organization: *Der Völkische Beobachter* (The Nationalist Observer).

Clearly, Sebottendorf played a role in laying the groundwork for what was to become the National Socialist movement. It also seems obvious that Sebottendorf and others received outside guidance and financial assistance for their activities. Were the Thule men the shapers of events, or were they pawns of greater forces? An overview of Sebottendorf's entire life demonstrates that he was primarily an adventurer and esotericist and that the activities of 1916 to 1919 as a political operative were a departure for him, and even these activities were carried out under the cover of occult organizations. These facts only deepen the mystery surrounding him.

---

*Curiously, it was on this same date twenty-six years later that Hitler committed suicide in the bunker, a few days before Germany's surrender to Allied forces.

In July 1919, Sebottendorf departed from the Thule Society and Munich. He once more devoted himself to esoteric studies, and during the following fifteen years he wrote and published the bulk of his major works. These included novels, histories of astrology, technical astrological texts, and his famous book on Sufi exercises. A brief overview of his works from this period will be instructive. His astrological manuals include *Die Hilfshoroskopie* (1921), *Stunden- und Frage-Horoskopie* (1921), *Sterntafeln* (*Ephemeriden*) *von 1838–1922* (1922), and *Astrologisches Lehrbuch* (Astrological Textbook) [1927]. Perhaps to be counted as his masterpiece in astrological studies is *Geschichte der Astrologie* (History of Astrology), volume 1 (1923). His other major works are *Die Praxis der alten türkischen Freimauerei* (1924), *Der Talisman des Rosenkreuzers* (The Talisman of the Rosicrucian; 1925), and finally, *Bevor Hitler kam* (Before Hitler Came; 1933).

Then something strange happened: after Hitler became Chancellor of Germany in 1933, Sebottendorf went back home to Germany and tried to reactivate the Thule Society. In December of that year, he published the book *Bevor Hitler kam,* which actually seemed to try to claim responsibility for getting the National Socialist movement started from within the Thule Society. The NSDAP was not pleased. Sebottendorf was arrested twice, the book was officially banned on March 1, 1934, and all copies confiscated and destroyed. He finally returned to Turkey. This whole misadventure would appear on the surface to be an attempt to take personal advantage of the success of the Nazis, an attempt that seems to have failed—or perhaps not. Sebottendorf's life after 1934 remains an enigma. It is known that he was on the payroll of the German Intelligence Service in Istanbul. His contact person was a man by the name of Herbert Rittlinge. Turkey had been an ally of Germany in the First World War, but in the Second World War it had remained neutral until the very end of the conflict. When the outcome was clear in 1944, the Turks joined the Allies in August of that year. The German embassy was closed in Turkey, and Sebottendorf was given a severance package of one year's support. About ten months later, on May 8, 1945, Germany surrendered unconditionally and—so the official story goes—Sebottendorf committed suicide by jumping off a bridge in Istanbul that same day.

Controversy surrounds Sebottendorf's death. The subtext of the story is that he was so depressed by the defeat of Germany that he took his own life. But it is just as likely that it was an act of desperation by a seventy-year-old man with no hope for the future. However, it must also be said that the possibility exists that he was *assassinated* after his sponsors had vanished along with any special protection he might have enjoyed. Such an assassination could have been carried out by Nazi free agents who wanted to insure his silence about the origins of Nazism or by the enemies of the Nazis who finally took their revenge.

Sebottendorf's Ideology

Three of Sebottendorf's books are of special importance to our study. The first two of these are *Die Praxis der alten türkischen Freimauerei* (1924) and the novel *Der Talisman des Rosenkreuzers* (1925). The novel is a semi-autobiographical text used to fill in details of Sebottendorf's often shady life story. Then there is the doomed book, *Bevor Hitler kam*. Each of these works seems to have a specific mission. In *Der Talisman* he wishes to bolster his image as an adventurer, while in *Bevor Hitler kam* he clearly wants to take some of the credit for the recent successes of National Socialism. Only in the *Praxis* does he seem to reveal something of his particular path, a path that is difficult to comprehend as having anything to do with the mainstream of National Socialist ideology.

The following passage from my introductory remarks to *Secret Practices of the Sufi Freemasons* goes a long way in explaining Sebottendorf's relationship to Sufism and the role he saw it playing in post-WWI Germany.

Those who have been paying attention to events in the Orient over the last few years must continually wonder in amazement: "How is it possible that a people such as the Turks, who aren't even a homogenous people, have been able to develop such perseverance, turn it against a world of enemies, and eventually carry it to victory? Anyone knowing how exhausted the people already were by the ongoing burdens of war, which only a Muslim can bear, when they entered the World War must also be amazed by their patience and endurance under the most difficult conditions. What is then the difference between Germany, which has almost had to succumb under the yoke of a horrendous peace, and Turkey, which rejected a similar peace and fought on to obtain different conditions?"*

The modern intellectual, schooled in materialism, will thanklessly strive to find the underlying reason for this because he is always focusing on externalities.

He can in no way understand that it is the spiritual guidance and training alone, which every Muslim strives for from his youth forward, that have born him through these hard times. We are experiencing the shameful spectacle of a great part of the German people throwing themselves into the arms of the Bolsheviks expecting every sort of benefit from those who have declared materialism to be God, and we see that Turkey, this small, weakened land, certainly made use of the aid of the Bolsheviks afforded them, but that they were far from throwing themselves into the arms of Bolshevism. On the contrary, it finds no place among them.

We see that one people, which had been counted as one of the most intellectually advanced, decided to take just such a step backward, while another people—previously scorned as being inferior—clearly recognized this step as ruinous and declined to participate, and not only rejected the step in its particulars, but in its entirety as well.

"Just tether your ass and commend it to God," goes a Turkish proverb. The West has always been of the belief that Islam is stagnant as a religion. Nothing is further from the truth; Islam is more viable than the Christian religion. It has proven its viability. The following exploration clearly shows us the wellspring of the power of Islam; it is up to us to make the wellspring useful to the Christian religion as well. It was living water from this wellspring that brought everything to fruition in the early period of the Church, and which

---

Here Sebottendorf is referring to the unfavorable Treaty of Sèvres, first imposed upon the Ottoman Empire after the conclusion of WWI, a treaty not unlike that of Versailles. This sparked a nationalist revolution among the Turks, led by Mustafa Kemal Atatürk, and the establishment of the Turkish nation-state, the Republic of Turkey.

produced the most glorious flowering of the Middle Ages; only rationalism and materialism blocked this wellspring. (Sebottendorf 2013, 60–61)

The vast majority of the written material produced by Sebottendorf had little or nothing to do with politics. However, both his life story and one of his books, *Bevor Hitler kam* (1933), show his involvement in founding and directing insurgent political operations. In the introductory sections of his 1933 book, Sebottendorf describes his devotion to two ideas: *Deutschtum* (Germanism) and socialism. We have already become familiar with the outlines of the concept of Deutschtum. For men such as Sebottendorf, it was also bound up with concepts of anti-modernism. Modernism was seen as coterminous with industrialization, commercialism, and democracy—all considered destructive to the nation and to Deutschtum.

It would appear that Sebottendorf provided only glimpses of parts of his whole occult ideology. One factor of great importance to him was a sort of unified field of reality, which connected things such as the stars with the fate and character of individual humans. Here we see an echo of the Islamic insistence on the essential unity of being (Arabic *wahdat al-wujûd*). This is also a clear reflection of the Monism popular in his day, although he sometimes overtly appears to disavow "bogus Monism."* This idea of the unity of being also gives Sebottendorf the rationale for his focus on tradition and individual national traditions, it makes the concept of alchemy possible (since the base and noble, lead and gold, are all parts of the same substance of being) and explains why and how the stars can affect the soul and destiny of men and nations.

---

*The word *monism* is used in a variety of ways in philosophical parlance. We can assume that Sebottendorf as a Sufi ascribes to the doctrine of Ibn al Arabi (wahdat al-wujûd), which teaches the unity and hence reality of Allah and that all things that exist borrow their unity and reality from the central source of being. But monism was also a term used by materialists who hold that everything that exists is material, and therefore anything that appears to be nonmaterial is either erroneous or represents something material that has been misunderstood as "mental." This type of materialistic usage is what Sebottendorf refers to as "bogus monism."

Sebottendorf focuses on the idea of the perfectibility of the individual, which is the aim of the Sufi exercises, and it follows that he thought this could be extended to greater organic units such as nations. The results of individual work are seen to be transferred to the larger society in which the individual lives. This, we are told, is the original mission of the *Praxis*. Alchemically, the individual becomes a living Philosopher's Stone. Contact with him can then function as a catalyst for widespread transformation. Is this how Sebottendorf worked? So much influence has been ascribed to him, yet his biographical details do not seem to reflect that level of power. How did an obscure occultist exert such historical influence in a short time and disappear from activity years before the results of his operation were manifest? And why did he return at the moment of the operation's dark triumph only to then fade into final obscurity?

Sebottendorf's work was mysterious. Beyond written documents, he also worked in the formation of groups and movements. If we analyze what he did, we can arrive at some semblance of understanding of his worldview. On the one hand, he was a dedicated nationalist, but on the other he was a lover of the exotic who spent a large part of his life outside his home country and even converted to Islam.

Politically, Sebottendorf was an adherent of two main ideas, Germanism and socialism, both of which were sweeping through Germany. Hitler was motivated by a combination of these same two ideas as well. Indeed, they are reflected in the very formula of National Socialism.

THE GERMAN(IC) FAITH IDEOLOGY

The way had been prepared for the advent of openly neopagan philosophy. During the time before WWII, in the early part of the twentieth century, there arose in Germany a variety of ideologically and often organizationally related groups that made use of similar terminologies. The main ones, and the ones we will discuss in some detail here, were the Germanische Glaubens-Gemeinschaft, founded by Ludwig Fahrenkrog, and the Deutsche Orden, founded by Otto Sigfrid Reuter, which later melded in part with Jakob Wilhelm Hauer's Deutschgläubige Bewegung in 1933. In general, these various groups competed with each other, but were also constantly trying to coordinate and consolidate their efforts to present a united front in a struggle for state recognition. Groups would periodically ally themselves with one another, then split apart again. In the end, the only real unifying force was that provided by the NSDAP itself. The ideas that united these groups were their common rejection of Christianity as a proper myth for the guidance of the people in the German nation and their embrace of the idea of an autochthonous Germanic faith based on racial and historical/cultural factors. The tone of all of these groups tended to be abstract, academic, philosophical, and artistic, which reflected the natures of their leaders. Although these groups are rightly characterized as being neopagan, there is little of the perhaps expected focus on historical Germanic paganism with regard to ritual or practical spiritual customs.

These groups and the ideas that inspired them were understandable given the particular mixture of ideological developments coming out of the nineteenth century: (the Christian) God was dead, which left people freer than before to seek spiritual or religious solutions outside the confines of Christian mythology; nationalism and national identity was the rising ideal, which urged some to seek for that meaning in specifically autochthonous or culturally authentic ways of thinking. This combination of factors led certain individuals of considerable intellectual development to find their ways into what could be called a *national* German religion.

Ludwig Fahrenkrog and Die Germanische Glaubens-Gemeinschaft (1908–1964)

Ludwig Fahrenkrog (1867–1952), besides being a founder of the völkisch and neopagan organization known as the Germanische Glaubens-Gemeinschaft (Germanic Faith Community; GGG), was also a well-known artist and poet. After an apprenticeship as a decorative painter in the Altona area of Hamburg, he studied art at the Academy of Arts in Berlin. He was eventually named as a professor of art in 1913, and he was also a visiting professor of art at the University of Dakota in 1925.

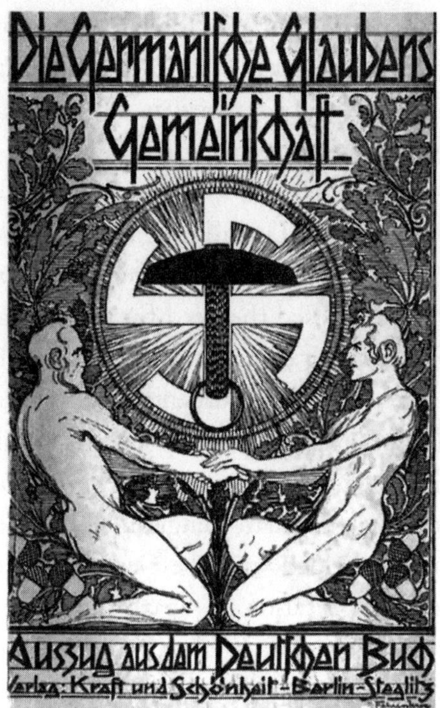

Fig. 4.7. Cover art by Fahrenkrog for a condensed version of *Das Deutsche Buch*

His early work was greatly influenced by the Life-Reform movement and by the art nouveau style (Ger. *Jugendstil*) that was sweeping the art world in the late nineteenth century. He rejected modern trends in art and embraced a symbolist style with themes of nature, Germanic mythology, and the subjective contents of the soul. By 1900 he was committed to a neopagan vision. In that year, he officially resigned from the church, and by 1908 he was calling for the creation of a religious community based on Germanic principles. He founded the Germanische Glaubens-Gemeinschaft in 1913, a group he led until the end of his life. In the same year the GGG was founded, his volume titled *Lucifer* appeared, followed by *Ludwig Fahrenkrog: Seine Schöpfungen und ihre Bedeutung für unser Volkstum* (Ludwig Fahrenkrog: His Creations and Their Meaning for Our Folk; 1922).

He wrote several dramas with Germanic-heroic themes and published a journal called *Der Weihwart* (The Holy Warden) beginning in 1922.

Although Fahrenkrog saw Christianity as a foreign creed rooted in Judaism and therefore incompatible with the Germanic spirit, he was not a National Socialist. The Nazis kept him at a distance, and his works of art and his philosophy were neither partisan nor did they glorify war.

As mentioned, the history of the GGG really began with an article written by Fahrenkrog in 1908 in the periodical *Der Volkserzieher* (The Folk-Educator) in which he proposed the need for the formation of a Germanic religious congregation to compete with the traditional Christian confessions in order to reestablish an authentic and autochthonous religious faith specific to the German people. By 1911, Fahrenkrog had gathered a number of fellow enthusiasts, and something called the Deutschreligiöse Gemeinschaft (German-Religious Community) was formed in theory, which soon melded with the German Order of Reuter. But after a short while the unification fell apart.

In 1913, Fahrenkrog's group received its final name, Germanische Glaubens-Gemeinschaft, and a new charter. At this time, the artist known as Fidus (Hugo Höppener, 1868–1948) became a member of the group and began doing some artistic work for GGG publications. As time went on, Fidus became more active in the group, and he and Fahrenkrog developed a close friendship. The artistic styles of Fahrenkrog and Fidus shared many common elements. The community of the GGG was hierarchically organized into households (in which the father was the head), local congregations headed by a Weihwart (Holy Warden), regional or tribal areas headed by a Gauwart (District Warden), and finally the community in general with the Hochwart (High Warden) at its head. Fahrenkrog was the Hochwart of the community. By the beginning of the 1920s, there were several hundred members and about thirteen local congregations.

In the early 1920s the community was in cooperation with various other groups, such as Otto Dickel's Deutsche Werkgemeinschaft (German Working Community) and the Nordisch-religiöse Arbeitsgemeinschaft (Nordic-Religious Work Community) led by Norbert Seibertz and Wilhelm Kusserow, which was closely connected to National Socialism from the beginning. These organizations were united in their opposition to Christianity, "Asianism," Judaism, and Marxism. Jakob Wilhelm Hauer's Arbeitsgemeinschaft Deutscher Glaubensbewegung (Alliance of the German Faith movement; ADG), founded in 1933, absorbed much of the membership of these organizations.* The ADG was always a rather heterogeneous organization that included many different points of view and directions, spiritually and philosophically. What the German identity was, and what it meant to an individual's spiritual life, remained a matter of individual conscience. This trait stems from the Protestant and Pietistic roots that informed much of the tenor of the organization.

Throughout the war years there were repeated efforts to unite the various German Faith groups, including one in 1941 held at Erbsen, near Göttingen. The GGG survived the war, and Fahrenkrog continued to be active as an artist. He received a commission to paint the portraits of Hans and Sophie Scholl, who had been executed by the Nazis as dissidents. After Fahrenkrog's death in 1952, the GGG continued to exist as a small group until it finally officially came to an end in 1964.†

Doctrines of the GGG

The spiritual universe of the GGG partook heavily of the ideas and practices of medieval German mysticism, such as that of Meister Eckhart, albeit stripped of its overtly Christian aspects. The direct experience of the presence of God and the existence of the divine in the natural environment and in the human soul were the foundations of their beliefs. One of the leaders of the movement, Wilhelm Schwaner (1863–1944), an important author and publicist for the movement, looked to more modern paradigms of German thought in the works of German statesmen and philosophers, whereas Fahrenkrog saw the foundations of German spirituality more in Nordic and medieval German sagas, legends, and folk art.

---

*The ADG will be discussed in more detail in chapter 7.
†The GGG has since been revived in the 1990s by Géza von Neményi and remains active today.

The following manifesto, which appeared in 1921 in *Das Deutsche Buch,* was addressed to all of the Germanic peoples throughout the world.

THE "CONFESSION" OF THE GGG

1. We acknowledge the powers of the spirit and of life, which permeate the All and ourselves, as well.

2. And recognize the formational powers of life in the All, which condition the variety of all phenomena, and therefore also acknowledge all separate phenomena in their natural necessity as revelations of the powers of life.

3. Since, however, the truth and the sense of its existence is itself just as naturally necessary in phenomena, it is thus also the import or function of all phenomena to fulfill themselves.

4. Therefore, we too recognize the meaning and the duty of our existence—as a grain of seed arisen with us and trusting in its fulfillment—existing with us.

5. Hence, we believe and know that a religion of the German folk can only arise from within itself.

6. For us religion is the pure, world-affirming relationship of the soul to the entities of the All and to their forms of phenomena and revelation, joyous in deed and knowledge.

7. Our knowledge and experience of the gods as the ultimate truths and essences and as forces working in us and through us is for us at the same time knowledge of a moral law within us and the foundation of our trust in their leadership and the cause of our belief in the exalted destiny of the German folk.

8. Out of such knowledge also germinates within us the will to do the good, the will to purity, truth and justice, to self-salvation and self-fulfillment, and thus arises in us also the will to free and moral action including self-sacrifice.

9. Therefore, we perceive in our reflection upon our own essence as the special operative phenomenal forms of the gods and in the maintenance of health and strength, of the progressive and higher development of this essence toward ever purer,

nobler forms and aims, the most exalted task of each and every Germanic person inside as well as outside of the German borders.

10. Beyond the grave, however, we gaze in complete trust into infinity, whence we came. Our task is to fulfill this existence—to allot this task is the right and power of the gods, who permeate the All and us as well, in time and eternity. (Fahrenkrog 1923, 31–35)

Fahrenkrog saw himself as a sort of prophet among the Germanic peoples of the world. He had as his aim the reversion of the Germanic people to their indigenous national faith and communion with their own actions and love in this the world of the here and now—in the *Diesseitigkeit,* or "this-worldliness," as Nietzsche would have called it. It is clear, however, that Fahrenkrog and the school of which he was an essential part often looked more to contemporary German philosophy and personal experience rather than to the myths and legends of the ancient Germanic past for their guiding principles.

GGG Customs

The rituals of the GGG under the leadership of Fahrenkrog are not very well documented. In the Romantic spirit, the practitioner sought to experience nature directly on a regular basis. It would appear that the heavily syncretic nature of the organization lent itself to the radical inner reinterpretation of outwardly Christian rituals, customs, and sacred times. For example, the Christian calendar was reinvested with völkisch significances, as follows:

Church Festival	GGG-Interpretation (1913–1964)
New Year (January 1)	Honoring the All-Father
Good Friday	Memory of the Mass Execution of Alemannic and Saxon Nobility at Cannstatt and Verden
Easter	Victory of the Light over Darkness and the Resurrection of Nature

Ascension (40 days after Easter)	The Bringing Home of the Hammer in Memory of the Restoration of Germanic Belief
Pentecost	The Presence of God in Nature and the "Awakening of the German Spirit"
St. John's Day (Midsummer)	Festival of Abundance
St. Michael's Day (September 29)	Harvest Festival
Sunday of the Dead (between November 20 and 26)	Memory of Those Who Have Passed Away
Christmas (December 25)	Rebirth of the Light

DER DEUTSCHE ORDEN

At approximately the same time as Fahrenkrog began to formulate the GGG, Otto Sigfrid Reuter (1876–1945) founded the Deutsche Orden (German Order), which existed officially until 1933. Reuter was the son of the director of a navigation school in Leer. While working for the German postal system, Reuter began to study history and law at the University of Bonn in 1901. He eventually found himself in Bremen as the telegraph and phone-system director. Partially due to his activities as a political agitator, he was forced into early retirement in 1924.

Reuter wrote an influential book in 1910 called *Sigfrid oder Christus?* (Siegfried or Christ?), which was a rejection of Christianity in favor of an autochthonous form of Germanic spirituality. The next year he founded the German Order in Berlin. This occurred in the offices of the *Staatsbürger Zeitung,* the organ of the Deutschsociale Partei (German Socialist Party). The group was immediately allied with Fahrenkrog's Deutschreligiöse Gemeinschaft (which would change its name to the Germanische Glaubens-Gemeinschaft three years later).

Membership in both the German Order and the German Faith Community required the so-called Aryan Certificate proving the member's ethnic heritage as being purely German going back to at least 1750. Such genealogical proof was certified by Bernard Koerner (1875–1952), who published the *Deutsche Geschlechterbuch* (German Book of Genealogy).

Reuter himself continued to gain prestige in völkisch circles, not so much as a leader or organizer, but more as a thinker and scholar. Reuter became increasingly involved with prehistoric Germanic studies in an academic setting, and even studied at the university with the Old Norse expert Gustav Neckel in Berlin and with Gustaf Kossinna in archaeology, and wrote articles for Kossinna's journal, *Mannus*. Reuter's enduring legacy was built upon his studies of Germanic astronomy, which was the topic of his 1934 magnum opus titled *Germanische Himmelskunde*. An undated summary of this was published by a National Socialist press titled *Der Himmel über den Germanen* (The Sky over the Germanic Folk). Reuter received the Gustaf-Kossinna Prize for Prehistory in 1935, and, with the support of several scholars, he also received an honorary doctoral degree from the University of Jena in 1939. Reuter did not become a member of the NSDAP until that same year, after which he worked to some degree within the context of the Ahnenerbe.

In the final analysis, differences in philosophy between the approach of Reuter and Fahrenkrog prevented continuing cooperation between the two. Reuter was laxer in the particulars of doctrine and felt that the recognition of one's belonging to the Germanic race was the simple essence of doctrine, whereas Fahrenkrog strove to develop a more complex set of tenets.

The German Order dissolved itself in 1933 after the National Socialists had gained control of the government of Germany. It was thought that the order had accomplished its mission.

Reuter was killed on April 5, 1945, by Allied bombs in an attack on his neighborhood in Bremen-Huchting.

THE ARTAMANEN MOVEMENT

The Artamanen movement was an early twentieth-century sociocultural initiative that greatly influenced Heinrich Himmler along with a

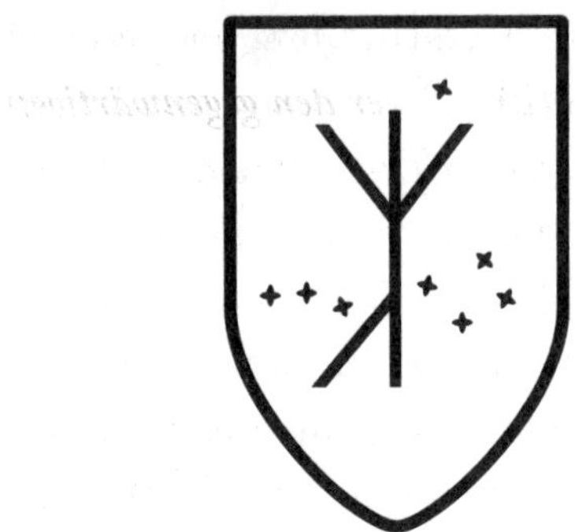

Fig. 4.8. Artamanen badge

number of other National Socialist leaders. In many respects the movement was rooted in the general Reform ideology of Germany at the turn of the century. The original visionary for the movement was Willibald Hentschel (1858–1947). The most insightful study of the group has been offered by Michael Kater (1971).

The unusual word *Artamanen* received several explanations over the years. At first glance it appears to be based on the German word *Art,* which means "kind," as in "our own kind." This is suggested by the postwar organization founded by a former SS-man, Wilhelm Kusserow, called the Artgemeinschaft (Kindred Community). However, Hentschel at times derived it from the Middle High German word *art,* "agriculture; agricultural yield; innate characteristics," compounded with the word for "man." In his book *Varuna,* Hentschel says he originally derived it from a Persian word, *Artam.* Old Persian has *Arta-,* "truth, existence, right working," which is cognate to Sanskrit *r̥tá,* a term that figured greatly in List's ideology (reformulated as *Rita,* "right, cosmic law"). With certainty, the word *Artamanen* can be identified as an artificial construct by Hentschel, but one that seemed to attract followers with a mysterious power.

The motto of the Artamanen is:

> *Gläubig dienen wir der Erde*
> *Und dem großen Stirb und Werde!*

"Faithfully we serve the Earth and the great dictum: Die and Become."

Hentschel studied biology with Ernst Haeckel in Jena and received his doctorate in 1879 with a dissertation titled *Über den gegenwärtigen Stand ursächlicher Erklärung in der Vererbungserscheinung* (On the Present State of Research on the Causal Explanation of the Phenomenon of Heredity).

After completing his studies, he began to acquire rural property in Germany's eastern provinces. When he was twenty-three years old, he married, had five daughters with this wife, and was survived by thirteen grandchildren and twenty-seven great-grandchildren upon his death in 1947. His academic and scientific work provided a good income along with earnings on patents in the field of chemistry. After 1890 he began to be involved in völkisch and anti-Semitic political circles and was a leader of the Deutschsozialen Partei. This caused friction in academia so he retired to his properties in Silesia.

Hentschel first outlined his vision for what would become the Artamanen-Gesellschaft (Artaman League) in his seminal books *Varuna* (1901) and *Mittgart* (1904), in which he advocated the colonization of territory by means of spreading polygamous agrarian communities, especially into the eastern frontiers of Germany. The farms established by this movement would be places for the breeding of a healthy, superior Nordic stock of new humanity.

According to Hentschel's plan, the farms making up the Mittgart-settlement network would have ten women for every man—a polygamous system that he believed had been the rule in ancient Germanic society. Although there was initial success for the movement as far as establishing farms was concerned, the polygamous aspect had to be abandoned because not enough women could be recruited!

Hentschel was good friends with Theodor Fritsch, the anti-Semitic founder of the Germanen Orden and the author of the *Handbuch der Judenfrage* (Handbook on the Jewish Question; 1893). Fritsch published some of Hentschel's books, and he even periodically lived with Hentschel on his estate at Seiffersdorf (present-day Kozy, Poland). Hentschel wrote for Fritsch's journal *Hammer* and the *Deutsch-Sozialen Blätter*.

As a consequence of events connected to WWI, Hentschel lost his means of livelihood and estates in the east and had to reorganize in northern Germany near Westerwanna at what he named Keim-Siedlung (Seed-Settlement) Niegard. In 1923 he published a call to action to organize activities.

Hentschel did join the NSDAP in 1929 (member no. 144,649) but relinquished membership in December 1932. He did, however, continue to enjoy good relations with Party officials, including Hitler himself. Hentschel's direct influence on Party programs and customs include the *Lebensborn* (Wellspring of Life) program, and it was actually Hentschel who promoted the practice of the "Hitler-greeting," or salute.

A formal and legal organization was founded in 1926 called the Bund Artam (Artam Association), which was directly inspired by Hentschel's 1923 call to action in his publication *Blätter aus Niegard*. The Artamanen farms were seen as populated by black-clad warrior-farmers who formed an order of knights for the defense and expansion of the Fatherland. As noted, several leading Nazis were involved in one way or another with this ideology.

It was the visionary aim of Hentschel and his followers to create a practical system of agricultural development, which would also be a cultural context for the breeding of a higher form of man based on the principles of eugenics and biology learned from the theories of Haeckel. Modern urban life was seen as a degenerate form of life, which encouraged degeneracy. The Artamanen ideology and practice gave full form to the philosophy of *Blut und Boden* (blood and soil). The word *Artam* was interpreted as "renewal out of the primeval power of the Volk, out of blood, soil, sun and truth" (Sünner 1999, 26). The attitudes of the movement were decidedly anti-Semitic and anti-Slavic. The aim of the push to the east was to secure living space for the German Volk and to act as a protective shield for the Fatherland. Voluntary agrarian work was intended to make migrant workers from Poland unnecessary. The Artamanen would form an expanding wall against migrants from the east.

The first Artamanen farm was established in Limbach under the leadership of a Transylvanian agriculturalist August Georg Kenstler, and other farms were set up elsewhere after that. Artamanen men often worked as volunteers for large landowners in the eastern provinces. The members pooled their financial resources and bought their own land, and divided it equally.

The Artamanen recruited from a variety of German youth organizations, which included the Wandervogel, Kyffhäuserbund (Kyffhäuser League), Wehrverband Wehrwolf (Defense League Wehrwolf), and a dozen others. Many were members of the SA and NSDAP.

In 1927 Georg Wilhelm Schiele founded an organization called Gesellschaft der Freunde der Artamanenbewegung (Society of Friends of the Artamanen Movement). Its members included a number of prominent NSDAP activists, such as Himmler, Darré, and Rudolf Höss, who was later the commandant of Auschwitz.

By 1926 the organization had some 600 members, who worked on some 60 farms, mostly in eastern Germany. By 1929 there were approximately 2,000 members on about 300 farms. In a way, the group fell victim to its associations and successes, as in 1929 the NSDAP dissolved the Artamanen into the structure of the growing Party apparatus. But the Artamanen and their history remained an honored part of the history of the development of the Party and retained some identity within the Hitler Jugend (Hitler Youth) organization. It has been estimated that over the course of the movement's history between 25,000 and 30,000 young people were involved in the organization to one degree or another. The legal organization Bund Artam e.V. was officially absorbed into the Hitler Youth in 1934.

The Artamanen symbol, shown at the beginning of this section, is made up of a bind-rune that combines a Listian Man-rune and an Ar-rune. The Y-rune indicates "Man," while the Ar-rune (↑) can mean noble ideals and the field (acre)—if tilted horizontally on its side, it symbolizes a plow. It is placed on a blue field (sky) and also bears stellar symbols of the North, the polestar and the Great Wain or Big Dipper. As a symbol it was later used on the uniforms of certain Nazis who had previously been members of the Artamanen.

In the late 1960s there was an attempt to revive the organization and ideology of the Artamanen in Germany, with mixed success.

FRIEDRICH HIELSCHER AND THE
INDEPENDENT FREE CHURCH

Friedrich Hielscher (1902–1990) is a personality around whom a good deal of legend has been woven. Some of this legendary material, which we will discuss later, was made possible because relatively little was known of him. Happily, this defect is being remedied in recent years with major studies of him by Peter Bahn (2004) and Kurt Lehner (2015).

His hometown was Guben on the Neisse river, with half the city on the eastern side of the river. This became the Polish city of Gubin after 1945. He completed his college preparatory school in 1919, just after the end of WWI. He joined a Freikorps paramilitary group but left this life after his unit wanted to take part in the unsuccessful Kapp Putsch in 1920 and such paramilitary groups began being absorbed into the regular army. Hielscher then went on to study law at the University of Berlin.

Fig. 4.9. Friedrich Hielscher testifying at Wolfram Sievers's trial, 1946
(US Government Archives)

Hielscher does not fit neatly into any of the usual categories of thinkers from his time period. His views were highly spiritual, anti-materialist, and hence, in his mind, anti-Western. He saw everything from within a religious paradigm, which included what most would call "politics." His concept of the *Reich* (empire) was entirely spiritual.

He studied law at the University of Berlin, receiving his degree in 1926, after which he went into service with the state. At the same time, he began a career as a publicist for conservative causes, joined the Society for the Study of Fascism, and made friends with a wide range of conservative thinkers. He worked on a variety of journals such as *Arminius, Vormarsch* (Advance), and *Das Reich* (1930–1933)—often under a pseudonym.

Once the Nazis came to power in 1933, Hielscher concealed much of his work under the cover of the Faith community that he founded called the Independent Free Church (*Unabhängige Freikirche* [UFK]). This was founded a short time after his official resignation from the Protestant Church.

In one of Hielscher's main works, *Das Reich* (1931, 28), he makes it clear that in his view a Volk is not a defined by language or blood, but rather by culture in a larger sense: "Ein Volk ist Einheit des Bekenntnisses und des Schicksals" (A Volk is a unity of creed and fate). Hielscher's ideology was contrary to that of the National Socialists in many ways. His book and journal, both called *Das Reich,* were immediately banned upon the Nazi assumption of power in 1933. He was named an enemy of the regime. Over the years, he had made many good friends in spiritual circles who were later members of the NSDAP, such as Wolfram Sievers, and these apparently helped to protect him during the time of the Third Reich. He was certainly part of a group who resisted, in often subtle ways, the Nazi regime. He did not become a member of the Party but did participate in certain benign groups within the state apparatus—for example, the National Sozialistischen Volkswohlfahrt (National Socialist Volk Welfare) and the NS-Altherrenbund (NS Old Gentlemen's Club), which facilitated aid to older men and built bridges between the generations.

After the conclusion of WWII, he tried to remove himself from even a hint of the political. Much of his creative work stemmed from the writing of various autobiographical works. He wrote widely for several journals, but the vast majority of what he wrote after the war remains unpublished and stored in approximately six hundred archive boxes in the Kreisarchiv des Schwarzwald-Baar-Kreises in Villingen-Schwenningen. Most of this relates to his post-1945 production (Bahn 2004, 14). He lived a quiet rural life with his wife, keeping up a lively correspondence with friends, including Ernst Jünger, until his death at the age of eighty-eight in 1990.

Hielscher's Teachings

Hielscher's intellectual and spiritual influences were numerous and complex. Oswald Spengler was essential. He was able to meet and talk with Spengler during the time when he was a law student writing his dissertation. He also spent time at the Nietzsche Archive in Weimar and became acquainted with the philosopher's infamous sister.

Other influences on Hielscher's thought were John Scotus Erigena and Johann Wolfgang von Goethe. At the heart of his pagan theology stood God, the absolutely real (*Alleinwirkliche*) and almighty, the primeval one. This was not understood in terms of the Judeo-Christian anthropomorphized God, but in a panentheistic pagan sense in line with the attitudes of the ancient Greek philosophers and others. All of the special entities that exist in the world enjoy a cycle of existence between the divine and material worlds. Underlying this construct was the essence of the Nietzschean idea of the "eternal return" (*ewige Wiederkehr*). Hielscher's Messengers (*Boten*) were eventually given names from Germanic/Nordic mythology and were twelve in number, six masculine and six feminine.

In many ways Hielscher's theology resembles the Iranian/Zoroastrian system, with a high-god of abstract unified qualities and an array of angels, which help the one god carry out the divine mandates.

Hielscher did come to favor names and attributes of his Messengers drawn from Germanic, specifically Eddic/Norse sources, as these seemed more *natural*. However, he was not opposed to the religious system of other peoples and rather saw that all faithful people, regardless of system, belonged in a common struggle against the materialistic forces of atheism. It was upon this basis that he formed his strongest theoretical opposition to National Socialism, the racial doctrine of which he saw as purely materialistic. His was a spiritual, heathen, all-inclusive system.

The credo of the UFK, formulated in 1929, reads:

I believe in God the absolutely real, our foundation and father.

I believe in His twelve divine Messengers, our reconciler and perfector.

I believe in Their eternal Reich. God's world and our Church.
(Schmidt and Breuer 2005, 96)

Politically, Hielscher proposed a sort of theocratic system (in his version of the new heathen religion) opposed to the materialistic Modern political rationale of the Enlightenment.

Unfortunately, Hielscher's own works are relatively inaccessible, and few translations of his work exist.

But fortunately for the English-reader, Michael Moynihan has made one of Hielscher's most stimulating texts, *The Real Powers* (2015), available. In it the author vividly describes the seeker's approach to the concept of *mystery* (Ger. *Geheimnis*).

After describing how the sense of mystery suddenly "flashes up" in the consciousness of an individual Hielscher goes on to say:

Such a person is capable of this confession in his work to the degree that he is not merely a seeker of his mystery but one who—in the same moment—finds it.

If it becomes conscious to him, if he sees the form in which it is concealed flashing up in his world, if the great wonder enthralls him, then the first stage of revelation is reached.

The second stage involves battle. The powers of the higher orders take part in this battle, in which the struggling soul and the mystery are entwined. The greater the abundance of power that we possess, the stronger we feel these forces and the more surely we know to engage with them in friendship or animosity. Whoever is not up to their ranks must fail. . . .

As this battle unfolds, the question of whether the soul remains steadfast is dependent upon the nature of the mystery. If the mystery is hostile, then the moment nears when the opponents have become so embattled with one another that the mystery has penetrated the soul with its powers, and vice versa. All that remains is victory or defeat. Either the mystery shatters the soul and seizes control of its abandoned powers now drifting about in terror, fear, and dismay—or the soul shatters the mystery and gains the glory, outfitting itself with the powers of the mystery. Here we are at those borderline states of madness where the battle plays out on a razor's edge. The shapes seen in madness are the signs of a dreadful reality: the mystery that would swallow the soul. The visions of Nietzsche and of Hölderlin, the sheer radiance and brilliance of their final pronouncements, bear testament to the rare and unheard-of victory of a being that was, when confronted with the magnitude of the chosen enemy, incapable of doing enough and so sacrificially, as a victor, gave itself over to the gods. The higher order—the order to which the soul belongs—overcame that of the mystery.

But if the mystery befriends the soul, then the battle of the second stage becomes a struggle for the mystery against the other, the unknown, with respect to which the soul and the mystery safeguard and actualize the selfsame order. For how can they befriend one another unless they both agree at their deepest core? And how would this agreement be possible unless it is common to both? From the battle, then, a deeper understanding always comes about between soul and mystery. They are open to one another; they penetrate one another. Willingly, the mystery unveils itself in an exhilarating ecstasy of yearning, dissipation, and benevolence.

Following the second stage of battle is then the third, that of ecstasy. The soul becomes ecstatic like someone overwhelmed, or like the vanquisher of an enemy: this is the ecstasy of one who loves and unites with the befriended mystery.

It is no longer alien to us now. It lives inside us. We ourselves have become the mystery. We ascend up into ourselves; and the self we discover is more than the self that was seeking. And yet it exists within that same self. The soul finds itself to be the spark of an infinite fire. Its borders disappear in the great flame. (Hielscher 2015, 5–7)

One of the students or acolytes of Hielscher was Wolfram Sievers (1905–1948), who will become an important part of the Hielscher legend later on. He was the son of a Protestant church musician who was expelled from school for his membership in the Deutschvölkischer Schutz- und Trutzbund (German-völkisch League for Protection and Defense) but went on to study at Stuttgart's Technical University. He remained active in the Bündische Jugend and the Artaman League.

Sievers became a member of the NSDAP in 1929, and beginning in 1933 he administered the Externsteine-Stiftung (Externsteine Foundation), for Heinrich Himmler. The Externsteine, the "Stones of Extern," constitute a monument thought to have great historical and cultic significance for the ancient Germanic peoples.

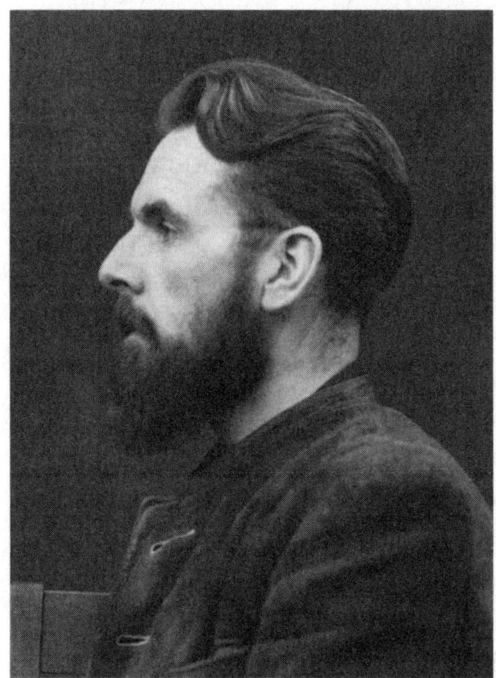

Fig. 4.10. Wolfram Sievers as defendant during the Doctors' Trial, 1946 (US Government Archives)

Himmler appointed Sievers as the General Secretary (*Reichsgeschäftsführer*) of the Ahnenerbe in 1935, and he continued to manage the operations of that organization to the end of the war. Regrettably, he also was the director of the part of the organization that dealt with "military scientific research," which conducted many grisly experiments on human subjects and also participated in a program in which Jewish prisoners were killed for purposes of collecting their skulls and skeletons.

For these and other crimes Sievers was tried at the so-called Doctors' Trial at Nuremberg. Sievers attempted to defend himself by insisting that he was part of a movement to resist the Nazi regime, with plans to assassinate both Himmler and Hitler. This was, as we have seen, in part a reflection of his relationship with Friedrich Hielscher and his Independent Free Church. The defense had no effect, and he was sentenced to death and hanged on June 2, 1948.

Hielscher's Independent Free Church continued on after the war and enjoyed its greatest successes in the 1950s. All of its mysteries still await exploration.

THE GROWTH OF POSITIVE CHRISTIANITY

In chapter 1 we witnessed the birth of what would come to be called Positive Christianity, rooted in the higher criticism of the nineteenth century. By the dawn of the twentieth century, such ideas had become increasingly popularized. The mainstream churches, the Roman Catholic Church and the Evangelical Lutheran Church, had been encouraged by the generally anti-Semitic content of this movement to emphasize their age-old enmity against the Jews. But, of course, the main thrust of the idea of Positive Christianity was set against the traditional churches themselves. The main thing all sides could agree upon was the idea of anti-Semitism. Over the centuries, the Christian churches had promoted anti-Semitism (since the beginning of Christianity as an organized religion), and there had been times and places where the Christian Churches had protected the Jews (for their own temporary reasons)—from the very persecution that the churches themselves had been responsible for generating. After the evidence of the Holocaust had been uncovered, the churches claimed that the Nazis had been motivated by the devil or by paganism to do these crimes, when history shows otherwise. David Kertzer, in his *The Popes Against the Jews: The Vatican's Role in the Rise of Modern Anti-Semitism* (2001), outlines in some detail the history of anti-Semitism leading up to WWII.

Generally, the church promoted anti-Semitism—openly and officially as well as in a clandestine manner through the press outlets it controlled—for reasons similar to those other forces, conservative or revolutionary, opposed the Jews: they were considered to be agents for *modernism*. Modernism called into question the authority of God, the churches, and all sorts of traditional cultural features. The Modern, and in the mind of church authorities, the Jews who they saw as promoting the Modern, posed a great challenge to the continued domination of the spiritual life of citizens of countries belonging to Christendom. Of course, as we pointed out in the introduction to this book, the emancipation of the Jews was a feature of modern reforms, which the Jews did benefit from in a secular way. They did not *cause* the changes in society; rather, they were simply a beneficiary of such changes. But for the churches, who had spent centuries blaming the Jews for every malady and shortcoming, from plagues to famines—old habits died hard.

In 1956, Adolf Leschnitzer offered an insightful study that in part compared the persecution of the Jews under the Nazis with the witchcraft mania in Germany during the late Middle Ages and the early modern age. The witch was seen as an opponent of Christian culture and values, just as the Jews were cast in this role anew in the early twentieth century. It is a mistake to see this in any way as a German phenomenon. It was a universal Christian attitude inherited from the teachings of the early church, which found violent expression at various times in history whether in Spain, England, Russia, France, or indeed Germany. The new component was the introduction of the "racial" idea: that the Jews were scientifically and biologically different from other people.

Anti-Semitism and Lutheranism had a historically close relationship. Luther wrote two extensive works, both published in 1543, one titled *Von den Juden und ihren Lügen* (On the Jews and Their Lies) and the other *Vom Schem Hamphoras und vom Geschlecht Christi* (On the Holy Name and the Lineage of Christ). These were virulent anti-Jewish works in which the Reformer wrote that the Jews were no longer the "chosen" people, but rather they had become "the Devil's people." His opinions went beyond theology and entered the realm of public policy. He advocated the burning of the Jews' synagogues, destroying their books, and either confiscating or destroying their property—"we are at fault for not slaying them." Ironically, but typically, he cited the Bible (Deuteronomy 13) as justification for such actions. These attitudes were, of course, nothing new: they are the standard and orthodox teachings regarding the Jews throughout the Middle Ages. When a plague came, the church typically taught that the pestilence was visited upon the people by God for the people's impiety and that by "avenging Christ" on the Jews, the plague could be lifted. Luther's writings prefigured the Twenty-Five Points of the program of the NSDAP by saying that such policies would force these venomous serpents to work for a living for the first time or be expelled from the country. Luther's message only reinforced medieval forms of anti-Semitism. It must be emphasized, however, that his attitudes were nothing new. The anti-modern trend among conservatives in the late nineteenth and early twentieth century was well stocked with quotes from the works of Luther. Lutherans tended to vote disproportionately for the NSDAP, as compared to Roman Catholics.

Of course, after the end of the war, official Christian institutions successfully recast themselves as pure victims of the Nazis. Whereas Christianity had invented anti-Semitism and promoted it as a pious attitude for many hundreds of years, after it had borne its bloody fruit for all to see and the side that had represented the idea so radically had been relegated to the losers of history, the church secretly switched sides in the dark while no one was watching.

One of the most significant truths about religion in the Third Reich is that most of the major leaders of the Party were hostile to all religion as it stood. On the one hand, they were culturally enmeshed in Christian thinking in many ways that remained unconscious even to them, but the by-then popularized intellectual revolutions ushered in by

Darwin, Haeckel, Marx, Wagner, Nietzsche, and even Freud had profoundly altered these men's attitudes toward religion and myth. It had made them unsympathetic to the church and to Christianity, yes, but it had also soured most of them on the idea of reviving the religion of the Germanic past as being somehow backward, barbaric, and decidedly unmodern. The Protestant spirit was especially skeptical about ritual and cult practices. National Socialism saw itself as a forward-looking, revolutionary movement, and the past, along with its symbols, were mostly valuable (whether Christian or pagan) as tools for manipulating the masses and segments of the masses to undertake the program of the NSDAP with enthusiasm. A good deal of the actual practice of Nazi occultism was connected to the use of metalinguistic paradigms to communicate the will of the Führer to the masses in a persuasive manner.

The complexity of the occult roots of Nazism is often overlooked in favor of a one-sided view. Most commentators focus on the ideas of men such as Guido von List and Lanz von Liebenfels. These are important figures in the early twentieth century völkisch movement, to be sure. However, the entire stream of thought represented by men such as Fahrenkrog, Reuter, and Hauer is often virtually ignored. The key difference between these two streams of ideology lies in the decidedly spiritualistic and certainly theosophical basis of Ariosophy and Armanism and the more academic and philosophical roots of the *Deutschgläubige,* the "German Faith" advocates. In the final analysis, it must be recognized that the deeper pedigree for occult Nazi roots are to be found among the German Faith movement rather than the theosophical branch represented by List and his followers and the rune-esotericists. There appears to have been little friction among all of these equally völkisch factions, as the differences were more of culture, intellect, and temperament rather than aims. One might be tempted to say that the Listian heritage seemed to approach the mystical aspect in a more accessible and doctrinal manner (more along the lines of Catholicism or Theosophy), while the German Faith lineage also accessed mystical and occult dimensions but did so more along the lines of Protestant Pietism—on a more individualized basis.

The Listian/Lanzian stream was smaller and less influential, with little direct influence on what can actually be characterized as Nazi occultism, than was the larger, highly connected, and directly influential force of the German Faith movement on the shape and direction of National Socialism. Although they differed in the conclusions they reached, the German Faith movement and so-called Positive Christianity shared many of the same deep cultural and intellectual roots in German academia.

Events surrounding WWI took on portents of greatness and potential disaster for the Pan-Germanic and Ariosophical ideologies. At first the war was seen as a great march to victory for the heroic forces of Aryanism—but when the war turned out badly and events led to the downfall of the aristocratic regimes in Austria, Germany, and Russia, a sense of foreboding spread through the movement. This defeat of the Central Powers and the subsequent dissolution of the social fabric of Germany and Austria could not help but have a profound effect on the thinking of the participants in the Germanic Rebirth movement. Certainly, the most fundamental change was that they now increasingly began to identify the source of their plight in the world as something allied with a conspiracy of Jewish, Freemasonic, and Bolshevik forces. In the jargon of today, they became greatly "radicalized."

Some have misinterpreted the German movement as something born of the defeat in WWI. The book *Was tut not? Ein Führer durch die gesamte Literatur der Deutschbewegung* (What Is Needed? A Guide through the Whole Literature of the German Movement), published in 1914, shows that most of the elements present in the interwar era leading to the establishment of the Third Reich were already well developed before WWI, so the movement could hardly be characterized as a reaction to the defeat in that war. However, it is correct to say that anti-Semitism grew in importance within this movement as a result of the negative outcome of the war and its aftermath. The desperate times certainly also led to a willingness on the part of a great number of people to reach out to more radical solutions to political and economic problems.

The greatest single aspect that caused significant weakness in the whole Germanic Rebirth movement was its general lack of a strong basis in the study of what Germanic beliefs and culture actually *were* and a corresponding heavy reliance on the revaluation of ancient Germanic culture in terms of modern German philosophical traditions. One does not need to go beyond the example of the way in which right-leaning scholars such as Gustav Neckel or Bernard Kummer rejected the image of Óðinn that emerges from the authentic and autochthonous texts of the *Edda* in favor of a more conventional and conservative image to understand how this worked contrary to the interests of a genuine Germanic reawakening.*

*Many scholars of Germanic myth and religion around the time of the Nazi regime, men such as Eugen Mogk and Bernard Kummer, took a dim view of the god Wodan/ Óðinn due to his dark aspect and strange activities. It became fashionable to see him as a foreign (Asiatic) influence.

CHAPTER 5

PRELUDES IN SCIENCE AND PSEUDOSCIENCE

Science as Symbol and Weapon

The nineteenth century had been one in which many new approaches to matters of human life and culture had been introduced, hinted at, and suggested in theory—the new century, the twentieth century, would be one in which these ideas would be increasingly accepted and actualized. The action came lightning-fast and with great claps of thunder. The scientific foundations had been laid, and now the ideas not only found more practical applications, but they also began to have a direct effect on the cultural and political lives of people in Europe and America.

In this chapter I will delve into several topics: (1) the growth in the biological sciences under the guidance of Ernst Haeckel, who is thought by some to have been pivotal in the racial doctrines of National Socialism; (2) the unusual theories of physics and geology of the time; and (3) the development of German pseudoarchaeology. All of these sorts of ideas had significant effects on the popular imaginations of Germans at this time, and among these we will find some of the leaders of the NSDAP.

Here it will be important to realize that the age of science and technology, one that we now so much take for granted, was a new and often startling way of life for the great masses of people in the West. The whole of culture was in flux. Even in times of peace, such technological changes would have been difficult to absorb—but these were not decades of peace but rather of war. Life and culture were pressed

156

to their maximal levels of tolerance for change and most of the major states in Europe would crack under the pressure—Russia, Germany, and Austria. Problems came with the application of science and technology—as the Romantics had predicted—and people were ready to have science and technology fix those problems as well. The *Modern* had been established.

MONISM AND THE PHILOSOPHY OF SCIENCE

The scientific giant Ernst Haeckel has been mentioned several times in this book already. He is a man that belongs to the nineteenth century, but it was in the beginning of the twentieth century that he gained status as a figure of popular culture and became known for his forays into politics and religion, as well as evolutionary science. After decades of investigation and publication of ideas related to the theory of evolution as first suggested by Charles Darwin and Jean-Baptiste Lamarck, decades in which he became a leading German scientist in the field of evolutionary biology, in the last part of his life Haeckel became more

Fig. 5.1. Ernst Haeckel, circa 1904
(Wellcome Collection)

active in political and religious affairs. In 1909 he retired from teaching and the next year he actually resigned from the Evangelical Lutheran Church of Prussia.

Two of his works published during the latter part of his life, *Die Welträthsel* (The World Riddle; 1895–1899) and *Gott-Natur* (1914), clarify Haeckel's philosophy in virtually religious terms. He sees the complexities and mechanisms of nature as being encoded with a form of cosmic (= world-order) consciousness that is the true and real God—not an anthropomorphic entity with all the psychological foibles of every human being.

Through his works, which reached a wide public, Haeckel became a well-known person in the latter years of his life. He died on August 9, 1919.

Haeckel's philosophy was a product of, and beloved by, the greater German Romantic movement. As such, there was from the beginning an interest on his part in political and religious activism. Although Haeckel was a proponent of Darwin's theory of natural selection, he also accepted and synthesized elements from the theories of Lamarck, who had put forth the idea of acquired characteristics, which Darwin's theory of natural selection opposed. Therefore, although Haeckel was an important agent for the introduction of Darwinian ideas into German science, he was himself not a strict Darwinian. He championed elements of the theories of Lamarck, which held that organisms acquired inheritable characteristics, characteristics they developed in their interactions with their natural environments. To simplify, Darwin would say that the giraffe has a long neck because only the long-necked specimens survived to reproduce, whereas Lamarck would say that the creature stretched its neck and passed the longer necks on to its offspring.

Beyond the sphere of biological studies, however, Haeckel also ventured into politics and the social sciences, as well as what might be called religion. He coined the concept of "applied biology," which indicated his intentions and dreams of using his ideas and discoveries in a practical manner to cause revolutionary (evolutionary?) changes in the world. To facilitate this venture, he founded the Monist League (Deutscher Monistenbund) in 1906.

As a Monist, he was reluctant to posit a distinction between what is popularly or theologically called "matter" and "spirit." For example, he considered psychology a branch of physiology. The grand and complex mechanism of nature is the essence of what men call "God." Haeckel's beautiful illustrations of the marvelous variety of nature's forms had the purpose of demonstrating that evolution proceeded in an aesthetic and planned way under the guidance of some impersonal consciousness. As a rule, he supported the Lamarckian idea of acquired characteristics over Darwinian natural selection.

Haeckel, building on the earlier theories of Étienne Serres, asserted the theory that "ontogeny recapitulates phylogeny"—that is, the development of the embryo of a creature from fertilization to birth or hatching (ontogeny) reflects the evolutionary stages of the creatures' remote ancestors (phylogeny).

Haeckel was a proponent of bold theories that often seemed to be intuitive rather than scientific. In response to Darwin's *Origin of the Species* (1859), he postulated that the region of earliest human evolution was in the island of Indonesia. Archaeological investigations in the region by his students resulted in the discovery of the Java Man in the 1890s.

Haeckel's hypothesis would ripple through the occult world and would also influence certain obsessions in the SS connected to the supposed Asian origin of human beings. At one point, Haeckel held that the area presently called India was the original home of the human species. Into this theory he also introduced the idea of a lost continent of Lemuria, a landmass in parts of where the Indian Ocean is now. This acted as a land bridge between Africa, Asia, and areas of the East Indies. He even later claimed that perhaps Lemuria was the actual cradle of humanity. In his 1884 book *The History of Creation,* he speculated about the migration routes made from Lemuria by the first humans. Of course, many will be familiar with the role Lemuria plays in the theosophical theory of Root Races.*

---

*In Theosophy the Lemurians are identified as the Third Root Race, with their home, as prefigured by Haeckel, in what it now the Indian Ocean. They were followed in dominance by the Fourth Root Race, the Atlanteans.

Haeckel's pronounced racism was largely a product of the time period in which he lived. Whether in science or in mysticism (e.g., Theosophy), concepts of evolution supported by different theories were dominant in nineteenth-century thought. Both Darwinian and Marxist theory was devoted to the idea of some sort of teleological development, the idea of progress toward a better future—biologically, politically, and economically.

Darwin's presentation of his theory of evolution was marked by great restraint in the claims he made, largely because he was sensitive to the objections that might be raised against these theories by religious interests. He was right in this, but Haeckel had no such restraints on his mind. In his monumental two-volume work *Generelle Morphologie* (General Morphology; 1866), he put forward a bold synthesis of Darwin's theory and the German system of thought known as *Naturphilosophie* (natural philosophy). This went back to Goethe and was greatly refined by Friedrich Schelling and others. He then adds to the mix the progressive evolutionism of Lamarck to create his own theory, which he still called by the term *Darwinismus*. He is credited with inventing new concepts and terms, such as ontogeny and phylogeny, in the process of presenting his recapitulation theory.

As we have touched upon earlier, there are scholars who see in Haeckel's ideas the hidden genesis of what was to become National Socialist ideology, while others claim that there is no linkage at all between Haeckel's Monism and National Socialist ideology. As he died before the NSDAP was founded, it can be said that he had no personal link with it—but the same can be said of Guido von List, who died the same year. Haeckel's influence was greater and more global. He was an advocate of scientific racism and held that the races were unequal in quality and therefore unequal in value. Haeckel was also an advocate of what is called social Darwinism. This means that the races are in a struggle with one another and only the ones most fit to survive will thrive. As such he was also a promoter of the idea of eugenics and supported a program whereby tens of thousands of congenitally defective (whether mentally or physically) individuals were to be euthanized. Of course, this idea was eventually put into practice in the Aktion T4 program of the Nazis. However, it must be cautioned that Haeckel was certainly not alone in these ideas and that they were actually quite common at the end of the nineteenth and the beginning of the twentieth century on both sides of the Atlantic.*

One of the problems Nazis had with Haeckel is that the scientist was not an anti-Semite. Haeckel was a racialist who ranked different races in terms of their supposed evolutionary status, but Jews were near the top of such rankings, not at the bottom, where Nazis placed them. A second problem was that for most of his life Haeckel was a dedicated pacifist and did not believe, as did Clausewitz or the Nazis, that war is the "mother of all things." In the end, it is most likely that as a result of Haeckel's long and productive life, and after decades of his ideas being further popularized by others, that he was in fact more of an indirect, rather than direct, influence on National Socialist ideologies.

As we saw in chapter 2, Gasman makes a case for Haeckel's influence on the Nazis, but more comprehensive research done by Robert J. Richards (2009) calls this direct connection into serious question. Richards points out that the Nazis would eventually reject Haeckel due to the fact that the old scientist opposed anti-Semitism and also supported various ideas that the Nazis vehemently opposed, such as atheism, feminism, internationalism, and pacifism. On an anecdotal level, Richards also notes that Haeckel was known for making good friends on his travels in Asia with native individuals, even the "untouchables" in India, rather than the European colonists.

Because Haeckel was such an established figure in German science, and one who enjoyed universal prestige, it is telling that the attitude of the National Socialist ideologues toward this scientist was not all that positive. Some praised him, but others actually condemned him.

---

*For an interesting view of the history of the eugenics programs in the USA, see Isenberg (2016, 174–205). It is remarkable that over the centuries the American establishment has targeted all sorts of people as "undesirable" and in need of limitation on their population. These were not always people of color, but also Caucasians of Anglo-Saxon and Celtic heritage whose culture made them "deplorable" to the establishment. Many of these had originally been forcibly relocated to North America as indentured servants or debtors from Britain.

In 1935, his books were placed on a forbidden list. Haeckel's ideas were probably too complex and nuanced and could not be made to conform to the NS approach to eugenics and evolution, which was simpler and more pragmatic—an approach that others might dismiss as belonging more to the barnyard than the laboratory.

As with so much else in the course of this study, simple and direct answers to questions are often impossible, and the truth is frequently understood only by those who are willing and able to understand complexity and nuance regardless of the idea, object, or person under discussion. Simple answers make for sensational texts and are tailor-made for political propaganda and rhetoric. Hitler understood this principle and used it in his day, but now so do those who seek to mythologize and demonize the Nazis for fun and profit.

The 1909 Nobel Prize–winning chemist Friedrich Wilhelm Ostwald (1853–1932) was a Baltic-German scientist influenced by Haeckel and someone who had a wide scope of influence himself. He was born in Riga and studied in Estonia, where he received his Ph.D. in chemistry in 1875. He became a professor at Leipzig in 1887, where he spent the rest of his life. He was responsible for many breakthroughs in the field of chemistry over the years and was also known for his interest and activity in a variety of fields including peace movements, color studies, and artificial languages (Ido, Esperanto). Ostwald also adopted the Monist philosophy of Ernst Haeckel and became the president of the Monist League in 1911. In this context, he used his influence to promote the values of Social Darwinism, eugenics, and the use of euthanasia. His version of Monism is said to have influenced Jung's classification of psychological types. He was also initiated into the Scottish Rite of Freemasonry and became the Grand Master of the lodge in Bayreuth called Zur Aufgehenden Sonne (Toward the Rising Sun).

Monism and Racial Doctrine

Haeckel extrapolated from biological ideas that the political structure of the nation should be based, if possible, on an authoritarian foundation that would allow the strong, healthy, and intelligent members of society to have a greater share of power than the weak, sick, and dull-witted. In so doing, laws and politics would be an aid to evolutionary progress rather than a hindrance to it. With regard to the relationship among nations, Haeckel also asserted that certain cultures (races) were naturally superior to others. Much to the chagrin of the later Nazis, he ranked the Jews as highly as the Nordics in this respect.

Faced with the extreme diversity in appearance among the various types of humans on the globe, an earlier generation of scientists assumed that humanity had evolved in the form of distinct races in a variety of places around the globe. This attitude was born of a new scientific criticism of the biblical version of the origin of humanity from a single source. Darwin again argued for a single-source, or monogenesis, for humanity and placed the point of this genesis in what is now called Africa. This theory has come to dominate science today. It is a biological fact that all current humans belong to the same species in the sense that they *can* interbreed with one another. Darwin's theory was taken as being highly linear. More recent evidence using DNA research has proved that various subspecies of man, such as the Neanderthal, did interbreed with *Homo sapiens* (and now account for up to 2 percent of the DNA in non-African populations). Therefore, the process of human evolution is not as linear as once thought.

Haeckel, despite his general support for Darwin's theory of evolution, posited his own polygenetic theory. Curiously, he used as his theoretical underpinning the newly generated ideas in historical linguistics posited by August Schleicher (1821–1868). Schleicher was an early specialist in Indo-European studies and developed a *Stammbaum* (tree of descent) showing the descent of all Indo-European languages from a single common ancestor—an *Ursprache* (primordial language) today called Proto-Indo-European. The importance of this theory for Haeckel was not the model itself (Schleicher had taken it from fields of natural science to begin with) but rather the fact that it showed an independent origin for a family of languages discrete from all others. All of the languages of the world did not have a common ancestor, so why should man have a common biological set of ancestors? (Again, the biblical account of the origin of languages posits an original Ursprache for all humans before they split up, as accounted for in the myth of the

Tower of Babel [Gen 11:1–9]). The polygenetic theory would hold that the different language groups had originated among various divisions of prelinguistic protohumans. In such a model these different biological groups would have evolved under the influence of different branches of language.

The races of humanity were divided and actually ranked by Haeckel with the "Caucasian race" being the highest and most developed, and the Negros of Africa being the lowest and most primitive—that is, closest to the simian ancestry common to all humans. He further posited that the more primitive races were actually destined to eventual extinction. As we have seen in the case of many schools of thought, these ideas were extremely common and popular. Haeckel did not originate these ideas, he merely endowed them with a more scientific veneer. The same ideas are enshrined in the theosophical doctrine of Root Races.

PRE-1933 EUGENICS

The concept of eugenics is an ancient one, known in Greece and Rome in classical times and practiced in one way or another by many ancient peoples. Disabled newborns were customarily killed. But it could hardly have been called a science; it just belonged to the general customs and laws of the ancients.

Modern eugenics really begins with Francis Galton (1822–1911), who attempted to apply in a practical and active way the evolutionary theories of his half-cousin Charles Darwin. Galton coined the term *eugenics* in 1883.* In Galton's view, character and abilities were genetically determined with little influence by training or education. By the late nineteenth and early twentieth centuries, the idea had many powerful proponents in American and British academic circles.

In 1907 the British Eugenics Education Society was formed to help

---

*The term *eugenics* is a compound of the Greek prefix *eu-*, meaning "good," and the stem *genēs,* "come into being, generation." The word is a modern scientific coinage, but the concept is an extremely ancient one that we know from the customs and laws of ancient European cultures from the Greeks to the Germanic folk of antiquity. Plato championed the idea as well.

educate potential parents in matters of eugenics. A similar group was founded in America in 1921 called the American Eugenics Society. Eugenics conferences were held and societies formed around the globe. The concepts of positive eugenics (i.e., the encouragement of people with desirable traits to reproduce at a higher rate) and negative eugenics (i.e., the prevention or limitation of reproduction by those with less desirable traits) was developed. This latter kind came to include the practice of sterilization (voluntary or coerced), abortions, and euthanasia in extreme cases.

Eugenics as an ideology and in practice was not without opposition, mainly from the Catholic Church and Socialist or Labor politicians. However, support for the idea was generally widespread and its popularity significant in both America and the United Kingdom, where none other than Winston Churchill was a supporter and honorary vice president for the British Eugenics Society. Eugenics was seen as a bulwark against "race deterioration" and as a passive way to reduce both crime and poverty. In general, eugenics practices included things such as genetic screening, birth control, marriage restrictions (which included prohibitions on racial mixing), coerced sterilization, and abortions.

Germany was relatively slow to get involved in the eugenics craze. It was the object of scientific investigation by the Kaiser Wilhelm Institute of Anthropology, Human Heredity, and Eugenics, founded in 1927 in Berlin with the financial support of the American Rockefeller Foundation. This is just one more area where Hitler would eventually see that America and Britain had leaped ahead of Germany, and some of the racial policies of the NSDAP were designed to catch up. It would, however, be a mistake to see that the Nazis would be focused on the eradication of the Jews as primary, despite the lack of any evidence that the Jews exercised a dysgenic influence on the German population.

The main blow against eugenic practices in the Anglo-American world would come later, in the wake of WWII, with the case of Nazi Germany and the demonstration of just how far such things could be abused and misused.

HANNS HÖRBIGER AND
THE WELTEISLEHRE

Johannes "Hanns" Evangelist Hörbiger (1860–1931) was an Austrian engineer and inventor who also dabbled in cosmology. He was the illegitimate son of Amilia Hörbiger. His formal education took place at the Mechanical Engineering School in Vienna. He was employed as a draftsman in 1881, and after a short time of military service there was a period when he earned his living as a wandering zither-player. But from 1884 onward he worked in his profession as a mechanical engineer for various major companies in Austria.

Hörbiger married Leopoldine Janák in 1887 and they had four sons, two of whom became well-known actors (Attila and Paul).

In 1894 he envisioned a new design for a blast furnace and invented a new type of steel valve for operating the furnace. This invention was patented in 1896 and became a source of considerable wealth, especially through licensing to foreign manufacturers. The new technology made steel production and mining operations much more efficient. The Hörbiger valve was used in chemical plants and natural-gas pipelines.

Fig. 5.2. Hanns Hörbiger

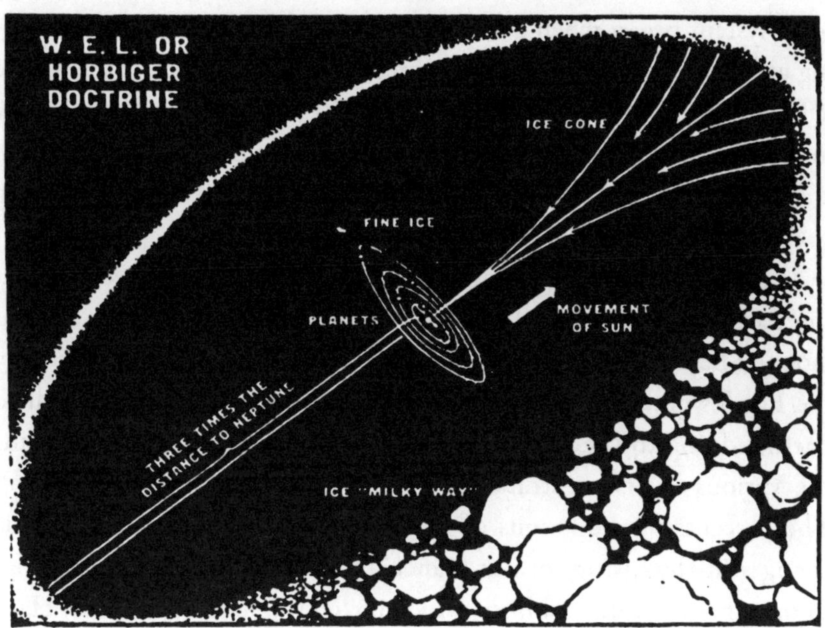

Fig. 5.3. Diagram of the universe according to the World Ice Theory
(from *Astounding Science Fiction*, May 1947)

In 1900 a corporation was founded for administrating the business side of Hörbiger's endeavors and the inventor was able to devote himself more and more to his cosmological passions. The company, Hoerbiger & Co., still exists as an important supplier of compression technology.

In 1925 a street in Vienna, Johann-Hörbiger-Gasse, was named after him. Hörbiger is buried in the Mauer Cemetery in Vienna.

The Welteislehre—"World Ice Theory" or "Glacial Cosmology"— first explicated in his 1913 work *Wirbelstürme, Wetterstürze, Hagalkatastrophen und Marskanal-Verdoppelungen* (Whirlwinds, Weather Disturbances, Hail Catastrophes, and Martian Canal Doublings), appears to have been mostly a sort of mystical cosmology wrapped in pseudoscientific jargon and presentation. This is not to say that many thinkers have not imagined things that eventually were proved to be scientifically accurate—for example, Alfred Wegener's theory of continental drift. It is just to say that the Welteislehre does not appear to fall into this category. Hörbiger's theory posits that the solar system began when a watery body fell into a gigantic star, causing an explosion that hurled the watery material out into space, where it froze into titanic bodies of ice. The Milky Way is a ring of this icy material. All planets slowly spiral inward, toward their points of origin, and meteors are actually ice blocks that regularly fall to earth causing "hail storms."

One of the most important aspects of the World Ice Theory is that the Earth had had several satellites before the arrival of our current moon. These bodies began as planetary objects that were captured by the Earth's gravitational pull and eventually disintegrated and fell to Earth, adding to the substance of our planet. This allegedly explains the various layers or strata of earth seen in the geological record. The descents of the moons of Earth are responsible for catastrophic changes in the history of our planet. In this regard Hörbiger belongs to the school of catastrophists, which includes Ignatius Donnelly, Hans Schindler Bellamy (an English follower of Hörbiger), and Emmanuel Velikovsky. Most of these theories were never given a second thought by academic scientists. In these thinkers we can discern a sort of quasi-religious pattern that might be called catastrophism. Such concepts have once more made themselves felt in the current belief in climate change. These ideas usually secularize, and put into scientific jargon, paradigms inherited from ancient mythologies, and most directly from biblical prophecy. Hörbiger seemed to command some level of respect in postulating his views, no doubt due to his successes in engineering, but nevertheless his ideas were rejected by mainstream science.

Hörbiger's theories are a precursor to peculiar Nazi approaches to science. They play a part in the actual history of alternative sciences in the time of the Nazi regime and will be seen to be an important piece of the mosaic of myths that permeate the postwar narrative of Nazi occultism.

VRIL

Despite the fact that the concept of Vril has its origins in a work of complete fiction by the English writer and politician Sir Edward Bulwer-

Lytton, who made this extraordinary power a feature of his 1871 novel *The Coming Race*,* and despite the fact that the word became a fetish around which Pauwels and Bergier would weave one of their major yarns of Nazi mythology in 1960, the concept of Vril and research into it did apparently draw some attention from German pseudoscientists in the years just prior to the advent of the Third Reich. In 1930 a book appeared titled *"Vril": Die kosmische Urkraft—Wiedergeburt von Atlantis* ("Vril": The Cosmic Primeval Energy—The Rebirth of Atlantis) by Johannes Täufer. It was published by an astrological publishing company owned by Otto Wilhelm Barth. This author's name, likely a pseudonym, is the equivalent of "John the Baptist" in German. Peter Bahn (1996) asserts that Täufer is a pseudonym for Barth himself, while others identify the author as Hans Janik. The work appears as an extension of a supposed group called the Reichsarbeitsgemeinschaft "Das kommende Deutschland" (Imperial Working Group: "The Coming Germany"). Supposedly, this group was founded in 1925 to study Vril energy. The existence of this small group does little to dispel the general assessment that the invention of the supposedly powerful Vril-Gesellschaft (Vril Society) is a pure hoax perpetrated by Pauwels and Bergier, who appear to have known nothing about Barth's work, which is the only positive evidence for the existence of any real interest in the Vril before their mythologizing efforts. Other members of this group were more concerned with the inventions and speculations of the Austrian Karl Schappeller (1875–1947), who claimed to be able to access "free energy from the atmosphere" (*Raumkraft*).

The 1930 booklet is a foray into the ideas of the production of free energy, which the author sees as something necessary for the German people to pioneer, research, and eventually produce to fulfill its destiny on the world stage. Such a position proved prophetic as the Germans can be said to have largely lost WWII due to a lack of energy and blunders made in the search for such energy. The book contains

---

*The novel originally titled *The Coming Race* (Edinburgh: Blackwood, 1871) was published anonymously by Edward Bulwer-Lytton and instantly struck a chord in the imagination of readers. It was later republished under the title *Vril: The Power of the Coming Race*.

various formulas, which attempt to explain how this energy works and how it is to be actualized. One of the main purposes of the production of this Vril energy was said to be the ability to create material things out of what is apparently "nothing." In other words, the Vril could actually replicate the power of God as described in the books of Hebrew mythology—a divine power by which beings could create things *ex nihilo*! Although the pamphlet in question is fitted out with pseudoscientific jargon and what appear to be formulas of mathematics and physics, it is also full of ideas relating to what we can recognize as theosophical concepts and other familiar myths, such as that of Atlantis. The word and concept "Vril" will have a lively existence in the "fantastic realism" of Pauwels and Bergier, which will be further discussed in chapter 11.

HOHLWELTLEHRE

The Hollow World or Hollow Earth theory is a pseudogeological notion that the planet Earth is not a solid core of molten elements but rather is actually in one way or another hollow, or contains spaces that allow access to an inner world beyond the surface. This theory is not new, having its origins in the sixteenth century and having been elaborated by earlier writers such as John Symmes (1780–1829) and Cyrus Teed (1838–1908), nor is it in any way particularly German, with theorists holding related views from around the world. (No one needs to be reminded of Jules Verne's 1863 novel *Voyage au centre de la Terre* [Journey to the Center of the Earth]). The theories cannot be described as following a single model. Some held that the Earth was hollow, some that it had various concentric layers of spheres beneath the surface, while still others speculated that we are actually on the inside of the Earth's sphere and the "heavenly bodies" are floating in the center of the internal void.*

In American popular culture we even get a zany foray into the theories of the hollow Earth in the science-fiction adventure film *The*

---

*One of the few sober general studies of this topic is David Standish, *Hollow Earth* (Boston: Da Capo, 2006).

Mole People (Universal, 1956), which, to give the film the air of "scientific plausibility"(!), is introduced by Professor Frank Baxter of the University of Southern California, who reviews theories of the hollow Earth, complete with diagrams.

Several German writers of the early twentieth century wrote about these ideas in one way or another. These included Johannes Lang, Robert Henseling, Peter Bender, and Karl Neupert. Of these, Johannes Lang is the most noteworthy here. His book *Hohlwelttheorie* was published in a second edition during the Nazi regime, after the crackdown on occult groups and theories. Clearly, his theories, which were fitted out with mathematical computations and complex theorems of optics, and so on, were not considered occult by the NS authorities. Fundamental to his theory is the idea that the fixed stars are actually gathered in a sphere at the center of the cosmos—a sphere that is also, incidentally, seen as the abode of the divinity, God or All-Father.

The Hollow Earth theory would become increasingly important in the postwar mythologizing of Nazi Germany, and far more so than it ever was during the time of the Third Reich itself (see chapter 11).

THE ROOTS OF NAZI PSEUDOARCHAEOLOGY

Imaginative interpretations of archaeological sites and data were a strong inheritance from the Romantic Age in Germany. Archaeology as we know it today as an academic science is of fairly recent development. Even men such as Heinrich Schliemann, who proved that the city of Troy was a factual reality and not, as most had come to assume, a mythic fantasy of some blind Greek poet, were hardly the scientific analysts of data we have today. Most archaeologists in the early twentieth century were still what they had been in the past: learned grave robbers and treasure hunters.

Romantic German archaeology is very much in evidence in works such as Guido von List's *Deutsch-mythologische Landschaftsbilder* (German Mythological Landscapes; 1891), in which he interprets things from megalithic structures to Catholic shrines in terms of ancient Germanic, or "Armanic," ideology. Here, as in other fields, List set a certain tone for the development of the esoteric enchantment of the Central European countryside. The mystical effects of such literature were the formation of increasing bonds between the spirits and minds of the people and the land upon which they lived. Also, with the ever-expanding Aryan mythologizing that was going on in the early twentieth century, some of these researchers began to project similar ideas onto more *global* landscapes.

When it comes to the science and academic discipline that has become archaeology, the völkisch interests of German Romantics both founded many of the most objective scientific procedures and practices and were also subject to wishful thinking and highly charged imaginations. (All the same could be said of the founders of Egyptian archaeology.) A figure central to this is Gustav Kossinna (1858–1931) of Berlin, who was an ardent nationalist but also one of the main geniuses behind the establishment of archaeology as a true science. He was the creator of the techniques of what is called settlement archaeology. Because of his political and cultural attitudes, he and his work were condemned immediately after the war, but in the meantime many have had to conclude that his methods were in fact sound and that he revolutionized the field of study—this admission of his correctness and genius has been referred to as Kossinna's Smile. So, while some postwar critics were moved to denounce his ideas as "pseudoscience," they did so largely based on the mob-mentality of criticizing as illegitimate *anything* that became connected with the National Socialist ideology. But in fact, Kossinna brought archaeology out of the category of glorified grave-robbing and treasure-hunting and into the realm of critical scientific thinking.

Other archaeologists with some connection to Nazis also continued to develop the scientific dimension of their work in ways independent of total ideological domination. Most notable among these is perhaps Herbert Jankuhn (1905–1990), who pioneered excavation and analytical techniques of great importance—for example, while working on the Haithabu site in Schleswig. (Jankuhn was also in the Waffen-SS in the panzer division Wiking on the Russian Front and fought in the tank battle of the infamous Cherkassy Pocket.) It will be found that just as German scholars did pioneering work in philology because so little of their linguistic and literary heritage remained (in contrast with the Greco-Roman world), so, too, was it necessary to develop refined modes of archaeology to extract maximal information from minimal evidence to be discovered beneath the surface of the soils of the Germanic world.

One of the monuments that obsessed Romantic, and later Nazi, archaeologists are the Externsteine (Stones of Extern). These will be discussed in more detail later in chapter 7 under SS projects. What should be said about them here is that they are a conspicuous natural rock formation in the Teutoburg Forest near Horn (North Rhine–Westphalia). In the Middle Ages the Externsteine were greatly modified by Christian clerics and made into a pilgrimage site. The alignment of surfaces and openings in the architectural features indicate certain astro-archaeological aspects—for example, the circular window over the altar in the (now ruined) chapel carved out of one of the stones, sites the rising sun on the summer solstice. Of course, the fact that the medieval Christians did do so much work on this remote site is perhaps the best indication of all that it was indeed a sacred site to the pre-Christian pagan Germanic (or perhaps Celtic) tribesmen, as it was the policy of the medieval church to make use of old sacred sites as a mode of propaganda.*

As we will see in part 4 of this book, the text of *The Morning of Magicians* contained many fantastic references to ideas connected to Nazi Germany, but the origins of these concepts are often left vague.

---

*It is a well-known and documented fact that early evangelists of Christianity in Europe used a strategy of replacing traditional, indigenous sacred places with Christian churches, just as the sacred times of the year important to the pre-Christian Europeans were systematically substituted by festivals with a Christian interpretation. The most conspicuous example of the latter is Christmas, which was not celebrated or observed by early Christians but had to be instituted to appease Germanic converts. It was originally called the Gothic festival. The archaeological record almost always reveals a pagan substratum below every Christian church established at around the time of the Christianization of the area in question. There is a famous letter from Pope Gregory to Abbot Mellitus (ca. 597) describing how to disestablish pagan sanctuaries in England and Christianize them.

One of the ideas made current in that book is that the legend of Atlantis is based on a cataclysmic event in which an advanced Aryan culture, whose home (known as Thule) was in the Atlantic, and that when the land was submerged the inhabitants spread out to higher mountainous regions remaining above water—what are now the Himalayas and the Andes. Such ideas were associated with those of Hörbiger in that it was an event connected with cosmic ice (e.g., a descent of a moon to the surface of the Earth) that caused the catastrophe. This theory was attractive to enthusiasts for Aryan nationalism because it could account for sources of high civilization outside the Middle East. If traces of the Aryan survivals in the Himalayas and Andes could actually be found, this would help prove many pet theories of völkisch pseudoscientists, such as an alternative origin of high civilization and the Welteislehre of Hörbiger.

These concepts were closely tied in the popular imagination to the innovated mythology and cosmology of the Theosophical Society, especially as expressed in Blavatsky's magnum opus, *The Secret Doctrine*. There much is made of supposed secret, subterranean cities, such as Agartha and Shambhala in the Himalayas or in the heart of Central Asia. This, coupled with Blavatsky's pro-Aryan stance, led imaginative völkisch thinkers in German-speaking lands to suspect that some sort of primeval Aryan homeland might lie in the mountains of Tibet.

The amateur and eccentric archaeologist Edmund Kiss wrote several books (some of them novels) about the Aryan migrations from Thule/Atlantis to the high plateaus of South America, where they built structures such as those now in ruins at Tiwanaku (Spanish: Tiahuanaco) near Lake Titicaca. These ruins were the subject of the work of an Austrian investigator named Arthur Posnansky (1873–1946). Posnansky was educated in Austria at the Imperial and Royal Academy of Pola as a naval military engineer. During his training, he participated in voyages to South America. He immigrated there in 1896, first to Brazil, then to Bolivia. In Bolivia, he became a successful entrepreneur and was involved in politics in the city of La Paz. Posnansky introduced the first automobile to Bolivia. However, he earned his

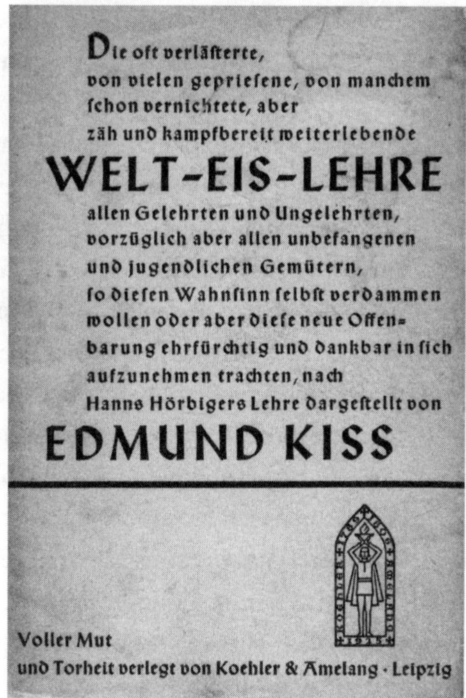

Fig. 5.4. The cover of *Welt-Eis-Lehre* (World-Ice Theory)
by Edmund Kiss, 1933.

greatest respect and notoriety as a researcher and writer in the fields
of American archaeology and ethnography. He published several books
including *Die Osterinsel und ihre praehistorischen Monumente* (Easter
Island and Its Prehistoric Monuments; 1895), *Razas y Monumentos
Prehistóricos del Altiplano Andino* (Prehistoric Peoples and Monuments
of the Andean High-Plateau; 1908), and his last book, *Tihuanacu, the
Cradle of American Man* (1945). He also lectured widely in Germany
and Austria. In the 1920s he made the acquaintance of Edmund Kiss
in Bolivia. Kiss would further popularize Posnansky's theories and con-
nect them to völkisch ideology. According to Posnansky, Tiwanaku
was built circa 15000 BCE by American peoples, although he did not
think that the ancestors of those then living in the area, the Aymara,
were the builders. Posnansky theorized that Tiwanaku was the point
of origin for high civilization throughout the Americas. Subsequent

investigations have shown that the Tiwanaku site probably dates from between 200 BCE and 200 CE, with the culture reaching the peak of its power about 800 CE.

Despite the fact that many of Posnansky's theories have been discredited by later research and despite the questionable usages of Posnansky's research by a series of eccentric popular writers throughout the twentieth century—Kiss, Pauwels and Bergier, Erich von Däniken, Graham Hancock, and others—his original research, conservation efforts at the sites, and recording of data in a scientific manner have all remained valuable. The popular writers using Posnansky's original research have become part of an occult or esoteric dimension to the academic science of archaeology, which we can refer to as pseudo-archaeology. The Nazis and their völkisch predecessors, such as Guido von List in his *Deutsch-mythologische Landschaftsbilder,* were enthusiastic purveyors of this particular occult art, but they are hardly alone in these obsessions. In the same category we can also place theories of Black Egypt, beliefs about British Israelitism, and repeated discoveries of Noah's Ark. Beginning in the late twentieth century, pseudo-archaeology became a thriving international cottage industry in publishing and video production. (Aliens have most often replaced Aryans in these narratives.)

Some readers might question the occult dimension of subjects such as biology, physics, or even of archaeology. Others will understand it immediately. In the effort to transform the being of the individual or the collective body of a group or even a nation, mythologizing or re-mythologizing the subject in question can be essential. Working models of who the subject is in his very flesh and blood (his biology), and of where the subject resides and functions in space (his physical context), and finally of what he or his ancestors might have been capable of in the far distant past—these are all extremely useful tools in the esoteric work of development and transformation. These tools are constantly being used all around us even today. It is really all part of the human condition and the human adventure on this planet. If people believe that they are evolving to something greater, if they believe they exist in a world in which miracles are possible, and if they feel reassured that they have been great in the past and therefore the prospect of future greatness is all the more possible—then people are generally happier, or at least consoled in their present unhappy state. Here again German-speaking esotericists, artists, and thinkers seemed to have been ahead of the curve with respect to this understanding in the early part of the twentieth century.

CHAPTER 6

OCCULT CULTURE IN GREATER GERMANY
The Fantastic Occulture of the Age

The interest of the individuals responsible for National Socialism in matters occult, to whatever degree it existed, was in many ways reflective of the zeitgeist of the early twentieth century. Radical and revolutionary solutions to problems—personal, social, political, or cultural—were in the air. The occult subculture expressed a broad spectrum of interests from astrology to spiritualism and from ritual magic to volkisch ideologies. Here we will leave the most unique aspect of occultism in the German-speaking world, the Armanen and Ariosophists, out of the discussion, because they have been treated in chapter 4. It should be noted that the word *Ariosophy* has more recently been used as an umbrella term for all individual writers and organized groups who had as their main operating and theoretical principle the idea that the secrets and mysteries of life were to be found in connection with the biological descent and present composition of a person or a people. Many recent writers have focused on this aspect of German occultism exclusively, whereas the picture was actually more complex than a concentration on Ariosophy alone would imply. In this chapter we are concerned with the broader spectrum of German occult activity because this, too, was a conditioning factor for the culture at large. A survey of these groups shows that there was much overlap between and among them as far as membership, goals, and organizational principles were concerned. It also demonstrates just how obscure the activities and histories of most of these organizations were.*

---

*For a catalog of these varied groups and organizations, and the basic data known about them, see Glowka, *Deutsche Okkultgruppen 1875–1937.*

178

With advent of the twentieth century, the German-speaking world virtually exploded with occult groups, many of the most extreme sort. Often those involved with them appear to have also been entangled with spy work or intelligence. This may also partially explain why authoritarian regimes typically have looked askance at such occult groups and orders. The Bavarian Illuminati had, after all, been directly involved in such things in the late eighteenth century under Adam Weishaupt.

During the years of the Weimar Republic (1918–1933) in Germany, and especially in the city of Berlin, there was a great proliferation of alternative forms of politics, religion, and philosophy, as well as experimentation with various kinds of sexuality, indulgence in drugs, and all sorts of entertainment possibilities. Weimar was a world of extreme prospects. The alternative side of Weimar culture is well illustrated by Mel Gordon's *Voluptuous Panic* (2006). This period of German history is rife with eccentric gurus and visionaries, each with a new view of humanity and how to save or perfect it. In many ways, Hitler and his Brown Shirts were for a time seen as just one more of these eccentric factors.

Astrology had become a very popular topic, but it often served more as a form of entertainment than a serious school of esotericism. Professional astrologers abounded in the years leading up the Third Reich, but they would not find a generally favorable place in the world of National Socialism.

In the early part of the twentieth century there was a dozen major groups and societies dedicated to psychic phenomena—that is, to parapsychology or "scientific psychology," in the German-speaking world. These were essentially offshoots of the spiritualistic movement. What had for the most part begun in the last decade of the previous century expanded rapidly after 1900. Interesting among these is the Loge Psyche (Psyche Lodge) founded by a theater director named Karl Weiss in Berlin, which began organizing public meetings and activities in 1904. The group did not admit women, yet it made an effort to indicate that it was based on brotherly love, and that all people, regardless of their ethnicity, religion, or class, were welcome. The motto of the lodge was "Faith–Love–Hope."

NUDIST CULTURE AND REFORM IDEOLOGIES

One significant part of the Life-Reform movement (1880–1933), and an aspect of it closely tied to what we would today call alternative spiritualities, was the culture of nudism (*Nacktkultur*) also termed *Freikörperkultur* (Free-Body Culture; FKK). There were many different attitudes toward this activity and aesthetic among its practitioners, and it ran the political gamut from the right to left. However, in every case it was an exercise meant to alter the prevailing norms of society and its attitudes toward the human body, shame, and sexuality. Nudity could be seen as a way to emphasize the equality of humans; it could recall the primitive tribal traditions of the Germans or act as a revolutionary act against prevailing church-dominated morality. (Recall that in the Book of Genesis, humans were characterized as being ashamed because they were *naked*.) If humans could learn not to be ashamed, it could be a harbinger of profound change in the whole species.

Organized nudism had its inception just after the beginning of the twentieth century. Berlin, and especially a lake in the southern part of the city called the Motzener See, became a focal point for the public practice of nudism, especially among young and athletic people. In certain German circles, the cult of *nudity* was closely tied to that of *beauty,* and hence to that of eugenics. So, the practice of nudism could be brought to bear on a variety of causes or directions, but its dramatic social and cultural effects are unmistakable.

Certain writers, theoreticians, and practitioners such as Heinrich Pudor (1865–1943), Hans Surén (1885–1972), and Richard Ungewitter (1869–1958) belonged to völkisch currents within the movement, whereas Ernst Schertel, the author of the book *Magie,* was a promoter of the idea of a more erotic and sexualized view of nudism.

By the end of the Weimar Republic, there were an estimated one hundred thousand members of organized groups or clubs connected to nudism, and, of course, many more who were only casual participants. Often the participants seem to have had a background in the mixed gender youth culture such as represented by the Wandervogel. What they had first experienced in a spontaneous way on their youthful travels, people now did so in a more organized and ideologically supported manner.

In general, nudism can be seen as a part of the larger Reform movement, which included vegetarianism, alternative medicine, and so on. It was also closely tied with certain alternative spiritualities, such as the New-Spirit movement, Mazdaznanism, as well as various völkisch interests. But because it was ideological and because it was not under the total control of the NSDAP, when the Nazis came to power the practice was initially forbidden (by a decree of March 3, 1933), but then it was quickly transformed into an official National Socialist form as the Kampfring für völkische Freikörperkultur (Militant Ring for Racial Free-Body Culture). Under the leadership of Hans Surén, nudism also found a place among members of the SS itself.

THE OTO AND THE FRATERNITAS SATURNI

Of great interest to readers today is the whole organizational complex that became involved in sexual mysticism and magic. Due to the fact that the Englishman Aleister Crowley (1875–1947) became absorbed by it, the German order called the Ordo Templi Orientis (Order of Oriental Templars; OTO) has in more recent years become extremely widespread in the world and very well known. Its popularity today can be traced to certain developments in the 1970s rather than anything that happened in the earlier part of the century. The OTO was founded by the Austrian industrialist Karl Kellner and the entertainer and police spy Theodor Reuss. It likely gestated over the years between 1895 and 1906. The first objective evidence for the existence of the organization, even theoretically, appears with the publication of the first number of the journal *Oriflamme* in 1902. Reuss had also earlier been involved with the attempt to revive the Bavarian Illuminati under the name Der Illuminaten-Orden. The main distinguishing feature of the OTO is its teaching of the idea of sexual magic as a key to the understanding of Freemasonic symbolism. This idea had been pioneered earlier in America by the remarkable and bold Paschal Beverly Randolph (1825–1875) and his follower Reuben Swinburne Clymer. Most likely

Reuss learned of Randolph's methods from documents in the possession of Jonathan Yarker. Crowley became involved with the OTO in 1912 and had a strong influence on the direction of the order after that. Chiefly this can be seen in his emphasis on the teaching of his Aeonic Word, *Thelema*—"True Will." This teaching became known as the Law of Thelema ("Do what thou wilt shall be the whole of the Law").* Clearly, the influences of men such as Nietzsche and Freud can be seen in some of these developments. Crowley's voluminous and widely published written works formed the basis for the latter-day popularity of the OTO.

The teachings of sexual magic within the OTO are difficult to trace because they appear to have evolved from disparate influences that included Indian tantrism, Randolph's system, and Judaic teachings, as well as being heavily admixed with the personal sexual fantasies of the various participants in the process. Clearly, however, the OTO form of sexual magic is focused on sexual pleasure, the orgasm, and the products of orgasm—not procreation. The VIII° OTO teachings involving a sex-magical technique in conjunction with masturbation, the IX° with vaginal intercourse, and the XI° with anal intercourse. Images of the Holy Grail are invoked in which the combined sexual fluids of the male and female are ingested from the vagina (Grail) and the substance is referred to as the Elixir.

Closely associated with this stream of thought was that which came to be identified with the concept of Pansophy. Here we again have a word based on a variation of the successful coinage of *Theosophy*. In this case, Pansophy can be understood as "Wisdom of the All." It is a perfect umbrella term for the kind of highly eclectic systems that many of these

---

*The Greek word θέλημα (*thélēma*), "will, volition, desire," appears sixty-three times in the New Testament. The phrase "do what thou wilt" is derived from a passage in *Gargantua and Pantagruel* by François Rabelais (1494–1553), in which the French phrase *Fais çe que vouldras* ("Do what you want") appears as an inscription over the door of the Abbey of Thelema. Crowley substantially reinterpreted the meaning and made it the basis of a magical and initiatory teaching. Crowley's philosophy also owes a debt to the German philosopher Friedrich Nietzsche (1844–1900), whose works, style, and philosophy made an often unacknowledged impression on the English mage. Nietzsche's philosophy, like that of Crowley, hinged on the concept of *Will*.

occult groups practiced, ranging from the Golden Dawn in England to the Fraternitas Saturni in Germany. In the early 1920s, Heinrich Tränker and his colleagues Eugen Grosche (= Gregor A. Gregorius) and Albin Grau organized groups called the Collegium Pansophicum or the Pansophische Gesellschaft (Pansophical Society). The personal practicalities of having such an eclectic approach appears connected to the fact that these men were often dealers in occult books of all sorts, which were much needed and demanded by students of these then obscure subjects. The Fraternitas Saturni absorbed many of the OTO teachings of sexual magic, but is not entirely dominated by these concepts and practices.

The Fraternitas Saturni (Brotherhood of Saturn; FS) was founded in 1928 from within the Collegium Pansophicum in the aftermath of the failed so-called Weida Conference of 1925, at which Aleister Crowley had attempted to absorb the Pansophical group that included many of the most advanced German adepts of magic. The FS accepted the Law of Thelema and Crowley's *Book of the Law* as a teaching and theory but rejected Crowley as a leader of the order. The Pansophical Lodge was closed in 1926. The FS developed its own system of initiation (with 33 degrees) and curriculum of study mainly as designed by Gregor A. Gregorius. The areas of emphasis in the FS were different from those of the Golden Dawn or the OTO. Kabbalah and Tarot were deemphasized and Gnosticism, astral lore, and Luciferianism were given

Fig. 6.1. Fraternitas Saturni seal

more importance. The FS was prohibited by the NSDAP in 1936, and the order would not be renewed until 1950.*

Significantly, when the concept of sexual mysticism or sexual magic is mentioned in the Ariosophical context it is most usually connected to the natural function of sexuality—that is, procreation or reproduction—and as such the operative magic involved amounts to a form of eugenics. Such a type of sexual religion was outlined by both Maximilian Ferdinand Sebaldt von Werth and Lanz von Liebenfels.

There is something that might be characterized as a sexual obsession in the German-speaking world during the early twentieth century. This obsession creates a framework for many of the phenomena we discuss throughout this book, ranging from the magical to the political and embracing the world of human fantasy and repressed desires of all kinds. Sexology, as an academic field, first developed in Central Europe in first decade of the twentieth century. It was spurred in part by the writings of Freud and the work of the Life-Reformer Karl Vanselow, the physician Iwan Bloch, and others. Albert Eulenburg, Magnus Hirschfeld, and Iwan Bloch founded the *Ärztliche Gesellschaft für Sexualwissenschaft und Eugenik* (Medical Society for Sexology and Eugenics) with its journal the *Zeitschrift für Sexualwissenschaft* (Journal of Sexology). Such studies went beyond pathologizing deviant behavior, as Krafft-Ebbing had done in the previous century, and really began to explore the possibilities of human sexuality in all its varieties. Such studies would be officially condemned by the Nazis after they came to power, but there can be little doubt that the leading theoreticians of National Socialism made use of this kind of psychological research on a certain level. For example, Hitler remained unmarried and—as far as the public knew—an unattached bachelor in order to stoke the fantasies of the female NS electorate.

According to Mel Gordon (2006, 203), statistically there were approximately two hundred various cults and alternative sects operat-

---

*The philosophy and magical system of the Fraternitas Saturni, some of its rituals, and its relations with Crowley and the OTO are outlined in my book *The Fraternitas Saturni* (2018).

ing in Central Europe during the interwar period. Some two million (other sources say as many as four million) individuals were members of these groups, with more than eight million people being subscribers to the publications put out by these groups. These statistics would suggest that the influence of such alterative ideas may have extended to somewhere around ten million on one level or another. Even with these sizable numbers, it has to be noted that the movement remained a minority. The total number of German-speakers in Central Europe in 1920 was approximately seventy million. So, those interested in alternative lifestyles constituted a minority, what we would call as special interest group today, that had to be appealed to and whose ideas had to be accounted for in partisan politics, but there were larger concerns and groups that remained more important, such as the confessing (orthodox) Christian sects, pure economic interests, and those concerned primarily with issues of home and hearth.

One of the best general presentations of the situation under examination here is that by Treitel (2004, 210–42). It is clear that the core of National Socialist ideology was not rooted in what we would call occult ideas and that many of the usual suspects (e.g., Guido von List or Lanz von Liebenfels) cannot be clearly identified as direct influences. Rather, the key is to be found in the fact that the general culture of the German-speaking world during the late nineteenth and early twentieth centuries was permeated with ideas from the Reformkultur and various occult or magical concepts. While men such as Hitler or Himmler were free to incorporate these concepts into their projects, under the radar as it were, in general overt occult concepts were rejected for dissemination by the Nazi censors. Treitel (2004, 228–29) discusses the publication of a 1935 book called *Arisches Weistum* (Aryan Wisdom) by Ernst Issberner-Haldane, which tries to co-opt all occult sciences into a Germanic and Aryan orbit and suitably expresses an orthodox anti-Semitism. But the NS authorities condemned the book as being "Anthroposophical" (a favorite bogeyman for the Nazis) and "spreading false information about the racial history of Germany." The way in which the Nazis dealt with occult topics is reminiscent of how the subject of magic was treated by the

Vatican in centuries past—books of magic were destroyed among the public, where found, but the Vatican Library has the greatest collection of such books known to man.

THE WORLD-LODGE TANATRA

As an example of the kind of groups that proliferated in Germany in the Weimar era, the Weltloge Tanatra was a religious community that promoted ideas of sexual freedom. Curiously, most of its members were also members of Lutheran congregations. It appears that Protestants were often involved to a greater extent than Catholics in various experimental spiritualities at the time. Tanatra believed in reincarnation and practiced a form of spiritualism using mediums. Special mediumistic talents were ascribed to male homosexuals because it was thought that they combined a male-female polarity.

Tanatra had its own periodical called *Der Freitag* (Friday), which was only published between 1930 and 1934. The symbol of the group was the Eye of God.

As an organization, the Gottesbund Tanatra (League of God: Tanatra) was founded by a businessman named Fedor Mühle circa 1922 in the city of Görlitz. The organization was quite successful and attracted several thousand followers and participants.

At the peak of its membership, there were several thousand adherents of Tanatra, with a higher concentration of members in northern Germany. The group voluntarily disbanded itself and then was officially banned in 1936 by the National Socialist regime. Many members of the group emigrated to South America after this time. The organization was especially targeted due to its positive assessment of male homosexuality. The founder, Fedor Mühle, was killed in the Buchenwald Concentration Camp in 1941.

Tanatra claimed itself to be an inheritor of the traditions of Egyptian Aten temples, Zoroastrian teachings, Gnostics, and Manicheans. Although the sect understood itself as a Christian religion, texts from all sorts of other traditions were acknowledged as being sacred.

THE ADONISTS

The Adonists are a school of magical and religious thought largely invented by the Viennese scholar Franz Sättler (1884–ca.1942), who usually wrote under the pseudonym Dr. Musallam. He created a whole magical system based on an idiosyncratic neopagan pantheon led by Adonis. Musallam equated Adonis with Satan, or the devil, and took a markedly anti-Christian stance. This Adonis was to be worshipped through sexual enjoyment, both heterosexual and homosexual. Dr. Musallam clearly stated that "Adonism is the worship of the devil" by means of erotic activity. He founded the Adonistische Gesellschaft in Vienna, active between 1925 and 1931, and published numerous written works. This organization had definite aims and methods but had no vows or restrictions. This was because the whole purpose of the movement was the liberation of humanity from every sort of inhibition and limitation. Adonism was a libertine philosophy coupled with magical ideology. According to Musallam-Sättler's esoteric vision, he retrieved these teachings from the *Bit el Nûr* (House of Light), a sort of monastery situated in the semi-mythical land of Nûristân. There a high priest maintained a college of priests and there was a temple containing a great museum and library. Musallam claimed to have spent years in this facility and only returned to Europe to spread Adonistic knowledge in order to bring about a new Golden Age. This age of world salvation was to be symbolized by the serpent and characterized by the qualities of freedom and truth.

The Adonists worked magically for their aims but also were involved directly in social questions and reforms. Below is a partial list of the reforms promoted by Franz Sättler and the Adonists:

1. Abolishment of marriage as a social norm.
2. Absolute equal civil rights for woman.
3. Unlimited right of individual women to become mothers.
4. Acceptance of love-friendships.
5. Mothers' rights to raise their children.
6. State support of mothers; reduced responsibility to fathers.
7. State support of pregnant women.

8. Institution of a prohibition against reproduction in cases of infectious or hereditary diseases.
9. Compulsory sex-education for youths 14–15 years of age.
10. Legalization of abortion in the first trimester.
11. Outlawing of all public or secret prostitution.
12. Abolishment of laws against homosexuality. (Gregorius 1958, 9–11)

In the minds of the Adonists, these and other reforms would lead to a healthier society. The idea of virginity as a virtue was rejected and steps taken to ensure that the initial sexual experiences of young people were to be filled with a sacred attitude. The very notion of sexual activity being some sort of a sin was to be eliminated.

Adonists supported the practice of polygamy with the additions of so-called Haustöchter (house daughters) to primary partnerships, to be regulated by the state to ensure that the man was healthy and capable of producing offspring. These reforms had no racial component: "The ideal aim is a healthy human species that includes all peoples and races of the earth" (Gregorius 1958, 11). Here we see a universalistic application of some of the ideas that abounded among völkisch Reformers as well.

MAZDAZNAN

Mazdaznan is an eclectic neo-Zoroastrian system. It only has a few essential philosophical points of contact with historical forms of orthodox Zoroastrianism, however. It was shaped by a German immigrant to America named Otto Hanisch (1844/1856–1936), who used the pseudonym Otoman Zar-Adusht Ha'nish. His system was a mixture of dietary theories, breathing exercises, meditation, physical exercises, and postures, as well as a whole alternative view of history and religion, East and West. The name of the organization is explained as a combination of Persian terms: *ma,* "good," *zda,* "thought," and *znan* (from *jasnan*), meaning "masterful." Following this explanation, the whole is supposed to mean "master of the divine thought."

Few certain facts are known about Hanisch, as he wove many myths around his biography. His activities began in Chicago about 1890 but quickly spread to Europe. Upton Sinclair wrote about him critically and derisively in his 1918 work *Profits of Religion,* in Book Six: "The Church of the Quacks." Hanisch first organized a church called the Mazdaznan Temple Association of Associates of God in 1900 in Chicago. The organization was handled in Germany by a married couple named Frieda and David Ammann. They founded the lodges of the Mazdaznan-Tempel-Vereinigung für Deutschland und die deutschsprechenden Länder (Mazdaznan Temple Union for Germany and the German-speaking Countries) in several German cities. Later these were known as the Zarathustra-Bund. In 1914 the Ammanns were exiled from Germany for publishing indecent material in the book *Inner Studies.* David Ammann died under suspicious circumstances in 1923, and his followers believe this was the result of a conspiracy against him. Hanisch himself is known to have visited Germany regularly up to 1932.

Mazdaznan had a lasting influence on German culture and was revived after the war. In the early part of the century an important proponent of the philosophy was the Bauhaus designer and teacher Johannes Itten. The Swiss Karl Heiser, also an anthroposophist, was an active leader in the organization after 1900. Heiser was moreover connected with Guido von List and ran a commune near Zürich called Aryana. The ONT brother Detlef Schmude was also an associate of the group. In the German-speaking realm Mazdaznan expressed itself in a friendly manner toward National Socialism and its racial policies. Despite this, however, the organization was outlawed in 1935 when their literature was also withdrawn, and their meetings were eventually entirely forbidden in 1941. It remained banned in East Germany but was revived in the West in 1959. Its postwar membership has never exceeded more than a few thousand followers.

Although there was a strong racial teaching in the German branch after 1919, in general this racial component was not dominant in the American branch. Curiously, Mazdaznan taught that the Semites (Jews) were also Aryans. Of course, this could not have endeared them to the

Nazis! Most of the teachings of the group were well within the scope of the typical Lebensreform ideology, with an emphasis on body-culture, diet and breath control, and exercises.

THEOSOPHY AND ANTHROPOSOPHY

Theosophy continued to grow in Germany in the early part of the twentieth century and was an active participant in the whole Reform movement. At the dawn of the new century, an Austrian named Rudolf Steiner (1861–1925) became a very important leader of the Theosophical Society in the German-speaking world. Steiner was an avid student of the work of H. P. Blavatsky, but he also brought many of his own innovative and practical ideas to the table.

Steiner's disagreement with Theosophy stemmed from its emphasis on *Eastern* ideas, its official acceptance of Krishnamurti as a messiah, and its general antipathy toward Christianity. Steiner broke away from Theosophy in 1912 and formed the Anthroposophical Society. It must also be remarked that Steiner did leave a positive mark on the world—this includes his devotion to the idea of individual freedom and his concept of education, which resulted in the system of Waldorf Schools that are still thriving in the world today. Even more than Theosophy, Anthroposophy was a part of the great German Lebensreformbewegung.

Especially in the time period immediately after WWI, Steiner proposed the idea of a tripartition of society called Social Threefolding or Threefold Division of Society. The three parts were the cultural, the political, and the economic. Each of these spheres was to act independently from, but in natural cooperation with, the others and have the freedom to develop within its own set of values. Steiner drew support from Hermann Hesse on this idea. Steiner based his structure on the threefold motto of the French Revolution: Liberté, Equalité, Fraternité—freedom in cultural life, equality with respect to political and legal rights, and cooperation in economic life. Steiner's main work on this topic is a 1919 book translated into English as *Towards Social Renewal.*

Although Steiner wrote and believed some things that seemed in keeping with the völkisch ambience of the times, such as works on the "folk soul" (Ger. *Volksseele*) and the importance of the blood in spiritual development, he also felt that humanity was to evolve away from these biological constraints, not more deeply into them. Steiner was also very much opposed to the development of national states in Europe after the First World War, for example. He favored zones in which different sorts of political organizations might be instituted. These and other ideas brought Steiner and the Anthroposophical Society into direct conflict with the National Socialist movement. Steiner's de-emphasis of the nation and accentuation of the freedom of the individual were concepts diametrically opposed to NS ideology.

Many might have thought that Steiner had based the name of his movement, Anthropo-sophy, from Theo-sophy; however, the word was already attested as early as the sixteenth century and was frequently used in the nineteenth century as a corollary to theosophy, which was also an old term. In any event, the names of these groups certainly must have led Lanz von Liebenfels to formulate the term *Ario-sophy* in 1915.

The clairvoyant methods used by Steiner and the theosophists to divine the secret histories of the past were very much akin to those utilized by men such as Guido von List in the service of völkisch mythology. A certain metanarrative could be discovered, which made some sort of intuitive sense of historical events, and this metanarrative then became the subject of an almost dogmatic faith about the past and the true heritage of a people. Such a method appears irrational—and it is—but we should recognize that it is hardly unique. Similar sorts of metanarratives have been and continue to be employed by mainstream religions and political philosophies of all kinds throughout history, right up to the present day.

ERNST SCHERTEL

The work of Ernst Schertel (1884–1958) came to the attention of the English-speaking world most recently due to the publication of a book by Timothy Ryback called *Hitler's Private Library* (2008). This book makes the reading habits of the Führer clear. He read as many as one book a day, spending most evenings in solitude turning pages. There it is also revealed that Hitler owned a copy of Schertel's seminal work on occultism titled *Magie: Geschichte, Theorie, Praxis* (Magic: History, Theory, Practice).* The author, or his publisher, had actually sent this copy of the book to the then fledgling political leader, Adolf Hitler, in 1923 with a personal inscription: "[To] Adolf Hitler respectfully dedicated by the author."

I will devote more space to Hitler's engagement with the writings of Schertel in chapter 11. However, it would be a gross error to see Schertel in any way as a part of National Socialism. He certainly deserves study in his own right, independent of the serendipitous connection with Hitler as a student of Schertel's writings.

Throughout the Weimar period Schertel enjoyed a heightened popularity and attention and was a well-known proponent of sexual liberation, experimental trance-dancing, occultism, and sadomasochistic themes in literature, art, and practice. He came to be known as the Philosopher King of Weimar Germany. And by 1933 it was clear that Schertel and Hitler stood many miles apart in their approaches to life. Here we will present a brief overview of Schertel's life and ideas.

In his youth, Schertel was bothered with severe inhibitions. While his imagination was free and sensual, he could not actualize these ideas due to a fear of eternal damnation. In 1911, he received a Ph.D. in philosophy from the University of Jena. Immediately thereafter he wrote a semi-autobiographical gnostic novel titled *Die Sünde des Ewigen: Dies ist mein Leib* (The Sin of Eternity: This Is My Body). The process of writing this work appears to have worked like magic to liberate him from his inhibitions. He says of himself after completing the work:

---

*The initial English publication of this book (Cotum, 2009) appears to have been produced by means of a (digital) machine translation, the results of which are often inaccurate and misleading. The significant feature of this edition is, however, that the lines of the book highlighted by Hitler (with marks in the margins) are set in boldface type. This renders this translation to an extent a piece of Hitler memorabilia rather than the radical and innovative take on magic that Schertel's book represents in its own right. An entirely new translation, and one more sympathetic to the meaning intended by Schertel, appears in my book *Dancing with the Demon: The Magical and Erotic World of Dr. Ernst Schertel* (2022).

"I threw myself into life like an unchained predatory beast, without inhibition, in a frenzy of enjoyment and real action."*

Schertel spent a few years as a teacher in a progressive college preparatory school. There he led the students in performances of dance he called "Mystery Plays." After this he set out on a career as an author, publicist, lecturer, and teacher of dance. He was quite successful with these activities as he published works on nudism, occultism, and the history of culture as it relates to the expression of primal urges and instincts. But above all he became well known for the works he published on his favorite topic: the art and literature of sadomasochistic sexuality. He rose to his highest level of notoriety on the eve of the Nazi takeover of the German government.

Initially, Schertel fled Nazi Germany and moved to France. But inexplicably he returned to the Fatherland only to be imprisoned for a time. His books were banned and his doctorate was officially revoked by the Nazi authorities in 1937. He survived the war years as a copyeditor. After the war, he was able to reissue some of his old erotic material, including his magnum opus *Der Flagellantismus in Literatur und Bildnerei* (Flagellantism in Word and Imagery), which appeared in a new edition the year before his death. Postwar West Germany was generally focusing on the efforts necessary to accomplish their famous *Wirtschaftswunder* (economic miracle) of the late 1950s and early 1960s, so the the old, dark enthusiasms of the Weimar Era were generally less appealing than they had been before! He died of a heart attack in relative obscurity in Hof/Saale in 1958.

Schertel's philosophy was constructed out of a triad of eroticism, magic, and sadomasochism. Among his voluminous writings nowhere did he completely outline the secrets of his inner work, but certainly the text of *Magie* comes closest to this if one is able to incorporate the other aspects of his thought with what is expressed in that book.

A brief summary of Schertel's magical theory is that powerful and distinctive personalities could actually be developed by means of certain

---

*This quote is cited from Gerd Meyer's essay "'Verfehmter Nächte blasser Sohn'—Ein erster Blick auf Ernst Schertel" (in Farin 2003, 496).

techniques designed to break down the division between what is called the "body" and the "spirit," between the "real" and the "ideal." His idea of magic grew out of the application of integrative processes effected by techniques of corporeal experience: eroticism, nudity, indulgence in exhibitionism and voyeurism, unconventional dance movements, and the use of pain and pleasure in an erotic context.

From the passages Hitler highlighted in his personal copy of the book *Magie,* it is clear that among other things the Führer remained interested in the role of a magician in the transformation of the age in which he lives. This is illustrated by the following highlighted passage.

> The magician . . . is the expressly ectropic man, that is, one who condenses energy; he is the guardian of ectropic energy sources, he works contrary to all entropic tendencies of the age and he—and only he—represents the point of origin for possible innovations. Therefore, the magician always works contrary to all prevailing entropic tendencies of the age and is therefore perceived to be "evil," however, physiologically he appears as an atavism, as does every genius. Magic always means plunging back into conditions that have been "superseded" by the dominant age, and which the ordinary crowd of this age no longer knows how to handle. Just as temples and palaces of great epochs decay in subsequent ages because the younger grandchildren are no longer the equals of their great ancestral works, thus too original conditions sink into a forgotten realm, because the age "rises up" over these things, which is to say, it swims on the surface. The magician is the man who is always able to enter into the *status nascendi* [state of being born] in a renewed way and break through in latent energies in ever new ways like dark memories. (Schertel 1978, 98; translation mine)

HANUSSEN AND THE PALACE OF THE OCCULT

Nowhere else is the connection between what most people think of as the occult and the Nazis more apparent than it is in the story of one Erik Jan Hanussen (= Hermann Steinschneider [1889–1933]) and the

NSDAP. Here the word *apparent* is operative! Hanussen was a master of illusion and showmanship. Both of these factors are very much in play when it comes to the sagas of both Hanussen and the Nazis. This tale has been recently told in two highly respectable books, Wilfred Kugel's *Hanussen* (1998) and Mel Gordons's *Erik Jan Hanussen* (2001). Hanussen was a very popular figure in Weimar Berlin in the years leading up to the Nazi seizure of power and so it is not surprising to see this stage and cabaret magician linked to the mass-manipulator working on the political stage at the same time, in the same city.

Erik Jan Hanussen was the alter ego, or stage name, of a man born to a family of Moravian Jews on June 2, 1889, and given the name Hermann (Herschel Chaim) Steinschneider. The place of his birth was Yppenplatz 8 in Ottakring, a village just outside Vienna, which at that time was being incorporated into the City of Vienna as its sixteenth *Bezirk* (district). His father was an actor and a caretaker for the synagogue, and his mother was a singer; the family often traveled around Central Europe as an entertainment troupe. During World War I, he was drafted into the Austrian Army in the 54th Infantry Regiment. Already during the war years, he began his career as an occultist and entertainer with an act involving mentalism and hypnosis. He supported his own fame by writing books on topics of telepathy and clairvoyance. These titles include: *Worauf beruht das—?!—Telepathie, ihre Erklärung und Ausübung* (How Did You Do That?! Telepathy Explained and in Practice; 1917), *Das Gedankenlesen, Telepathie* (Thought-Reading: Telepathy; 1920), *Die Weltseele* (The World Soul; 1922), *Das Gomboloy: Mein System zur Beherrschung der Nerven* (The "Gomboloy": My System for Controlloing the Nerves; 1927). Later, around the years 1932–1933, he would even publish his own journal, *Hanussen Magazin,* and a weekly tabloid paper, *Berliner Wochenschau,* with occult and astrological content. Since Hanussen's star was rising at the same time as that of Hitler, it is almost inevitable that they should be linked in fact or fiction.

Hanussen's activities made him a very wealthy man. He played to packed houses at La Scala in Berlin and was much in demand from wealthy patrons for his psychic readings and astrological charts.

Hanussen was a friend of the writer Hanns Heinz Ewers, who was himself a member of the NSDAP, and both were supporters of the Brownshirts, the *Sturmabteilung* (SA), who formed a massive private army for the Nazis from the beginning of the movement through the 1930s, although their role was severely diminished after the Night of the Long Knives (June 30, 1934). Hanussen had many contacts in the SA and was known to have lent money to a number of its leaders. He entertained members of the organization, often lavishly on his yacht, *Ursel IV.* Hanussen was also a procurer of sexual partners (of both sexes) for these SA men.

Hanussen's motives for supporting the Nazis appear rather inexplicable. Perhaps it was a manifestation of the obscure "Jewish self-hatred syndrome," but it was certainly unwise on many levels. His staff members who were Jewish made plans to leave Germany when they saw the Nazis come to power. Did Hanussen, in his arrogance, believe he was impervious? Or did he secretly wish to be destroyed? If that was his wish, it certainly came true.

In 1932, the Communist press in Berlin went on an all-out offensive against Hanussen, as they thought this was an indirect way of attacking Hitler. This strategy (a common one used by Communists, for example with the campaign against Rasputin in Tsarist Russia) backfired in this instance as it pushed more people into the Nazi camp in reaction to their antics against the popular clairvoyant. But Hanussen also felt he must act against the Marxists in his own way. He did everything he could to bring the Nazis to power, knowing that they would outlaw the Communist Party and thus end the threats on him being mounted by the Reds. This banning of the Communist Party of Germany did indeed occur on February 28, 1933.

Hanussen supported the Nazis with his own form of propaganda, which appeared in his publications in the form of predictions about Germany's future. His tabloid-type weekly, *Hanussens Berliner Wochenschau* (later called the *Bunte Wochenschau: Die Hellseher Zeitung* [Newsreel in Color: The Clairvoyant Times]), carried regular stories about Hitler. While these articles were not always flattering, they were generally designed to predict a glorious and successful future.

Below is the front page of the *Berliner Wochenschau* for March 25–31, 1932, which advertises that Hanussen predicts Hitler's future in a trance.

On several occasions Hanussen's newspapers published horoscopes for Hitler and for the NSDAP, all predicting significant struggles but ultimate success. Such occult propaganda was only indirectly manipulated by the Party itself, for, as we have seen, it appears that Hanussen had his own reasons, however misguided, for supporting the Nazis.

As a showman, Hanussen seems to have wanted to create the impression that he was an intimate adviser and even teacher to the Führer. Solid reports indicate that Hanussen held a few private sessions

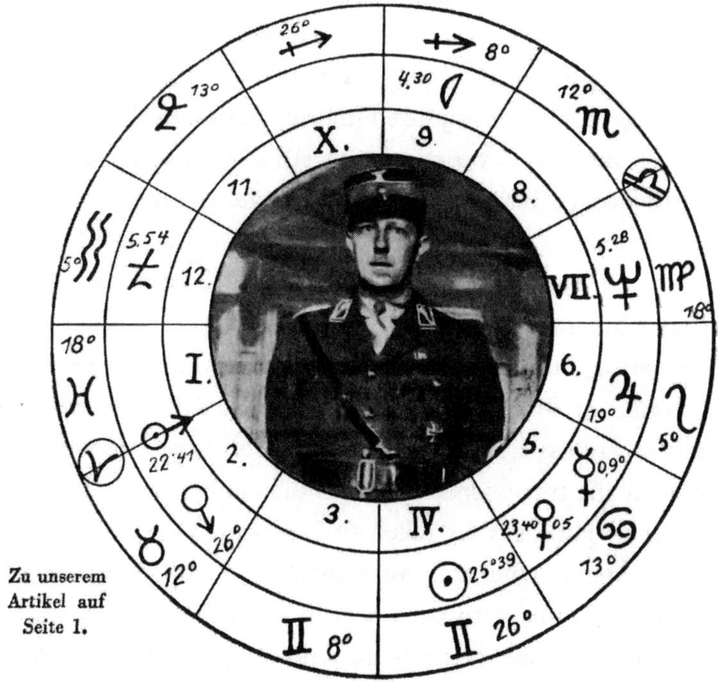

Fig. 6.2. A 1932 horoscope forecasting "The Future of the S.A." from Hanussen's *Berliner Wochenschau*

with Hitler in 1932/1933. The substance of these sessions seems to have been assurances by Hanussen of Hitler's glorious destiny, and there were perhaps some vague promises given by Hitler to create an occult university with Hanussen as its head! Other rumors abounded at the time, and even found their way into Walter C. Langer's 1943 psychological profile of Hitler that he worked up for the Office of Strategic Services. This report was later published in 1972 as *The Mind of Adolf Hitler.* There, with regard to Hitler's involvement with the occult, we read:

> It is true that it looks as though Hitler might be acting under some guidance of this sort that gives him the feeling and conviction of his own infallibility. These stories probably originated in the very early days of the Party. According to [Otto] Strasser, during the early 1920s Hitler took regular lessons in speaking and in mass psychology from a man named Hanussen, who was also a practicing astrologer and fortuneteller. He was an extremely clever individual who taught Hitler a great deal concerning the importance of staging meetings to obtain the greatest dramatic effect. As far as can be learned, he never had any particular interest in the movement or any say on what course it should follow. (Langer 1972, 40)

This sort of report might have been taken more seriously in the past, at a time before we knew how untrustworthy military intelligence can be. Of course, Langer was just picking up on insider reports (such as those of Strasser or Rauschning) written by men with personal axes to grind and rich fantasy lives of their own, as well as on misinformation being spread at the time by manipulators such as Hanussen himself.

The famous photographs taken of Hitler in 1925 or 1927 showing him rehearsing exaggerated poses for his speech-performances have sometimes been rumored to have been symbolic magical poses being taught to him by Hanussen, or some other occult guru. The photos were actually taken by his personal photographer, Heinrich Hoffmann. They were indeed self-teaching tools for the purpose of refining the Führer's performances, to make them more effective before large audiences. In that sense, they were a sort of performative magic, but not an example of occult mumbo jumbo. Hitler told his photographer to destroy the photos, but he kept them secreted in his studio. Hitler controlled his image legally and the rights to that image made both him and his photographer millionaires.

There are a number of reasons as to why the SA might have assassinated Hanussen. These range from the mundane (and most likely) motives—such as a way for the Nazis involved to avoid having to repay monetary loans made to them by the entertainer—to more esoteric reasons that are not entirely implausible. One motive that falls in the latter category would be that of silencing Hanussen regarding a possible role in the Reichstag Fire of February 27, 1933: he may have known about the plot to burn the building—which led to Hitler's assumption of expanded emergency powers—and wrote about it as if it were one of his psychic predictions! Another angle, and one that finds resonance in later political intrigues, is that Hanussen actually hypnotized the Reichstag arsonist (supposedly a Communist named Marinus van der Lubbe), causing him to commit the act in a trancelike state. This last possibility seems to come right out of the fantasy life of Weimar-era films about a "Dr. Caligari" or "Dr. Mabuse." The Reichstag Fire is later envisioned as a textbook example of the false flag operation.

The events of the first three months of 1933 both brought Hanussen to his peak of power and to his ultimate destruction at the hands of the very forces he helped to call forth. During January, the Nazis maneuvered to seize power; in February, Hanussen converted to Catholicism and joined the NSDAP and the SA (even receiving his own uniform!). On Sunday, February 26, Hanussen opened his elaborate Palace of the Occult—a mansion he had converted into a venue for his occult performances, and one worthy of any UFA film set. On the evening of the next day, the Reichstag was burning. On March 25, 1933, Hanussen was abducted from his apartment, taken to an SA barracks, and shot. His body was dumped in a remote area north of Berlin. The corpse was later found by a farmer on April 7. He was buried with Catholic rites in the Südwestkirchhof Cemetery in Stahnsdorf near Berlin.

Erik Jan Hanussen has become an intriguing figure in the postwar mythology of Nazi occultism. His case provides a prime example of the mixture of truth and fantasy fed both from the side of the pro-Nazi sympathizer and the anti-Nazi propagandist. However, his story would not be one of the most exploited in most recent times, even in popular culture.

One of the most persistent themes in the general tenor of Nazi occult mythology is that Hitler had some sort of power to control the masses in an almost hypnotic way. This theme of hypnotic control was a major feature of German-speaking popular culture, especially as expressed in the motion pictures of the day. Hanussen's stage hypnotism act in Vienna was outlawed in 1919 as it was judged to be a public danger. At that same time, the great film *The Cabinet of Dr. Caligari* was being made in Germany. The film depicts how a stage magician and hypnotist is able to use an unconscious somnambulist to commit murder at his command.

One of the episodes in the Hanussen saga that does not get much attention in the literature about Nazi occultism is recounted in the obscure book *Die Lösung des Rätsels Adolf Hitler* (Solving of the Riddle of Adolf Hitler) by Johannes von Müllern-Schönhausen (1959, 133–86). It involves the supposed transference of a magical mandrake root to Hitler from Hanussen on January 1, 1933, along with the prophecy that Hitler would succeed within a month. Belief in the success-bringing power of the mandrake root (Ger. *Alraune*) was a well-established part of German popular culture of the time as a result of Hanns Heinz Ewers's bestselling 1911 novel *Alraune,* which was also adapted into several films that were produced between 1918 and 1930. Hitler was a fan of Ewers and had inducted him into the NSDAP on his birthday (November 3) in 1931. The meticulous researcher Wilfrid Kugel concluded after examining von Müllern-Schönhausen's "evidence" that it was based on forgeries.

The place of Hanussen in a study of this type is not to be ignored or diminished. However, it must also be noted that in Hanussen we have an individual who was famous in his own right at the time the Nazis were rising to power in that atmosphere of chaos and excess that characterized the Weimar period and who appears to have been a person who was simply caught up in, and quickly destroyed by, the virtually gangland aspects of the NSDAP. Hanussen actually did play an important role in bringing the Nazis to power on January 30, 1933, as his predictions and suggestions were instrumental in manipulating public opinion in those critical months. Here we have another verifiable connection between the Nazis and the occult.

Hanussen was a popularizer of astrological ideas. In the first decade of the twentieth century, astrology had undergone a major revival in the German-speaking world largely under the sponsorship of theosophical interests. Works by astrologers such as Karl Brandler-Pracht, Ernst Tiede, and Otto Pöllner were published by the Theosophical Publishing House and Brandler-Pracht established the Astrological Society in Vienna in 1907. At about the same time the Kosmos Society was founded in Germany. Periodicals began to appear as well. These included the *Zentralblatt für Okkultismus* (the organ of the Kosmos Society) and the *Astrologische Rundschau* (founded 1909). In 1920, Rudolf von Sebottendorf became the editor of the latter organ. Typical of the German culture, there was also the Academic Society for Astrological Research, which published *Astrologische Studien*. To be a member of this society, one had to hold a Ph.D..

THE CALIGARI SYNDROME

One aspect of occultism that had penetrated deeply into the popular culture of Germany in the early twentieth century is what I will call the Caligari Syndrome. As I have already alluded to, this term is based on the content of the Weimar-era German film *The Cabinet of Dr. Caligari* (1919), in which it is demonstrated how a carnival hypnotist controls a human instrument of his will in order to do the master's (often nefarious) bidding. This theme of an object (a person or thing) being manipulated to perform actions as the agent of its master's extended will is repeated in many films of the German golden age of Expressionist cinema in the 1920s and early 1930s, such as the Dr. Mabuse series *The Golem* and *Metropolis*.

It is rather ironic, as such things so often are, that the apparent *subject* (doer) of these manipulations (the NSDAP) may not have been ultimately the active party at all but rather the virtual victim of yet another operator, hidden in plain sight—the Christian Church. The point of having an extended agent is to be able to deflect guilt from one's self, while the agent acts as an unseen hand in some criminal activity. It is well known that the Christian churches in Germany, both Catholic and Protestant, were virulently anti-Semitic in the years leading up to the First World War. Indeed, they had been active promoters of anti-Semitism over the centuries leading up to this time in history. In this they were matched by churches in Eastern Europe, especially in Poland and Russia. Christian religious sentiment forced the hand of the czar to conduct numerous pogroms against the Jews in Russia (especially in 1905–1906), and the famous book called *The Protocols of the Elders of Zion* was originally concocted by Russian secret agents to foment anti-Semitism as well. The NSDAP can be seen as an external agent created to do the will of its ecclesiastical masters, but like another figure that perhaps belongs to this paradigm, Frankenstein's monster, it got well out of control and destroyed the whole laboratory, as it were. On the other hand, there can be no doubt that Hitler, like Lenin or Stalin, saw *himself* as the master manipulator whose will would ultimately triumph on the stage of history. Such hubris on the part of political and military leaders is, of course, nothing new.

* * *

The occult world and the realm of the esoteric in early nineteenth-century Central Europe can be said to have had an unusual degree of activity focused on nativistic, neo-Germanic symbology, to be sure. However, the scene was no way entirely dominated by this aspect. Then as now, the German-speaking world exercised great interest on a wide spectrum of esoteric topics—often of the most universalistic or exotic bent. Peculiar systems such as those of the Adonists or Mazdaznanists showed the innovative attitude of the universalistic German spirit, while others—such as the OTO or Fraternitas Saturni—represented German approaches to age-old systems. All of these sorts of ideas and organizations would be targeted for elimination by the Nazis. On the other hand, the völkisch brand of esotericism had a bifurcated fate, as we will see. Since many of the leading Nazis had contacts with such organizations, had belonged to them in the early days and had sympathies with their general tenor and motivations, such individuals and groups faced a choice: dissolve themselves into the official construct of the NSDAP or meet the same fate as the universalistic or idiosyncratic types.

PART III

Myth of the
Twentieth Century
(1919–1945)

INTRODUCTION TO PART III

In this third part of the study, we come to discuss the heart of the matter: the actual ideas and practices of the NSDAP that can be considered to one degree or another *occult*. This section will take into consideration the entire history of the Party, not just the time period when the National Socialists ruled in Germany. The NSDAP was officially founded on February 24, 1920, but its immediate predecessor, the DAP (Deutsche Arbeiterpartei) had been established in January 1919, and Hitler became a member (no. 55) of that organization in September 1919. This time period, immediately after the end of hostilities in World War I and the collapse of the monarchal regimes in both Germany and Austria, also saw the establishment of the Weimar Republic as a bulwark against the impending threat of Communist revolutions in various parts of Germany.

The political institutions of the Weimar Republic are generally seen to have been an abject failure in historical retrospect, but the same cannot be said of the cultural scene. In many ways it represented a virtual renaissance of certain aspects of German culture. The failure of the Weimar Republic as a political and economic system was inevitable given three factors: Germany's inexperience at the practice of modern representative government; the constant attacks by extremists of both the left (often directly connected to the Soviet system of Russia) and the right (fueled by disaffected veterans of the war); and, finally and most devastatingly of all, the economic hardships imposed by the stipulations of the Treaty of Versailles. The period of hyperinflation in the early 1920s was a time when people had to have wheelbarrows full of money to buy a loaf of bread. The Germans felt themselves to have been politically betrayed, as they had not been decisively defeated on the battle-field, but rather in the backrooms among politicians and diplomats. It was in this political and economic environment that the philosophy of National Socialism gained its advantage.

That is only one side of the story of Weimar, however. It was also a time of tremendous cultural vigor, artistic energy, and scholarly expansion. In spite of the ongoing economic and political troubles, nowhere on earth did the 1920s *roar* more than they did in Berlin. For a general overview of this culture, see Peter Gay's *Weimar Culture* (1968) and, for a more sensational and visual perspective, Mel Gordon's aforementioned *Voluptuous Panic.* Gay's observation is that the value of Weimar culture can be measured by the quality of the exiles who left Germany at the time of the Nazi assumption of power. These exiles, many of whom ended up in the United States, virtually transformed various aspects of Western culture in the fields of art, literature, filmmaking, scholarship, and the sciences. This was the "heart drain" from Germany, which would arrive before the famous brain drain that came after the Second World War.

National Socialism and the National Socialists themselves were—to a greater extent than most commentators today might like to admit—also a part of this Weimar Culture as a culmination of those trends we have already traced in German social and cultural history from the late nineteenth century. To understand fully the context of the contents of this book, one needs to understand the general history of Nazi Germany. To summarize those twelve years, we might say that the NSDAP with Hitler as its Führer (leader) seized the

Fig. Pt3.1. Nazi Party
heraldic eagle

apparatus of government by democratic means on January 30, 1933. Hitler was named chancellor with the limited functions delegated to that office, but, with the burning of the German Parliament Building (the Reichstag Fire) on February 27, Hitler demanded and got extraordinary powers, which he never relinquished, consolidating authority and making Germany a National Socialist state by the end of 1934. Power was further solidified in 1935, and Germany systematically ignored the provisions of the Treaty of Versailles and began a massive rearmament campaign, leading to full employment and general economic renewal.

Ultimately, however, Hitler was bent on war. So, after more or less peacefully expanding the Third Reich through various means (the annexation of Austria in 1938 and the takeover of Czechoslovakia in 1939), the Führer finally went too far, too fast with his invasion of Poland on September 1, 1939, precipitating the beginning of the Second World War. For the first three or four years of this war, Germany was apparently invincible: overrunning most of Western and Eastern Europe. In the Far East, Japan, an Axis ally of Germany, attacked the United States Navy at Pearl Harbor on December 7, 1941. When the United States declared war on Japan, Germany, bound by treaties with Japan, declared war on the US. The victorious tide of the Nazis was turned in the east at Stalingrad in February of 1943. The Allies invaded Italy (an Axis ally of Germany) in September 1943. The Allied invasion of Normandy in June 1944 opened the second front in the war. Under mounting military pressure from the Allies and the Red Army, the depleted Nazi state was completely crushed by the beginning of May 1945. Germany unconditionally surrendered on May 8. Hitler and Goebbels committed suicide. Himmler tried to escape but was captured and likewise committed suicide by means of cyanide. Other leading Nazis—including Hermann Göring and Alfred Rosenberg— were tried for crimes against humanity and sentenced to be hanged on October 16, 1946. (Göring avoided the noose by taking cyanide the night before he was to be executed.)

In what follows I will again devote three chapters to the questions of symbolic or mythic content, scientific issues tinged with occult significance, and finally the occult itself as conventionally understood. Here, as elsewhere, these categories are on one level distinct from one another, but in the minds of many—both then and now—the lines between these fields of human endeavor are often blurred into non-existence. Separating them for individual discussion simply brings the whole picture into sharper focus.

I will utilize a good deal of space discussing the often elaborate liturgical aspects of the NSDAP movement. It is in these sometimes pageant-like rituals that a good deal of the magic of the Nazi spell-casting acumen can be discerned. Even if only viewed on film, these rituals still bewitch many today. By studying the rituals from an objective angle, we can perhaps effectively demystify them. But, on the other hand, experience has shown that if one is dealing with true *mysteries,* they are actually largely impervious to demystification.

There are two occult dimensions to the scientific branch of occult Nazism. The first concerns the occult aspects of the theories used by scientists to explain phenomena or even to create technological innovations using these theories. The second dimension concerns the occult beliefs *about* scientific and technological innovations created during the Nazi era.

These are two very different things. The first supposes that discredited or as yet objectively undiscovered constructs, or ones created in ways that lay outside the accepted scientific model, were used by professional or lay scientists to shape theories or produce technologies. The second speaks only to the occult mania focused on the Nazis—both by their sympathizers and opponents. In this regard, the scientific branch of occult Nazism falls into the exact same pattern of thinking as the other branches of this historical examination.

When we come to consider the more conventional dimensions of the occult during the time period of the Third Reich, the field becomes very murky. Despite the idea that there exist orders or lodges of practicing magicians, in general the occult is a highly individualized and subjective field of human endeavor. In his seminal 1952 study *A General Theory of Magic,* the French sociologist Marcel Mauss characterized the practice of magic as an anti-social behavior. By *anti-social* he means that magic is oriented toward the fulfillment of the will of the individual, independent and apart from society in general. Clearly, whether one considers orthodox religions (e.g., Judaism, Christianity, Islam) or socialistic political philosophies of the left or right, the will of the individual is to be subordinated to the will of the religious leadership—or in political contexts, to that of "the people"—and so the free practice of magic and occultism will always present a problem for such systems. The greater the control of the centralized church or party, the less it desires to have individualized interpretations and experiences usurping the dogma and the party line. This is not to say that the centralized power rejects occult principles per se—although it certainly may do so officially. Indeed, it may make use of such principles in practice. It just does not want renegade individuals competing with it.

CHAPTER 7

SYMBOLIC ELEMENTS IN THE NSDAP

How Signs, Symbols, and Ceremonies Were Wielded to Gain and Maintain Power and Control

The Third Reich was an empire of applied symbology. This is clearly visible in things such as its use of the swastika or runes, but it went well beyond that into every aspect of its formulations and expressions. Many of these may have been unconscious, or examples of things that were "accidentally" effective, such as the Nazi obsession with militaristic uniforms, but most of them were to some extent conscious and willful efforts. The quasi-military look of the Storm Trooper's dress probably just stemmed from the fact that the early members were WWI veterans who had nothing else to wear than their old uniforms. The effect of it was, however, that the Nazis exuded to the public the image of discipline, of law and order, whereas their Communist opponents generally appeared as rag-tag unemployed workers. One image inspired confidence in the general public; the other, despair. These, too, are symbols and signs in the acts of magical communication.

The symbolic elements of the NSDAP were rich and varied. Many of them stemmed from the personal interests and even obsessions of the men who led the many departments and organizations within the vast and to some extent surprisingly amorphous whole that made up the Party. As we will see, the two most dominant personalities and factions within this overall structure were those of Hitler himself, and his loyal-(almost)-to-the-end chief enforcer on a cosmic level, Heinrich Himmler. These men, along with several others, will be the touchstones of our discussion here. It will be seen that Hitler represented a pragmatic and

Fig. 7.1. NSDAP logo

largely classical aesthetic, while Himmler was of the more Romantic school—but no less lethal.*

THE FÜHRER

When studying any aspect of National Socialism—and the supposed occult dimension is no exception—the personality and position of Adolf Hitler must take center stage. Without him and his personality, National Socialism, as history came to know it, probably would not have existed. He had a tremendous influence on the twentieth century. It would certainly be a mistake to think that Hitler was some sort of calculating and cunning genius who made things happen despite everything being against him. A cunning genius he may have been, but much more than this he was a man in the right place, at the right time. The

---

*This aspect of Hitler's character is clear both from the evidence of his own writings and his designs for the renovation of German cities, as well as on a more deeply philosophical level; see Birken's *Hitler as Philosophe* (1995) and Spotts's *Hitler and the Power of Aesthetics* (2003). The Romantic reenvisioning of the Germanic past, its aesthetics and art forms, was almost a private obsession of Himmler's and one that Hitler did not much like.

zeitgeist and Hitler's own character aligned perfectly, and the world was hurled deeper into catastrophe. Certainly, if there had been no Hitler, someone of a similar sort would have probably come to power in Germany, but perhaps it would have been no worse than your average fascist such as Mussolini or Franco. Hitler was not by nature a politician. Then as now, politicians are generally only interested in gaining and keeping power for themselves. Hitler was a far more dangerous type: an *artist* and visionary, influenced not by previous generations of politicians, but by men such as Wagner. Thus, Hitler would set the stage for his own Gesamtkunstwerk, in which the greatest "Twilight of the Gods" ever seen would play itself out over the whole globe.

The Life and Times of Adolf Hitler

The life, activities, and ideas of Adolf Hitler (1889–1945) are among the most documented in history. Many biographies of the man have been written from many different perspectives. But it is well to survey some of the most essential facts here.

Fig. 7.2. Hitler striking an oratorial pose, photographed by Heinrich Hoffmann, circa 1925
(German Federal Archive)

He was born in Braunau am Inn in Austria. His father was a customs official with whom Adolf had a difficult relationship. Hitler remained an Austrian citizen until just a few months before becoming Chancellor of Germany. Most of his youth was spent in Linz, Austria. After his parents' deaths, he was on his own and spent years in a bohemian lifestyle in rooming houses and men's dormitories in Vienna. His youth and early life in Vienna is well documented but leaves many questions unanswered. His friend August Kubizek is thought to be a reliable source on many things but questionable on others. For example, Kubizek reports that Hitler was always a dedicated anti-Semite, but other evidence suggests that this did not happen until after the Great War. In any event, Hitler was a lover of music (Wagner) and architecture and evolved these into political interests.

During his time in Vienna, it is said he read anti-Semitic pamphlets. These have been thought by some to be the publications of Lanz von Liebenfels (e.g., *Ostara*). Lanz himself tried to make this idea credible. The only problem is, of course, that Lanz's pamphlets were *not* anti-Semitic at all. Such literature abounded in Vienna at the time, but Lanz's work was not a prominent part of it. It is likely that Hitler did read all sorts of nationalistic or völkisch literature, which surely included Guido von List and perhaps even Lanz.

Hitler found himself in Munich when WWI broke out and he joined the Bavarian army. (This was an administrative mistake, as Hitler was not eligible to join as an Austrian citizen.) Hitler spent the war on the Western Front, participated in many battles, and was wounded several times.

In a poem, ostensibly written on the war front in 1915, he would already show some of his basic ways of thinking, which would suggest elements of neo-Germanic religious or mystical conceptions, although the work is likely a forgery.

> *Ich gehe manchesmal in rauhen Nächten*
> *Zur Wotanseiche in den stillen Hain,*
> *Mit dunklen Mächten einen Bund zu flechten—*
> *Die Runen zaubert mir der Mondenschein.*

*

Und alle, die am Tage sich erfrechten,
Sie werden vor der Zauberformel klein!
Sie ziehen blank—doch statt den Strauß zu flechten,
Erstarren sie zu Stalagmitgestein.

So scheiden sich die Falschen von den Echten—
Ich greife in das Fibelnest hinein
Und gebe dann den Guten und Gerechten
Mit meiner Formel Segen und Gedeihn.

IN EINER RAUHNACHT 1915 IM FELDE

Which can be translated as:

I often go on bitter nights
To the Wotan's oak, into the quiet grove,
With dark powers to weave a bond—
The moonlight casts the runic spell over me.

And all who are full of impudence during the day
Are made small by the magic formula!
They draw shining steel—but instead of going into combat,
They solidify into stalagmites.

Thus, the wrong ones are separated from the genuine ones—
I reach into a nest of words
And then give to the good and just,
With my formula, blessings and prosperity.

[WRITTEN] ON A *RAUHNACHT** 1915, ON THE FRONT

The only known source for this text is Johannes von Müllern-Schönhausen's book *Die Lösung des Rätsels Adolf Hitler* (1959, 210). It

---

*The *Rauhnächte* (sing. *Rauhnacht*) are the twelve days of the Yuletide in Central European folklore.

appears only as a photocopy, and the whereabouts of the original are unknown. The Dutch investigator Jaap van den Born seriously doubts the poem's authenticity and ascribes it to Müllern-Schönhausen himself, who is known to have fabricated other evidence connected to the Nazis and the occult.

After the war, he was discharged and returned to Munich, where he worked with the army as an informant on radical political groups. He went undercover to attend meetings of the German Workers Party (Deutsche Arbeiterpartei) and was converted to their cause. His mentor was Dietrich Eckhart, to whom he dedicated *Mein Kampf.* Hitler undertook the direction of the design of the Party and was instrumental in reforming its name and in endowing the organization with its striking logo: the swastika. The new name, *The National Socialist German Workers' Party,* expressed various key symbolic contents of the organization's ideology. *National* referred to the idea that it was *völkisch*—that is, oriented toward the racial identity of its members and those they seek to lead and serve. The *socialist* component was double-edged. On the one hand, it was a diverting tactic from the other forms of (Marxist) socialism popular on the street at the time. But for the Nazis, socialism was a more basic concept, as expressed in the Party's program (the 25 Points) with the formula "The common good before the individual good." The word *German* in the name made it clear that the Party was for Germany and Germans only. The 25 Points define a German as a *Volksgenosse* (folk comrade) to exclude Jews specifically, both from Party membership and even citizenship in the new Reich. The meaning of *worker* in the name is also complex. It alludes to the labeling popular on the Left, but more specifically, a *worker* is one who does not profit from the practice of *usury*—lending money in exchange for interest. This was *ideally* to be outlawed by the Nazis. And finally, it is a *party*—that is, an ideological faction—that stands behind these concepts and represents them in the public sphere in a disciplined way. The abbreviated form NSDAP was the Hitlerian response to the Roman insignia SPQR, *Senatus Populusque Romanus* (Senate and People of Rome).

This reference to the imagery and symbolism of Rome should come as no surprise. The symbolism and aesthetics of the NSDAP were thoroughly imbued with a *Roman* air, despite the much-publicized supposed obsession of the Nazis with things *Germanic* or Norse, they owed far more of their style and imagery to Rome than to the ancient North. Hitler's own sense of aesthetics, which was well developed, ran firmly in the direction of the classical Greco-Roman rather than Germanic. Hitler undoubtedly would have viewed *actual* Germanic art as somewhat *entartet*—"degenerate." In the work of magical communication (propaganda), the Roman aesthetic projected the disciplined, ordered, unidirectional thrust he desired. Actual Germanic art exudes a spirit of individual liberty, which was undesirable for him (except in his own case and those of his close associates!).

The ancient Roman connection to Germany is complex and symbolically powerful. Rome is, of course, considered by many to be the symbolic opponent and opposite of Germania—an attitude stemming back to ancient times when Rome and the Germanic tribes were embroiled in centuries-long warfare. (But even there, many Germanic tribesmen sided with Rome, so much so that by the end of the Roman Empire most of its army was made up of Germans!) Centuries after the collapse of the original (Western) Roman Empire, in 800 the Holy Roman Empire was formulated under Charlemagne (Karl the Great, a Frankish king). This was the first German empire, which lasted until 1806. The kaisers (emperors) of the Holy Roman Empire considered themselves to be just as much *Roman* emperors as Augustus or Tiberius had been. In the Middle Ages, Germania *became* Roma. The Third Reich (third empire) saw itself as the inheritor of the original (first) Holy Roman Empire, as carried through the second empire, that of kaisers Wilhelm I–II (1871–1918). The idealistic-sounding statement in the nineteenth point of the Party Program that "we demand the substitution of German Common Law for Roman Law; Roman Law serves a materialistic world order" shows little sign of ever having been seriously implemented. "German Common Law" was akin to "Positive Christianity"—difficult for the general populace to define, so open to all sorts of pragmatic and ideologically facile redefinitions and applications. The NSDAP could not have existed in a state that was actually governed by Germanic common law.

It is also known that Hitler designated the design of the swastika as the insignia, or logo, of the Party. The sign was adopted for the Party in 1919 and the swastika-emblazoned flag was made the national symbol in 1933. As is well known, the symbol is a universal one found in many cultures. A book detailing this from a National Socialist perspective is that of Jörg Lechler (1934). There the author makes specific reference to the sign as one that functioned for Hitler and the Party like an operative device to promote and ensure victory and success: "Through Adolf Hitler it was elevated to the symbol of the National Socialist movement in 1919 and so commenced his victorious march, so that it became the symbol of the new Germany fourteen years later" (Lechler 1934, 14).

Hitler's first attempt to wrest political control away from the establishment was carried out in Munich during the so-called Beer Hall Putsch of November 8–9, 1923. Inspired by Mussolini's March on Rome the previous year, Hitler led a force of two thousand men from the Bürgerbräukeller* to try to take over the Bavarian government. They were met at the Odeonsplatz in front of the Feldherrnhalle by a police force and a shoot-out ensued. Sixteen NSDAP men were killed. The flagbearer was hit and dropped the swastika banner and another man, Andreas Bauriedl, was killed and fell on top of the flag, staining it with his blood. This flag—which came to be called the *Blutfahne* (Blood Flag)—was eventually given to Hitler, who transformed it into a talismanic object.

As a result of the attempted coup in Munich, Hitler was sentenced to a prison term, which he spent in Landsberg prison mostly in the company of his secretary Rudolf Hess. There they put together Hitler's book *Mein Kampf* (My Struggle). This was to act as a presentation of Hitler and his ideas to a wider public. When Hitler was released after serving only nine months in 1925, the NSDAP was reformed and once more began its progress toward power—now according to legitimate electoral means, coupled with organized street action. The economic failures and political turmoil characteristic of the Weimar Republic played into his hands. The Nazis remained a minority party, winning 37 percent of the

---

*The building was demolished in 1979.

vote in the 1932 elections, but eventually the president of the Weimar Republic, Paul von Hindenburg, asked Hitler to be chancellor and form a government. Hitler became chancellor on January 30, 1933. Within a month the German parliament building, the Reichstag, was burned in an act of arson. Communists were blamed and Hitler suspended basic civil rights as an emergency measure. This process continued until on August 1, 1934, when the cabinet decreed that upon the death of the President (Hindenburg), Hitler would assume an office that combined both the chancellorship and the presidency. Hindenburg died the next day and Hitler became "Führer und Reichskanzler" of the Reich.

In 1935, Hitler instituted what is called the *Gleichschaltung* (coordination), which involved making the symbols of the NSDAP the same as those of the German state, so the swastika flag became the national flag of Germany and on a practical level the system of administering the state was subsumed by the administrative structure of the Party. Other parties were outlawed. Hitler was the absolute dictator of Germany.

Hitler was opposed to the interests of the church, both Protestant and Catholic, mainly because they could interfere with the effectiveness of the implementation of NS ideology in the populace over the long term. Julius Caesar, in his development of the institution (Emperor) that would bear his name in Rome (Caesar), saw that he had to subsume three offices in the Roman Republic to assume complete control of the state: (1) the *Imperator* (leader of the army, commander in chief); (2) the *Dictator* (speaker of the senate), who in the Republic had a limited term, but under the empire his office would be for life; and, finally, (3) the *Pontifex Maximus* (the head of the college of *flamens,* or priests of the pagan Roman cult). Hitler was not so bold, but understood the principles, and so began to limit the power of the church. The church was suffering in the early part of the twentieth century from a lack of popular support. Church attendance was dwindling. Hitler forged what is known as the *Konkordat* with the church in Germany. Financially, Hitler would fold the church and support for it into the taxing authority of the state. This ensured control of the church by the state, and the church was assured of financial support from the state and did not have to depend on free-will donations from the ever-declining faithful. This was similar to the way in which Mussolini had made a pact with the Roman Church to establish Vatican City as a sovereign state. Hitler's *Konkordat* is basically the way in which the church and state relate to one another in Germany to this day.

Hitler as **Philosophe**

Many are surprised about the degree to which Hitler exemplified Neo-Classical proclivities. He loved the Greco-Roman aesthetic and loathed the artistic sentiments of the ancient Germanic people. This stemmed not only from his sense of aesthetics (see below), but from a basic and fundamental adherence to the philosophical principles of the Age of Enlightenment school of thought, the exemplars of which were known as *Philosophes,* such as Voltaire, Rousseau, Diderot, Locke, and Hobbes. This thesis is the topic of a book by Lawrence Birken, *Hitler as Philosophe* (1995). Although many of the ideas of these philosophers became the bedrock of conventional political and secular thinking in the West, the use of this template to clarify what appears to most observers to be unrelated to these ideas, constitutes a revelation of occult, or hidden, dimensions to Hitler's thought process.

Certainly, the greatest overriding characteristic of the Enlightenment way of thinking is the drive to understand things in terms of logical *systems*. Whether Marx or Hitler, modern revolutionaries make fetishes of their systems. In the case of Hitler, however, this system must be inferred from the evidence.

According the Birken (1995, 14–17) three characteristics of Hitler's philosophy relate to the Enlightenment:

1. The juxtaposition of egalitarianism and hierarchy, with a view toward social egalitarianism and biological hierarchy.
2. The juxtaposition of a conservative idealization of nature and a revolutionary attitude toward technology.
3. The juxtaposition of (traditional) religious faith and (modern) revolutionary secularism.

God had become, in an almost Wagnerian manner, equated with man, but not just any Man—rather, the German Volk.

The Enlightenment logic held that there was a correct and an incorrect—a true and a false—answer every question. For Hitler, the poles were between the real, which he equated with the natural, and the unreal, which he equated with the unnatural. For him, the Aryan man was the natural man, awaiting only the correct manner or breeding of selected specimens with others marked by their strength and beauty in order to artistically achieve the higher and more perfect form of the species. Enlightenment thinking, however, requires a counterpart to this element. For Hitler, of course, this role was filled by the Jews. The natural man was creative and engaged in productive work; the Jews, as embodiments of anti-nature, were non-productive (or destructive), parasitic, and lazy.

The mode of thinking exemplified by Hitler had long since become passé among philosophers of the twentieth century. He was reviving with full force the kind of ideas that might have been held among eighteenth-century Philosophes. In this sense, these ideas qualify as occult, because they are largely rejected by those aware of the history of philosophy. However, they are potent ideas and ones that still exercise a powerful attraction to the mind.

As history has shown us, the Enlightenment had two faces: the measured and reasoned approach of the American Revolution, and the excessive and impassioned application of what appears to be reason in the French Revolution. The fetishizing of Reason can and quickly did pave the way to a Reign of Terror. No matter whether by faith or reason, if persons endowed with great power are convinced of the *correctness* of their ideas, and those ideas are *revolutionary,* violence and criminality cannot be far behind.

HITLER THE ARTIST

Hitler was the dictator, formerly known as the artist. In so many ways Hitler was not what he appeared to be. He was the Führer of Germany, yet only became a German citizen a few months before he was appointed its political leader. He was the political head of the German state, yet up until that point had identified himself on official documents as an artist professionally. Popular culture of today tends to excuse radical or bizarre behaviors or beliefs when the subjects of these acts identify themselves as artists. The interpretation of Hitler as primarily having the temperament of an artist is not speculative. His own contemporaries and intimates often knew the same thing.

In his book *Hitler and the Power of Aesthetics,* Frederic Spotts outlines the Führer's deep and abiding interest and activity in a variety of artistic areas: graphic arts and design, music, architecture, as well as ceremonies. His approach to politics and leadership was also tinged with the same temperament. Hitler was not just a passive fan of the arts, rather he was an active agent in the endeavor in much of what he did.

Hitler's own surviving paintings, mostly depicting cityscapes, have been criticized by art historians and lawyers alike in terms which themselves seem inspired by a kind of mania or madness. Spotts (2003, 401) reports: "In an argument submitted in the spring of 2001 to the Federal Appeals Court in Washington, the United States Justice Department maintained that the very brush strokes of Hitler's watercolors have such incendiary potential that they must be guarded from the gaze of all but screened experts." What a testimony to the occult power of the evil genius of Hitler! Of course, this power is mostly in the weak minds of the victims of these reputedly diabolical brush strokes.

But Hitler's artistic undertakings went well beyond his watercolors of quaint European buildings. These included the concepts to redesign whole cities in his own aesthetic architectural taste. Areas of Munich were reconfigured, and he planned to rebuild the Austrian city of Linz, where he spent much of his boyhood. But the most ambitious of these plans was the rebuilding of the capital city of Berlin and renaming it *Germania,* to be the capital of a vast Pan-Germanic or worldwide empire. Hitler's plans to rebuild Berlin echo the architectural renovation of the City of Rome by Emperor Trajan (53–117 CE). The connection goes beyond that, however. Any examination of the actual plans Hitler had for this new Berlin (designs and models exist showing the final vision), clearly demonstrates his total dedication to the aesthetic of

Rome and the classical style. Hitler also designed the logo of the Nazi Party and the general contours of the Volkswagen Beetle (Type 1)—he wanted to live up to the genius of his hero Henry Ford. He was constantly working on artistic projects of one kind or another.*

All artists exercise a sort of magic. They translate their concepts into forms and execute them in the world so that they may communicate their effects to the cosmos. They impress their wills upon the world and gain pleasure and fulfillment from the act, from the changes in consciousness that their artistic work forces upon the viewer or listener. This artistic dimension of Hitler's character is one of the most obvious examples of the presence of the occult and the magical in the National Socialist movement.

HITLER: RELIGION AND THE OCCULT

For years, controversy has raged over the questions of Hitler and his religion, his position toward religion and the occult. So many agendas are being fed by these speculations that they have come to form a whole modern mythology of their own. These range from Hitler being a pagan Wotan-worshipper or a Satanist—the most far-fetched of the myths—to him simply doing the Lord's work in a completely Christian sense, to him being an atheist, to him being in league with various occult groups, and so on. Each of these various paradigms of interpretation have some grain of truth to them, perhaps. The best sources for gaining any real insight into these questions can be found in his own words, such as in *Mein Kampf,* his speeches, and his "Table Talk" and other utterances where he touches on religious matters. These quotes have been conveniently collected in the 1977 book *Hitlers "Religion"* by Manfred Ach (with a collection of original sources by Clemens Pentrop). The authors of this book put the word "religion" in quotes because their analysis shows that the aspect of Hitler's thinking that might be called "religious"

---

*One idea that should perhaps be understood in the same context—especially given the prevailing popular culture in Germany at the time—is the design of a beautiful, strong, and healthy population based on ideals of the Aryan prototype (Spotts 2003, 97–112).

could not be categorized under the heading of any known and established faith or church. As with most men in history with similar stories, their religion seems to have been understood in terms of their individual selves—a steadfast belief in their own personal meaning, purpose, and mission in the world. Hitler's religion is summed up in the formulaic mantra uttered by one of his greatest disciples, Rudolf Hess, when he introduced his Führer with the words: "The Party is Hitler! But Hitler is Germany, just as Germany is Hitler!" Thus, three entities are equated: the NSDAP = Hitler = Germany. This, and this alone, was probably the essence of Hitler's *religion*. There was simply no room in his being for any other. This Trinitarian formula is reminiscent of another which was used at the time: *Ein Volk—Ein Reich—Ein Führer* (One People—One Empire—One Leader), which was directly inspired by the medieval Catholic formula "One God, One Pope, One Church" (Lat. *unus Deus, unus Papa, una Ecclesia*). One does not need to go beyond this formula to realize the depth to which Hitler would reject any actual sense of authentic *Germanic* spirituality with its emphasis on tribal loyalty and individual liberty.

Certainly, one of the most important books on the topic of Hitler and religion is Steigmann-Gall's *The Holy Reich* (2003). This book clearly demonstrates the two religious strains present in the Third Reich: the Christian (Positive or orthodox) and the neopagan (which we have clearly seen was not the traditional worship of mythic Germanic gods and goddesses, but rather a pseudoscientific nationalism). Both were *equally* seen as being völkisch. As Hitler was the Party, these same tendencies were present in his worldview. Steigmann-Gall comes to the conclusion that the Christian component was dominant, but it has been ignored and underplayed in the postwar political and cultural climate. The idea that Nazism was an anti-Christian movement is seen as a nonfactual but useful truism for Christians and the liberal elite in the postwar climate (Steigmann-Gall 2003, 266).

The aforementioned book *Hitlers "Religion"* is useful, but it was produced by churchmen with their own agenda as well. They put too much stock in the early twentieth-century Germanic rebirth movement of List, Liebenfels, and others. Nevertheless, the final analysis provided by Pentrop, based on the actual sources, is most useful for its general categorical breakdown: "Hitler's personality," "Hitler's philosophy," "race-folk-masses," "science and nature," "Providence," and "will-responsibility-conscience." An almost fatal flaw in this study, however, is the fact that the authors take the spurious writings of Hermann Rauschning as a reliable source.

Two of the most important words used by Hitler in a quasi-religious manner are *Vorsehung* (Providence) and *Schicksal* (Fate). These are semantically closely related. Hitler uses the word denoting Providence five times in *Mein Kampf,* but the word *Schicksal* occurs many dozens of times. In Roman Catholic doctrine, *providentia* is an attribute of the omnipotent and omniscient divinity that has preordained events. In this sense, it becomes virtually synonymous with the colloquial use of the German word *Schicksal,* "fate, destiny." These concepts were essential to Hitler's view of himself and his mission in the world: he will succeed because it has been *preordained.* Interestingly, in the ancient Roman religion, the goddess Providentia governed the fates of the emperors, and with them the people of Rome. Hitler always ascribed his survival of over forty assassination attempts to the power of *Providence.* This heightened sense of *Vorsehung* and *Schicksal* related to Hitler personally as a sort of ego cult, but he thought that he was putting this special dispensation in the service of the German Volk, and this alone would be his moral justification.

With respect to Hitler's beliefs in the occult and occult powers, these seem to be intimately bound up with the religion just described. But in connection with the practical application of occult or magical ideas, some of which he may have absorbed from the text of *Magie* by Ernst Schertel and similar sources, the text of *Mein Kampf* bears considerable testimony.

As the following preliminary analysis of the practical occult ideas contained in the text of *Mein Kampf* amply illustrates, Hitler was versed in magical and occult principles in a highly utilitarian way. His information on this was gleaned from the books he read so voraciously, his observations of society, and especially his close analysis of recently successful political revolutions in Russia and Italy.

SOME MAGICAL NOTES ON *MEIN KAMPF*

Many would-be writers on the idea of the Nazis and the occult almost entirely ignore the most powerful grimoire of the movement—Hitler's book titled *Mein Kampf* (My Struggle). If the book is read from a magical, or *operative* perspective, many of the secrets of how Hitler worked his will can be clarified. Certainly, a whole book-length study could be written about the methods implied or stated in Hitler's widely disseminated but little-read book.

The German word for "magic" or "sorcery," *Zauber(ei)*, appears in one form or another around twenty times in the text of *Mein Kampf*.

Mein Kampf was written at a time just after the failed Beer Hall Putsch, when the NSDAP was in tatters and the task at hand was to revive it and recruit capable men in great numbers. The book was written mainly to convince would-be active members of the Party, not the general electorate. For this reason, Hitler constantly tries to demonstrate how clever and astute he is as a leader and manipulator of the masses, and in so doing he frequently gives the present-day reader access to his methods and thought processes.

In this section, the page-number references are to the now standard Ralph Manheim translation and edition. It is curious to note that in the introduction to that edition (1971, xix) by Konrad Heiden, he says of the volume: "The book may well be called a kind of satanic Bible." This would later be echoed by Anton LaVey.

About *Mein Kampf* it can generally be said that it is full of references and allusions to Christian religion and sentiment, sympathetic to a common folksy kind of Christianity—as we have seen, there are those frequent references to the power of Providence (*Vorsehung*), which seems to be connected to Hitler's belief in himself and his sense of a special personal mission in the world. But there are even more uses of the term "fate" (*Schicksal*), which was the focus of many philosophers of a völkisch orientation in the years leading up to the Third Reich. The word *Schicksal* appears more than one hundred times in the German text of *Mein Kampf*. He frequently refers to Bible quotes: "daily bread," "their sword shall become our plow" (p. 3), "camel pass through a needle's eye" (p. 88), and so on. He also frequently refers to Greco-Roman mythology; for example, "goddess of eternal justice" (p. 15), "Goddess of Suffering" (p. 21), "Aphrodite" (p. 87), and "the Pantheon" (p. 91). By contrast, he never mentions any figures of Germanic mythology.

Hitler takes great pains to separate his movement from the neopagan völkisch fashion of the day. He spends several pages (359–64) making disparaging remarks about those who "toss around old Germanic expressions," and the like. In these pages, he refers to those who "fight with spiritual weapons" and who want to reform religion or culture on a völkisch basis and indicates his lack of respect for them. He also frequently uses terms related to occult practitioners in a scornful manner.

Hitler repeatedly refers to what the NSDAP is doing as a "new philosophy of life" or a "new world conception" (p. 378). He wants to emphasize that his path is a modern and scientific path—not a reference to old and ancient things.

His method is "to have that great magnetic attraction which alone the masses always follow under the compelling impact of towering great ideas, the persuasive force of absolute belief in them, coupled with a fanatical courage to fight for them" (p. 377). It is his purpose to "fill people with blind faith in the correctness of [our] doctrine" (p. 459).

Another methodological outline is presented on pages 380–81 when he posits the necessity of having a great idea, coupled with a fighting organization with definite goals—it is only with this approach that a victory is possible.

Not infrequently Hitler refers obliquely to the aim of developing a "higher humanity" (e.g., p. 392), but what this would entail is left to the reader's imagination. But on pages 404–5, for example, he does refer to planned and programmatic state-run efforts to regenerate the original human form made by the Almighty Creator by eliminating the "original sin of racial poisoning" (p. 405).

There are also several fragmentary examples of where Hitler actually explains how he cast his spell on the world.

Chapter 6 of the book is generally devoted to Hitler's methods of communication—especially the spoken word.

Elsewhere I wrote about the conscious use by the Nazis of symbols and signs as modes of effecting meta-communication as a form of magic. This is not merely an interpretation on my part, but rather was an actual intentional act on the part of Hitler. It is quite evident from the text of *Mein Kampf,* where this idea is emphasized. At one point, Hitler reminisces about the generation of the Party symbol.

> Up until then [1920] the movement possessed no party insignia and no party flag. The absence of such symbols not only had momentary disadvantages, but was intolerable for the future. The disadvantages consisted above all in the fact that the party comrades lacked any outward sign of their common bond, while it was unbearable for the future to dispense with a sign which possessed the character of a symbol of the movement and could as such be opposed to the International.
>
> What importance must be attributed to such a symbol from the psychological point of view I had even in my youth more than one occasion to recognize and also emotionally to understand. Then after the War, I experienced a mass demonstration of the Marxists in front of the Royal Palace and the Lustgarten. A sea of red flags, red scarves, and red flowers gave to this demonstration, in which an estimated hundred and twenty thousand persons took part, an aspect that was gigantic from the purely external point of view. I myself could feel and understand how easily the man of the people succumbs to the suggestive magic of a spectacle so grandiose in effect. (p. 492)

Hitler later explains how he designed the flag of the movement. The colors of the flag are the ancient colors of the German standard,*

---

*The symbolic use of the three colors—black, red, and white—in connection with ancient Germanic culture and society is well documented. Ancient evidence for the symbolic colors can be found in, for example, the Old Norse poem called the "Rígsthula," which outlines the mythic origin of the three classes of society and associates them with colors: thralls (black), warriors (red), and kings (white). This is the subject of a special study by Jan de Vries (1942). These are also the three pigments most often used in the painting of runestones in ancient times.

but Hitler explains the colors as "in *red* we see the social idea of the movement, in *white* the nationalistic idea, in the *swastika* the mission of the struggle for the victory of the Aryan man" (pp. 496–97).

Elsewhere Hitler shares his idea that the nighttime rallies he so favored were especially effective because the mind of an individual becomes more receptive and susceptible to suggestion after dark. This nighttime staging of speeches was also essential in the early days when he was trying to change people's minds about National Socialism: "At night . . . they succumb more easily to the dominating force of a stronger will" (p. 475).

Hitler's field of mastery was, as all have recognized, as a speaker before an audience. He himself says, "But the power which has always started the greatest religious and political avalanches in history rolling has from time immemorial been the magic power of the spoken word, and that alone" (pp. 106–7). He also gives insight into how the act of speaking before an audience, friendly or hostile, has a transformative effect on the psyche of the speaker.

> The man who is exposed to grave tribulations, as the first advocate of a new doctrine in his factory or workshop, absolutely needs that strengthening which lies in the conviction of being a member and fighter in a great comprehensive body. And he obtains an impression of this body for the first time in the mass demonstration. When from his little workshop or big factory, in which he feels very small, he steps for the first time into a mass meeting and has thousands and thousands of people of the same opinion around him, when, as a seeker, he is swept away by three or four thousand others into the mighty effect of suggestive intoxication and enthusiasm, when the visible success and agreement of thousands confirm to him the rightness of the new doctrine . . . then he himself has succumbed to the magic influence of what we designate as "mass suggestion." (pp. 478–79)

Here he is apparently teaching his followers how to proceed, but in fact he is giving us insight into his own inner experience. He concludes this section by saying that such a speaker succeeds in becoming a "member [*Glied*] of a community [*Gemeinschaft*]." As such a member he forges a link between himself and the community and between and among all other members of that mass.

Hitler has rightly been characterized as a master of the use of *hate* in his political system. He acknowledged this on many occasions. His use of this was not altogether emotional, however. It was part of his understanding of how to lead and manipulate, if you will, the masses. He shaped information with the following philosophy:

In general the art of all truly great national leaders at all times consists among other things primarily in not dividing the attention of a people, but in concentrating it upon a single foe. The more unified the application of a people's will to fight, the greater will be the magnetic attraction of a movement and the mightier will be the impetus of the thrust. It belongs to the genius of a great leader to make even adversaries far removed from one another seem to belong to a single category, because in weak and uncertain characters the knowledge of having different enemies can only too readily lead to the beginning of doubt in their own right. (p. 118)

Here we see Hitler's propaganda strategy for the equation of the Jews with Bolshevism (an equation already made by Dietrich Eckhart, Hitler's mentor). No matter how many enemies the movement seemed to have, it all led back to one simple foe: the Jews. It is uncertain as to how much Hitler actually believed this. The text of *Mein Kampf* appears to reflect an underlying and well-thought-out strategy for the manipulation of the masses. The Jews were the only convenient cultural element that could play this all-important pivotal role in his formula.

Chapter 6 of *Mein Kampf* is dedicated to "War Propaganda." He states: "The art of propaganda lies in understanding the emotional ideas of the great masses and finding, through a psychologically correct form, the way to the attention and thence to the heart of the broad masses" (p. 180). In his analysis, the messages have to be simple, short, and repetitive: "The receptivity of the great masses is very limited, their intelligence is small, but their power of forgetting is enormous" (p. 180). He admires the English anti-German propaganda of WWI, with its repeated lies about German war atrocities aimed at blaming the Germans as the "sole guilty party for the outbreak of the War." The anti-German propaganda campaign is further analyzed.

> [It was] limited to a few points, devised exclusively for the masses, carried on with indefatigable persistence. Once the basic ideas and methods of execution were recognized as correct, they were applied throughout the whole War without the slightest change. At first the claims of the propaganda were so impudent that people thought it insane; later, it got on people's nerves; and in the end, it was believed. (p. 185)

Through the course of this book we confront the Nazi obsession with the creation of what amount to sacred sites for the movement. That this was a well-considered point of occult thinking on Hitler's part is frequently substantiated. One passage in *Mein Kampf* reads:

> The geo-political significance of a focal center in a movement cannot be overemphasized. Only the presence of such a place, exerting the magic spell of a Mecca or a Rome, can in the long run give the movement a force which is based on inner unity and the recognition of a summit representing this unity. (p. 347)

At one point Hitler gives the reader his formula for "personal success."

> *In all cases where the fulfillment of apparently impossible demands or tasks is involved, the whole attention of a people must be focused and concentrated on this one question, as though life and death actually depended on its solution.* Only in this way will a people be made willing and able to perform great tasks and exertions.
>
> This principle applies also to the individual man in so far as he wants to achieve great goals. He, too, will be able to do this only in

step-like sections, and he, too, will always have to unite his entire energies on the achievement of a definitely delimited task, until this task seems fulfilled and a new section can be marked out. Anyone who does not so divide the road to be conquered into separate stages and does not try to conquer these one by one, systematically with the sharpest concentration of all his forces, will never be able to reach the ultimate goal, but will be left lying somewhere along the road, or perhaps even off it. This gradual working up to a goal is an art, and to conquer the road step by step in this way you must throw in your last once of energy. (pp. 249–50)

Toward the end of the book, Hitler gives his ideas on leadership and the methods of controlling an organization as well as the methodology of propaganda. Clearly, he sees these endeavors as efforts in mastery over a certain set of human laws—psychological laws of human behavior, both individual and within the masses. As opposed to Marxists who constantly harp on various (mostly fictitious) economic laws, Hitler focuses on psychological motivation. His methods of working with the human mind at all times border on the *magical*. He never seems to operate as a current politician, by offering special interest groups or factions within an electorate promises of material gain or security (although such things would come later). Rather, he challenges his would-be followers to engage in a heroic crusade. This method is only intelligible given the main target audience of his motivational efforts: the great body of disaffected WWI veterans and the average German citizens insulted and humiliated by the terms of the Treaty of Versailles.

Presaging Orrin Klapp's theory of the "Hero, Villain, or Fool" (1962), Hitler says in *Mein Kampf*:

It makes no difference whether they laugh at us or revile us, whether they represent us as clowns or criminals; the main thing is that they mention us, that they concern themselves with us again and again, and that we gradually in the eyes of the workers themselves appear to be the only power that anyone reckons with at the moment. (p. 485)

Curiously, the book was dedicated with the date October 16, 1924. I am sure it was no accident that the Nuremberg defendants were hung on that date in 1946.

The Leader Who Did Not Lead

Hitler's title was that of Führer, which simply means "leader," but his style of leadership tended to be ineffective. He extolled and practiced the *Führerprinzip*—the "leader principle." This first placed the personal authority of a leader above the written or customary law of the land. It made the leader responsible for the success of the state, but also had to be applied rigorously in order to work. Its application involved the absolute obedience of those under the leader to follow the orders of their superiors. Hitler did not invent the principle, obviously, and the term was coined by the German-Baltic philosopher Hermann von Keyserling (1880–1946). Keyserling held that history was made by certain gifted individuals who had the courage to use this principle rooted in Darwinian reality. This pyramid of power is built up out of a vast array of smaller such pyramids. Each element is to be obedient to his or her immediate superior—with all authority ultimately resting with the Führer at the top. In practice, however, the chain of command was not entirely disciplined because Hitler delegated so much power and leeway to those immediately below him in the system. He often gave contradictory orders (or suggestions) to various subordinates and then placed them in positions where their duties tended to overlap and be redundant. This was only effective in so far as it kept him as the central focus and ensured disarray in the ranks just below him. In other words, it was a strategy for holding onto power with the state and in the NSDAP but not a winning strategy for Germany or his theoretical cause. Hitler never met with his cabinet after 1938, the other leaders under him were discouraged from meeting, and orders were typically issued orally. Later Hitler also often conveyed orders through his secretary, Reichsleiter Martin Bormann, who controlled access to the Führer. Bormann seems to have used this position more for his own empowerment than the ultimate success of the Third Reich.

The role of the political leader as a psychologist of the masses is an idea that Hitler overtly expresses in *Mein Kampf* (p. 580). Hitler became the exponent of the will of the Volk using the following technique. The forty-two *Gaue,* or administrative districts into which Germany was divided, was a system of regional Party leaders, *Gauleiter.* Hitler regularly received informal reports from these leaders, digested the reports, and knew which way the popular sentiment was leaning—and then, in an apparently miraculous manner, expressed that very "unspoken" popular will. This magic trick was essentially the same one used by Hanussen and other mentalist magicians who had an informant in the audience: the informant conveyed things about audience members to the stage magician in a secret code, then the magician could "read the audience members' minds." (Today politicians attempt to use the same technique using polls, but the population quite often lies to pollsters, so this method frequently just plays tricks on the politicians themselves!)

A fundamental part of National Socialism as practiced in Germany from 1920 forward is the concept of anti-Semitism. The Nazis did not invent anti-Semitism, to be sure, but it was a key part of their ideology on all levels, which is why it was discussed already at some length in chapter 1 of this book. For Hitler and the political strategists of the National Socialist movement, it was essential for the German people to be defined not only in positive terms as to who and what this Volk was but also to have a contrasting negative archetype, a clear and defined "other," with which the Volk could be contrasted. This model was seen as a method for intensifying the building of identity and solidarity among a people who, it was felt, were weak in this regard after the fall of the Second Reich. In many respects, anti-Semitism served an almost mechanical function as a weapon in the magical arsenal of psycho-political manipulation. The Nazis mastered the use of the "other" as a symbolic reality to forge solidarity within a target group. They did not devise this concept, but virtually perfected it, and now this technique is widely practiced in politics today. Ironically, the word *Nazi* has become just such an ideological fulcrum in the manipulative jargon of many progressives today. Such terms are used across the political spectrum to label "enemies" and such enemies run the gamut from the concrete and well-defined to the vague and ephemeral—or even the nonexistent, residing solely within the imaginations of the target group. The way in which the medieval church invented and then persecuted the cult of Satan-worshipping "witches" gave them leeway to prosecute (and confiscate the property of) all sorts of individuals of their choosing, because no evidence could be produced proving that this or that individual was *not* in league with the devil!

Hitler's War

Hitler, in defiance of the terms of the hated Treaty of Versailles, rearmed Germany with state-of-the-art armaments during the rest of the 1930s. Through bold political maneuvers and gamesmanship, he took advantage of the fear and weariness of the Western nations of Britain and France, and capitalized on the instability of the Soviets. Austria was annexed into the German Reich in 1938 and Czechoslovakia was absorbed in March of 1939. A nonaggression pact was concluded with Stalin in August of 1939. On September 1, 1939, he went too far and invaded Poland. A false-flag operation was used by which SS men dressed as Polish soldiers engaged in a skirmish with German troops on the border and this was used as the excuse for the invasion. German intentions on Poland were only to take the western half of the country at first. Nevertheless, Britain declared war on Germany two days later. The Second World War had begun—or, better said, the Great War had been resumed. Stalin invaded Poland from the east sixteen days after Hitler had invaded—which was little noted by the West. Poland had effectively been partitioned by the Nazis and Soviets as part of the Molotov-Ribbentrop Pact.

Initially, over the next few years (1939–1942), Germany had spectacular success on the battlefield. France was defeated in six weeks of Blitzkrieg—a task that could not be completed in four years of trench warfare in 1914 to 1918. Most of Europe was under German control by 1942. Hitler's confidence was swelled by almost ten years of unstoppable triumphs. Then he made the same mistake as Napoleon had before him and invaded Russia, launching Operation Barbarossa on June 22, 1941. The tide turned at Stalingrad at the end of 1942. Two and a half years later the Red Army would be entering Berlin. The Eastern Front was the bloodiest and most horrific war in human history. Most of the German war machine was dedicated to this theater of war. The Germans were eventually overcome by a combination of weather, dwindling resources, overwhelming numbers of Russian men and tanks—and the grim determination of a people motivated to defend their Motherland.

As Germany was being defeated on two fronts, Hitler pursued a policy of "victory or annihilation," in which he seemed unconcerned about the destruction being visited on the German cities and armed forces. On Walpurgisnacht—April 30, 1945—Hitler ended his own life and that of his new bride, Eva Braun, in the *Führerbunker* with the Red Army just yards away. The War in Europe would be over in a few days. For years after the war there were legends about Hitler's escape, but all that belongs to the realm of myth.

DIETRICH ECKHART

Before discussing the many significant followers of Hitler and members of the NSDAP and their esoteric pursuits or roles, we would be amiss if we found no place for Hitler's only real acknowledged mentor, Dietrich Eckhart (1868–1923). He was acknowledged by Hitler as the "spiritual founder" of National Socialism itself.

Fig. 7.3. "Follow Hitler! He will dance, but it is I who have called the tune!" Deathbed utterance ascribed to Eckhart.

Eckhart was born into a Catholic family and studied law and later medicine in Munich. But in 1891 he decided to be a writer. By this time, he was already a heavy drinker and addicted to morphine. He lived with his affluent brother, Wilhelm, after 1907 and in 1913 married a wealthy widow, Rose Marx. His first great success had come in 1913 with his adaptation of Ibsen's *Peer Gynt*. This made him a wealthy man in his own right and provided him with the social contacts he would later use in the development of Hitler and the NSDAP.

Over time, Eckhart developed an ideology of anti-Semitism coupled with a doctrine of a heroic race of supermen. His ideas were rooted in writers such as Otto Weininger, Lanz von Liebenfels, and the German philosophical traditions from Schopenhauer to Nietzsche.

Eckhart's best-known work of art was his adaptation of Ibsen's play *Peer Gynt*.* In it the hero struggles against the trolls, who are clearly identified with the Jews, to become king of the world, only to meet his fall due to his own selfishness and deceit. Later Eckhart would construct the "Hitler Myth." The poet seems to have based his structuring of this propagandistic myth on the archetype of Peer Gynt, and he made this explicit in things he wrote to Hitler himself. He emphasized to Hitler the greatness of his cause and that he will be forgiven for all of the destruction and death he will cause.

Eckhart's feelings of anti-Semitism developed over time. This aspect of his thought became extreme only in the wake of the loss of WWI and the conditions of the Versailles Treaty. At the very end of 1918, he founded a weekly newspaper called *Auf gut Deutsch* (In Plain German). Here he began his publicizing of the anti-Semitic resistance to the events leading to the end of the war. Alfred Rosenberg and Gottfried Feder were coworkers on the newspaper. They resisted the so-called German Revolution, the Weimar Republic, and helped spread the popular *Dolchstosslegende*—the "stab-in-the-back legend," which held that since Germany was not decisively defeated on the field of battle,

---

*The story of Peer Gynt is taken from Norwegian folktales that concern a lonely hunter figure, his identity, and his relationships. The stories relate various adventures of the character. For example, he rescues three dairymaids from trolls and kills a troll called the Bøyg, which assumes the shape of a serpent and plagues travelers.

the defeat was more a matter of an internal governmental conspiracy. Of course, the Jews were seen as being behind it all. It was also around this time that Germany was introduced to *The Protocols of the Elders of Zion,* a book concocted by Tsarist anti-Semites in the Russian intelligence service and first published there several decades earlier.

Hitler's path first crossed that of his "pole star" at a 1919 meeting of the DAP where the younger man gave a speech. Eckhart recognized the raw material present in the younger one. Eckhart was a member of the fledgling Party, which had been formed as a political adjunct to the Thule Society, although he was not a member of the Thule himself.*

Hitler became Eckhart's student: the teacher gave the student books to read, introduced him to important contacts, guided his thoughts, helped him dress and look the part, and educated him in his manners, oratory style, and writing.

Eckhart and Hitler formed a symbiotic relationship along the lines of a father-son bond. Both men thought of themselves as *artists* first and foremost. Both shared an ambivalent feeling about the Jews; neither was a natural anti-Semite but rather saw this approach as a pragmatic political stance. Eckhart considered the Aryan-German and the Jew as forming a historical dyad and that the tension between the two was essential to the existence of each. It is also worth noting that Eckhart and Rosenberg (who had been educated in Russia) were not rabidly anti-Slavic as many other Nazis were; they saw Germany and Russia (minus the Jewish philosophy of Bolshevism) as natural allies.

One of Eckhart's most important moves was the purchase of the *Münchener Beobachter* from Rudolf von Sebottendorf and transforming it into a Party organ for the NSDAP—the *Völkischer Beobachter.* Eckhart also created the Party slogan: *Deutschland Erwache!* (Germany, Awake!).

Eckhart's most significant written work with respect to National Socialist ideology is his little book *Der Boschewismus von Moses bis Lenin* (Bolshevism from Moses to Lenin). It was published after his death in 1924 as an unfinished fragment. In this work, Eckhart shapes a

____

*On the Thule Society, see chapter 4.

form of anti-Semitism that clearly identifies Bolshevism with the Jewish people. He claims that the ideology of the Communists has been virtually created by the Jews and imposed upon the Russians; in fact, Moses could be considered as the first Bolshevik.

The reason that relatively little attention is paid to Eckhart is that he died in 1923 and so was never part of the Third Reich itself. Also, Eckhart belonged to a culture and a generation very different from those upon which National Socialism was based. Hitler learned effective ideas and modes of behavior from Eckhart, his considerable rough edges were smoothed by his mentor's influence, but in the end what the NSDAP was and what it became was something well beyond what Eckhart might have envisioned.

Hitler was quickly educated in many skills, not only by Eckhart himself but also by people Eckhart introduced him to, such as military leaders, his photographer Heinrich Hoffmann, and the socialite Helene Bechstein, who tutored the Führer in matters of etiquette.

Eckhart schooled Hitler in gathering men around himself whom he may not like or might even find repulsive, such as Julius Streicher (publisher of the semi-pornographic paper *Der Stürmer*), because a movement such as National Socialism requires many different kinds of participants. Hitler kept Streicher to the end.

In many ways, Eckhart treated his mentorship of Hitler as a work of art. He fashioned the Hitler Myth mainly in the pages of the *Völkischer Beobachter*. The Hitler Myth consisted of these elements: Hitler is a self-created genius who has emerged from the common folk, he is the leader not just of the Nazi Party but also of Germany itself, he is the awaited messianic savior figure promised by the Kyffhäuser movement.*

---

*The legend of the Kyffhäuser Mountain, recorded by Jacob and Wilhelm Grimm in the collection of German legends titled *Deutsche Sagan* (1994, 55–56), has it that the Holy Roman Emperor Friedrich Barbarossa (reigned 1155–1190) did not die but slumbers in the Kyffhäuser Mountain and will reawaken to return in the hour of Germany's greatest need. A monument to Kaiser Wilhelm I was built on the mountain and dedicated in 1896, thus making the inference that the old emperor had returned and the prophecy was fulfilled in 1871 with the unification of the Second German Empire. Nationalist interests continued to use the legend of the Kyffhäuser Mountain as a rallying point, and after the end of WWI there was renewed interest in this myth.

Already by 1922, Hitler had learned his lessons from Eckhart and was rising in his new role, while Eckhart was physically, mentally, and spiritually on the decline. While hiding out in the Bavarian Alps, Eckhart was visited by Hitler at Berchtesgaden and this became Hitler's hideaway from then on. Hitler relieved Eckhart of his position as editor of the *Völkischer Beobachter* and replaced him with Rosenberg. But Hitler kept his mentor involved as much as possible, and the old man even participated in the Beer Hall Putsch and spent a short while in Landsberg Prison for his role.

Eckhart's lifestyle eventually caught up with him. Shortly after being released from Landsberg Prison, he died of a heart attack at the age of fifty-five and was buried in Berchtesgaden.

ALBERT SPEER

Albert Speer (1904–1981) was the son of an upper-middle class architect and was educated as an architect himself. He joined the NSDAP in 1931, believing, as did so many others, that Hitler was the only way out of Germany's problems. Because Hitler was a frustrated architect himself, he and Speer had a close bond personally. In the 1930s Speer's main role was that of a designer and organizer of the great Nazi rallies and spectacles. He designed the mass movements of people, decorations of whole cities with the emblems of the Party, and even created innovative lighting techniques for spectacular effects. Among these was the famous Cathedral of Light using air raid lights in the night sky. During the war itself, Speer was assigned the task of being the Minister of Armaments and War Production, a role that he fulfilled most efficiently. He kept wartime production high even in the face of relentless Allied bombing of German munitions facilities. Hitler also had Speer working on the total redesign of the city of Berlin into a future world capital called Germania.

After the war, Speer was tried with the rest of the surviving Nazi hierarchy. Speer acknowledged his guilt and was sentenced to twenty years' imprisonment. The Soviets wanted him hanged, because his efficient work as Armaments Minister had cost so many Russian lives. He

Fig. 7.4. The Cathedral of Light at an NSDAP rally in Nuremberg
(German Federal Archive)

served the full twenty years. Released from Spandau Prison in 1966, he became the author of several books about his experiences, most notably *Inside the Third Reich* (1970).

RUDOLF HESS

Rudolf Hess (1894–1987) was born in Alexandria, Egypt, where his father, a prosperous Bavarian merchant, had business interests. He was educated in Germany and the École supérieur de commerce in Neuchâtel, Switzerland. When WWI began, he enlisted and fought in an artillery unit in WWI, distinguished himself, and was wounded several times. Late in the war he began aviation training but did not fly in combat before the end of hostilities. Immediately after the war, he enrolled in the University of Munich. There he studied and became

Fig. 7.5. Rudolf Hess
(German Federal Archive)

friends with Professor Karl Haushofer and his son Albrecht. He joined the NSDAP in the summer of 1920 and became closely associated with its new leader, Adolf Hitler. Hess was by Hitler's side during the Beer Hall Putsch and both were arrested and sentenced to prison. They served partial sentences together in Landsberg Prison, where Hitler began to dictate the book that was to become *Mein Kampf* to Hess, who acted as his secretary.

Hess was instrumental as a loyal aid to Hitler during his rise to power, and after 1933 he became the deputy Führer, Hitler's personal secretary and cabinet minister without specified duties. Hess often signed legislation as Hitler's representative (*Stellvertreter*). Hess was a trusted minister in whom Hitler placed a great deal of trust and confidence. Hess named his only son Wolf Rüdiger in tribute to Hitler, whose code name was "Wolf." (Hess called his son "Buz.")

Hess, like Hitler and so many other Nazi leaders, was a typical product of the Reformbewegung. He was a vegetarian, obsessed with his health and health food, as well as things such as astrology, clairvoyance, and the occult. (It should be noted that among the things Hess brought with him on his later mission to Scotland were twenty-eight different alternative medicines and other homeopathic treatments.) All these things indicate interests that Hess shared with his friend Albrecht Haushofer (son of Karl Haushofer*). It was a friend of Haushofer's, Douglas Douglas-Hamilton, Duke of Hamilton, whom Hess attempted to meet on his ill-fated rogue endeavor to negotiate a peace treaty with England. As we will see, the younger Haushofer would later be involved the July 20 plot to assassinate Hitler. Hess's interest in alternative medicine was also an aspect of his hypochondria and obsessive-compulsive personality.

It is most noteworthy that Hess, unlike all other top- or even mid-level Nazi leaders, did not follow the dictum "Enrich yourself!" He lived modestly on his salary and did not build a cadre of followers or develop a vast bureaucracy around himself. His main motive seems simply to have been to serve Hitler. One of his greatest functions was to introduce Hitler's speeches, which he did with a great deal of conviction and enthusiasm. Before such a speech he might cry out the mantra:

> *Die Partei ist Hitler! Aber Hitler ist Deutschland,*
> *wie Deutschland Hitler ist!*
> *Hitler!*
> *Sieg Heil! (x 3)*

After *that,* the crowd was typically already in a receptive mood to be swayed to the Führer's will.

At the beginning of actual hostilities in September 1939, Martin Bormann, Hess's chief of staff, was named Hitler's secretary, replacing Hess, who was deemed to be second in line to succeed Hitler.

From the time the war began, Hess increasingly found himself on the outside looking in as far as the top-level decision-makers in the Third Reich were concerned. It seems that Hess did not have the hardened and cynical character that Hitler somehow trusted more and more as time went on. This may have played a part in what happened next.

---

*On Karl Haushofer, see chapter 10.

In advance of Hitler's invasion of Poland, he had signed a non-aggression pact with Stalin. Few realize that the Soviets had invaded and seized parts of Poland from the east after the German invasion. In the spring of 1941, however, Hitler was poised to launch Operation Barbarossa—the invasion of the Soviet Union. Hess was well aware of this, of course, and this was the context in which his flight to Scotland took place. After the war, Albert Speer reported that Hess told him that the mission had been inspired by supernatural forces appearing to him in a dream—but Speer is not the most objective source for this sort of information. Apparently without the knowledge of Hitler, Hess took off in his private Messerschmitt Bf 110 on May 10, 1941. Apparently Hess had a strong premonition (!) that Germany could not win a two-front war against superior numbers and larger industrial capacity. Perhaps Hess's lessons from Haushofer had taught him things that Hitler, in his megalomania, could not understand.

Hess flew his plane over Scotland, and as it ran out of fuel he parachuted out of the plane and was captured in the countryside. There are many enigmas and controversies surrounding this mission to Scotland. None of it appears to have had an occult dimension. The alternative interests of Hess were largely private matters. However, this part of his life was well known to Hitler and other leaders—many of whom disapproved of them. At one point Hess ate with Hitler regularly at the Berghof. But because Hess—who, like Hitler, was a vegetarian and did not smoke or drink alcohol—also insisted on bringing and eating his own "biologically dynamic" food, these common meals had to be discontinued because Hitler did not approve of the special alternative diet. One important connection to the occult did arise after his flight and capture. Hitler blamed Hess's action on his strange interests, and the occult became a sort of scapegoat for the whole affair. There ensued what came to be called the Aktion Hess (Operation Hess), which involved the widespread arrests of hundreds of still-practicing astrologers, faith healers, and occultists around the date of June 9. This has all of the appearances of Bormann, Goebbels, and even Himmler (through Heydrich) simply wanting make use of the crisis to tie up some loose ends. The Nazis had raised this technique of not letting a crisis go to waste into a political and propagandistic art form.

As soon as it became apparent that his mission would be a failure, Hess began to slip into bouts of paranoia—he believed the British were trying to poison him—and amnesia (apparently feigned). On several occasions while in custody he attempted suicide.

At the Nuremberg Trials, Hess was brought up on the same charges as the other top NSDAP leaders but was only convicted of two counts and sentenced to life in prison. The Soviets demanded the death penalty but were outvoted. The Russians resisted all attempts to release Hess toward the end of his life. Controversies surrounding Hess's death, his true identity, and his gravesite all added notes of outlandishness to the last chapter of his life. His suicide was just the last in many attempts made over the years, and in this instance he was probably successful due to his advanced age and frailty. DNA tests proved that he was indeed the man he was purported to be and not some "double" whom the Allies substituted for the real Hess. His grave, which bore the inscription *Ich hab's gewagt* ("I dared),"* was destroyed, his body cremated, and the ashes scattered at sea in 2011.

ALFRED ROSENBERG AND *THE MYTHOS OF THE TWENTIETH CENTURY*

Alfred Rosenberg was born and raised in Tallinn (then called Reval; now the capital of Estonia) in the Russian Empire. He finished his education in Moscow on the eve of the revolution in 1917. After WWI he became a refugee and fled to Munich, where he became active in the anti-Bolshevik movement there. He joined the DAP just eight months prior to Hitler joining. After Eckhart, Rosenberg became the editor of the NSDAP newspaper, the *Völkische Beobachter*. In the wake of the Beer Hall Putsch he was appointed leader of the Party until Hitler could return to his post. Hitler later said he put Rosenberg in control because

---

*This was undoubtedly inspired by the personal motto of the knight, poet, and Protestant reformer Ulrich von Hutten (1488–1523).

Fig. 7.6. Alfred Rosenberg in 1939
(German Federal Archive)

he was weak and not a threat to Hitler's own position. Hitler rewarded Rosenberg's loyalty and used him as he could but had little respect for him or his writings, which Hitler called unintelligible—although his assessment was probably not an honest one but merely another dimension of control.

Rosenberg's position in the history of the Party largely hinges on his authorship of the popular book titled *Der Mythus des Zwanzigsten Jahrhunderts* (The Mythos of the Twentieth Century)—an ideological survey of human history from a National Socialist viewpoint. An almost symbolic office in the Party apparatus called the Dienststelle des Beauftragten des Führers für die gesamte geistige und weltanschauliche Schulung und Erziehung der NSDAP (Station of the Deputy to the Führer for General Intellectual and Philosophical Schooling and Education), commonly referred to as simply "Amt Rosenberg" (the Rosenberg Office), was created for him. Within this was the Amt für Volkskunde und Feiergestaltung (Office for Folklore and Ceremonial Design). There was always friction among the various elite leaders of the

NSDAP. For whatever reason, Hitler tolerated the circular firing squad represented by men such as Goebbels, Himmler, Rosenberg, and Göring.

In terms of its tone and content, Rosenberg's *Der Mythus* owes a great deal to *The Foundations of the Nineteenth Century* by H. S. Chamberlain. But Rosenberg was grappling with the difficulties of actually having to design a new religious expression suitable for the envisioned future of the National Socialist state. His book was much criticized by outsiders as well as some within the Party.

In the preface to the third edition of *Der Mythus,* Rosenberg wrote in response to his critics:

It was omitted [by critics] that I rendered Wotanism as a dead religious form (but naturally have respect for the Germanic character which gave birth to Wotan as well as Faust) and, in an unscrupulous manner, the fantasy was concocted that I wished to reintroduce the "pagan cult of Wotan." (Rosenberg 1982, liii–liv)

Rosenberg focused his religious zeal almost entirely on the concept of a new "religion of the blood." This was to be based on what he believed were deeply seated biological patterns in the "Nordic soul." The latter must defend its noble character against the degeneration to which it was subject, both racially and culturally, from the influence of less noble human types. He admitted to the Aryan qualities of other Indo-Germanic peoples (e.g., the Slavs, which made him suspect to some) but placed the Nordic as the highest exemplar of the Aryan race.

He was especially hostile to the beliefs and institutions of Christianity, which was rejected due to its supposed universal nature (equally good for all humans regardless of race or culture), its doctrine of original sin, its belief that sins could be forgiven, and its tenet that the soul was immortal. Rosenberg traced the negative aspects of Christianity to its Jewish roots. He accepted the teachings of Chamberlain, who argued that Jesus was a Nordic non-Jew from the Galilee and resisted Jewish religion. (In this, Rosenberg, or Chamberlain, somewhat followed along the Jewish criticisms of Christianity many centuries earlier [see Smith 1978, 21–67.]).

Curiously, Rosenberg had a soft spot for heretics such as Marcion (ca. 85–ca. 160) and the medieval French Cathars. This latter group was also the obsession of Otto Rahn. Marcion was a Christian heretic who rejected the Old Testament as being incompatible with the teachings of Jesus, whom Marcion saw as a non-Jewish teacher, and the Cathars were a dualistic sect in the same vein as the Manicheans. These interests are odd simply because such sects actually held philosophies even further away from Rosenberg's concepts than orthodox Christianity—as the dualism of Gnosticism rejects in no uncertain terms the world of matter and flesh as *evil*. In essence, for Rosenberg, at least as he expressed it officially, religion was simply to be a theory for advancing and enforcing racial purity in the Nordic folk.

As a sort of private study Rosenberg attempted to work with the ideas of G. I. Gurdjieff. He may have been involved with the mysterious Gurdjieff group active in Bavaria and may have learned of the Gurdjieff work through a Nazi anti-occult propagandist named Gregor Schwartz-Bostunitsch. Schwartz-Bostunitsch wrote an attack on the Anthroposophy of Rudolf Steiner in a book called *Doktor Steiner ein Schwindler wie keiner* (Dr. Steiner, A Swindler Like No Other; 1930). It is likely that Schwartz-Bostunitch studied with Gurdjieff around 1917 (Webb 1980, 186–87).

Gregor Schwartz-Bostunitsch was born in Russia in 1883, and the date and circumstances of his death are unknown, but he was probably killed in 1944. He was a staunch anti-Bolshevik and avid conspiracy theorist, who had studied with Gurdjieff in the Caucasus. Schwartz-Bostunitsch wrote a book on *Freemasonry and the Russian Revolution* in 1922 and left Russia for Germany immediately afterward. He lectured widely on the Jewish-Masonic-Bolshevik conspiracy and the *Protocols of the Elders of Zion*. For a while after 1923 he became an anthroposophist, but rejected the system by 1929 as an expression of the great conspiracy. It was then that he converted to Ariosophy in one form or another and contributed to Georg Lomer's journal called *Asgard,* which had a theosophical and neopagan orientation. In this context, he also worked for Alfred Rosenberg and eventually joined the SS. His lectures won him an honorary professorship from the SS in 1942. He appears to have been one of Himmler's unorthodox pets. But eventually he ran afoul of the SS hierarchy.

As for Rosenberg himself, he outlined the future of religion in Germany to be implemented after the war. These was delineated in his Thirty-Point Plan.*

ROSENBERG'S THIRTY-POINT PLAN FOR THE NATIONAL REICH CHURCH OF GERMANY

1. The National Reich Church of Germany categorically claims the exclusive right and the exclusive power to control all churches within the borders of the Reich; it declares these to be national churches of the German Reich.

2. The German people must not serve the National Church. The National Church is absolutely and exclusively in the service of but one doctrine: race and nation.

3. The field of activity of the National Church will expand to the limits of Germany's territorial and colonial possessions.

4. The National Church does not force any German to seek membership therein. The National Church will do everything within its power to secure the adherence of every German soul. Other churches or similar communities and unions, particularly such as are under international control or management, cannot and shall not be tolerated in Germany.

5. The National Church is determined to exterminate irrevocably and by every means the strange and foreign Christian faiths imported into Germany in the ill-omened year 800.

6. The existing churches may not be architecturally altered, as they represent the property of the German nation, German culture, and to a certain extent the historical development of the nation. As property of the German nation, they are not only to be valued but to be preserved.

---

*The translation presented here was received in the fall of 1941 by President Roosevelt from a source in Europe and was later published in US media outlets in 1942. Only minor adjustments have been made to punctuation.

7. The National Church has no scribes, pastors, chaplains, or priests but National Reich orators are to speak in them.

8. The National Church services are held only in the evening and not in the morning.

9. In the National Church German men and women, German youths and girls, will acknowledge God and His eternal works.

10. The National Church irrevocably strives for complete union with the state. It must obey the state as one of its servants. As such it demands that all landed possessions of all churches and religious denominations be handed over to the state. It forbids that in the future churches should secure ownership of even the smallest piece of German soil or that such ever be given back to them. Not the churches conquer and cultivate land and soil, but exclusively the German nation, the German state.

11. National Church orators may never be those who today emphasize with all tricks and cunning, verbally and in writing, the necessity of maintaining and teaching Christianity in Germany. They not only lie to themselves but also the German nation goaded by their love of the positions they hold and the sweet bread they eat.

12. National Church orators hold office as government officials under civil service rules.

13. The National Church demands immediate cessation of the publishing and dissemination of the Bible in Germany as well as the publication of Sunday papers, pamphlets, publications, and books of a religious nature.

14. The National Church declares that to it, and therefore to the German nation, it has been decided that the Führer's *Mein Kampf* is the greatest of all documents. It is conscious that this book contains not only the greatest, but that it embodies the purest and truest ethics for the present and future life of our nation.

15. The National Church has to take severe measures in order to prevent the Bible and other Christian publications being imported into Germany.

16. The National Church has made it its sacred duty to use all its energy to popularize the coeternal *Mein Kampf* and to let every

German live and complete his life according to this book.

17. The National Church demands that further editions of this book, whatever form they might take, be in content and pagination exactly similar to the present popular edition.

18. The National Church will clear away from its altars all crucifixes, Bibles, and pictures of Saints.

19. On the altars there must be nothing but *Mein Kampf* (to the German nation and therefore to God the most sacred book) and to the left of the altar, a sword.

20. The National Church speakers must during National Church services propound this book to the congregation to the best of their knowledge and ability.

21. The National Church does not acknowledge forgiveness of sins. It represents a standpoint which it will always proclaim that a sin once committed will be ruthlessly punished by the honorable and indestructible laws of nature and punishment will follow during the sinner's lifetime.

22. The National Church repudiates the christening of German children, particularly the christening with water and the Holy Ghost.

23. The parents of a child must only take the German oath before the altar. This oath is worded as follows. The man: "In the name of God I take this Holy oath that I (name), the father of this child, and my wife, are of proven Aryan descent. As a father I agree to bring up this child in the German spirit and as a member of the German race."

The woman: "In the name of God I take this Holy oath that I (name) bore my husband a child, and that my husband is the father of this child and that I its mother, am of proven Aryan descent. As a mother I swear to bring up this child in the German spirit and as a member of the German race." The German diploma can only be issued to newly born children on the strength of the German oath.

24. The National Church abolishes confirmation and religious education as well as the communion, the religious preparation for the communion. The educational institutions are and

remain the family, the schools, the Hitler Youth, and the Union of German Girls.

25. In order that school graduation of our German youth be given as especially solemn character, all National Churches must put themselves at the disposal of German youth. The Hitler Youth Day will be on the Friday before Easter. On this day only the leaders of these organizations may speak.

26. The marriage ceremony of German men and woman will consist of taking an oath of faithfulness and placing the right hand on a sword. There will not be any unworthy kneeling in the National Church ceremonies.

27. The National Church declares the tenth day before Whitsunday to be the national holiday of the German family.

28. The National Church rejects the customary day of prayer and atonement. It demands that this is to be transferred to the holiday commemorating the laying of the foundation of the National Church.

29. The National Church will not tolerate the establishment of any new clerical religious insignia.

30. On the day of its foundation the Christian cross must be removed from all churches, cathedrals, and chapels within the Reich and its colonies, and it must be superseded by the only unconquerable symbol of the *Hakenkreuz* (swastika).

It is doubtful this kind of draconian program would have worked in any practical way. Its tone resembles the sort of policies that were implemented by Stalin with regard to the church in Russia. Although Rosenberg's concepts leaned heavily on those developed by the German Faith movement in general, his concepts lacked any approach to the numinous and appeared to be just what they were: power and control mechanisms for the NSDAP. The occult dimensions of this program are those connected to the exercise of the symbolism of the cult of personality—it is surprising that a picture of Hitler was missing from his altar icons! As extreme as Rosenberg's plans might seem, when put into the context of the historical events set off in his mind from that "ill-omened year 800" when Charlemagne became the Holy Roman Emperor and set out on a bloody military campaign to convert the German tribes to Christianity, kill their leaders, and destroy their sanctuaries, a little church redecoration might actually seem quite restrained. This whole effort by Rosenberg was just another that earned him the nickname given to him by Goebbels—*fast Rosenberg*, meaning "almost Rosenberg," because everything he did was *almost* good enough, but not quite.

In 1933, Rosenberg became head of the Nordische Gesellschaft (Nordic Society), which had originally been founded in 1921 and head-quartered in Lübeck. The intent of this organization was to foster cultural connections between Germany and Scandinavia. Clearly, it was Hitler's plan to incorporate all of Scandinavia into a Greater Germany. Externally, the society appeared to be a cultural group, but it was really a front for National Socialist inroads into Scandinavian culture, economics, foreign policy, and politics. Heinrich Himmler was also a member of its board of directors.

The main activity of the Nordic Society was the prediction of written works: books, pamphlets, and brochures, as well as the journal called *Der Norden* (The North). All of this aimed at a conceptualization of a Baltic and Scandinavian region closely connected to Germany, which drew on the historical and cultural links forged in the age of the Hanseatic League. Its monthly circulation was around seven thousand. Cultural exchange activities of the Nordic Society were especially effective in Sweden, which remained officially neutral during the war, but economically cooperated with the Germans as well. Less effective were the efforts of the society in Norway and Denmark, since the Nazis occupied those countries and thus generated tremendous ill will there.

Rosenberg was tried with other highest ranking members of the NS elite, on a standard battery of charges—namely, "conspiracy to commit crimes against peace (planning, initiating, and waging wars of aggression); war crimes; and crimes against humanity." His crimes were almost entirely theoretical and intellectual. But his rank and position in the NSDAP was simply too high for him to avoid execution.

HEINRICH HIMMLER: REICHSFÜHRER-SS

Heinrich Luitpold Himmler (1900–1945) certainly became the second most powerful individual in the NS regime. Without the existence, obsessions, and interests of this *one* individual, any history of Nazi occultism would have to stand on pretty flimsy evidence. He came from a conservative Catholic family, and his father was a teacher and school administrator. Himmler was studious, and his early interests were in religion, mysticism, sex, and dueling—although he was a poor physical specimen. He was too young to enlist in the army at the outbreak of WWI, so he trained with the local cadet corps and was still in training when the war ended. After the war, he studied agronomy (the science and technology of producing and using plants) at the Technical University in Munich. There he became more deeply involved in mystical, racist, and anti-Semitic thought. He became involved in the world of the Freikorps, the paramilitary organizations mostly made up of war veterans and that were usually dedicated to fighting the Marxists. There he met Ernst Röhm, early leader of the Sturmabteilung (Storm Division;

Fig. 7.7. Himmler in 1929
(Photograph by Heinrich Hoffmann,
courtesy of German Federal Archive)

SA) of the NSDAP. Himmler joined the Party in 1923 and the SS in 1925. Hitler appointed him leader of the SS in 1929, and he grew it over time from 290 men to a force of more than a million.

In the early 1920s Himmler's diary entries indicate his private reading materials consisted of many anti-Semitic works, coupled with ones on Germanic myths and works of occultism. He drifted more and more to the radical Right, began to be active in street demonstrations, and in August 1923 he joined the NSDAP. At first Himmler was under the tutelage of Ernst Röhm. Röhm's SA men, his Storm Troopers, formed a paramilitary division of the Party. After the Beer Hall Putsch, in which he took part, but for which he was not imprisoned, Himmler took the intervening years until Hitler's release from prison as an opportunity to consolidate power within the Party apparatus. His political activity led to the loss of his job as an agronomist, and so he had to move in with his parents in Munich. He organized for the Party under the leadership of Gregor Strasser in Bavaria.

Already by 1923 to 1924, Himmler had abandoned Catholicism and embraced an unorganized set of ideas centered on the concepts of anti-Semitism, Germanic mythology, and the occult. He was, like so many others of his generation, involved to one degree or another with the ideas of the Lebensreform movement.

In 1925 when Hitler was released from prison and the Party was refounded, Himmler joined the Schutzstaffel (Protection Division; SS) with membership number 168. The SS was originally a subgroup of the SA with the specific function of protecting Nazi leaders (especially as Hitler's own bodyguard) and acting as security for their meetings and speeches, which were always subject to attacks by Socialist forces. He rose quickly in the ranks, creating his own internal bureaucracy that served as a power base for him in the Party. In 1927 he proposed his vision of the SS as an elite unit. The Führer promoted him to deputy Reichsführer-SS.

In the late 1920s also, Himmler became personally involved with the Artamanen Gesellschaft (outlined in chapter 4). It was there that he met Walter Darré (see page 288) and Rudolf Höss, who would both also be instrumental in the history of the NSDAP.

Already in early 1934, Hitler and others had become wary of the leader of the three-million-men strong Sturmabteilung, Ernst Röhm, whom they thought might be plotting a coup. Röhm was a populist, socialist, and, by the way, homosexual. Hitler had overlooked the latter fact in the past. Röhm was a wounded WWI veteran of extreme toughness and an exemplary leader of men. He was one of the few men with whom Hitler used the familiar *Du*-form of address. Röhm was angling for more power, and he had the men to mount a revolution within the Reich, so on June 21, 1934, Hitler decided to eliminate this potential threat to his leadership. It would be the SS who carried out this hit between June 30 and July 2, a time that came to be known as the Night of the Long Knives. This operation catapulted Himmler to a more important position and the SS into a more prominent role as a national police force. Eventually the state and local police forces were brought under the control of the SS Sicherheitsdienst (Security Service).

Himmler also developed his own independent army called the Waffen-SS. These were the "knights" in his order, which he thought of as being analogous to the chivalric orders of the Middle Ages. Service in this knighthood was also racially restricted, with Nordic types finding favor who could prove their Aryan lineage back to 1800 or 1750. Himmler recruited men from the Netherlands, Norway, Belgium, Denmark, Sweden, Switzerland, and Finland. There were also units from Spain and Italy. As the war wore on and losses became hard to replace, recruiting was extended to the Balkans and other areas of Eastern Europe. Eventually, the greatest number came from the Balto-Slavic states, with Lithuania contributing fifty thousand men. Early in the war these were among the best troops at the disposal of the Third Reich, but as time went on their performance in combat deteriorated.

Racial Policies—Eugenics and Mass Murder
National Socialist eugenics policies were essentially ramped-up versions of the ideas that had become popular (among physicians) and accepted in America. Contrary to the image of the Nazi eugenics program, it was never that well organized or thought out. Its most formal expression was found within the rules and customs of the SS.

The racial policies that Himmler was mainly in charge of carrying out formed a two-pronged mission. One was the extermination of elements undesirable to the target model of the Nordic/Aryan racial type. The theories pursued in these breeding practices were directly based upon the tenets of stockbreeding as practiced in animal husbandry and farming; both Himmler and Darré were well schooled in these principles. One aspect of this is the so-called culling of undesirable traits in the breed in question, which involves killing examples of that trait. This is the negative side of the practice of eugenics—"good breeding." The second part is the affirmative or positive side, which entails encouraging the birth of desirable examples. As the SS men were theoretically proven to be of the best Aryan stock, it was customary in Nazi culture for Aryan girls to unquestionably accept the sexual advances of SS men as partners. Bearing children out of wedlock to SS men was a virtue in which girls could take pride. Such births could take place in remote locations in the facilities of the Lebensborn (Wellspring of Life) program. (This program was responsible for only about 11,000 births over the course of its existence.)

The use of concentration camps, another feature borrowed from the Soviet system, was begun right at the inception of the Nazi regime. These camps clearly became a method of separating out (and eventually even eliminating) those elements of society that the Nazi theory deemed unfit for reproduction. But the main purpose initially was merely to segregate political opponents from general society.

It would be a mistake to think that the Nazis immediately began exterminating the Jews and other disfavored people. This was a grim task to which they warmed only slowly. At the beginning of the war in 1939 it is recorded that the six camps run by the SS housed "merely" twenty-seven thousand inmates. The lives of these people were held in little regard, and survival in such institutions was difficult. The first camp to be opened was Dachau, which served as a model for all future camps. These camps were a mechanism for the Nazi eugenics program in that any and all types of persons deemed undesirable for the future construction of the NS state were subject—often at the whim of some official—to be interred there. This included not only Jews but also

Romani (Gypsy) people, communists, Jehovah's Witnesses, homosexuals, and criminals of various kinds, even vagrants, and generally anyone who might run afoul of any NS official.

The occult dimension to this policy is that such ideas remained unestablished, regardless of how widespread they might have been in European and American culture among the highly educated class. Their acceptance by the latter was the result of the popular reception of the work of Charles Darwin. The ancients of many cultures knew and practiced in one way or another similar ideas but did so through various cultural customs, such as the right of *prima nocta*–type traditions or the notion of Sarmatian girls having to kill a man in battle before she could wed and bear children in the tribe.

One of the ironies of the whole idea of breeding for Aryan characteristics is that the Poles, for whom the Nazis appear to have had a special enmity, are among the most Aryan populations in the world. This is also very much true of the Balto-Slavs.

It was within the SS itself that Himmler had his maximum level of ability, when he chose to apply it, to select a population for its racial characteristics. Members—and their wives—had to show a pure Aryan (i.e., Christian, non-Jewish) bloodline back to 1750. This date was specified because it was at that time that the Jews began to be emancipated and began to take part in the civic and public life of Central Europe. Therefore, sexual contact between Jews and non-Jews increased, and the mixed offspring became more possible. Himmler saw the SS as a warrior society, but part of how war was to be waged against the ultimate foe of the *Untermenschen,* "subhumans," was through vigorous and numerous offspring produced by the SS men and women of identical racial quality. This concept was at the root of many of the innovated customs and organizational principles of the SS. Some were Romantic inventions, but more were actually based on old Germanic concepts—men bound together in warrior-bands, sworn loyalty to a leader, belief in reincarnation in their descendants. This last point was researched by Sturmbannführer and scholar Karl August Eckhardt. The SS was a military order, an elite conventional fighting unit, but also a *Sippengemeinschaft*—a "clanic community."

In general, it has to be said that the SS did not become the breeding ground for the Aryan superman that Himmler had hoped for. Almost 60 percent of the SS men were still unmarried in 1938, and only about a quarter of them had even fathered a child at all. Himmler's goal had been for every SS man to father at least four children, under whatever circumstances.

Himmler did recognize the necessity of recruiting the best fighting men to his elite Waffen-SS units, and so many were taken from non-German populations as volunteers, with the promise of being incorporated in the German Volk—should they survive. Half of the men of the Waffen-SS were not Germans. (In this the Third Reich followed in the footsteps of the original Roman *Imperium,* which recruited heavily from among the Germanic tribes. There, too, the glory of Roman citizenship could lie at the end of a twenty-year career, contingent again on survival.)

Evidence clearly shows that Himmler, the SS, and the regime in general were aware of the criminal nature of their endeavors to exterminate non-Aryan elements in the areas of Europe they controlled. The best evidence for their attitude is reflected in a series of speeches made by Himmler in 1943 to SS officials. The motive for these speeches seems to be that of making the hearers culpable in the acts so that they will be motivated to defend Germany and themselves from capture at the end of the war. They could not maintain that they "knew nothing." This and other techniques used by the SS are typical of traditions of criminal gangs, then or now. Men engage in antisocial, usually violent behaviors in groups, which bond the participants together psychologically and also make them have a sense of solidarity with their fellow participants. These were called *Sonder-Aktionen* (special operations) in NS jargon.

Germanization

Himmler and the SS were heavily involved in the program to Germanize regions to the east of Germany. This would be the manifestation of the theory of Lebensraum as outlined by the geopolitician Karl Haushofer, and ideally and theoretically this process would take place in a manner inspired by the Artamanen ideology Himmler had absorbed in his early days. The general plan for the East mandated the enslavement, expulsion, or extermination of the current population and their replacement by Germans to be moved from the German homeland into these regions. As a program, it was based more on the biblical narrative of the Hebrew mythology of Exodus than it was on the Great Migrations of the Germanic peoples in ancient times. Few Germans voluntarily participated in the program. The few who did participate were never established on the envisioned farms but instead spent their time in camps or in requisitioned homes in Poland. By 1943 more than half a million Germans had been relocated into Poland. The program also recruited ethnic Germans (*Volksdeutsche*) from among the Polish population. There were vast numbers of people in Poland who were German, but Polish by nationality due to the historically shifting borders of Poland. Himmler developed an elaborate system of ranking this population racially. Some were considered by Himmler to be German who refused to be so classified. These people had their children taken away and made part of the Lebensborn program. Children so removed from their families who were judged to be of high quality were adopted out to German families; those who did not make the grade were sent to a children's concentration camp, where most died. This whole program has its origins in the ideas of Hentschel and Haushofer—but certainly was implemented in ways either of these men would have found abhorrent. In the general plan for the East, Himmler took the Romantic dreams of his youth and made them subject to criminal impulses. So it was with many things that occurred in Nazi Germany.

Himmler's Religion and Mysticism

Himmler appears to have been motivated at every step by some profound—if vague and emerging—sense of heroic and mystical purpose. He was himself not a visionary, thinker, or philosopher in most senses of these words. His skills were those of organization and the implementation of ideas into some sort of action. He had a collection of ideas gleaned from his early readings, but instead of working these out himself, he collected men of greater knowledge, talent, or vision to marshal into various bodies of action. Some of these were military men; others were scholars, mystics, and visionaries.

Fig. 7.8. A *Julleuchter* on the cover of an SS booklet about celebrating "Christmas in Wartime," circa 1943

Of course, Himmler was interested in incorporating ideas of the Germanic warrior-societies (*Männerbünde*) into the ideology, customs, and rituals of the SS. We must hasten to add, however, that these ancient tribal societies and their members would have little recognized the motives and thought patterns of the imperial, nationalist Reichsführer. They would have been loath to give up their liberty for the sake of a distant ruler. What he and Hitler did understand was the archaic power of the *oath*. There is an ancient and powerful magic in the swearing of oaths of loyalty to a war-band leader, and both Hitler and Himmler made use of this magic formula.

Himmler also wanted to promote the cult of ancestor worship among his SS men. One of Himmler's SS men and a participant in the Ahnenerbe, Karl August Eckhardt, wrote a book called *Irdische Unsterblichkeit: Germanischer Glaube an die Wiederverkörperung in der Sippe* (Earthly Immortality: Germanic Belief in Reincarnation in the Clan; 1937). Himmler ordered twenty thousand copies of this book but then cancelled the order.* It does appear that he did buy copies and distributed them to officers in the SS. This book was an entirely scholarly study of the ancient Norse belief in rebirth of the ancestors in their descendants. It was this kind of solid research Himmler wanted to foster and put into *action* in the institutions of the SS.

The SS constituted its own form of religion. There were ceremonies for the stages of life: birth (name-giving), wedding, and funerary rites. Also, there were special SS forms for the celebration of the festivals of the year, especially for the summer and winter solstices. Some of these are outlined in the book *The SS Family* (1998), which is a translation of an SS tract by Fritz Weitzel from 1939.

One object that captured the imagination of people after the war is the SS *Julleuchter* (Yule lantern). These were produced in porcelain and issued to SS men for Yuletide ceremonies. The candle of the old year burns out and the one for the new year is ignited. About this the presentational document reads: "May every SS-man watch the little light go out with a pure heart and light the new light of the year with renewed vigor."

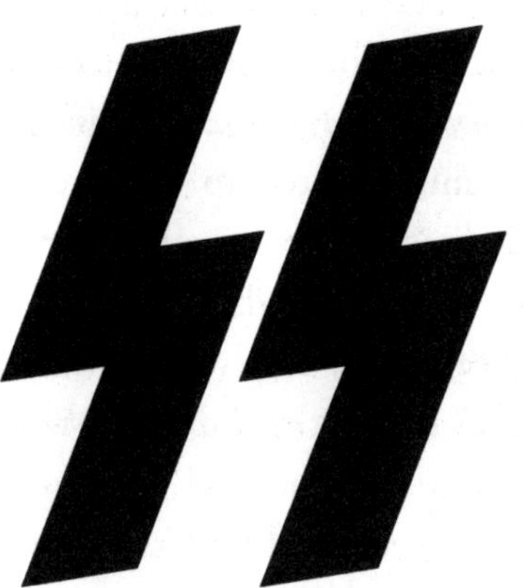

Fig. 7.9. SS Sig runes

---

*Padfield (1990, 192) makes it sound like Himmler was somehow involved in making money for himself through this contract, which is possible. The cancellation of the order may have been due to financial appearances, or it might have been for ideological reasons. The Norse doctrine of rebirth discussed in the book (not a new idea) may have been far too pagan for most National Socialists to support at the time. If so, here we would have yet another example of how Himmler tried to push the pagan agenda, only to have to retract it in short order.

Ultimately, the level of completeness and formality with regard to the neopagan or mystical dimension of the SS was rather sparse. Most of this was made up of Himmler's personal dreams and fantasies (e.g., that he was the reincarnation of Heinrich the Fowler), but with the apparatus of the Ahnenerbe and the other parts of the SS there to aid him, the amount of material and infrastructure to support these ideas was impressive.

Symbolism of SS Regalia and Uniforms

The uniform of the SS (as well as some other NS uniforms) was created by none other than the fashion designer Hugo Boss. This perhaps goes a long way in accounting for the extra sense of style displayed in the appearance of SS units.

SS uniforms were black because they were supposed to represent a *peasant* army. Black was determined to be the emblematic color of the farmer class. This symbolism was practiced by the Artamanen, to which Himmler had belonged. This symbolism is also supported in the folk traditions and can even be seen in the Old Norse poem called the *Rígsþula* (Lay of Rig). The ancient Germanic symbolism of colors shows: white = priesthood, red = warriors, black = farmers. Or as Guido von List would have expressed it the *Lehrstand, Wehrstand,* and *Nährstand* (Teacher Class, Defender Class, and Nourisher Class).

The almost art-deco-style double lightning bolt version of the two ᛋ-runes signifying the SS was drawn by an unemployed artist named Walter Heck in 1929 and was at first used only as a civilian insignia. In 1932 it gained wider use. This was employed on banners and on the collar tabs of uniforms, for example.

SS-Obersturmbannführer Karl Theodor Weigel gave a description in 1929, which was repeated by Fritz Weitzel in his *Die Gestaltung der Feste im Jahres- und Lebenslauf in der SS-Familie* (1939, 41), which explained the *symbolic* meaning of the SS as follows:

> ᛋ Sig-rune means "Victorious sun" and signifies the indwelling strength that assures victory. "The two Sig-runes on the banners of

the ᛋᛋ express the old formula '*sig und sal*,' which is the salvation that lies implicitly in the certainty of the sun's victory."(K. Th. Weigel)

The designation of the ᛋ-rune as meaning "victory" (i.e, the "*Sieg*-rune"), enters runelore with the interpretation of Guido von List (1908) and is in keeping with his methods of linguistic interpretation. The old rune-name for the ᛋ-rune always meant simply "sun." The NS symbolism never completely strayed away from the interpretation of the rune as a solar symbol. (Originally, the symbol of the SS was simply a swastika.)

The meaning of some of the most conspicuous aspects of SS symbolism is often misunderstood. As we have noted, for example, the black uniforms were indicative of the idea that the SS was to be a peasant army (reflective of Himmler's agrarian vision). Another such case is the *Totenkopf*, the "death's head" symbol, which was not originally a sign of intimidation but rather one that is explained below.

The SS Totenkopf Ring

The detailed symbolism of the Death's Head Ring of the SS will be discussed in more detail when we come to examine the activities of Karl Maria Wiligut, who designed it. However, Himmler's own ceremonial and formal customs surrounding this object are clear attempts to instill a sense of the sacred to this talismanic object.

The official explanation of the use of the death's head is that the symbol is a sign of the wearer's own willingness to die for his honor and for the cause of National Socialism in loyalty to the Führer.

When a man received a Death's Head Ring, it was accompanied by a document, signed by Himmler, which read:

I award you the Death's Head Ring of the ᛋᛋ.

A sign of our loyalty to the Führer, our steadfast obedience to our duty, and our solidarity and comradeship.

The Death's Head reminds us that we should be ready at any time to offer our own lives for the good of the collective.

The runes opposite the Death's Head are symbols from our past of the prosperity that we will restore through the philosophy of National Socialism.

The two Sig-runes stand for the name of our Protection Division.

The Swastika and the Hagall-Rune represent our unshakable faith in the ultimate victory of our philosophy.

The ring is wreathed in oak, the leaf of the ancient German tree.

The Death's Head Ring cannot be obtained by purchase, and must never fall into the hands of outsiders.

Upon departure from the ᛋᛋ, or from life, the ring must be returned to the Reichsführer-ᛋᛋ.

Copies and imitations are punishable by law and it is your responsibility to protect same.

Wear the ring with honor!

So, this is the official explanation of the significance of the ring that every recipient was issued. Further details of the symbols as designed by Wiligut are explained below.

Among militaria collectors of these rings a legend grew up around the idea that there was a huge cache of the rings at the Wewelsburg castle at the end of the war. The rings were supposedly to be returned to the castle upon the death of the SS man to whom it had been issued. One story related in Gottlieb's *The SS Totenkopf Ring* (2008, 131–33) has it that at the end of the war there was a box of these rings that was hidden and then lost somewhere on the grounds of the then ruined Wewelsburg. Its whereabouts remains a mystery.

The SS Dagger

Similar to the mystique surrounding the ring was that of the SS dress-dagger. It, too, was presented in a ritualistic manner and played an interesting role in envisioned SS funerary rites. At the burial of an SS-man, his ceremonial dagger was removed from the coffin and replaced with the dagger of another SS-man who had died earlier. This was to represent the "continuity beyond death" of the brotherhood. This feature was taken from research on the ceremonial use of so-called heirloom swords in Germanic antiquity.

The dagger was a symbol of loyalty. The motto inscribed on its blade is *Meine Ehre heißt Treue,* "My Honor is Loyalty." Therefore, the oath connected to the blade was that which was given to Adolf Hitler as the Führer. This was typically carried out in an elaborate ritual at the Feldherrnhalle in Munich on November 9.

A fundamental part of the spiritual life of the ancient Germanic peoples, and especially that sociological phenomenon known as the *Männerbund,* or "warrior-band," was the swearing of oaths of allegiance to the chieftain. It was in ancient times, for example, considered to be a mark of dishonor for a warrior to survive his lord on the battlefield. The Nazis, and especially Himmler, wanted to make use of this feature to strengthen the solidarity and loyalty of SS-men. To this end they swore the following oath, different from that sworn by the ordinary soldier in the Wehrmacht. The swearing of this oath was often done in a midnight ceremony at the Feldherrnhalle in Munich, which had been redesigned as a memorial to the sixteen NSDAP men who had fallen near that location during the Beer Hall Putsch.

This oath read:

Ich schwöre Dir, Adolf Hitler, als Führer und Kanzler des Reiches Treue und Tapferkeit. Ich gelobe Dir und den von Dir bestimmten Vorgesetzten Gehorsam bis zu den Tod, so wahr mir Gott helfe.

Usually translated as:

> I swear to you, Adolf Hitler, as Führer and Chancellor of the German Nation, loyalty and bravery. I vow to you and to my superiors designated by you, obedience to the death. So help me God.

This oath includes reference to the *Führerprinzip* and most powerfully makes it a personal oath to the personhood of Adolf Hitler, who is addressed as a comrade with the grammatically familiar form of address. Notably, and much to the chagrin of those who want to see Nazism as a purely pagan or Satanic organization, it also invokes the conventional Christian God in a traditional form.

Himmler was enthusiastically active in the efforts of the NSDAP to control and/or eliminate the power of the church and Christianity in German culture. But here as elsewhere there was no coherent and unified vision of what the religious doctrine of the future would be exactly. Himmler and his aides, such as Karl Maria Wiligut, established some rituals and customs, but they were weakly and unevenly applied and practiced. The main reasons for this were Himmler's own indecision and lack of vision, and the distractions of the war effort. For Himmler, the main religious exercise on a practical level can be said to be the elimination of subhuman elements in the population (through incarceration in concentration/labor camps or murder). The exercise (on paper) of merciless ruthlessness appears to have been a sort of spiritual discipline for Himmler. He was not, like so many of his recruits, a homicidal sadist. He was known to become ill at the sight of real violence. Rather, he was willing to sign papers and put policies into action that would result in the deaths of hundreds of thousands of people at a time for their biological or ideological status.

Clearly, Himmler's own attitude toward religion was anti-Christian, especially anti-Catholic, and he and his organization were on the search for patterns and rituals that would be the basis for a new, Germanic-based (as he saw it) religion of the future.

The SS had no Christian clerics or chaplains, although the

Wehrmacht or regular army had them. The SS never took direct action against Christian institutions, however, and allowed and respected the rites of Christianity if men wished to participate in them. But the SS itself would not aid in this activity.

Himmler patterned the organizational principles of the SS on the Jesuit Order (Society of Jesus) as a practical and pragmatic decision. The SJ had demonstrated over centuries the core elements of a hierarchy of unconditional obedience in a cultic context. Himmler's pet project was to construct a neo-Germanic order for the future. The Christian model for him was unacceptable because Jesus was a Jew.

Himmler immediately began to institute a liturgy of rituals for the celebration of life events (marriage, child-naming, etc.) in an SS format, such was also done for the cycle of the year so that there were rituals of the SS celebrations of the Yuletide, summer solstice, and so on. Most of these were to be celebrated privately, so actual participation rates among SS-men is unknown.

It is important to realize that Himmler, with all his hostility to the church, was not an atheist. In fact, such a stance was forbidden to the SS-men. They had to acknowledge a god, and atheism was banned on the basis that it was an expression of egoism. This was because atheism placed the individual at the center of that individual's universe and not the Volk, which would violate one of the main tenets of National Socialism: "The Common Good before the Individual Good."

An important and revealing statistic about religion among the Nazis is revealed by the data gathered from SS membership. To be a member, a man had to list his religion: only three were officially possible—Protestant, Catholic, or *gottgläubig*.* In 1938, the following figures appeared: Protestant 54 percent, Catholic 24 percent, and gottgläubig 22 percent. As these were the most hardcore men, the statistics should be sobering to those who want to see the Nazis as a pagan or even Satanic(!) movement. Now, it will also be remembered

---

*The term *gottgläubig* (which literally means "god-believing") referred to those who had left the established churches yet still professed belief in a higher power or divinity.

from elsewhere in this book that among many National Socialists new interpretations of both Protestantism and Catholicism existed below the surface. But those who rejected Christianity in a formal way were few. Among the highest NS leaders it was notably Himmler, along with Hess and Rosenberg (but not Hitler [!]), who took the step to resign from the church formally.

These statistics are important to the larger picture, but with regard to our special interest in this study, we may inquire as to the reality of neopagan ideology within the SS and elsewhere in National Socialist Germany. At the highest level and within a certain inner circle, neopaganism (which ranged from the teachings of Friedrich Hielscher, to J. W. Hauer, to Ernst Bergmann,* and to Rosenberg himself) was clearly in evidence and despite being statistically a small minority, it was a *powerful* minority. But it is very important to keep in mind there were two distinct kinds of neopagans: (1) those who actually have some sort of religious connection with the indigenous gods of the ancient ancestors of the Germanic peoples; and (2) those who may be atheists or merely gottgläubig in the vaguest sense. The latter type of neopagan was far more common among the Nazis than was the former.

HIMMLER AND THE WITCH HUNTS

Himmler invested considerable energy into what might seem to be a surprising avenue of investigation with his obsession concerning the history and meaning of the extensive witchcraft persecutions and prosecutions that occurred, especially in Germany, during the sixteenth and seventeenth centuries. This investigation was not undertaken, as one might have expected, mainly by the Ahnenerbe, but rather by the policing arm of the SS—the Sicherheitsdienst. This was doubtless because the research was conducted through an analysis of court records and municipal archives, along with those of museums and libraries. The data continued to be collected for this research right up until 1944. The

---

*Hauer and Bergmann are treated in detail in chapter 9.

investigation resulted in a vast archive of data comprising thirty-four thousand notecards. These survived the war and are now stored in an archive in Poznan (Poland) known as the *Hexenkartothek* (Witch Card Index). Himmler's interest was, on the one hand, a personal one, but the material was also to be used for specific purposes: anti-clerical, anti-Semitic, and promotion of the idea of neopaganism.

The links between the Nazis and the witchcraft persecutions has been a metaphorically rich one in the history of the interpretation of German history. As might be expected, the Nazis are often cast in the role of the witch hunters with the Jews playing the role of the persecuted scapegoats. We have met with this interpretation, for example, in the work of Leschnitzer (1956). But Himmler and the Nazis had a completely different assessment of the whole situation. They saw the church as persecutors of German women possessing certain kinds of knowledge—especially concerning breeding—which the church was determined to destroy.

The phenomenon of the witch persecutions and trials, and the craze surrounding them, had been extensively studied over the years in Germany since the eighteenth century. These historical events were largely treated as manifestations of the irrational fear among Christian theologians and laymen of nonexistent witch cults. The Romantic era brought new attention to the possibilities of the recorded instances of witchcraft actually being some sort of survival of earlier pagan beliefs.

This idea of the witches of European history as examples of the continuation of the pagan world was explored by several völkisch writers in the late nineteenth and early twentieth centuries. Guido von List, for example, wrote an article titled "Das deutsche Hexenthum" (German Witchdom) in 1900, and in 1911 wrote about witches being the survival of the ancient Germanic feminine priesthood in his book *Der Übergang von Wuotanismus zum Christentum* where witches (Ger. *Hexen*) are seen as a feminine branch of the Armanenschaft and called "wise women," which specifically referred to them as a feminine priesthood and as healers. List (1911, 104) clearly states that the purpose of the witch cult was "to breed a noble race in a conscious way." List was joined by other völkisch writers such as Hentschel and Sebaldt von Werth in these ideas. Even a member of the ONT and follower of Lanz von Liebenfels (a staunch anti-feminist), Theodor Czepl, wrote of Germanic woman in her role as *Zuchtmutter des Gottmenschentums* (breeding-mother of divine humanity)—that is, she possessed the secret knowledge for the breeding of a noble race and was in touch with the "primeval sources of life."

Himmler's project was not the only place where the witch-craze phenomenon was addressed in the NS and völkisch context. Alfred Rosenberg had his own theories about the origin of the Catholic Church from an Etruscan witch cult. Mathilde Ludendorff also expressed herself on the topic, where she contrasts the rational and scientific nature of the Germanic people with the Christian proclivity toward superstition and occultism. She wrote a 1934 essay, "Christliche Grausamkeit an deutsche Frauen" (Christian Cruelty to German Women), in which she addressed some of these issues.

The findings of Himmler's investigations were used against both the church and the Jews. The church, in Himmler's view, was a criminal organization of sadists and homosexuals whose mission it was to destroy the German Volk, and they sought to do so by directly attacking German women of pure blood who possessed traditional knowledge having to do with the reproductive process and selective breeding within the tribe (as matchmakers, for example).

Clearly, the meaning of the term *witch hunt* came to mean the unjust and irrational persecution of a person or persons whom the hunter hated or envied. In almost every instance such a persecution entails the preservation of the hunter's power and/or the deprivation of power from the hunted and its transfer to the benefit of the hunter. This pattern holds true, regardless of whom one sees as the hunter or the hunted, or in whatever epoch of history the witch hunt takes place.

HIMMLER'S "NEOPAGAN" PROJECTS

Himmler's ideas about the witch cult is a specific example of a broader model of understanding about the German past, of course. For the most part, his interest in discovering the lost beliefs and practices of the Germanic past was based on a desire that these might theoretically provide models for cultural reforms to take place in the present, to ensure a better future. The essential problem was that he and his fellow Nazis already had a firm idea about what the secrets of the past were, and already had a Master Plan for the future, regardless of what any research into the past might show. Many Nazis had already formulated a view of the Germanic past that was a mirror of the mind of the rational German of the nineteenth century.

The Wewelsburg

Himmler seems to have first concentrated on the building or remodeling of various cult sites for his planned new religion. These included the Wewelsburg castle, near Paderborn, which was to become the ideological center or school for the SS state within a state. More recently, in post-WWII literature, it has become one of the most overt symbols of Nazi occultism. This location was significant to the SS as one of its *Ordensburgen* (order castles), of which it was undoubtedly the most important. Himmler had plans to make this site the *Mittelpunkt der Welt*—the Center of the World in a future SS-state within the state. This castle, built on the site of an older one, was completed in its present form around 1609. Himmler acquired it for the SS in 1934 and envisioned it as a school for elite SS-men and a ceremonial center inspired by the legends and literature surrounding the Grail mythology, as in Wagner's *Parsifal* and Wolfram von Eschenbach's medieval romance *Parzivâl*.

The north tower of the Wewelsburg was the main ceremonial focus of the structure. It consists of three levels: the crypt or vault (also esoterically called the Walhalla) below, and the SS Generals' Hall and the larger meeting space on the upper levels. None of Himmler's plans were completed, and the spaces were never actually used for the purposes he intended. In the vault a central eternal flame was planned, and it was to be a place for honoring the dead, hence the name "Walhalla." The vault was fitted out with twelve pedestals and wall niches, and at the apex of the dome was a swastika. The space just above the vault is

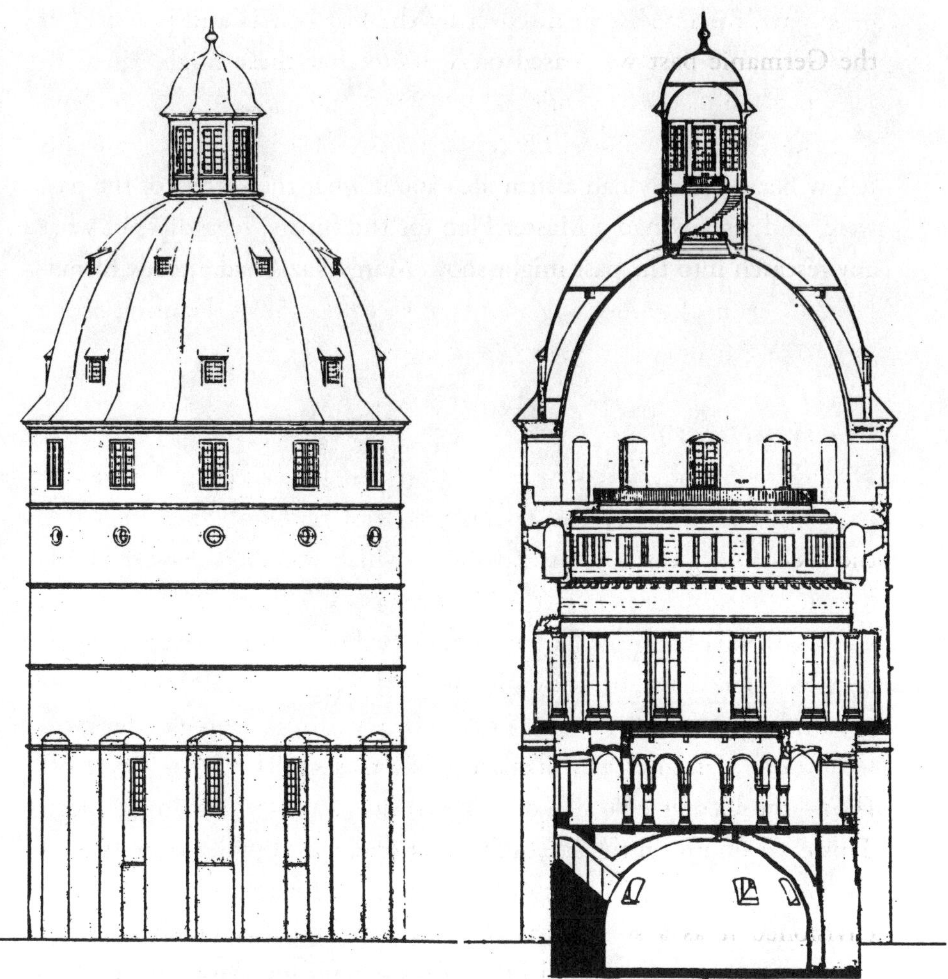

Fig. 7.10. Cross section of the north tower of the Wewelsburg

the SS Generals' Hall, on the floor of which is emblazoned a twelve-armed solar wheel based on an Alemannic brooch design.* It is assumed that this space was to be the ceremonial meeting place of twelve high officials of the SS based on the concept of an Arthurian model of the Knights of the Round Table. (It should be recalled that Arthurian-themed epics were just as important in medieval German literature as

---

*There will be more to be said about this design in chapter 13.

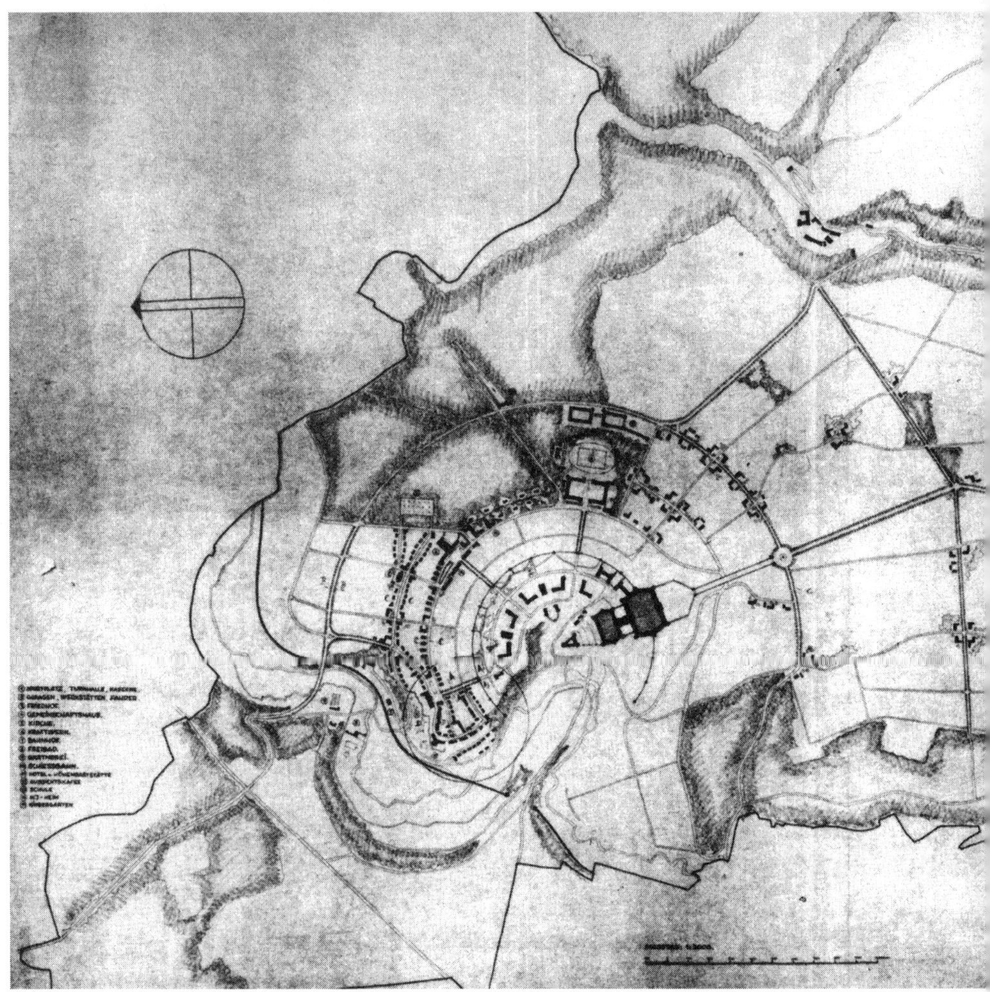

Fig. 7.11. Diagram showing the proposed development of the landscape around the Wewelsburg, emphasizing its role as the Center of the World (Note the spear-like design with the actual castle at its point.)

they were in French or British contexts.) The uppermost levels of the tower remained unfinished.

The Sachsenhain

Another sacred mythic location was that of the Sachsenhain (Saxon Grove) near Verden an der Aller, the supposed place where 4,500 Saxon

Fig. 7.12. A pathway of the Sachsenhain in Verden today
(photo by Gunther Tschuch, courtesy of Wikimedia Commons)

chieftains were beheaded for resisting Christianization in the year 782. The Ahnenerbe, in partnership with the Reichsarbeitsdienst (Reich Work Service), moved 4,500 boulders and arranged them in a vast oblong space (a mile and a quarter long, and eighteen feet across) to commemorate the fallen Saxon chieftains. This project, which was undertaken in 1934, involved both the Amt Rosenberg and Himmler's SS. For construction, local farmers were charged with finding and collecting the boulders, some of which, it is thought, were taken from megalithic monuments in the region.

Into the site was also incorporated a so-called *Thingstätte** (Thingstead) and various historical Germanic-style buildings in the southern

---

*The name is a reference to ancient Germanic assembly sites.

part of the complex. The grove was consecrated on Midsummer 1935 with Himmler and Darré in attendance. Ironically, the site was turned over to the Evangelical Lutheran Church of Lower Saxony after the war.

The Externsteine

For a number of years, as we have already seen, the site known as the Externsteine had been a place of great interest to völkisch enthusiasts. It had been singled out as the sacred site that the tribes of Arminius had defended in the Battle of the Teutoburger Wald in 9 CE. It was supposedly a place of sacrifice and cult in ancient Germanic times and the site of the *Irminsûl*—the sacred *axis mundi*—of the Saxons, which the Franks destroyed as part of the Christianization process. It had also been identified by writers in the 1700s as the cult site containing the tower of the seeress whom Tacitus named Veleda. The Nazis set about restoring the site to its original configuration under the guidance of the Ahnenerbe and lay experts such as Wilhelm Teudt (1860–1942) and the aforementioned Wolfram Sievers. The site was also of official interest to the Amt Rosenberg. Teudt had been researching and writing about the stones since the 1920s and had been active in various völkisch groups, finally becoming a member of the NSDAP in 1933, where he lobbied for the development of the Externsteine into a holy site of the new regime. So a special organization, the Externsteine-Stiftung (Externsteine Foundation), was organized under the auspices of the SS with Himmler as the chairman and Wolfram Sievers serving as the director from 1933. Excavations were undertaken to attempt to prove that this was an old Germanic cult site. The records of these excavations are inconclusive.*

Below is a sketch of the Ahnenerbe plans to restore the Externsteine to the way they might have appeared in ancient Germanic times during the pagan age. There is no hard evidence for such a reconstruction.

---

*Appendix E of my 2018 edition of *Rune Might* contains some interesting details on the esoteric history of the Externsteine.

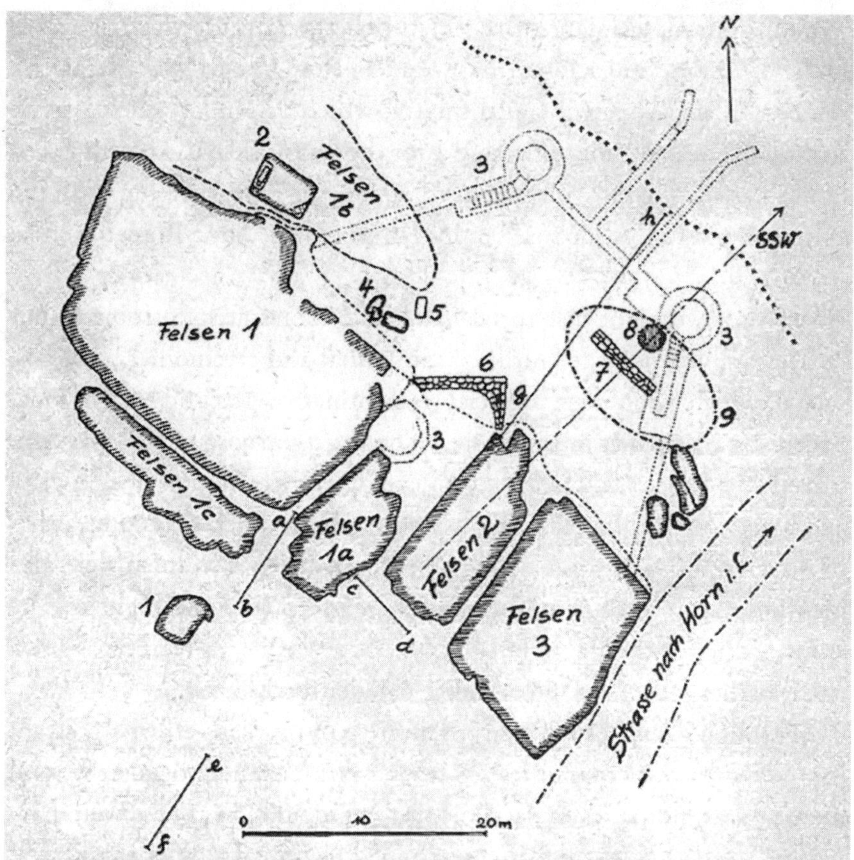

Abb. 2. Lageplan der Felsen 1—3 der Externsteine mit dem Grabungsgelände. a—b, c—d, e—f, g—h Querschnitte durch die Erdschichten. 1 bearbeiteter Sandsteinblock. 2 Sargstein. 3 „Jagdhaus" und Turm von 1660. 4 Steintisch. 5 Baumsarg. 6 Trockenmauer. 7 Trockenmauer. 8 Schacht. 9 mit weißen Sand bestreutes Oval um die Trockenmauer (7) und den Schacht (8). —— — Grenze des zerstörten Felsens 1b. ···· Grenze des sichtbaren festen Sandsteins. ++++ Grenze des Sandsteins unter Oberfläche. ➤ SSW Richtung zum Aufgangspunkt der Sonne am Sommersonnenwendtag (nach R. M ü l l e r).

Fig. 7.13. The Externsteine as envisioned by the Ahnenerbe

Karl Theodor Weigel led regular tours of the Externsteine for visiting SS dignitaries. After Weigel's release from postwar imprisonment, he worked near his beloved Externsteine at the regional newspaper *Lippische Landeszeitung* as a freelance writer.

One other cult site Himmler designated was a reflection of a somewhat private obsession of his: the belief that he was the reincarnation/descendant of the Heinrich the Fowler, who reigned as Duke of Saxony and King of East Francia from 912 to 936. Heinrich's tomb is in the Abbey of Quedlinburg, which Himmler ordered to be slightly remodeled and confiscated it for the SS as a shrine. This historical figure was admired by völkisch historians as the first true king of all the Germans and for his supposed refusal to be crowned by a Roman bishop.

These sites were not just to be inanimate monuments or objects but rather were intended to fulfill certain ritual and ceremonial purposes, each of which would have a special transformative effect on the National Socialist participants in these rites. The main purpose of the rites continued to be the encouragement of a sense and conviction of solidarity and belonging to a sacred militant and fraternal order. Of course, other sites sacred to Nazism, such as the Feldherrnhalle in Munich were also incorporated into SS ritual. It was there, deep into the night on the anniversaries of the Beer Hall Putsch, that Waffen-SS recruits swore a ritual oath of allegiance before Hitler under torchlight.

From an occult or magical perspective, Himmler's efforts to establish cult sites and ceremonies for performance at these sites go beyond mere propaganda or even psychological manipulation. These were neo-mythic rituals and sacred spaces designed to provide life-changing and transformative experiences for individuals who participated in them, and to bond the participants into a body of (usually) men whose bond would be lifelong and even extend beyond death. That was Himmler's intention, but how thoroughly he succeeded remains a mystery. After the war, SS-men (not unlike other veterans) did continue to meet regularly for fellowship, despite the intense efforts at denazification.

Later sensationalistic mythologizers of the "occult Reich" take Himmler's dreams, plans, and infrastructures not for the tentative experiments they actually were, but rather as a thoroughly established and widely practiced ideology and tradition.

In his 2015 history of the SS, Bastian Hein astutely cites two major reasons as to why Himmler's experiments in neopaganism generally failed: (1) Himmler himself was continually vacillating and in doubt about his own religious life or beliefs, and so presented no strong and unified message to his men; and (2) Himmler and Rosenberg were undermined and not supported from above, as the Führer publically and privately ridiculed the effort and often intervened on the behalf of traditional church interests for larger political reasons.

An interesting trait of Himmler, and one not discussed previously, to my knowledge, is his soft spot for the outcasts and outsiders he sponsored in the SS. Three prominent examples come to mind: Karl Maria Wiligut, Otto Rahn, and Herman Wirth. In each case, he gave the man a position in the SS, only later to bend to pressure to demote or expel him, but in all instances he continued to support them through back channels as best he could.

THE FALL OF HIMMLER AND THE REICH

In the final analysis, it can be seen that Himmler developed a whole parallel Reich over his years of service to his Führer. Himmler had his own parallel economy, controlled the national police force (Sicherheitsdienst, Gestapo, etc.), a parallel army of his own (the Waffen-SS), a scientific community (Ahnenerbe), and was constantly working on the development of a new Germanic religion or system of symbolic customs and culture. It really must be said that in the effort to create a new religion he met with the greatest failures. This is probably due to his own lack of personal vision, whereas his abilities in bureaucratic organization remained exemplary.

In the final stages of the war, as the Red Army was advancing on Berlin, Himmler was put in charge of various military operations—operations for which his only qualification was his apparent loyalty to Hitler, and reliability and sincerity as far as his effort was concerned.

But behind the scenes Himmler was preparing for the inevitable defeat of the Reich in the early part of 1945. He began to negotiate with Swedish representatives for the release of prisoners from the concentration camps. Everything came to a head on Hitler's birthday, April 20, 1945, when the Führer announced his intention to remain in Berlin to the bitter end. Himmler's peace negotiations with the West intensified—and he harbored vain beliefs that the West would unite with the Germans to fight the Bolsheviks! (A dream apparently shared by George Patton.)

When Hitler learned of what he interpreted as the great betrayal by the formerly "loyal Heinrich," he became enraged and dismissed Himmler from all his posts. Himmler tried to continue negotiations with the West but was rebuffed. After Hitler's own suicide (April 30) and the unconditional surrender of Germany (May 8), Himmler went underground under an assumed identity and wandered the countryside with no real direction. He had not even attempted to arrange an escape plan. Eventually, he was stopped at a checkpoint and brought to an interrogation camp near Lüneburg.

Upon interrogation, Himmler's identity was soon discovered, after which he bit down on a potassium cyanide capsule hidden in his mouth, and he was dead within fifteen minutes. He was buried in an unmarked grave.

THE AHNENERBE

The organization and facilitation of this corporation was Himmler's greatest contribution to the symbolic and scientific underpinnings of the Third Reich. It has erroneously been called an "occult bureau." The official designation of this vast bureaucratic office was originally the Studiengesellschaft für Geistesurgeschichte "Deutsches Ahnenerbe" (Society for the Study of Intellectual Prehistory "German Ancestral Heritage"). It was founded in 1935, and its main purpose was to investigate many of Himmler's private obsessions. It was a sort of independent think-tank segment of operations within the SS. The scientific scope of the Ahnenerbe was a wide net covering all of what we call the humanities (including history, folklore, religious studies, symbology, musicology, etc.), as well as racial and ecological studies of a more scientific nature. The history and enormous scope of this organization is substantially outlined in Michael Kater's 1974 book. In general, it appears that Himmler's vision was a broad one that included many mysterious areas of interest—and ones that also fascinated lay-investigators, who possessed only the most dubious qualifications. Himmler recruited these, yet planned to replace them once

Fig. 7.14. Ahnenerbe emblem

qualified academics could be developed to investigate these areas more scientifically and reliably. On the other hand, Germany was full of men with impeccable qualifications in many fields of study whom Himmler marshaled to his purposes.

One of the most active areas of Ahnenerbe research was that of archaeology, a subject we have already noted in chapter 5 and elsewhere in this chapter. This was an area that employed many trained academics and ones who developed new techniques making the study of archeology more into a true science, rather than mere treasure hunting or grave robbing. Many of the improvements stemmed, no doubt, from the attitude of the researchers toward their objects. Instead of having little sympathy for the people whose bodies or objects they were excavating, there was a high degree of reverence for, and identification with, the ancients being investigated.

A simplified version of the organizational structure of the Ahnenerbe appears as appendix A in this book.

The Dark Side of the Ahnenerbe

When most people think of the Ahnenerbe today, they perhaps think of the occult (based on the postwar sensationalist literature), or of investigations into things belonging to Germanic antiquity (Viking archaeological sites, runes, and so on), or of bizarre expeditions to Central Asia to seek the original Aryan homeland. The very name of the organization seems to speak to these sorts of pursuits. But there is a darker, criminal edge to the organization that is often glossed over.

Under the heading of "Purposed Research for the Military" in the division of the Ahnenerbe dedicated to the natural sciences, the organization undertook several medical-type experiments carried out on inmates of concentration camps. These were done in the attempt to determine under what conditions (atmospheric pressures, extreme temperatures, and so on) a person might die or be injured. Subjects of these experiments were doubtless chosen as a form of punishment or extermination. Not to draw a moral equivalency, but similar things are known to have been done in American prisons, carried out on African American prisoners before the middle of the twentieth century.

Because the Ahnenerbe was so heavily involved in the world of higher education, it was also a driving force behind the elimination of Jews from academic positions, replacing them with men of Aryan heritage. This constituted a sort of academic ethnic cleansing. Again, such policies are not unique to the Germans in the Third Reich. Ethnic criteria were known to be applied to the application process in universities in the East Bloc countries after the war, such as the exclusion of ethnic Germans in favor of "pure" Hungarians, Czechs, and so on. Again, such principles are not unknown in the USA. Examples of this run from earlier anti-Jewish quotas in Ivy League schools to the application of ethnically based "affirmative action programs."

This whole topic of the "Nazification" of academic departments in German universities after 1933 has become a cottage industry among Germanists and other academic historians.* The politicization

---

*For example, two extensive studies done on the Nazification of folklore are Dow and Lixfeld (1994) and Lixfeld (1994). Mees (2008) takes a wider view, as does Pringle (2008). Many of these studies, however, exhibit a philosophical and methological weakness in the assumption that there is something unique about the way academic studies were politicized by the Nazis, whereas these are really just case studies of how any powerful sectarian influences from outside the academy can quickly corrupt the fields of science or intellectual inquiry.

of academia through the power of the state is nothing new in Europe, regardless of the type of regime in question. It is often the controlling political party that determines the selection of professors and their continued employment. In the West today we have witnessed a politization of academia "from below"—which began in earnest around 1968.

The organizational chart of the Ahnenerbe presented as appendix A is a slightly simplified version of the description of the organization from 1944/1945. A survey of the topics singled out for investigation shows that these reflect the private obsessions of Himmler as well as a few practical military concerns. Such an overview of the fields of investigation should also quickly illustrate that this was no "occult bureau," as only a tiny part of it was concerned with the investigation of overtly magical or occult topics. Most of it was a sort of private university for prehistoric studies with a bureaucratic cover for certain military experiments (which got Sievers into trouble) and a budget for the private renovations of Himmler's pet architectural projects.

HERMAN WIRTH

Herman Wirth (1885–1981) was born in Holland and studied both in his native country and in Germany. He received a Ph.D. at the University of Leipzig in Flemish/Dutch philology in 1910 and became a professor in that field at the University of Bern in Switzerland. At the outbreak of WWI, he joined the German army but was discharged due to his support for Flemish nationalists in German-occupied Belgium. This activity did not harm his reputation among the Germans, however, as he was appointed professor by the kaiser. He was an honorary professor at Marburg but taught in the Netherlands in the 1920s. Wirth also formed a Flemish nationalist group after WWI. He joined the NSDAP in 1925, but in 1927 he relinquished membership through nonpayment of his dues. In 1928 he published one of his major books, *Der Aufgang der Menschheit* (The Ascent of Mankind), which brought him considerable notoriety. Wirth was supported both professionally and financially by sponsors within the NSDAP.

After the National Socialists came to power in Germany, Wirth rejoined the Party in 1934 with his old membership number sponsored by Hitler himself. He was thereupon immediately inducted in the SS. As we have seen elsewhere, the first few years of the NS regime were marked by ideological struggles among various factions: Christian, German-Christian, neopagan, atheist, nondenominational theistic (gottgläubig), those advocating warrior-society models, and, in Wirth's case, a radical departure into the realm of matriarchy and pacifism. Wirth was always at a disadvantage in this conflict because his ideas were at odds with the attitudes of the average rank-and-file member of the NSDAP and he was not a native German but rather Dutch. In this story, it is revealed just how *German* the NS ideology was, despite its (largely propagandistic) appeal to Pan-Germanism and ideas of Grossdeutschland (a Greater Germany) to include Scandinavia and Holland.

Between 1931 and 1936 Wirth published volumes of what was his masterpiece, the monumental work called *Die heilige Urschrift der Menschheit* (The Holy Primeval Script of Mankind). During the time when this work was being published, he tried to set up an institute called Deutsches Ahnenerbe, but he was unsuccessful. However, he was bought into contact with Heinrich Himmler and Walter Darré, and Wirth was among the founders of the Ahnenerbe in 1935 and headed that organization until 1937. Himmler reorganized the corporation in that year and made Wirth the "Honorary President." By 1939, however, Wirth was completely shut out of the Ahnenerbe due to his unorthodox views, which most especially included a belief in primeval matriarchy and a sympathy for pacifism. Another example of this was his interpretation of the *Oera Linda Book,* which is a forged document that purports to be the story of the ancient Goddess-worshipping Frisians as the founders of world civilizations. Interestingly, Himmler himself did not apparently find Wirth's ideas so abhorrent, as he continued to finance Wirth's endeavors and kept him in the ranks of the SS.

As Wirth saw it, civilization was a curse on mankind. He was a devotee of the Reform lifestyle—a vegetarian and proponent of a direct relationship to Mother Earth. He considered the origin of human culture to have been on the island of Atlantis, which had been located in the North Atlantic, inhabited by pure Aryans. With the demise of the island, the inhabitants not only influenced the populations of Europe but North America as well. Wirth held that the Atlanteans were worshippers of a single god, but that both Judaism and Christianity were corruptions of the true religion. Since the Germanic peoples were the most direct descendants of the Atlanteans, the study of Germanic antiquities and mythology was the best way to rediscover the old Atlantean culture. Wirth's ideology influenced the Expressionist artist Bernard Hoetger's design of the 1931 Haus Atlantis building in Bremen—a design that was criticized by Hitler and other Nazis. It was heavily damaged by fire and bombs and was rebuilt over the years with most of its unique features being lost. It is now a hotel owned by the Radison corporation.

Wirth's highly subjective methodology liberated his conclusions from the constraints of the rules of philology and archaeology. Wirth's influence was supportive of a wider interpretation of the Germanic runes as being "hieroglyphic" in nature. The concept of *Begriffsrunen*—the use of individual runes to stand for the meaning of their names or for related formulaic words—was intensely studied by more scientific runologists at the same time (most notably Helmut Arntz and Wolfgang Krause).

After the conclusion of World War II, Wirth was arrested and "interviewed" for two years. When he was released he went to Sweden, where he remained until returning to Marburg in 1954. He lived the remainder of life as a private scholar.

Wirth continued to express support for the philosophical principles of National Socialism until his death in 1981. The 1970s revival of interest in Germanic antiquities among a new generation of neopagans, very unlike those who were active during the NS regime, found many of Wirth's concepts appealing. He even made contact with North American Indian groups at that time.

KARL MARIA WILIGUT

By the time Karl Maria Wiligut (1866–1946) became involved with the National Socialists, he had already lived a long life. The best comprehensive treatment of Wiligut and his ideas in English is contained in *The Secret King* by Flowers and Moynihan (2007), which also contains translations of most of Wiligut's major esoteric written works. I will direct the reader to that study for more details. He is also treated at some length by Goodrick-Clarke (1985, 177–91).

Wiligut was a military man from an early age. In 1883 he was drafted into the army of the Austrian-Hungarian Empire and by 1888 he had been promoted to lieutenant. His career in the esoteric began to be formalized when he joined a Schlaraffia Lodge, a German-speaking group with connections to Freemasonry but dedicated to "friendship, art, and humor." This is really a satirical organization, but one that acted as a gathering place for German-speaking nationalists in an empire where they had become a minority. Wiligut's serious delving in the esoteric is first evidence by his epic poem *Seyfrieds Runen* (1903) and then the "Neun Gebote Gôts" (Nine Commandments of Gôt; 1908). Although Wiligut would later try to take pains to distance himself from the influence of Guido von List, claiming that List's version of Armanism and the religion of Wuotan were heretical offshoots of the true Irminist faith, Wiligut's personal mythology and methods of working actually show great influence from List.

Wiligut retired from the military after the First World War in 1919. He then devoted himself to his esoteric studies. He claimed to be the heir to a secret kingship and revealed a new religion called Irminism. All of this annoyed his wife of thirteen years, who successfully had him involuntarily committed to a mental institution in 1924, where he remained until 1927. With regard to Wiligut's actual mental health, it seems that he was the victim of an unhappy domestic situation. (His eccentricities are no more extreme than those of every second Wiccan high priestess in the 1970s who claimed to be the heirs of a family tradition going back to the Stone Age, with secret books of forbidden knowledge hidden in their basements.)

After his release from the asylum, Wiligut went to Germany and settled in Munich. There he had contacts with members of various völkisch groups, which included the ONT of Liebenfels, the Edda Society, and the Nordic Society. One member of the Edda Society, Richard Anders, was an SS-man and helped introduce Wiligut to Himmler, who met each other at a conference of the Nordic Society in 1933. After that Wiligut, who had assumed the pseudonym Weisthor, was inducted into the SS and rose in rank. In 1935, he was transferred to Berlin to be in Himmler's personal staff. "Weisthor" became Himmler's adviser on symbolism and ritual, contributed to liturgical aspects of the developing religion within the SS, and designed the SS Totenkopf ring (see the section below on runology). The old "rune master" also was active in the redesign of the Wewelsburg castle and undertook expeditions to study sites he thought were centers of the Irminist religion in the Black Forest region.

Toward the end of 1938, Himmler's second in command in the SS, Karl Wolff, visited Wiligut's wife, who got another chance to betray him and revealed his past in the mental institution. Wolff used this information to force Wiligut into retirement from the SS. He retired just prior to the beginning of hostilities in World War II and spent the war years moving around and living on a meager pension. He died after the end of the war in 1946.

RUNIC STUDIES

Besides the esoteric work by Wiligut, there was a good deal of other runic investigations undertaken within the program of the Ahnenerbe. Much of it can be characterized as amateur efforts by lay enthusiasts, but even that can be seen to be a far cry better than the kind of runic nonsense generated in the Anglo-American world beginning in the early 1980s!

Among the Ahnenerbe associates engaged with research into runes and symbols was SS-Hauptsturmbannführer Karl Theodor Weigel. He lacked any formal academic training but was a dedicated lay folklorist who collected images of medieval folk art supposedly connected with the ancient Germanic past. The collection of his images (drawings and photographs) is still housed at the University of Göttingen as the Weigel-Archiv im Seminar für Volkskunde (Weigel-Archive in the Department for Folklore). Weigel wrote books such as *Runen und Sinnbilder* (Runes and Symbols; 1937). He also headed the Lehr- und Forschungsstätte für Runen- und Sinnbildkunde (Instructional and Research Institute for Runology and Symbology) but was later subordinate to the great academic runologist in Göttingen, Wolfgang Krause.

Some of the older spirit of the Listian enthusiasm for the supposed runic aspects of heraldry could be found in the work of Karl Konrad Ruppel for the Ahnenerbe, such as *Die Hausmarke, das Symbol der germanischen Sippe* (The "House-Mark"—The Symbol of the Germanic Clan; 1939). Franz Altheim, who was primarily a Classicist, wrote *Vom Ursprung der Runen* (On the Origin of the Runes; 1939), a work that bolstered the North Etruscan theory of the origin of the runes, together with his partner Erika Trautmann for the Ahnenerbe.

More details on runic studies are addressed in the section "Nazi Runology" in chapter 8.

WALTHER DARRÉ

Richard Walther Darré (a.k.a. Ricardo Walther Óscar Darré; 1895–1953) was born in Buenos Aires, Argentina, to a German mother and Swedish father, who was a partner in a German import/export company. Darré became fluent in four languages: German, Spanish, English, and French, and he was sent to Germany to be educated when he was nine. He was an exchange student in England in 1911. Back in Germany he broke off his education in 1914 to join the army. He saw action and was lightly wounded several times. After WWI, he continued his studies and worked on various farms. In 1922, he began university studies at Halle in agriculture, specializing in animal breeding. He received a Ph.D. from that university in 1929.

It was also during the late 1920s that Darré became formally involved with the Artamanen-Gesellschaft (see chapter 4), where he met Heinrich Himmler and other future Nazis. This was a back-to-

Fig. 7.15. Darré speaking at a Reichsnährstand assembly in Goslar, 1937
(German Federal Archive)

the-land youth movement with the idea of colonizing the regions east of Germany to expand the necessary living space (*Lebensraum*) for the German Volk.

It was in this context of his formal studies in agricultural sciences, Germanic history and lore, and the ideas of the Life-Reform movement that Darré developed the idea of *Blut und Boden,* "blood and soil," as a philosophy. These two concepts—that of race, inherited racial characteristics, and so on, which constitutes the "blood" of the Volk, and that of the land or soil on or in which that Volk community is at home—form a harmonious and natural essence. It is this unity of Volk and land or territory that defines the nation. As a theory, this entailed a long-term relationship between the Volk and the land it both occupies and *cultivates* productively.

The Volk can be improved and developed through the same practices and principles by which animals are bred for beauty, utility, and strength. The very words *Blut und Boden* became a powerful mantra in and of themselves. They harbored a coherent philosophy and yet could be understood quite simply, directly, and on an unconscious level.

For the most part, Darré has remained in the historical shadows of more sinister images—those of Hitler, Himmler, and even Rosenberg. But Anna Bramwell's 1985 study *Blood and Soil* brought Darré to renewed prominence in a surprising and compelling context.

Darré's ideas will often not fail to remind the reader of thoughts that might have flowed from the pen of Thomas Jefferson, as noted by Bramwell (1985, 179), who invokes the idea of a "Jeffersonian republic of small farmers."

Darré's writing carreer also began in the late 1920s with works such as *Das Bauerntum als Lebensquell der nordischen Rasse* (Peasantry as the Life-Source of the Nordic Race; 1927) and *Neuadel aus Blut und Boden* (A New Nobility from Blood and Soil; 1930). It can be seen that the ideology of Hentschel and the Artamanen shines through much of his thinking. He specifically attacked Christianity for promoting the idea of the equality of men before God, which weakened the concept of a hierarchical nobility. Many of Darré's ideas could be criticized from a National Socialist perspective as well, as he seems to imply the values of the conservative monarchists, but he cleverly couched his concepts in notions of the nobility of the common (Aryan) man or the peasantry.

After a personal meeting with Hitler in 1930, Darré joined the NSDAP and the SS. It was his special mission to help recruit farmers to the cause of National Socialism. Darré had three main missions in his efforts to organize for the Party: (1) to exploit unrest among the farmers as a weapon against the urbanized establishment; (2) to convince the peasants to support National Socialism; and (3) to gain a constituency of people who could later be used as settlers to displace the Slavs in a future conquest of the East. Once the National Socialists gained control of the government, Darré was the leading blood-and-soil ideologist and served as Reich Minister of Food and Agriculture from 1933 to 1942. He was relieved of his post as the war effort began to go badly and his programs were not producing large enough quantities of food.

Darré was representative of an agrarian-idealist wing in the Nazi Party, and one that found kindred spirits in Alfred Rosenberg and, of course, Heinrich Himmler. This faction saw farming and agrarian development of the land in an expansive program toward the East as the core of NS development and policy. They tended to be anti-industrialist and anti-urban. Darré coined the phrase *Blut und Boden* to champion an anti-industrial and anti-urban ideology, expansion into Eastern Europe to win Lebensraum, an alliance with Great Britain to defeat the Soviet Union, and staunch opposition to restoring the pre-1914 German colonial empire. The agrarian faction held that pre-WWI German imperialism had been flawed by the fact that it tried to establish colonies in lands unsuited to German immigration—which also had the effect of turning Britain against Germany. The idea of colonizing the areas east of Germany became the agrarian ideal. This was a plan inherited from Hentschel and the Artamanen. Darré was made head of the Rasse- und Siedlungshauptamt (Race and Settlement Main Office; RuSHA) in 1932. Among other things, the RuSHA was concerned with regulating racial policies and practices within the SS. He resigned from this post in 1938.

With respect to the religious question, Darré definitely belonged to the pagan faction of the Party with men such as Rosenberg and Himmler, but for the most part Darré has been left out of discussions concerning the occult aspects of Nazism. This has been an oversight. Darré was a Romantic who had his own idea of what the ancient Germanic culture was like and how he wanted to reinstitute it for the development of a future state.

Many times, Darré's ideas were implemented in practical, legal terms and sometimes in a bloody and violent manner. One legal aspect was the promotion of the *"Erbhof* Law" (*Reichserbhofgesetz*). An *Erbhof* is a piece of inherited farmland. German farm life had long been at a disadvantage due to the fact that German law mandated that land could be inherited by all the sons of a farmer, so that if a man had three sons, his land would be divided three ways upon his death. Large farms were split up over and over again, making corporate farming difficult. In fact, this was ancient Germanic practice, or at least one of the old ways. The idea that German lords divided their estate among their sons is actually responsible for the shape of the European political map today. When the son of the great emperor Charlemagne (Karl the Great), Louis (Chlodwig) the Pious, died in 840, his empire was divided among his three sons as West Francia, Middle Francia, and East Francia, with West Francia becoming what we call France today and East Francia eventually becoming Germany. The idea that the oldest son of the king would inherit all of his kingdom is a Christian idea, but one that promotes national strength and continuity. Darré extolled the innate virtue of a Volk rooted in an ancestral soil and condemned what he thought of as nomadic people, by which he was targeting the Jews. He seems to have ignored the Germanic propensity for migration and global colonization.

"GREEN" NAZISM

By far the most controversial and interest-provoking aspect of the work and personality of Richard Walther Darré in recent years has been the assertion that he and his philosophy represented a sort of proto-"Green" movement in culture and politics. This controversy seems to have been generated initially by the aforementioned 1985 work of Anna Bramwell titled *Blood and Soil*. Because she treated the topic with such objectivity, with little of the expected (and obligatory) use of disparaging adjectives, and because her case was so well argued, other academic historians have rushed to criticize her work—for example, in the collection of articles edited by Brüggemeier, et al., titled *How Green Were the Nazis?* (2005). The main reason for the counterargument appears to be that the "Greens" (Ger. *die Grünen*) in today's political world certainly do not want to be connected to the Nazis. The real connection here is not so much with National Socialism per se but rather with the earlier Reform Movements out of which so much else grew. Clearly, the underlying philosophy of the Green movement is closer to that of National Socialism than it is to Marxism. In Nationalist Socialist ideology, *nature* and *biology* are the dominant myths (paradigms of meaning), whereas in Marxism these underlying myths are economics and political power.

That even the concept of "blood and soil" was not necessarily a right-wing concept is demonstrated in a poem, not published until 1939, titled "The Primacy of the Living," in which the anthroposophist Rudolf Steiner expresses these concepts:

> *We need a better knowledge of man,*
> *Health through natural living,*
> *Harmony between Blood, Soil and Cosmos,*
> *Life reform as national aim,*
> *Knowledge and Life,*
> *The Rule of the Living.*
> (QUOTED IN BRAMWELL 1985, 176–77)

The very word *ecology* was coined by our old friend Ernst Haeckel in the nineteenth century, but it was only later, in 1930s Germany, that the term took on the sense we usually associate it with today. In this whole complex of ideas, we come face-to-face with the etymological interplay among the words *natural, national, native, natal,* and *innate.* The Reform ideology understood well the idea of holism, of the natural bond between body and soul, matter and spirit. The neopagan elements of the NSDAP exploited this reasoning, which is theoretically impeccable as long as it is bound by the limits of legality and morality. But the Nazis did not respect such limits. They marshaled these conceptions, as well as every other idea, in a "total war" effort. The idea of a pure racial type was extolled, and anything that led away from the realization of that type was seen as a genetic flaw or simply a weed to be eliminated from the garden.

Many of the ideas held by ecologists, naturalists, environmentalists, and Green activists of today are ones that were first articulated within the Life-Reform movement of Germany and, by the same token, may have their parallels within Darré's ideology. For example, a typical naturalist of today will despair of the deleterious effects of invasive species in an ecosystem. The same logic might be used by National Socialist to argue against the presence of foreign elements (e.g., Jews or "Gypsies") in Germany. The Nazis combined ideas about ecology with the force of governmental coercion. This sort of combination is one that the world has become accustomed to more recently.

Darré was a major influence on Himmler with regard to the idea of creating a German racial aristocracy—a Master Race—with the use of selective breeding. But Darré's ideas were eventually rejected in practical terms because Himmler, under pressure to deliver tangible results in wartime, eventually found Darré's concepts too theoretical. Actual study of the National Socialist practices and policies regarding eugenics and selective breeding reveal a far more practical and simple view than certain fantastic authors from the 1960s forward might have us believe. No Nazi goal of breeding humans to restore the third eye or anything of the sort was ever part of an official program.

However, the occult and esoteric dimensions of the ideology of men like Darré should not be overlooked, either. Darré is the most prominent exponent of what might best be called biological mysticism. If the German race could be bred in a pure and isolated form—separate, healthy, strong, and beautiful—and placed in close proximity with nature and the natural productive cycles of the Earth (farming), with room to expand and develop, then the nation and the species would be transformed into something more perfect and happy than ever thought possible before. As we have seen, these and related ideas grew out of alternative ideologies of the late nineteenth century, which we have identified with the Reform movement. At the time, there was no established scientific or political support for these ideas. They were either ancient ideals, thought to have long since been overcome by history, or utopian dreams of wild-eyed eccentrics (such as Hentschel). But Darré and his supporters, who did not represent the majority of National Socialists, attempted to practicalize and realize these ancient and unestablished dreams—and were willing to stop at nothing to accomplish them. It is noteworthy that despite his efforts, Darré generally failed in these more ambitious projects and progressively lost power in the Nazi regime over the years. He did not deliver the goods. By contrast, Himmler only saved his position by doing the dirtiest of jobs asked of him with efficiency and zeal.

After the war Darré was arrested by American authorities and subsequently put on trial with twenty-one other defendants in the so-called Ministries Trials, which took place between 1947 and 1949. He was convicted on several counts and sentenced to seven years in Landsberg Prison. Released in 1950, he died three years later and is buried in Goslar.

OTTO RAHN

If the theories of Otto Rahn had not been mentioned and picked up by later writers in the mythology of Nazi occultism—writers such as Jean-Michel Angebert, Nigel Graddon, Miguel Serrano, and Howard Buechner—he would have been a fairly minor footnote in this study. Due to the undeniable quality and depth of Rahn's work, he did not fail to impress those who knew him and read his works in the 1930s. Rahn's contributions should be ascribed to the esoteric rather than strictly occult field, and they reveal a way of thinking that was common, but hidden, in the intellectual world of post-Wagnerian German neo-Romanticism, which a discussion of Rahn gives us the opportunity to explore.

Otto Wilhelm Rahn (1904–1939) was born into a middle-class family and he began his university studies in law in 1922, but these were interrupted in 1925 when he took a job as a traveling salesman for a publishing company. He probably went to work to help out his family financially. In 1928, he resumed his university studies with a new direction—that of literature and medieval philology under Friedrich Gundolf in Heidelberg. The NSDAP Minister of Propaganda, Joseph Goebbels also studied with Gundolf, whom Goebbels referred to as "the Jew Gundolf." Rahn did a good deal of traveling in these years as he visited the sites that were connected to his chief interests— the Cathar heresy and its possible connection to the Holy Grail. He sojourned in southern France and studied with the grail seekers Maurice Magres, Albert Cassou, the Countess de Poujol-Murat, and with her a host of *Polaires*. He never finished his university studies but made good use of what he had learned. In 1932, he tried to open a hotel (De Marronniers) Ussat-les-Bains. He quickly went broke and was suspected of being a German spy. Back in Germany he published his book *Kreuzzug gegen den Gral* (Crusade against the Grail), which helped him with debts and brought him a certain notoriety throughout Europe. It also brought him to the attention of another grail enthusiast, Karl Maria Wiligut—and thus into contact with Reichsführer-SS Heinrich Himmler. Rahn was sponsored by the SS for research and subsequently joined the organization in 1936 as a part of Himmler's staff under Wiligut. The two visionaries worked together on grail-related projects. He undertook a travel expedition to various places in Europe that he felt were connected to the Cathars and the Holy Grail. This resulted in the book *Luzifers Hofgesind* (Lucifer's Court). Himmler ordered one hundred copies and had some of them custom bound, and he gave one to Hitler for his birthday in 1937. A fact about Rahn was unknown to the Nazis—he was a homosexual. He also had questionable ancestry with respect to his pure Aryan pedigree. He had long been suspect as an apparent Francophile due to his interest in southern France and French medieval poetry. Basically, and to his credit, because Rahn was never suited to be a part of the National Socialist cause, he felt the noose constantly becoming tighter as time went on. He was thought not to have the right hardness to be a member of the SS and so was sent to Auschwitz to act as a guard to toughen him up. Rahn wrote a letter of resignation from the SS on February 28, 1939. On March 13, he committed suicide near Söll in the woods of the Tyrolian Alps by exposing himself overnight to extreme cold temperatures.

In Rahn's relatively short productive career he published only two major works, the aforementioned *Kreuzzug gegen den Gral* (1933) and *Luzifers Hofgesind* (1937). The first of these was produced before his official involvement with the NSDAP and is very scholarly in tone and content. The German edition of this book has more than sixty pages of footnotes. It purports to be a "history of the Albigenses" but is far more a scholarly yet also esoteric meditation on the medieval Minnesingers and troubadours and their works, connecting them with a perhaps Romanticized view of the Cathars, a dualistic sect of Christianity popular in the late twelfth and early thirteenth centuries in certain regions of Europe. His other important work, *Luzifers Hofgesind,* is a travelogue written as a sort of report for the SS with his reflections on the locations he visited in relation to his historical theories about the Cathars as a secret religion of Europe.

Rahn was a total Romantic. He put the elements of his vision together out of things that fired his imagination—heretics; the Grail; medieval love poetry; Greek, Celtic, and Germanic mythology; and anti-Catholic sentiment—and mixed these together, looking for connections to prove what he already "knew" was true. In his particular case, he combined most especially the epic poem *Parzivâl* by Wolfram von Eschenbach and the Cathar heresy, thus bringing together the Grail and the Cathars at the site of the Cathars' last stand at the fortress Montségur in March 1244. Rahn identified the Cathars' Montségur with Wolfram's Munsalväsche.

Much of Rahn's predilections and approach can be sorted out from a quote attributed to him: "My ancestors were pagans, and my grandparents were heretics" (Rahn 2006, x). This model of thought immediately suggests itself to anyone who is interested in the indigenous traditions of the Germanic peoples, but who finds himself at home in Germany rather than Scandinavia. The Germans have no *Edda* of their own, no version of the oldest Germanic pagan myths, so from the beginning of the study of their past they gravitated toward a special, sometimes esoteric, interpretation of the culture and literature of the High Middle Ages. On the surface this literature seems to be entirely Christian, but upon deeper examination a different story can be understood. The courtly culture of the German aristocracy, as well as the lives of the simple peasants of the day, often appeared to be at odds with orthodox Christian doctrine. This substitution of a Romantic understanding of the German Middle Ages for their (lost) more distant traditional past was a common theme in the late nineteenth and early twentieth centuries. It was a view also utilized and believed in by Heinrich Himmler, who spiritually identified with the medieval king Heinrich der Vögler.

For all of these reasons Rahn's vision and his writings were designed as an attempt to discover a hidden tradition of, and create and alternate mythology for, a pan-European identity rooted in the (sometimes perhaps imaginary) medieval world of heretics. Like many before him, Rahn used the past as a template for the construction of an ideal present and future state. This vision was in no way compatible with that of National Socialism.

It should also be noted that Rahn's ideas about the connection between the Grail and the Cathars seems suspect on the surface, because the Cathars were an offshoot of the Bogomil, Manichaean heresy, which did not believe in the ritual of the Eucharist or the role of the death and resurrection of Jesus as a part of their Christology. Rather it seems that all parts of Rahn's vision are new mythic constructions based on esoteric insight. The mythology suggested in Wolfram's *Parzivâl* is more compatible, which declares that the Grail is a stone that fell from Lucifer's crown during his war in heaven with the Trinity and is now guarded by an order of Grail-knights who use the stone to communicate with their supernal master by means of "heathen writing," which periodically appears on the facets of the stone.

In the end, it must be said that Rahn can only be considered a footnote in the history of Nazi occultism as practiced and understood in the period of actual National Socialist rule. He also belongs to a certain group, quite common among the names of individuals we come across in this study, who were part of the National Socialist movement in Germany but were for one reason or another profound misfits when it came to the particulars of the applied ideology of the NSDAP. Others in this category would include Hanns Heinz Ewers (bisexual, decadent), Karl Maria Wiligut (mental health record), and Erik Jan Hanussen (Jewish). Rahn will become important once more when we consider the postwar mythology of Nazi occultism.

CHAPTER 8

RITUALS OF NATIONAL SOCIALISM
Magic and Manipulation

Festivals and rites were used in Nazi Germany to forge the nation together and to shape and direct the general will of the Volk. These virtually cultic rites rites took on many forms—for example, Party rallies, and national celebrations, as well as more openly cultic celebrations. The Nazis, for example, instituted a "Morning Celebration" obviously meant to replace certain church services.

Of course, as we have repeatedly discussed in this work, so much mumbo jumbo has been written about occult Nazism, I can hear cautious readers now beginning to protest. Happily, with this branch of the study we have several good and reliable sources.* These include George L. Mosse's *The Nationalization of the Masses* (1975) and Klaus Vondung's *Magie und Manipulation: Ideologischer Kult und politische Religion des Nationalsozialismus* (Magic and Manipulation: The Ideological Cult and Political Religion of National Socialism; 1971). Mosse was a major scholar of Nazi culture, with other books titled *The Crisis of German Ideology: Intellectual Origins of the Third Reich* (1964) and *Nazi Culture* (1966).

One needs only to see Leni Riefenstahl's 1935 documentary chronicle of the 1934 rally of the Nazi Party titled *Triumph des Willens* (Triumph of the Will) to be convinced of the cultic aspects and

---

*Most academics have just as much of an ax to grind as do the New Age crackpots, but in the case of the academics at least they do provide a good deal of factual information about the topic, and their intellectual or theoretical templates are usually quite intelligible, which makes decoding their texts much easier.

intentions of such National Socialist political rallies. But this aspect was not unconscious or haphazard. The National Socialists willfully set out to establish a national cult of a kind that was perhaps intended in part to replace Christianity for the NS elite and members of the Party itself. Most sources on the phenomenon of NS festivals emphasize the idea that these rites and rituals were to be part of some ersatz religion being fashioned by NS ideologues. Curiously, Riefenstahl made an earlier version of the film with scenes from the 1933 rally titled *Triumph des Glaubens* (Triumph of the Faith), but because of the prominent role of Ernst Röhm in the film it was reshot the next year.

What is more, the sources on NS festivals tend to emphasize at one point or another the magical aspect of these rites and how they were intended to mold the masses into an instrument of the will of the leader(s). This will is usually seen as an expression of the general will of the Volk—an appreciation that is perhaps fundamental to any deep understanding of the Nazi mythos. Mosse writes:

> The pragmatism of daily politics lay within this cultic framework and for most people was disguised by it. But "disguise" is perhaps the wrong term in this context, for any disguise which utilizes regular liturgical and cultic forms becomes a "magic" believed by both leaders and the people, and it is the reality of this magic with which we are concerned. (Mosse 1975, 15)

From an operative perspective, these ceremonies could be seen as efforts to marshal the masses to do the will of a manipulative oligarchy. Interestingly, the theme of a mindless mass or automaton (organic or inorganic) that performs the will of its master is one which fascinated the German magical mind of the early part of the twentieth century. Again, we recall the famous films of the period with the golem of Rabbi Loew, Dr. Caligari's Cesare, Rotwang's robotrix Ultima Futura, or the uncanny powers of Dr. Mabuse. Another theme was, however, the specter of a shadow-self or Doppelgänger—this complicates the issue magically by posing the question of the ultimate character of the self.

But to return to the task at hand, what does the study of this material reveal about the practical magical application of certain psychological mechanisms to create rites of mass manipulation? First, it provides a historical understanding of how such a vast magical operation might be designed. Perhaps never before or since were such magical techniques so widely used to wield as much broad objective power as in Nazi Germany. It also allows the contemporary investigator to understand this mechanism, so that it is less likely to have effectiveness in the future—if only people can be educated in the subject *rationally*. In point of fact, the mechanism still seems to be at work, but it has been shifted away from mass rallies (for the most part!) and into rites of cyber-symbolism, mass media, and the art of memes—all working in a similar way, only through a different delivery system.

In any event, these may be the most solid ritual remnants of the National Socialist liturgy. In addition to these, NS liturgy provides a tremendous study in the ritual use of space (proxemic magic), and the melding of traditions of the past with those of the present in a pragmatic way.

Here we will look at a group of ceremonies that represent the Nazi effort to create a new national religion. Then we will examine the general structural features of NS liturgy used for almost every purpose.

RITES OF THE NSDAP

Although the NSDAP and all its various groupings, such as the SS and the Hitler Youth, had many kinds of rituals and festivals, we will concentrate here on the ones performed in the general public. Of these, there is obviously some public record that can be observed and utilized by those of us who study these liturgical forms for what we can usefully learn about them. As for the other more private, or secret, rituals—we are often dependent on sketchy or fragmentary written records. But in most cases the record has been totally lost. By the way, an official Nazi organ for the publication of aspects relating to its new experiments in religion was called *Neue Gemeinschaft* (New Community).

In the discussions of the various calendrical rites, we get a well-rounded picture of the kind of rituals the Nazis were developing. Besides the "Ceremonies of the Reich and the Course of the Year," other liturgical formats used by the NSDAP included "Morning Ceremonies" (*Morgenfeiern*), sometimes also called "Philosophical Hours of Celebration"; "Ceremonies of Life" (rites of passage); and the dramatic celebratory plays and so-called Thingspiele (Thing Plays). This latter type of ritual was an effort to create a mass drama in which the audience, or congregation, participated in poetic chants with actors or choral groups. Special open-air theaters, called *Thingstätten* (Thing-steads) were built for this purpose in the early years of the Third Reich. These might even be seen as a more Protestant-style liturgy (answering to the more Catholic style practiced at Bayreuth in the Wagnerian Gesamtkunstwerk), where the sacred action takes place in a transcendent space—with only spiritual participation by the audience (congregation).

At the outset, I want to emphasize that this liturgical calendar was never a completely standardized system, as it was regularly in flux and subject to changes. The short history of Nazism made such a traditional establishment impossible. Some elements were added at a later date, after the beginning of WWII, while others were deemphasized. It should also be noted that certain features tended to be practiced only by specific institutions within the Party apparatus. These variations clearly show that the Party was far from a monolithic organization. Variations in ceremonial were often dependent upon the aesthetic differences between the Romantic-Germanic style (favored, e.g., by Himmler and Rosenberg) and the Neoclassical style idealized by Hitler (and therefore by the majority of the Nazi elite). The Germanic imagery was most often found in the actions of the SS and the Hitler Youth. Among the most influential men responsible for the actual form of the rituals were Joseph Goebbels, Robert Ley, Alfred Rosenberg, and Albert Speer.

Ceremonies of the Reich and the Course of the Year

It was clear from the beginning of the Third Reich that the Party was actively trying to displace the role of the church in the lives of the people. One of the most significant methods it used in doing this was the development and institution of its own sacred calendar with attendant ceremonies and festivals. What must be understood about these rituals is that they were not entirely *religious* in character. That is, they were not merely rote repetitions of established formulas. Rather, they had a significant *magical* dimension. They were often performed with definite aims in mind, and they were periodically altered in their formulas to effect different modifications in the thought and behavior of the public or the Party faithful. Following is a list of the main days celebrated.

January 30: Day of Coming to Power

The principal liturgical act was the nighttime torchlight parade as a reenactment of the one that took place on that same night in 1933 in Berlin. Its significance was the final victory of the Party. Although that original one in 1933 was hardly an actual celebration of absolute power, rather its function was *magical,* for the Nazis celebrated as if they had already attained the power it would actually take them several months to acquire. During the war years, this celebration was moved to the 10,000-seat Sportpalast. This building at 172 Potsdamer Strasse was virtually destroyed by Allied bombing raid on January 30, 1944.

February 24: Proclamation of the Party Program

This was, in the early years, principally celebrated by Hitler and the "Old Guard" in the Hofbräuhaus in Munich in private ceremonies (in which they wore historical clothing). It was in the main hall of the Hofbräuhaus that Hitler had first proclaimed the twenty-five-point program of the Party on this date in 1920. This was only briefly a special day of public celebration (1934–1935). But in 1943 it once more took on greater significance as a celebratory meditation on attaining victory. Its significance was the mythic foundations of victory—which would come to fruition on the (following) January 30. Clearly, the Nazi festival year was formulated as a cyclical event.

March 16: Heroes' Memorial Day

As a holiday this was adopted from the days of the Weimar Republic when it was called "Day of Popular Mourning" (*Volkstrauertag*) and was a day for mourning the dead of the First World War. But under the Nazis it became a day for the remembrance of all those who have fallen in battle. The function of this day was national consolation "for those who have not died in vain," much in the same spirit as originally found in the American Memorial Day. During the war years this day took on added significance as new "fallen warriors" were being added to the ranks daily.

Last Sunday in March: Pledging of the Youth

This observation was developed to replace in a collective manner the day a person underwent confirmation in the confessing Christian churches. This became the day on which fourteen-year-old boys and ten-year-old girls could enter the Hitler Youth (Hitler-Jugend) or the League of German Girls (Bund Deutscher Mädel), respectively. Despite the fact that this was obviously an individual rite of passage, it took on a collective dimension as a time for celebrating the general commitment of young people to the movement. Liturgically, this was principally a private affair handled on a local basis. A special radio broadcast was used to support the private celebration.

April 20: Hitler's Birthday

This was never—or actually only once, on Hitler's fiftieth birthday—a legal holiday. Three significant liturgical events took place on this day: (1) the acceptance of ten-year-olds in the German Young Folk (Jungvolk) for boys and in the League of Young Girls (Jungmädelbund) for girls; (2) the swearing-in of Political Leaders of the Party (this occurred in liturgical splendor at night in the Königsplatz in Munich, with the darkness illuminated by torches and vessels of fire); and (3) military parades.

May 1: National Day of Celebration of the German People

Here is an example of a clear usurpation of the Internationalist-Marxist "workers' day" celebration—May Day. Although the name of the holiday was changed, the emphasis remained on the ideas of work and the worker. At one point this was declared the highest holiday of the German people by Goebbels. The German Workers Front liked to fill out the celebration with old Germanic folk customs and celebrated it as the "day of joy over the victory of eternally new life." The day was celebrated widely and officially in Berlin.

German Easter and High May

This was a general celebration of the concept of Spring, of rebirth of nature and the year. Efforts were made following 1944 to combine the Christian Spring festivals, Easter and Pentecost (*Pfingsten*). The latter was called "High May" in the folk tradition, and all of the customs attendant to this time period were combined and re-Germanicized as a Springtide festival. Celebrations were distinguished by folkloric events, centering attention on the national traditions of Germany as distinguished from the internationalistic rituals of Christianity. Alfred Rosenberg appears to have been the force behind this particular reclaiming of pagan celebrations from the Christian Church.

Second Sunday in May: Mothers' Day

The ceremonial features of this day were that, after the war had begun in 1939, mothers who had borne a certain number of children were invested with a cross of honor. Additionally, those mothers who had lost children in the fighting were escorted by flower-bearing Hitler Youth to the ceremonies, where they were recognized and honored for their sacrifices. As losses mounted in the war, the function of this day became the psychological reinforcement of the home front. Ultimately, this day of celebration has an American origin: Mother's Day was begun by the American activist Anna Maria Jarvis in 1908, who first established the date as the second Sunday in May.

June 21: Summer Solstice

Midsummer was especially celebrated by the Hitler Youth and the SS. Ceremonies typically had neo-Germanic trappings. Within the SS, this was the day for holding wedding ceremonies between Aryan brides and grooms. Various other neo-Germanic festivals were held by several groups. Even Goebbels got in on the act—but without the Germanic aesthetic, as the Neoclassical style was more to his taste. Central to the liturgy of the Summer Solstice was the lighting of the solstice fire. The Olympia Stadium in Berlin with its flame was the central location of this rite after 1937. Its function was again a völkisch one—with an emphasis on racial victory. Despite the significance of this observance, these rituals were held at night, with the open flame being its central symbol.

First Half of September: Party Day of the Reich

This was the most important celebration of the manifest power of the NSDAP—the victory of its collective will and that of its leader, as it were. Actually, this was not just a single day but rather an entire week of highly ritualized events. These are the ceremonial events that Leni Riefenstahl so infamously and beautifully recorded in her renowned documentary film in 1935—*Triumph of the Will*. These were truly the high holy nights of the National Socialist Party, in which every branch and root of its structure took part. Later in this chapter I will go into some detail on the structure of the rites performed during these days.

One rite that is recorded in Riefenstahl's film is the consecration of new Nazi banners by being touched to the Blutfahne (Blood Flag). This is referred to as the *Fahnenweihe* (flag consecration). The Blutfahne is the flag that was stained with blood during the Beer Hall Putsch (1923). As a sacred cult- object it was in the keeping of SS-Sturmbannführer Jakob Grimminger. When not in use, it was kept in the Party head-quarters called the Brown House (das Braune Haus) in Munich. This flag was last seen in public on October 18, 1944, after which it never surfaced again. It was most likely destroyed when the Brown House was burned during an Allied air raid in 1945. The ruin was later also plundered by Allied forces.

Beginning of October: Harvest Thanksgiving Day

As an expression of the balance between the farmers and industrial workers of the country, the beginning of October was set aside to honor the agricultural process and the farmers. (This balances the May Day celebration of the workers.) In keeping with the high honor given to the farmer (as a symbol at least) in the ideology of *Blut und Boden* (blood and soil), the Harvest Festival Rally was often an elaborate ritual. In the 1930s it was held on the Bückeberg, a hill just south of the town of Hameln. There, hundreds of thousands of German farmers were brought to participate in this festival, which also had a ceremonial ritual designed by Leopold Gutterer. The symbolic high point of the rite was the presentation of the harvest crown to the Führer. This represented a presentation of the harvest made by the farmers of the nation and offered to the entire community of the Volk. This large rally was reproduced on a smaller scale in various localities throughout the country, where a local Party official representing the Führer would receive the symbol of the harvest.

November 9: Memorial Day for the Fallen of the Movement

This day can be considered the holiest day of the NSDAP. It marks the anniversary of the attempted putsch of 1923. This was became the most significant cultic affair held by the Party. The ritual proceeded in this manner: The Old Guard (those who had been there on that day in 1923 and whom Hitler had awarded a special medal called the *Blutorden,* the "Blood Order"), gathered with the Führer before the Bürgerbräukeller beer hall. They then solemnly marched toward the Feldherrnhalle, where sixteen of them had been killed by gunfire. This march was led by those Old Fighters of the Blutorden, with one of their number bearing the famous Blood Flag (*Blutfahne*). This is a swastika flag carried on that day and stained with the blood of one of the slain. As they marched they went past pylons inscribed with the names of 240 "fallen of the movement." As they passed by each of these pylons, the names of the martyrs were called out. Throughout this procession, the sounds of the "Horst-Wessel-Lied" went out over loudspeakers. As they arrived at the Feldherrnhalle, sixteen cannon shots would ring out to commemorate the sixteen fatal shots of 1923. Hitler then laid a wreath on the memorial stone of the martyrs, as the "Lied vom guten Kameraden" followed by the "Deutschlandlied" ("Deutschland, Deutschland, über alles!"). This increased in intensity as the marchers continued their way to the Königsplatz—where the sixteen martyrs had subsequently been entombed in the Temple of Honor. Then a speech was given, usually by the Propaganda Minister Joseph Goebbels. At one point the names of the sixteen martyrs were read out as members of the Hitler Youth chorally answered, "Here!" After each name was read, a three-gun salute was given. The "Horst-Wessel-Lied" was repeated, followed by the "Badenweiler March" (said to be Hitler's favorite tune) and the "Deutschlandlied" again.

As the war went on, this holiday became more of a day of remembrance for all the dead ancestors, as some factions of the Nazi Party increasingly tried to displace Christian memorial days that fell around the same time of year. Not that this replacement ever got very far. The whole body of ritual elements found on the 9th of November have been compared to Catholic rituals connected to the Passion Plays (Vondung 1971, 84).

The SS also swore in new members during a nighttime ceremony held at the Feldherrnhalle on the night of this day.

December 21 and the "Holy Nights": Winter Solstice

Traditional German Christmas customs retained or had already redeveloped many pagan elements, but these festivities became the subjects of intense Nazi liturgical reinterpretation. Himmler was especially interested in the effort to re-paganize the Yule festival. The SS had a version of the Yule Fest that was unique to that organization. Both Goebbels and Rosenberg were in favor of utilizing subtler means in keeping with the overriding doctrinaire concept of Positive Christianity. A Nazi Christmas posed a new problem. Even in pagan times the Yuletide was a family matter, not one of public display. So, the usual marshaling of the masses for a typical rally-type ceremony was not suited to the occasion. The challenge became: how to develop new National Socialist traditions to be carried out in private homes? It took until 1942 before any sort of customs could be generated. The festival was to consist of three major celebrations: (1) of the "troop" (within Party organizations, military groups, etc.); (2) of the general community; and (3) of the family. This mirrors the normal way in which Germans typically today celebrate a three-day Christmas celebration with a day for friends, a day for extended family, and a day for the nuclear family. During the Christmas seasons of 1943 and 1944, the Ministry of Propaganda published and distributed a book called "A German War-Christmas" (*Deutsche Kriegsweihnacht*). This provided a full private liturgy with songs, poems, customs, and legends for the family to perform. This even presented a legend about a dead solider who returned for the holy nights to participate—albeit invisibly—in the celebrations of the family. (Here again is a purely ancient Germanic belief being revised and revived, with a definite nod to the more recently developed notions of spiritualism.)

Ritual Formulas

The calendrical cycle of rites and rituals sponsored by the NSDAP can not be said to have ever reached its intended level of performance across the nation. With the outbreak of the war, many of the celebrations mentioned here were eventually curtailed, or suspended entirely. As the public performances were discontinued, they were often observed in Party cells or as part of the regular Morning Celebrations (*Morgenfeiern*).

National Socialist ritual or ceremonial rubrics were greatly inspired by church liturgy in tandem with the free creative expression on the part of the individual designers of the rituals. A common underlying formula for a large portion of them, and clearly defining many of them, was a sixteen-point working outline, which can be divided into three constituent parts.

Part I

FANFARES
1. Marching-in of the Banners and Flags
2. Common Song
3. Poetic Invocation
4. Choral of the Troops (ritualized chants)

Part II

5. The Eternal Watch (Word of the Führer)
6. Choral of the Troops
7. Address of the Highest Ranking Official (*Hoheitsträger*)
8. Honoring of the Fallen

9. Oath of Obligation (to the dead, to the Volk, etc.)
10. Honoring of the Dead (ancestors, heroes, etc.)
11. Choral of the Troops

Part III

12. Solemn Vows
13. Common Song
14. Honoring of the Führer (threefold *Sieg Heil!*)
15. National Hymns (i.e., the "Horst-Wessel-Lied" and the "Deutschlandlied")

Fanfares
16. Marching-out of the Banners and Flags

To some observers, these ceremonies may not seem to be magical or have anything to do with the occult. This appearance can be deceiving. As we have seen in reading Hitler's *Mein Kampf,* he gives a variety of hints about his consciousness regarding some magical dimension to political gatherings and ceremonies. Such ceremonies are, in fact, among the best hard evidence for any sort of magical operations carried out by the Nazis. They constitute a sort of Realmagie that makes use of what have come to be called psychological mechanisms and types of communication to manipulate public will and emotion. Contemporary readers may not recognize this form of magic among the Nazis so easily, simply because it is the kind of magic that is constantly still used on us by politicians and advertisers.

From an operative perspective, these rituals had many functions. Among them were the forging of a focused general will of the Volk, the creation of a deep sense of self-awareness as an organic group, the bonding of that group to a set of symbols, the projection of the group through those symbols back in time to the ancestors and forward in time to the descendants—and to the ultimate victory of Hitler's new philosophy of life. In these mass liturgies, the German people were given a direct physical manifestation of the essence of their own version of heaven (or Walhalla)—its spaces, its sounds, its emotions, and its powers.

The ritual elements contained in these ceremonies formed a complex structure, but each element had a specific operative function. An analysis of these features demonstrates the underlying palette of elements: ritually shaped space, motion within that space, color, sound (music), and the spoken word. All this was played out in a pattern of dynamic tension between the individual and the gathered mass—nowhere is this more symbolically clear than in the sight of the Führer addressing the faithful at Nuremberg.

THE RITUAL OF THE *HITLERGRUß*

The Hitler-greeting (*Hitlergruß*), or Hitler salute, became the most common form of NS ritualism in the time of the Third Reich. It was the standard greeting between Germans who were members of the NSDAP and others who were adherents of the general philosophy. This ritual of greeting had the effect of setting NS members and sympathizers—or *Volksgenossen,* "folk comrades"—apart from all others at first and then became a mandatory ritual of folk and state solidarity in the time of the Third Reich. After the beginning of the war it became a legally punishable offence not to return the Hitler-greeting if it was offered. The magical function of this ritual gesture is often overlooked, and often misinterpreted.

The well-known form of the gesture is one that is shared with the Fascists of Benito Mussolini. Il Duce took the gesture directly from the *saluto romano,* the "Roman salute." Among the ancient Romans it appears to have been used both as a military salute and as a sign given when taking an oath. It seems likely that Hitler directly copied this gesture from Mussolini's Fascists. Later the Nazis were anxious to point out that this was not the case, and that the salute had been used as early as 1921, and Hitler even points out in *Mein Kampf* that the greeting *"Heil!"* was common among his friends as a youth in Austria. Indeed, the gesture as a form of honoring salute was not uncommon in the late nineteenth and early twentieth centuries.

In the United States, there was the so-called Bellamy salute, named after Francis Bellamy, given to the flag of the United States while

Fig. 8.1. American schoolchildren reciting the Pledge of Allegiance in May 1942
(US Library of Congress Archives)

reciting the Pledge of Allegiance. A version of this was used as early as 1887. Due to its similarity to the Nazi salute, the Bellamy gesture was banned by legislation in 1942.

The Hitler salute was introduced as official practice in the NSDAP in 1926. When greeting Hitler, the one giving the salute was to say, "*Heil, mein Führer!*" But normally the salute and response was simply "*Heil Hitler!*" or the motto "*Sieg Heil!*"

It is not unlikely that the gesture and the mantra was first introduced into völkisch circles by Rudolf von Sebottendorf in the Thule

Society. He was an avid student and practitioner of ritual gestures and mantric utterances. There, the mantra was *"Heil und Sieg!"*

In the case of the Hitler salute, we have another example of how the National Socialists created symbolic alternatives to Marxist-Socialist signs. In this case, the raised clenched fist was the international sign of Socialism, so the NSDAP countered this with the Hitler salute.

The magical/ritual effect of the practice of the Hitler salute was to remind the populace of their central allegiance to Hitler and to the cause of National Socialism, which was done in a rite that was repeated many times a day throughout all of Germany.

THE OLYMPIC TORCH RELAY

It is uncertain as to who designed the ritual of the inaugural torch relay that was first used for the Summer Olympics held at Berlin in 1936. Officially, the credit belongs to Wilhelm Haegert, a propaganda minister for the games. But several men took various sorts of credit for the idea—most notably the director of the games, Carl Diem. The Olympic Flame had been a part of the games since 1910, but the relay was a 1936 innovation. Many aspects of the relay were filled with opportunities for Nazi propaganda: the torch was lit using concave mirrors from the great German optics corporation Zeiss, and the object itself was fashioned by the Krupp steel company. The relay was staged to help raise awareness and anticipation for the games well in advance of their actual opening. The event was filmed by Leni Riefenstahl for the film *Olympia* (1938). As a ritual of operative propaganda, or magic, the Olympic torch relay can be seen as a mode of symbolic conquest, as all the lands through which the torch made its way from Greece to Berlin were under Nazi control by 1941. The ritual remains intact to this day as the Germans designed it in 1936.

In his book titled *Empire of Ecstasy,* Karl Toepfer offers some valuable insights in a section called "Nazi Concepts of Mass Movement" (1997, 314–20). He mentions several examples of choreographed performances in the Nazi era. Although they have often been forgotten about today, many of these events are surprising. At the 1936 Olympic Games there was a great nocturnal performance called *Olympische Jugend* (Olympic Youth). There were thousands of participants and one hundred thousand looked on in the Olympic Stadium. Unfortunately, this event was not recorded by Leni Riefenstahl for her epic film *Olympia,* because she thought the lighting would not be sufficient. Between the years 1933 and 1937, an extremely popular form of entertaining education was provided by the Thingspiele (Thing Plays). More than sixty amphitheater-like structures were built in and near towns for the performance of these plays, which Toepfer characterizes as follows:

> In the *Thingspiel,* the protagonist was always "the people" (embodied by choirs), who struggled, with simple, heroic pathos, against the evil inflicted by capitalism, bolshevism, Judaism, industrialization, unemployment, hunger, the "backstabbing" diplomats who contrived the Versailles Treaty, decadent intellectualism, gangsters, racial impurity, and the foolish, misguided administrators of democracy in the Weimar Republic. The salvation of the people depended on the emergence of the Führer, representatives of the SA or SS, or potent symbols of Germanic or Aryan heritage. (Toepfer 1997, 317)

After 1937, these Thingspiele were discontinued, despite their great popularity. They were popular because the represented the *revolutionary* side of National Socialism, but Goebbels saw that they were open to improvisation and lack of centralized control. Additionally, they were not conducive to the preparation for war that the Party was pursuing.

For the most part, the NSDAP staged spectacles involving the mass coordination of human bodies in motion, based on the liturgical model used for the 1934 rally at Nuremberg recorded in the film *Triumph des Willens* by Leni Riefenstahl. In these rites, the philosophy of the Party was exemplified in dynamic motion: the many becoming one, in coordination, under one aesthetic will.

Every time an individual participates in any one of these ceremonies, that person will go forth and act on the emotions evoked during the ritual. In this way, each "dynamized" participant goes out and actually reshapes the world in accordance with the will of the leadership. Again, we may detect shades of what I have termed the Caligari Syndrome (see chapter 6), but here it was a certain "psychological resonance" in the masses that was harnessed to effect the magical aims of the leaders. An example of a similar strategy in our present-day culture is evident in phenomenon of profit-driven rock bands that will tour extensively, even though the tours themselves often lose money. Why do they do so? Because their fans—the little "golems"—will go out after the "rally" and do the will of their "jukebox heroes" (or the latter's producers): they will *buy more records*.

Beyond this magical application, it is also possible that attempts were made to direct these collected energies by means other than psychological resonance—that is, by means of more traditional forms of ritual magic or direction by the magical will. These are the type of experiments we have some reason to suspect certain members of the Nazi Party might have practiced—but for which we have little hard evidence. Additionally, it must be remembered that for every Nazi leader, there was a different version of the envisioned aim of the Party. The lack of evidence may in part be accounted for because some of the secret files of the SS, for example, were known to have been destroyed. All we have left are traces and hints, and most importantly, the magical spaces they built to stage certain events and rites, such as the Hall of the Slain at the Wewelsburg.

NAZI RUNOLOGY

Certainly, one of the most conspicuous examples of occult symbolic phenomena from the Nazi era is the usage of runes. Runes constitute a system of writing used by the early Germanic and Nordic peoples largely for inscriptions.* The use of runes has become so closely associated with Nazism that even venerable academic institutions in Germany eventually discontinued their study in the twenty-first century due to

---

*For a general presentation of runology, see my book *Runes and Runology* (2022).

the "taint of Nazism." Of course, the runes, like all other aspects of early Germanic culture, were enjoying a high tide of popularity in early twentieth-century German-speaking countries, and the Nazis capitalized on this as part of their campaign in meta-communication to win over the hearts and minds of much of the population to their cause. Many in the leadership of the NSDAP, and especially Heinrich Himmler, were personally fascinated with the runes, as we have seen.

As Ulrich Hunger's detailed study (1984) shows, there never was an official National Socialist approach to the runes or runology. Several concurrent sets of ideas were present in NS circles and in the Ahnenerbe: some can be traced to Karl Maria Wiligut, others to Karl Theodor Weigel, but there were also the more purely academic runologists who continued to work relatively free of ideological constraints, such as Wolfgang Krause. Many runic, rune-like, and other ancient Germanic signs and symbols were used in the official insignia of the German government, the military, and various adjunct organizations, as well as within the NSDAP itself.

Partisan Runology within the NSDAP

From early on, National Socialists exercised an interest in utilizing runes and runic symbolism as a propaganda tool. This was effective due to the preexisting popularity of these symbols. The aim of this iteration was to differentiate German(ic) culture from other cultures and to a certain extent this had the effect of suggesting that Germanic culture was somhow superior to all others. The runes did this by emphasizing that the Germanic people in antiquity were in fact literate in their own form of writing and that this was in fact more ancient than other forms of writing. Such claims about the runes had been asserted before, but by the early twentieth century academic runology had already discredited these ideas. Therefore, the belief in an indigenous origin of the runes and dates of origin going back thousands of years—even to Atlantis!— clearly belongs to the occult realm.

Two separate groups within the NSDAP were officially interested in runic symbolism: the Rosenberg Office and the SS (and the Ahnenerbe especially). It should also be noted that it was perhaps in the

Hitler Youth, the youth organization for boys between the ages of fourteen and eighteen, where the runes were at the height of their visibility. Learning about runes and/or writing with runes at an exoteric level was a common activity in these organizations. As a matter of fact, the Nazis never sanctioned any runic system as being "official," runes were used in many formal capacities within Party symbolism.

As we have seen, perhaps the most obvious examples of runic *esotericism* on an official level can be seen in the activities of Karl Maria Wiligut, which have been outlined above. His situation is remarkable in that he clearly appears to be a representative of the earlier poetic or visionary views of the early twentieth century, such as also found in the work of Guido von List. This was not necessarily the case as regards

Fig. 8.2. Design of the Runic Death's Head Ring by Wiligut
(Wikimedia Commons)

the Nazis. He designed the SS honor ring with peculiar symbols that belonged to his own personal system of runology.

Wiligut himself provided an explanation of interpretation of the symbols found on the Totenkopfring of the SS. This appears in a document provided to Himmeler (see Hunger 1984, 149-51) as follows:

ᚼᚼ   =   "The creative spirit must be victorious."

ᛉ   =   "Man, be one with God, with the Eternal."

✳   =   "Enclose the All in yourself and you will command the All."

ᚼᚼ + ᛏ/ᚨ   =   [victory] *tyr* = os = "Be guileless, brave and true." "The power of your spirit makes you free."

Hauptsturmbannführer Karl Theodor Weigel often discussed and described the qualities of the runes in various publications for the SS as well as for the public. In books such as *Unsere Stellung zu den Runen* (Our Position toward the Runes; 1936) and *Runen und Sinnbilder,* he applied definite meanings to certain runes; for example, ᚼ = In the meaning of victorious power, ✳ = "For the protection of the wearer against an enemy," ᚼᚼ Misinterpreted as *gibor* = "victorious power of the personality," ᛏ/ᚹ = ᛏ = "Preparedness for self-sacrifice unto death + ᚹ = well-being, riches." Weigel pointedly referred to most of the rune-esotericists of the earlier time (List, Stauff, Gorsleben, etc.) and criticized them for their "unscientific" approach (1937, 75–78), although most readers would probably say that in the final analysis his approach was not much different.*

Archived correspondence between Himmler and various rune experts and other reputable academics during the years of the Third Reich

---

*Because Weigel lacked academic experience and credentials, he tried to make himself appear more scientific than his immediate predecessors by pointing out how unscientific they were. He also knew that despite Himmler's own lack of background in the fields he was obsessed with the Reichsführer was nevertheless bent on obtaining the best academic minds he could find to carry out his projects, so Weigel appears to have been in a struggle to maintain his position.

demonstrate that Himmler and other political operatives were not interested first and foremost in discovering the truth about what a symbol might have actually meant but rather that they looked at these symbols from a purely pragmatic, and virtually sorcerous, perspective. They wanted to know how to use them to mold the minds of those who observed them. Here as elsewhere we find examples of what might be referred to as magical propaganda and which we clearly recognize by concepts such as branding today. In this way NS concepts and programs could be provided with "runic memes" that were both ancient and atractive to the human eye. Among the common runic symbols used in this way were:

ᚻᚻ = *Schutzstaffel* (protection division)

↑ = *Hitler-Jugend* leadership badge

Y = Life, used for *Lebensborn* program

ᛉ = Death (origin of the Peace-Sign)*

ᛜ = Homeland

Several other runic explanations from Fritz Weitzel's *Die Gestaltung der Feste im Jahres- und Lebenslauf in der* ᚻᚻ-*Familie* (1939) include:

* Hagal-rune means: "The All-surrounding." Hagal (Germanic) literally means "I destroy." Through the destruction of the enemy, all-surrounding peace is ensured.

ᚻ Sig-rune means "Victorious sun" and signifies the indwelling strength that assures victory. "The two Sig-runes on the banners of the ᚻᚻ express the old formula '*sig und sal,*' which is the salvation that lies implicitly in the certainty of the sun's victory" (K. Th. Weigel).

ᛉ Gibor-rune is made up from the Sig-rune and the Is-rune. It is therefore a combined rune. The Is (ice)-rune is the north–south line

---

*See the appendix "On the "Runic Origins of the 'Peace-Sign'" in my book *The Revival of the Runes* (2021, 206–9).

of the circle of the year and symbolizes "life"; in human terms: the living personality. The Gibor-rune therefore stands for the victory-assuring strength of the personality.

↑ Tyr-rune: It symbolizes the Germanic god of war, Tyr (= Ziu = Zeus) and signifies preparedness to sacrifice oneself unto death for the redemption of honor.

Ϝ Fa-(Fe-)-rune: "Fe" is contained in the Germanic word *feod* = farm animals. It symbolizes all movable farming goods, livestock, wealth. The Fa- and Tyr-runes together mean: self-sacrifice unto death, despite any cherished material goods.

Y Man-rune: With its up-stretched arms, it shows the birth of a living creature. (Cf. the heraldic symbol of the Lily.)

ʎ Yr-rune: With its downward-pointing arms, it indicates the death of a creature. Man- and Yr-runes are taken from the six-spoked wheel of the year. (Cf. the Is- and Hagal-runes.)

ᛜ Ing-rune: Ing means "to be born," "to stem from," and can still be found in this meaning as a suffix to hundreds of words in today's German language. The rune shows the interconnection of two life-bearers and is therefore used as a wedding-rune.

ᛟ Odal-rune: Odal or Alod is the Germanic word for the allodium of the clan. It also stands for this meaning. It encompasses everything that we understand in the concepts allodium, soil, homeland. (Weitzel 1939, 41–43)

In general, many of the meanings ascribed here seem overly imaginative and highy subjective to modern academic runologists. But Nazi rune-symbolists were not overly concerned with accuracy; their main goal was *effectiveness* with regard to the communication of their subtle messages to the mind of the viewer. Runes and rune-like symbols were transformed into iconic versions of slogans, which were able to speak directly to the minds of people viewing them on an unconscious level. What is also obvious is that the interpretations of individual runes varied widely among NS writers and that no orthodox interpretations were ever established.

On an *esoteric* level the Nazi utilization of runic symbolism was more subtle and sophisticated than most people today realize. These symbols were not used to cast spells with runes or involved with chanting rune mantras or by performing rune yoga. The spell they were casting was part of a much larger operation. They were operating in ways we today recognize as branding and identification through logos and other tools of meta-communication. Runic and rune-like aesthetics had the power to fascinate and draw in those already attuned to this visual design-work—that is, those attracted to the Germanophilic symbolism. It might have also had the power to repel those not so attuned with this aesthetic and its message. Hitler himself had been instrumental in adopting the swastika design as the logo of the Party in 1920. Several cells or offices within organizations such as the Ahnenerbe may or may not have delved into the esoteric dimensions of the runes. In this case it was most likely a hangover from their more youthful enthusiasms.

Perhaps the closest thing to an official Nazi runology (a systematic presentation of the runes within a National Socialist ideological framework) was presented by Walther Blachetta in *Das Buch der deutschen Sinnzeichen* (The Book of German Symbols). This was published in 1941 by Widukind Verlag, which was an official organ of the NSDAP. For this reason, we can assume that the descriptions of the runes met with some degree of official approval. Blachetta concludes his introduction to the book with the words:

But one more thing must be said. A great degree of power resides in symbols. To bring them to life is a worthwhile endeavor. Only it would be childish to believe that they work all by themselves as if they were approved pills from the pharmacy. To carve a *feh*-rune into the leather of your wallet to ensure that this billfold will always be filled with money is a foolish undertaking. Even if somebody sticks a big swastika on his lapel, that is a long way from proving that he is really a National Socialist. He still has to put his will and work into an effective life serving the folk, fatherland, and Führer. But if this is the case, the symbol will radiate its power outward, flutter like a victory-banner, burn like a torch, and fulfill its purpose. (Blachetta 1941, 8)

This is how Blachetta describes the twenty-four runes of the Older Futhark:

1.	ᚠ	*Feh:* This is the rune of the masculine principle and stands for plenty and wealth, as well as abundant seminal power.
2.	ᚢ	*Ur:* This is the rune of the feminine principle and stands for origins and the foundation of all things and also for immortality.
3.	ᚦ	*Thurs:* This is a rune of the masculine principle and stands for the power over life and death.
4.	ᚨ	*As:* This is a rune of the feminine principle and stands for fruitful increase for humans, livestock, and the fields, as well as the healthy, fertile womb of women.
5.	ᚱ	*Rad:* This rune stands for judging, classifying, deciding, explaining, and advising.
6.	ᚲ	*Kaun:* As a chevron, it has the meaning of offspring, child—while the younger *kaun*-rune (ᚴ)is the sign of the masculine desire to procreate, instinct, ardor,
7.	ᚷ	*Gifu:* This is a rune of the procreative union and stands for marriage and increase.
8.	ᚹ	*Wenne:* This rune belongs to the masculine principle and stands for descendant, son.
9.	ᚺ	*Hagal:* The older *hagal*-rune stands for the union of man and woman, blessed with fruitful procreation; it is therefore the rune of procreative marriage. [Blachetta also notes that "The younger *hagal*-rune (✳), stands for humanity, which preserves itself by means of procreation. It is the holy sign that connects humanity and God."]
10.	ᚾ	*Naut:* This *naut*-rune stands for need, descent, defeat, inactive life, death.
11.	ᛁ	This *is*-rune is a rune of the masculine principle and stands for affirmation, the maintaining power, the decisive force, the active will, and the conscious "ego."
12.	ᛃ	The *jar*-rune is a rune of union for the sake of reproduction and stands for: the certainty, that at the end of every life stands the beginning of a new life. [Blachetta also gives another form of the *jar*-rune (⍭), which he says is "a rune of procreative union and stands for division and life-giving generation."]

13.	ᛊ	*Eoh:* Stands for fertility, increase, blooming, blessing, and salvation (*Heil*).
14.	ᛈ	*Peord:* Stands for generation, awaiting, and harvest.
15.	ᛉ	[For this rune, Blachetta refers the reader to the younger "*man*-rune." This, he tells us, "stands for the active, creative, generative principle; for freedom, unfolding, and life."]
16.	ᛋ	The *sig*-rune is a rune of the masculine principle and stands for clarity, but also for division; for solution, but also for dissolution; for liberation, but also for bursting open; and therefore, for life and death. [Blachetta also indicates an alternate form, the *sol*-rune (ᛋ), which he says stands for "knowledge, realization, illumination."]
17.	ᛏ	The *tyr*-rune is a rune of the masculine principle and stands for the deed of generation and completion.
18.	ᛒ	The *bar*-rune is a rune of the feminine principle and stands for the womb of the Mother (Earth), which contains death and life within itself.
19.	ᛖ	The *ehu*-rune stands for marriage and the family. [Here another form is also noted, the *eh*-rune (ᛇ), which Blachetta says "stands for ascension, upswing, elevation, and an honorable life."]
20.	ᛗ	The *man*-rune stands for the human and humanity.
21.	ᛚ	The *lagu*-rune stands for a law-abiding life in good-breeding, order, and law.
22.	ᛝ	The *ing*-rune is the rune of generative union and stands for unity, connection, interpenetration, and fusion. [Blachetta additionally notes the more usual form of the *ng*-rune as ◊ and interprets it as the "life-giving womb of a woman."]
23.	ᛟ	The *odal*-rune is a rune of the feminine principle and stands for destiny (*Schicksal*), aptness, heritage, inheritance, talent, and with this therefore birth.
24.	ᛞ	The *dag*-rune stands for succession, continuation, development.

(BLACHETTA 1941, 87–94)

Blachetta's work was meant for popular consumption, and it is remarkable to see the substantial degree to which there are traces of the ideologies of Guido von List and Herman Wirth to be found in his runology.

THE HITLER JUGEND

It was often in the context of Hitler Youth activities that runes were most prominently used and displayed. The Hitler Youth (Hitler-Jugend; HJ) was the organization for boys within the NSDAP. It originated in 1922 and was officially called the Hitler-Jugend, Bund deutscher Arbeiterjugend (Hitler Youth, League of German Worker Youth) after 1926. During the time of the Third Reich, this was the only legal organization for young men and also had a definite paramilitary aspect to its program and character. For younger boys between the ages of ten and fourteen, there was the preparatory organization called the German Young Folk in the Hitler Youth (Deutsches Jungvolk in der Hitler-Jugend; abbreviated DJ, or DJV). In many respects the Hitler Youth was the heir to the German cultural phenomenon of the late nineteenth century most exemplified in the Wandervogel movement, which had been extremely popular in the years before the Nazis came to power. But whereas the Wandervogel celebrated a wilder sense of wanderlust and was open to boys and girls, men and women, the Hitler Youth was a much more militaristic, disciplined organization exclusively for boys. Its purpose was the indoctrination of the youth into National Socialist ideology from a young age.

Fig. 8.3. Hitler-Jugend emblem

There was a corresponding girls' organization called the Bund Deutscher Mädel (League of German Girls; BDM). This organization was generally a disciplined group with training in various things such as political campaigns and gymnastics. For young women between the ages of seventeen and twenty-one, there was also the organization known as Glaube und Schönheit (Faith and Beauty). The separation of the sexes in these two organizations was officially to avoid the appearance of sexual promiscuity, which had been the reality among the earlier Wandervogel. But such was the case here as well, when it came to relations between the two Nazi youth organizations. Sexual contact between young men and women was not really expressly forbidden, nor were out-of-wedlock pregnancies of the girls treated as a matter of shame. At one Party rally, in which the camps of the two organizations were set up near to one another, nine hundred girls became pregnant.

During the 1930s the Reichsjugendführer (Leader of the Youth Organizations) was Baldur von Schirach (1907–1974). Interestingly, all four of Schirach's grandparents were Americans, and Baldur did not begin to learn German until he was five years old. In 1932 he married Henriette Hoffmann, the daughter of Hitler's personal photographer, Heinrich Hoffmann. This brought von Schirach into Hitler's innermost social circle. In 1940, he became the Gauleiter of Vienna. In that position, he was responsible for deporting great numbers of Jews to the concentration camps in the East. After the war, he stood trial at Nuremberg and was sentenced to twenty years, and he served the entire term.

CHAPTER 9

RELIGIOUS REVOLUTION IN THE THIRD REICH

The Rise of New Religions

One of the constant refrains heard leveled against the National Socialists is that they were attempting to overthrow Christianity and install a new pagan (Ger. *heidnisch*) religion in its stead. This charge began among German churchmen during the time of the Weimar Republic and became a regular feature of propagandistic attacks both during and after the war. Two early examples of this are P. Erhard Schlund's *Neugermanisches Heidentum im heutigen Deutschland* (Neo-Germanic Heathendom in Today's Germany; 1924) and Helmut Lother's *Neugermanische Religion und Christentum* (Neo-Germanic Religion and Christendom; 1934). As we know, and as statistical studies have shown, such a thing as "neopaganism" was never practiced by more than about 15 percent of the German demographic. Moreover, as Hitler himself pointed out in *Mein Kampf,* this practice was always so diverse and unfocused that it would have been useless as a tool for promoting German racial solidarity in line with National Socialist aims.

In the years leading up to the assumption of political power by the NSDAP, and especially in the early years of the Third Reich, religious visionaries were greatly inspired to attempt to formulate a new spiritual approach to life and culture that would be favorable to the Nazis and that they would see as promoting the agenda of the Party in one way or another. Here I will examine three such examples: the

Deutsche Glaubensbewegung of Jakob Wilhelm Hauer, the Deutsche Nationalkirche of Ernst Bergmann, and the Bund für (Deutsche) Gotterkenntnis led by Mathilde Ludendorff. Such efforts, even at the time, came to be called the "Professor Religions," because of the academic credentials of the leaders of these groups.

The most important organizations in this movement during the time period of the Third Reich were the older one led by the artist Ludwig Fahrenkrog (the GGG) and the newer one organized by the professor Jakob Wilhelm Hauer (the Deutsche Glaubensbewegung).

These radical new religious outlooks, if they were not already part of the apparatus of the NSDAP, found it difficult to become established in the ways they might have hoped. Even those intiatives that were firmly installed within the structure of the Party, such as the efforts of Rosenberg and Himmler, found that attaining a level of widespread public acceptance, or even approval within the Party or with Hitler, was in the end impossible.

DIE DEUTSCHE GLAUBENSBEWEGUNG (1933–1945) AND JAKOB WILHELM HAUER

In many respects the Deutsche Glaubensbewegung (German Faith movement) was an organization in the tenor of the Deutsche Orden and Germanische Glaubens-Gemeinschaft, which had been organized earlier in the century as discussed in chapter 4. One of the things that set the German Faith movement apart from the others was the leading stature of its founder, Jakob Wilhelm Hauer (1881–1962), and its close association with the agenda of the NSDAP. This organization was founded seven months after the Nazis came to power and was disbanded at the end of the war because it had been folded into the structure of the Nazi state apparatus. This organization had as its leitmotif the overt rejection of traditional Christianity and the embrace of an Aryo-Nordic faith as it was envisioned by Hauer.

Hauer's life and work has been studied in some detail over the past few years. One of the most informative of these studies is Margarete Dierks's *Jakob Wilhelm Hauer 1881–1962* (1986), while Ulrich Nanko's

Die Deutsche Glaubensbewegung (1993) places the movement in a larger context.

The Early Life of J. W. Hauer

As a young man, Hauer worked as a plasterer, but was later trained as a Christian missionary in Basel and served in British India from 1907 to 1911. While in India he began to study the history of Hinduism and lost his faith in Christianity. Upon his return to Europe, he studied Sanskrit at Oxford and Indology and religious studies at Tübingen. He became a professor at Marburg and then Tübingen. In the 1920s he was gravitating toward National Socialism. He formed a youth organization called the Bund der Köngener, which developed from Protestant Bible-study groups with links to the Wandervogel movement. Fellow Marburg scholar Rudolf Otto led this group for a while. By 1927, Hauer was outlining his own religious synthesis and to this end set up another organization named the Religiöser Menschheitsbund (Religious Human League) with the aim of trying to unify all German religion.

Attempted Cooperation with the NSDAP

Six months after the Nazi seizure of power, Hauer organized a conference of alternative religious movements and thinkers in Eisenach. These included Ernst Bergmann, Arthur Drews, Ludwig Fahrenkrog, Bernard Kummer, Gustav Neckel, Herman Wirth, Hans F. K. Günther, Hermann Mandel, Lother Stengel-von-Rutkowski, Otto Huth, Johann von Leers, Theodor Fritsch, Ernst zu Reventlow, Wilhelm Schwaner, and Georg Stammler. At that point, the Arbeitsgemeinschaft der Deutschen Glaubensbewegung (Alliance of the German Faith movement; ADG) was founded as a sort of umbrella organization but lacked focus or direction. Almost half of the major participants held doctorate degrees. Groups represented at the Eisenach conference included the Germanische Glaubensgemeinschaft (GGG), Volkschaft der Nordungen (Folk-Clan of the Nordungs), Nordische Glaubensgemeinschaft (Nordic Faith Community), the Rig-Kreis (Rig Circle), the Adler und Falken (Eagles and Falcons), Deutschgläubige Gemeinschaft (German Faith Community), the Nordisch-religiöse Arbeitsgemeinschaft (Nordic

Religious Alliance), the Freundeskreis der Kommenden Gemeinde (Friends of the Coming Congregation), and the Bund freireligiöser Gemeinden (League of Independent Religious Congregations). It must be said that although groups such as the more neopagan Nordungen and Deutschgläubigen drew and have drawn almost all of the attention, they represented a decided minority in this mixture of groups, making up no more than 15 percent of the total participation. The great majority was made up of the *Freireligiösen*—the "nondenominationals" among them all. Some of these were atheists, while others could be characterized as *gottgläubig,* meaning that they acknowledged a deity or divine power of some kind but were not part of a Christian denomination, nor necessarily Christians at all.

Within a year, when it became obvious that an overarching federation of these various groups was to be impossible, Hauer and Ernst zu Reventlow founded their own organization, the Deutsche Glaubensbewegung (German Faith movement) in 1934. What sets Hauer's ideology apart is its syncretism between German culture and Hindu mythology, with a heavy emphasis on the ideas contained in the second-century BCE Sanskrit poem called the *Bhagavad Gita.*

By the middle of 1935 most of the groups voted to consolidate themselves as the Deutsche Glaubensbewegung with Hauer as the leader. Adherents, who had to resign from other religious organizations to be full members, could fill out their legal paperwork with the word *deutschgläubig* when answering the question as to religious affiliation. But tensions among the various factions remained high: there were the ones who were oriented toward the völkisch symbolism and those who favored a more modernistic approach; some were strongly anti-Christian, others less so. The group was full of National Socialist activists who took full advantage of these tensions. In March 1936, Hauer was forced out of the leadership position by the NS members, and he resigned from the organization. Among the problems the Nazi members saw was Hauer's vehement and arrogant anti-Christian stance. Basically, the DGB was absorbed into the SS and remained without a leader for a period. The group became an operative wing of the SS in matters of religious questions.

Obviously, Hauer's greatest strategic error personally was that he did not even join the NSDAP until 1937, well after his efforts had been officially thwarted. Success in the Party often largely hinged on whether the person in question had joined before or after January 30, 1933.

With respect to ideology, the DGB drew a good deal of its ideas from the folk-based beliefs of the German (or Positive) Christians and was rooted in what was called "authentic piety": religious beliefs traceable to German cultural examples. This reflected a basic intellectual model of the time—that is, what was best was what was autochthonous and belonged to one's own culture or nation. Hauer notably introduced the idea of a wider Indo-Germanic identity, in which "Aryan" was equated with "Germanic," and did so in a way that included a strong link to the world of India and the Vedas.

The German Faith movement of Hauer was not what many might think it was. It was not, as intimated by Carl Jung in his essay on "Wotan," linked to the old Germanic pagan gods as such. It was rather a nontheistic, heroically ethical materialistic religion, oriented toward that which Nietzsche had called *Diesseitigkeit,* "this-worldliness," with an ambivalent relationship to Christianity and its symbols. Hauer had encouraged members of his organization to work together with Protestants and Catholics, finding their common ground in German-ness.

Theologically, many neopagan groups of this time made efforts to prove that the ancient Germanic or Nordic religion was not a polytheistic one, as most scholars assumed, but rather was originally monotheistic.*

It was Hauer's intention to create a corporate entity that would be accepted as having a coequal status with the confessional churches. The demographics of the so-called neopagans often included significant numbers of former communists and atheists.

---

*Earlier German Romantics sought to show that the ancient indigenous faith of their ancestors was monotheistic in nature, even if this monotheism was on an unconscious level (see Grimm 1966, I:13–28). This sort of monotheism could be focused on either an impersonal force or on a revision of a high god, such as Wodan, to the status of a sole creator-god. In this they appear to be (unconsciously) following the path of the ancients who focused their spiritual lives henotheistically on the god *Wōðanaz.

Hauer's organization was responsible for producing a number of journals or periodicals. Members received the journal *Deutscher Glaube: Zeitschrift für arteigene Lebensgestaltung, Weltschau und Frömmigkeit* (German Faith: Journal for an Authentic Life-Formation, Worldview, and Piety). It had a print run of four thousand. A more popular general magazine called *Durchbruch—Kampfblatt für deutschen Glauben, Rasse und Volkstum* (Breakthrough—Polemic for German Faith, Race, and Folk) was established in 1934. The latter publication was fiercely anti-clerical and had to cease publication in 1937.

Although Hauer seems to have had little success in establishing his version of German Faith within the apparatus of the NSDAP, he had stirred up so much notoriety for himself abroad during the years of the Third Reich that he was removed from his university post immediately after the war, imprisoned until August 1947 on the basis of so-called automatic arrest, and forced to pay the cost of his legal proceedings. He then formed the Arbeitsgemeinschaft für freie Religionsforschung und Philosophie (Alliance for Independent Religious Research and Philosophy) and later the Freie Akademie (Independent Academy) in 1955. He continued to write, and the old organization remained active—at least in theory—until his death in 1962.

ERNST BERGMANN AND
THE *DEUTSCHE NATIONALKIRCHE*

Ernst Bergmann (1881–1945) was the son of a Protestant pastor. He studied philosophy and philology in Leipzig, receiving his Ph.D. in 1905, and subsequently became a lecturer at the same university. In his early years, Bergmann was a disciple of Nietzsche's ideas and worked on the philosophy of the French materialist Julien Offray de la Mettrie. During WWI he volunteered but was unsuited to military service and released from duty in 1916. Bergmann was married to a Jewish woman from 1917 to 1921, and they had a son named Peter who later fell on the Western Front fighting for the Nazis. By the late 1920s he was more and more dedicated to some form of *Deutschglaube*—"German-faith."

In 1927, he married a woman with similar beliefs. He became a member of the NSDAP in 1930 and two years later he renounced the church. Bergmann then committed himself to the development of a religious and philosophical system within what he thought was a National Socialist context. He became a member of the leadership council of the aforementioned Arbeitsgemeinschaft der Deutschen Glaubensbewegung in July 1933.

That same year Bergmann composed his *Confessio Germanica* (Germanic Acknowledgment of Faith):

I believe in the God of the German Religion, which operates in nature, in the exalted human spirit, and in the power of his Volk. And [I believe] in the helper in time of need, Krist, who fights for the nobility of the human soul. And [I believe] in Germany, the land of development for a new humanity.

Bergmann promoted the elimination of Christianity and the return to an autochthonous mysticism in order to supersede Christianity, which in his view was far too tainted with Jewish concepts.

Bergmann acknowledged that the "Odin's religion" had been the most beautiful and authentic religion for the Germanic people, beside which Christianity appeared to be an unnatural religion of sickness and degeneracy, which he again traced back to its Jewish origins. But what he advocated bore little resemblance to things "Odinic" in any historical sense.

With Bergmann, as with most of those who promoted so-called neopagan religious views during the Third Reich, there is little to none of the mythic content of the ancient Germanic or Indo-European tradition. For the most part, the spiritual dimension hinged on eighteenth- and nineteenth-century German philosophy, and special readings or interpretations of medieval German mystics such as Meister Eckhart. Race and biology had replaced the mythic content of the old religion—in all of this, as we have seen, such neopagans were supported by the views of Hitler.

Bergmann's version of religion was especially dedicated to the practices of eugenics, of both the positive and negative sort. He supported elimination of degenerate life and saw a future where the cities would be cleared out of degraded genetic material. His works, along with many other ones expressing National Socialist philosophy, were placed on an index of forbidden literature by Pope Pius XI.

Despite his academic position and early support of the Nazis, his efforts to establish the German *Nationalkirche* (National Church) were not successful.

On April 18, 1945, as the Americans were entering the city at the end of the war, Bergmann committed suicide.

THE LUDENDORFF MOVEMENT

The Bund für (Deutsche) Gotterkenntnis (League for [German] Knowledge of God; BfG) was a group founded by General Erich Ludendorff and his wife, Mathilde. It is often identified with the name Ludendorff. Mathilde, who was a psychiatrist, was clearly the religious ideologue. After the First World War, in which the general was a hero, leading the German army to victory in the Battle of the Tannenberg (August 26–30, 1914). Ludendorff was a supporter of the Nazis and participated in the Beer Hall Putsch. In harmony with the ideas of Alfred Rosenberg, the Ludendorffs organized their ideas and formed the BfG. The religious self-designation of some people became *gottgläubig,* meaning that they believed in a deity, but not one that could be contained by any known denomination. The Ludendorffs and works they published were often critical of Hitler and the Nazis, and factions within the Party saw them as ideological competitors. The Ludendorffs, who generally demanded that their followers resign from the Christian churches they might have been born into, charged Hitler with being a co-conspirator with the churches given the *Konkordat* he concluded with the Vatican, which legitimized the churches in German political life. After the Nazi seizure of power in 1933, the BfG was banned as an organization. But eventually the Ludendorff organization received permission to reorganize after a personal meeting between Hitler and the general in 1937, shortly before the latter's death. Since the government finally outlawed most other organizations of this kind in that year, the BfG can be counted as one of the very few such groups that were allowed to continue to exist in the Third Reich.

With respect to ideology, the BfG can be generally placed within the neo-Germanic sphere, although a few traces of traditional cultic or mythic content are in evidence.* The idea of race and heredity of moral and psychological characteristics are central concepts, but the philosophical underpinnings provided by Dr. Ludendorff propel the league into the sphere of the esoteric.

The BfG represents an effort to create a system in which the philosophy of religion and the laws of science were in absolute harmony. The conception of God was a fully pantheistic one. A personal God is rejected, as is monotheism in the Judeo-Christian sense. God is seen as an all-pervasive force and set of laws of nature.

A fundamental aspect of religious activity is seen to be maintaining a strict separation between and among the various ethnic groups of the world. Mixing them or making hybrids is seen as something to be avoided, as it thwarts the will of the divine and causes whole cultures to be lost or corrupted. The Ludendorffs blamed the Jews, Jesuits, the Roman Catholic Church, Freemasons, and Socialists for the degenerate state of affairs, and Mathilde especially also targeted *occult* organizations and methods. She claimed that occult groups not only organize against the interests of the German race, but they also foster practices that lead to insanity in the individual. The Ludendorffs pejoratively criticized other völkisch religious groups, such as that of Hauer, as "occult."

The writings of Mathilde Ludendorff make it clear that she saw herself as a seeress of some kind, one who had discovered the laws of nature and of the human mind and soul. Her works were to be *absorbed,* not merely read.

---

*Because of the unique traits of the BfG in comparison with other organizations of the time, this group is treated in its own section in Puschner and Vollnals's handbook, *Die völkisch-religiöse Bewegung im Nationalsozialismus* (2012), 127–47.

As we will see, the BfG was revived after the war in an attempt to press forward with Mathilde's philosophy.

POSITIVE CHRISTIANITY

Contrary to the claims of postwar apologists and historical propagandists for Christianity, who have constantly tried to make Nazism appear to be pagan or even Satanic, it is important to keep in mind just how much of the National Socialist movement and the personal philosophy of Adolf Hitler was *a part of Christianity* as they and he understood it. An important study in this regard is offered by Richard Steigmann-Gall, *The Holy Reich* (2003). This book is subtitled "Nazi Conceptions of Christianity, 1919–1945" and details just how thoroughly a certain concept of Christianity, based on longstanding Christian traditions, shaped and motivated Nazi ideology.

Fig. 9.1. SA-men and Hitler Youth promote the
"German Christians" in 1933 church elections, Berlin
(German Federal Archive)

The only mention of religion made in the NSDAP program of the Twenty-Five Points is an explicit reference to the concept of Positive Christianity in point 24. Steigmann-Gall (2003, 14) observes that the wording of the point encompasses three key ideas: "the spiritual struggle against the Jews, the promulgation of a social ethic, and a new syncretism that would bridge Germany's confessional divide." The authors of the Party Program equated Christianity with the spiritual, whereas they believed that Jews and their religion were entirely defined by, and limited to, material existence.

Technically, the term *Positive Christianity* meant a Christianity shorn of its miraculous fables and its Jewish context. It posits the role of the historical individual named Jesus as an exemplary model of the Aryan Man.* The foundational documents of Christianity (i.e., the Bible) were subjected to text-critical examination by which all irrational elements were eliminated and the whole message and nature of the religion remade in the image of the philosophical approach of the nineteenth century.

The roots of the Nazis' conception of Positive Christianity lie in the late nineteenth century with the school of Richard Wagner and his son-in-law, Houston Stewart Chamberlain. They crystalized a vision of an Aryanized Christianity, devoid of what they considered Judaic elements. Jesus Christ was seen as the Aryan Man, and, commenting on his use of ancient pre-Christian Germanic imagery and myth in some of his operas, Wagner himself identifies Wotan and Christ (Steigmann-Gall 2003, 101).

Up to the time of the Nazi assumption of power in 1933, Positive Christianity seems to have been an unorganized concept or ideology. After the apparatus of the state came into in the hands of NSDAP officials (some of whom were part of the Christian denominational mainstream, while others were not), the situation began to change rapidly.

---

*Similar claims would underlie the early twentieth-century phenomenon of British Israelism or Identity Christianity. The thesis of Identity Christianity is essentially that the ethnic protagonists of the Old Testament, the ancient Hebrews, were not Semites but rather Aryans; their descendants are therefore not the modern Jews but the Caucasian Europeans.

With the support of the NSDAP, formal Positive Christian organizations soon began to spring up, although they never succeeded in forging a unified or well-organized movement during the Third Reich. In this regard, it mirrored other aspects of Nazi (dis-)organization on many fronts.

The current view of establishment historians is that the Positive Christian movement was a general failure due to the "fact" that the Nazi leadership was "anti-Christian" and that there was a significant resistance mounted by mainstream churches to the idea. Both of these assumptions are generally false. The idea that the "pagan" aspects of Nazism were so strong is significantly modified when we look at certain statistics: The membership of "German Christian" organizations in Nazi Germany numbered around a half a million, whereas the leading so-called pagan organization, the German Faith movement, had around forty thousand members with an additional thirty thousand sympathizers (Bergen 1996, 2, 14). Enthusiasm for the church, whether Protestant or Catholic, was waning significantly in the early part of the twentieth century in Germany. (Today only about 13 percent of Germans attend church regularly, and these are generally of the older generations.) During the period of the Weimar Republic, an arrangement was made between the church and state for the support of churches by means of taxes collected by the state. The arrangement was generally followed in the period of the Third Reich, although not as smoothly as it is today. Hitler asserted in a speech in 1933 that Christianity was a foundation of German culture, and the many references to Christian concepts and verbal formulas in *Mein Kampf* show the degree to which his mind in particular was shaped by (pseudo-)Christian concepts. Hitler's famous agreement (the *Konkordat*) with the Vatican in September 1933 even remains in force today. It ensures the loyalty of the church to the state and preserves the quasi-independence of church activities. It gave religious legitimacy to the Nazi regime and formed a working relationship between the Vatican and the German government.

A telling document regarding the deep-seated views of at least one member of the highest Nazi leadership toward Christianity and its symbols is the novel *Michael* by Joseph Goebbels, published in 1929.

It is written in the form of a diary in which the protagonist, Michael, ruminates over the state of Germany in the years following the Great War. There are many overt positive references toward Christianity and to Christ. Michael declares at one point that the Germans ought to become something like "Christ Socialists" (Goebbels 1987, 65). By the same token, he also states that modern man must become what he called a Christ-man, an emulation of Christ whom Goebbels identifies as a "great man." The name of the novel's protagonist was undoubtedly chosen as an allusion to the archangel Michael, whose name means "Who is like God" in Hebrew and is seen as a soldier of god and the one who conquers evil influences. Although most dismiss the novel as something written before Goebbels "lost his Catholic faith," the date of its publication (which was several years after Goebbels had become a leader in the NSDAP) and the fact that it was published by a Party publishing house, all would indicate that the contents of the book were considered within the bounds of National Socialist thinking.

Tenets of Positive Christianity

Since the days of Emil-Louis Burnouf and Paul de Lagarde, and on to Richard Wagner and H. S. Chamberlain, the tenets of what would come to be called Positive Christianity in the Twenty-Points of the NSDAP were developing in a detailed but disparate way. With the organization of groups of German Christians in the age of the Third Rich, these tenets became more established. Perhaps one of the best summaries of what this all meant in Nazi Germany is expressed in the book *Positive Christianity in the Third Reich* by the theologian D. Cajus Fabricius, an English translation of which was published in 1937.

Fabricius answers the question "What is Positive Christianity?" as follows:

> It means at any rate the religion that has grown and become as one with the spirit of the German nation throughout the history of the centuries. The utterances of the Führer have made this perfectly clear. . . .
>
> "Positive" means here as everywhere "the real thing," but in the

case of a spiritual power like religion, it means what is a historical reality. (Fabricius 1937, 23)

Fabricius continues to define the term *positive* in this way:

[Positive] may be understood as something opposed to what is artificial, supposed or pretended. Thus a difference has been made between the positive, historical religion and a rational, philosophical trend of thought. Taken in this sense, to profess "Positive Christianity" would be to reject all systems of freethought and free religion together with all would-be rationalistic interpretations of Christianity. Again "Positive Christianity" may be taken to mean what is universally known as "practical Christianity," which is a Christianity not exhausting itself in expressing convictions of faith but one active in loving one's neighbour. (Fabricius 1937, 23–24)

Obviously, the author understands "one's neighbor" as a fellow German and "Christian"—that is, an Aryan (non-Jew).

Fabricius asserts that "Positive Christianity is the innermost life, the spirit, the soul of the National Socialistic German People, or in other words, National Socialism itself has its roots deep in the Christian spirit; it is a movement determined by Christianity" (1937, 32–33). Furthermore, he makes clear the triangular nature of the struggle for the soul of the Party when he writes:

[I]t must be determined in how far the forces proceeding from freethought [atheism] are inadequate or detrimental to the life of the *Volk*. And above all, we must keep in view in how far Christian forces are conducive to success in the present heroic fight of the German *Volk* for life and honour, and to what extent pagan forces are a hindrance. (Fabricius 1937, 35)

In the section of the book called "Kinship with God and Dominion over the World," Fabricius argues that the connection of the German Volk to the Christian God is its true source of strength and heroism in the many struggles it has faced. He sees connection with this higher power as the surest source of victory. Furthermore, he again alludes to the idea that atheistic scientism and paganism are less than adequate, and even impractical, in this process. In some ways Fabricius argues from a pragmatic stance.

In a section called "God and *Volk*," he writes:

We must now investigate the question as to how the Christian's belief in God harmonizes with belief in the German *Volk*, one of the basic principles of the National resurgence. There are certain people, those to whom the Führer alludes as "men in bear-skins," who would appear desirous of establishing a new Germanic "Folk-religion." Our standpoint with regard to this matter is as follows:

Since in religion man rises to the superhuman, which means he advances beyond human limitations and communes with the Power recognized by him to be the Ruler of the world, so is the horizon of the world which man conceives in experiencing God of great vastness at every stage of religion. (Fabricius 1937, 43–44)

Fabricius also addresses the function and role of the Führer in this new German understanding of religion and politics.

[I]n this important point National Socialists, as is compatible with their whole attitude of mind, are on the side of Christianity and not of free-thought. For like Christians they have not gained their views of life from any system of philosophy, but from the stern realities of life. One fact in this struggle for existence has become to them an overpowering reality: the Führer. In him they have experienced the incontestable fact that all great happenings in history do not originate in the universal but in the particular, not in crowds but in some great personality. In him too, they have experienced that great historical deeds are not only planned in the magnificence of royal palaces, or at the official boards of parliaments and ministries, or even in the buildings of large banking-houses, but they may have their source in one simple life that started in modest circumstances, having to struggle onward through poverty and privation, and after much hard fighting finally reaches the height, and even on the height thinks only of self-denial and sacrifice.

. . . The Führer himself belongs to those who fulfil the will of God and realize the life of Christ in this life in an extraordinary degree. The Führer in uniting the nation and helping it to rise from the laxity and neglect into which it had fallen, to a sense of moral discipline, fulfils the law of Christ respecting love in a way few mortals could ever hope to emulate. By defending with a strong hand the spiritual heritage of the German nation against the powers of darkness, he also protects our most sacred possession, the Gospel, guaranteeing moreover, the further spread of its power. (Fabricius 1937, 70–71)

Positive Christianity was mainly anchored in the Protestant areas of Germany, but it recognized that Germany was made up of "two great churches," the Protestant and Catholic. The confessing, or mainstream and orthodox, churches in Germany had been engaged in a decades- and centuries-long anti-Semitic campaign, so that dimension of the German Christian movement was not at the crux of the conflict between the Positive Christians and the confessing churches. Rather it appears that the opposition of many churchmen to the whole National Socialist movement and its auxiliary features, such as atheistic scientism and what was seen as paganism in one form or another, was a response to the movement's rejection of the historical underpinnings of the church: its Judaic roots, its universality, and its supernatural avenue for human redemption from a "Fallen" state.

Clearly, the intellectual and spiritual antagonisms that arose between various religious forces in Germany during the time of the Third Reich were real. It was not merely a struggle of two opposing sides, however. It was a battle royal among several divergent views, and often the conflicts were inner ones, felt by the individual leaders involved and played out in the culture of this short-lived political movement. The combatants can be described as pagans, Positive Christians, atheists, the gottgläubige (those who believed in an unspecified deity), and—most importantly—those for whom the Party itself and its Führer had come to replace that part of themselves that might have otherwise been occupied by "religion."

The Wagnerian vision of a new form of the Christian faith, purified of its Jewish origins, was obviously ideally suited to the purposes of the National Socialists. The masses of the German people could not be moved by messages of a return to paganism, and only a few of the leaders of the NSDAP showed any real interest in paganism or the occult. A small number of them formally resigned from the church into which they had been baptized. These included Himmler, Hess, and Rosenberg, but most notably, Hitler did not make such a formal renunciation. The masses were still moved by Christian imagery, and so this is the imagery the Nazis most effectively used and exploited in their efforts to fold the will of the masses into the will of the Party. This process, after all, was the true "holy grail" of Nazi propaganda, or its "magic."

In the final analysis, however, Positive Christianity was a general failure as a movement. In many respects, it failed simply because the mainstream Catholic and Protestant Churches were already doing the kind of work this organization was supposed to do. We have seen how the anti-Semitic writings of Martin Luther were obviously mainstream ideas in the Evangelical Lutheran Church. Himmler admired them, and the city of Nuremberg presented a gift of the first edition of Luther's *On the Jews and Their Lies* to the hyper-anti-Semite Julius Streicher on his birthday in 1937. In 1941 seven Protestant regional confederations published a document agreeing with the law forcing Jews to be marked by the yellow badge. The infamous *Kristallnacht* (November 9–10, 1938) was meant to coincide with Martin Luther's birthday (November 10). And while Positive Christianity can be to some degree classified as an occult idea, due to its peculiar set of beliefs (including the Aryan Christ), anti-Semitism cannot be so classified. Anti-Semitism was part of the warp and weft of establishment, consensual thinking in Europe and America until after the end of WWII.

CHAPTER 10

OCCULT DIMENSIONS OF NAZI SCIENCES

The Weaponization of the Occult

As we have seen, Germany was a scientific mecca during the late nineteenth and early twentieth centuries. The country was more scientifically advanced than perhaps any other in the world. It therefore will come as no surprise that this science and technology would be brought to bear in the war effort during the Nazi regime—and this includes some of the fringe areas of science that bordered on what could be considered occult beliefs. In this chapter I will focus on disciplines that we associate with the hard sciences, and even in some cases the so-called social sciences, of today. As will become apparent, there is also an occult dimension to these scientific and technological pursuits in Nazi Germany, either as practiced at the time or as they were later mythologized. Despite the astounding facts of what the Germans accomplished in the technical fields during the period of the National Socialist regime, the facts in no way can compete with the fantastic myths that developed surrounding these scientific advances in the postwar years. I will treat this postwar mythologizing of Nazi secret technologies in chapter 13.

There are what might be called hard sciences, which are usually based on quantifiable and mathematically rooted realities—for example, chemistry, biology, physics, and the like. The Germans came to call these the *Naturwissenschaften* (natural sciences). The scientific approach to the humanities, on the other hand, hinges mainly upon linguistic knowledge and the theoretically based observation of related symbolic cultural patterns. Such sciences are called *Geisteswissenschaften,* literally "intellectual sciences," in German. An undisciplined approach to these intellectual sciences can soon fall under the domination of political or religious ideology and then descend into mere propaganda. Such was often the fate of the humanities in Nazi Germany. The natural sciences have math to check this drift, but as we see even today, this is not foolproof. The humanities are always more subject to ideological pressure, because there can be the appearance of the practice of the Geisteswissenschaften without having done the basic qualifying work to undertake the discipline. This is how men such as Wiligut or Weigel could gain the positions they did in runic or symbolic studies. The natural sciences, too, have always been subject to ideological pressures. This pressure usually comes from religious or political interests that are motivated either to gain or maintain power over the people. The medieval church fought against Copernicus and Galileo to preserve the Aristotelian geocentric model to make *itself* the center of the universe. More recently, similar types of manipulation have occurred in different scientific fields for political reasons. The Nazis certainly engaged in such manipulations, as did the Soviets and other totalitarian regimes. I leave it to the reader to examine whether we in the West are likewise subject to this phenomenon today.

Outside of the regular scientific spectrum, there are the *Geheimwissenschaften,* the "secret" or occult sciences, which lie either beyond the limits or below the surface of the established sciences of the modern consensus reality.

A pioneering effort in the study of Nazi Geheimwissenschaften was Nigel Pennick's 1981 survey titled *Hitler's Secret Sciences.* This work takes into account much of the "Nazi occult" literature that had been produced in the 1970s, but it is particularly strong in the field of the author's area of expertise: geomancy and the study of sacred sites. The Nazis were especially passionate about establishing such sites, as had been mandated by Hitler in *Mein Kampf:* "The geo-political significance of a focal center in a movement cannot be overemphasized" (p. 347). This field of propagandistic interest then opened the gates for those interested in accessing the powers of the Earth and mysterious "lines of force" in the landscape. For our purposes in this chapter, however, we will try to limit ourselves to the occult dimensions of intellectual traditions that were seeking to become established within the National Socialist state. It will become apparent that discovering the occult side of the natural sciences is often a difficult task. Most investigators are quickly drawn into the highly romanticized worlds of runes, Vikings, Templars, and Tibet, much to the detriment of the study of the Nazi uses of science and technology. There are several likely reasons for this. First, science is difficult to study and understand. It is difficult for me as well. Another reason is that the Romantic side is more interesting and holds a dark fascination now, just as it did then. Finally, perhaps, the Romantic aspects can easily be rejected and denied as being weird and sinister, whereas the scientific dimensions were actually often embraced and utilized by the Allies as well.

Heather Pringle's 2008 work titled *The Master Plan: Himmler's Scholars and the Holocaust* has a rather misleading title. If anything, the book demonstrates that there was no master plan, but rather a jumble of projects fueled by private and personal agendas and obsessions. The title obviously evokes the notorious idea of a Nazi plan to create the Master Race through eugenics programs, but the book says virtually nothing about this. Instead the author is quickly seduced into discussing the sexier bits of Nazi lore having to do with paganism and neopaganism, with extended digressions into the work of Herman Wirth—apparently forgetting the fact that Wirth was himself eventually rejected by the Nazis and that his ideas were generally not implemented in any NS plan, masterful or otherwise. The scholars she chooses to discuss are from certain fields of the Geisteswissenschaften, with no place for physicists, biologists, and so on. There is not even a mention of Karl Haushofer. Despite these shortcomings, the book is a solid source for what the author has handpicked to discuss.

The best and most convenient review of how scientific issues played out in the world of National Socialist Germany is that of John Cornwell's *Hitler's Scientists* (2003). With respect to the use of secret and innovative technologies in the German war effort in general, it will be found that there existed an Achilles heel of irrational ideology and an *occult* dimension as applied to science throughout the history of this topic. German scientists of the orthodox Nazi sort were always looking for some way to construct an "Aryan physics," for example, and some scientific findings (e.g., Einstein's Theory of Relativity) were denounced and rejected as "Jewish physics." This ended up hampering certain technological developments and was a real disadvantage for the war effort. By contrast, pragmatic and utilitarian Anglo-American scientists historically were not encumbered by such ideological baggage. The politicizing of science and its coercion into fashionable ideological causes is an extreme impediment to actual progress. It should be noted that Soviet scientists were similarly encumbered by ideology—as everything had to conform to a theory of historical materialism, which caused the Soviet Union to lose tremendous ground to the West over the years. Both the Nazis and Soviets were in many ways defeated by their own self-imposed ideological limitations.

KARL HAUSHOFER, *GEOPOLITIK,* AND *LEBENSRAUM*

The science—or some might say pseudoscience—of geopolitics was not an invention of Karl Haushofer, nor was it originally a German idea. It was pioneered in America by both the Monroe Doctrine and the work of the naval strategist Alfred Thayer Mahan (1840–1914), and in the service of the British Empire by Sir Halford Mackinder (1861–1947). It was formalized and coined as a technical term by the Swedish political scientist Rudolf Kjellen in 1905. Kjellen was a student of the German Friedrich Ratzel (1844–1904), who can be seen as the direct forerunner of Haushofer's *Geopolitik.* As for Mackinder, he became best known for his work "The Geographical Pivot of History," in which he described the geography of the world as constituting a "World-Island" (Eurasia), with its epicenter in Eastern Europe. The medial zone surrounding it included Britain and Japan, for example, and then there was an outermost zone that included the Americas and Australia. The "heartland" of the world according to this theory is located between the Volga and the Yangtze Rivers. Mackinder stated: "Who rules East Europe commands the Heartland; who rules the Heartland commands the World-Island; who rules the World-Island commands the world" (1996, xviii).

This formulation can be seen as the ultimate rationale for Operation Barbarossa.

Geopolitik had enjoyed a considerable evolution in German thought over the years. Its deeper roots can be traced to the works of Carl Ritter (1779–1859), who developed an organic conception of the state. The state, like the individual, had a compelling interest in survival and desire to thrive, even at the expense of other competing neighbors. Ultimately, Haushofer's ideas can be seen to be a synthesis of the ideas of Oswald Spengler, Alexander von Humboldt, Carl Ritter, Friedrich Ratzel, Rudolf Kjellen, and Halford J. Mackinder.

The concept of Geopolitik was, however, elaborately systematized, refined, and promoted by a German general and professor at the University of Munich named Karl Haushofer (1869–1946), about whom many a fantasy has been spun in the literature of Nazi occultism. Haushofer was born into a family of artists and scholars. By the end of his life he was a household name in Germany due to his nationally broadcast monthly radio lectures, which aired between 1925 and 1931, and again between 1933 and 1939. In addition, he wrote major books,

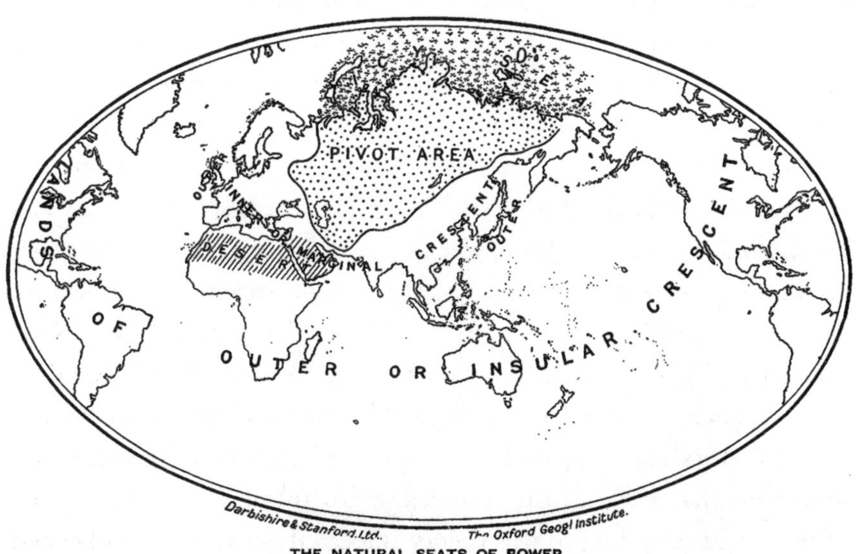

Fig. 10.1. A map from Mackinder's article
"The Geographical Pivot of History"

hundreds of articles, and had his own journal, *Zeitschrift für Geopolitik*. In the early part of his life he was in the military and served as military attaché in Japan, where he was received by Emperor Meiji. In 1911 he was given leave from the military for health reasons. He took the opportunity to undertake academic studies and received a doctorate in philosophy from the University of Munich. During WWI, Haushofer served on the Western Front and retired as a major general after the war. Back at the University of Munich in 1919, he made the acquaintance of a student who subsequently served as his assistant—Rudolf Hess. Through this connection, Haushofer became directly involved with the affairs of the NSDAP. Both German military leaders and leaders of the Nazi Party were sent copies of all of Haushofer's works throughout the years.

The scientific context of the theory of *Lebensraum* (living space) is discussed by John Cornwell (2003, 174–77) under the heading of "*Geopolitik* and *Lebensraum*." He expresses his doubt that geopolitics is a science at all and can rather be ascribed to "an idiosyncratic version of cultural and political history." Nevertheless, it penetrated to governmental policy makers in many countries, and remains a factor in today's world.

Fig. 10.2. Prof. Karl Haushofer and Rudolf Hess, circa 1920

By 1933, Haushofer was named a full professor at the university, and after the Nazi seizure of power his link through Hess remained strong. Hess protectively assisted the Haushofers with regard to the fact that the professor's wife was deemed to be "half-Jewish" according to Nazi racial laws. However, Haushofer's son, Albrecht, himself a professor of geopolitics in Berlin, became active in the conservative resistance to Hitler and may have been instrumental in the failed attempt by Rudolf Hess to make peace with Britain in May 1941. Due to the close connection between the elder Haushofer and Hess, the old professor lost much of his influence on the Lebensraum policies after Hess undertook his bizarre mission. Albrecht also participated in the July 20 plot to assassinate Hitler in 1944 and was arrested and later shot at Moabit Prison in Berlin by the SS in April 1945. Haushofer himself, along with other family members, was arrested and spent time in Dachau on suspicions of some connection with his son's activities.

After the war, Haushofer was informally interrogated by Allied authorities and deemed not to be culpable of any war crimes, although it was also determined that Haushofer's theories had a significant influence on Hitler's strategic thinking. Despite all this, on the night of March 10, 1946, both Haushofer and his wife committed suicide in a secluded spot on their estate in Bavaria named "Hartschimmelhof."

GEOPOLITIK AND THE OCCULT

Geopolitics is difficult to really characterize as an *"occult* science." It can be seen as an underlying principle at work in many of the successful (and several of the failed) attempts to establish empires in the world, both ancient and modern. John Dee can be seen to be a practitioner of the theory in his advising of Elizabeth I. The fact that its principles often are applied in secret and the fact that as a concept it often runs contrary, or as an alternative, to both modern globalist and nationalistic theories of politics, qualify it as a nonestablished, visionary science, and hence one that has occult dimensions.

There remains controversy over how much influence Haushofer had on Hitler's ideas. Haushofer's theories seem to have influenced

Hitler's plans for Eastern Europe, as expressed, for example, in chapter 14 of *Mein Kampf,* but the professor's influence was not of a direct or mentoring sort. Hess was a student of Haushofer, and this may have been the indirect route the ideas took in entering Hitler's thinking. Haushofer may have also played a pivotal role in the relationship between the Empire of Japan and the German Reich in the formation of the Axis. The main contributions of Haushofer's Geopolitik to Nazi strategic ideology are: (1) the idea of the necessity of Lebensraum; (2) the promotion of an organic state; (3) the desirability of an autarky (self-sufficiency); (4) the development of *Panideen* (panideas)* and "panregions" (enlarged regional spheres of economic and military power based on a panidea); and (5) the usual dichotomy between land powers (such as Germany sought to develop) and sea powers (such as Britain represented). In Haushofer's mind, the Reich was a cultural rather than a biological reality, and it was culture (language, customs, etc.) that could guide the areas of expansion beyond Germany's borders, rather than military or purely economic factors. He saw statistics of high population density, decreased birthrate, and heavy urbanization as signs of a weakening state. The solution to these problems was increased "living space," or *Lebensraum.*

Haushofer's most conspicuous connection with the actual inner circle of Nazi hierarchy obviously came in the form of his relationship with his former student, Rudolf Hess. Hess was imprisoned with Hitler and acted as his secretary in the writing of *Mein Kampf.* The two were visited by the professor while they were in Landsberg prison after the failed Beer Hall Putsch in 1923. They had a six-hour meeting, during which Haushofer provided them some reference materials, including Friedrich Ratzel's 1897 work *Politische Geographie* (Political Geography).

Although Haushofer would become a central figure in the postwar mythologizing of Nazi occult connections, there is no consensus from established historians about the extent of his actual influence on Hitler.

---

*Panideas are ideological frameworks that can serve as the basis for geographical-political units, such as "Panislamism," "Panasianism," or "Pangermanism."

Immediately after the war, the professor himself downplayed any role he might have had. The fact that his son Albrecht was executed by the SS and that he and his whole family often had a contentious relationship with Nazi authorities (including his own eight months in Dachau) probably markedly affected his attitude.

One important fact to keep in mind is that Haushofer was never a member of the NSDAP. It is also known that he voiced disagreements with the Party. He was friendly with left-wing members of the Party, such as Georg Strasser, and advocated a German-Russian alliance at one point. Haushofer was not anti-Semitic and actually believed more in a regional and cultural definition of the Volk, rather than a strictly biological one.

A revealing article by Edmund A. Walsh, "The Mystery of Haushofer," was published in *Life* magazine in September 1946, shortly after the professor's death. Walsh, who was Haushofer's interrogator at Nuremberg and exonerated him from war crimes, describes how the professor felt trapped by the Nazi regime. On page 114 of the article, a diagram appears that purports to show how Haushofer supposedly sat at the center of a web of influence in Nazi Germany. Given many known facts about Haushofer's life, activities, and personal relationships, this idea of his influence seems to be a combination of partial truth and wishful thinking. Haushofer himself did not believe that Hitler understood his theories and only counted Rudolf Hess and Konstantin von Neurath, the one-time Minister of Foreign Affairs, among the Nazis who "had a certain understanding of geopolitics—without being able to apply it successfully" (Walsh 1946, 117).

These facts all tend to cast a great a shadow of doubt on claims about Haushofer's continuing close linkage with Hitler, as well as the postwar stories that he was a member of the Thule Society, a student of Zen Buddhism, or an initiate of Tibetan lamas, and so on.

Geopolitik as a concept, with its ideas of Eurasia being the "pivot area" or even called the "heartland," can be seen to lie in the occult spectrum. That this particular region, which likely corresponded to the original homeland of the Indo-Europeans, would still have a mystical hold on strategists in the twentieth century is striking. These ideas seem to run counter to any logical assessment of global power, yet they are persistent. That is, the ideas of Geopolitik just described tend toward a theory of separate autochthonous regions with internally based economies and security concerns, as opposed to a global market-place controlled by multinational corporations with little to no concern for national or regional boundaries.

As we will see in part 4 of this book, Haushofer became a favorite topic for postwar mythologizers of Nazi occult. The reasons for this are probably that he was already the subject of speculation during the war (e.g., in the 1943 American propaganda film *Plan for Destruction*) and the fact that Haushofer *was* a powerful member of the academic establishment in Germany. Haushofer, as a person, certainly does form an interesting connection between what could be described as occult beliefs and the regime of the NSDAP. But postwar Nazi mythologizers will make even more of his influence and importance than was ever the case in reality.

MILITARY TECHNOLOGIES

The main innovative technologies used by the German military during the war were the V-1 ("buzz bomb") cruise missile, the V-2 long-range missile, and the Messerschmitt Me 262 jet fighter. All of these constituted military technologies that the Allies were unable to match but would later become the basis of advanced weapons development in America after the war. At the time when these devices were being tested and deployed by the Germans they were not anything that could be considered "occult," although they did give rise to the plausibility of other stranger technologies. Such speculations crept into the minds of people on all sides, both official and civilian—*if* the Nazis had flying bombs, rockets, and jet aircraft, what *else* did they have that remained secret?

The V-weapons were so dubbed because they were thought of as instruments of vengeance (Ger. *Vergeltung*). Of course, the causes of the idea that the National Socialists and the German Volk had reason to avenge themselves on someone were numerous. However, the direct reference in regard to the naming of these weapons was vengeance for the bombing of civilian targets in German cities, which was inaugurated at Churchill's direction beginning in May 1940. There is some controversy over who started bombing whom in WWII, but the book *The Bombing War* by Richard Overy (2009) makes it clear that it was originally a concerted Allied strategy to target civilians, which only intensified as the war went on. It was thought that the German will to fight could be broken if enough of their wives and children were killed. This strategy was not entirely successful, although many hundreds of thousands of civilians were killed in German—as well as Japanese—cities. The madness of this strategy was later acknowledged by the Allies after the war, and it is perhaps responsible for the current obsession among Americans with the avoidance of civilian deaths in contemporary warfare.

The V-1 was a pilotless pulse-jet bomb that delivered a 1,870-pound warhead and reached a maximum speed of 400 mph. The first of these hit London on June 13, 1944. Some 10,000 of these weapons were launched in all by the Germans, mainly at London, but also Antwerp. Six thousand Londoners were killed by these bombs, and 18,000 injured. The V-2 was a true ballistic missile with a warhead of 2,220 pounds and a maximum speed of 3,580 mph. It was first launched on September 8, 1944. Between that date and the last launch on March 2, 1945, it is recorded that 1,054 rockets hit London and 900 hit Antwerp. Figures show 2,700 Londoners were killed with this weapon. The weapons were designed and deployed as instruments of terror and propaganda and had no effect on the English will to fight.

The Messerschmitt Me 262, or Schwalbe (Swallow), also called the Sturmvogel (Storm Bird), was the world's first operational fighter jet to see combat action. The jet was first flown in July 1942, but its use was mismanaged by the Germans (mainly due to Hitler's own misjudgments concerning this craft) and it was not brought into combat operations until two years later, in July 1944, by which time it was too little, too late. It continued to be used for the wrong kind of missions.

The Messerschmitt Me 163 Komet was a rocket-powered aircraft intended as a bomber interceptor. Its flying performance was unparalleled, reaching speeds of over 1,000 mph. In actual combat, it was not that spectacular, but as a work of aeronautical engineering it was a success.

A staple of the literature of what will be called Nazi Mythology is that which is best classed as "occult Nazi technologies" or "secret sciences" are those directly connected to the war effort: the production of *Wunderwaffen* (Miracle or Wonder Weapons). Sometimes it is difficult to know where science and technology in any practical sense ends and we enter into the realm of science fiction. This difficulty arises due to the fact that the actual pressure to produce such weapons within the Nazi regime after 1942 became so great that a significant number of impractical and fabulous weapons were not only proposed and designed, but many were actually produced and tested, especially in the final months of the war (Cornwell 2003, 377–88). None of these more fantastic efforts had much of an effect on the battlefield, but they do seem to have become designs and prototypes for future weapons in the arsenals of the Allied militaries.

WESTERN ALLIES' SECRECY
ABOUT GERMAN TECHNOLOGY

The dramatic and undeniable evidence of the V-1s, V-2s, and the Me 262s flying through the sky belongs to one class of weaponry and technology. But the German scientific experiments and developments leading to technological innovations in the service of the war effort went well beyond these highly visible examples. After the war, it is recorded that boxcar loads of scientific data and hardware, records, patents, and prototypes were loaded and sent westward, mostly to end up in the United States for assessment and further development.

During the war, there was good reason to keep what was known of the German scientific development secret. Such knowledge, if generally appreciated, would have had a negative effect from a propaganda standpoint. The Western Allies also had reason to keep what they knew from their Russian counterparts, as awareness of the coming conflict between the East and West was already looming on the horizon. It was this latter factor that drove the postwar urge to secrecy. Such security blankets were usually made up of two components: denial and classification. First of all, it would generally be denied that anything special existed in the German arsenal or laboratories, and then through the classification of these matters as "top secret," access to any information about them was restricted. The first component is more powerful than the second. Soviet spies could more easily penetrate security if they suspected something was there to be found, but if it was thought nothing existed, an effective smoke screen was better established. In chapter 13 we will see how these techniques played a part in the UFO craze of the late 1940s onward.

Many of the extraordinary developments of German science and technology during the Second World War are outlined in Henry Stevens's book *Hitler's Suppressed and Still-Secret Weapons, Science and Technology* (2007). This book has its own occult edges as well, but it is a good starting point for research.

The experimental weapons technology pioneered by the Nazis was enormous. Only a small part of what was designed ever saw any practical application in actual combat. These programs were often stalled by more conservative military policies and at a certain point the war was a lost cause. The best known of these weapons that became operational were the aforementioned V-1, V-2, and Me 262. But there were dozens of other projects that largely remained secret until well after the war—and even after the end of the Cold War. Many of these innovative designs served as prototypes for American weapons designers, who went on to perfect numerous experimental ideas first dreamed up in Nazi weapons labs. The V-1 became the cruise missile, the V-2 the intercontinental ballistic missile, and so forth.

Perhaps some of the most shockingly advanced weapon systems are what evolved into our current "smart bombs." There were prototypes and tested systems that included air-to-surface, air-to-air, and air-to-ship guided bombs or missiles. These included the Henschel Hs 293 anti-ship guided missile, which was a radio-controlled glide bomb that also had a rocket engine. The Ruhrstahl Ru 344 X-4 was a wire-guided air-to-air missile, which was never deployed, while the Ruhrstahl SD 1400 X (nicknamed the "Fritz X" by the Allies) was an air-to-ship bomb that actually was tested and sank and damaged several Allied ships. There were experiments with video cameras in the noses of these bombs.

Another strange rocket-propelled weapon was the Natter (Viper), which was launched from a scaffold and attained an altitude above that of the incoming bombers. Then the Natter would glide down among the oncoming Allied aircraft and fire its load of anti-aircraft rockets from its nose cone. This was a highly experimental craft and was difficult to operate.

In the field of general technology, the German scientist Konrad Zuse (1910–1995) pioneered innovation in digital computing. He invented the world's first programmable computer, the Z3, using the first computer language, called Plankalkül, which became operational in May 1941. Because these developments took place in wartime Nazi Germany, they were largely unnoticed. IBM optioned Zuse's patents in 1946, and the rest is history. In a way, Zuse was following a long line of German computer scientists, as Gottfried Wilhelm Leibnitz (1646–1716) had perfected the

Fig. 10.3. A 1944 test flight of the Natter rocket plane from its launch scaffold

binary number system, worked out the first algorithms, and even invented the first mechanical computing device.

Other technological innovations included infrared night-vision devices (to be used on tanks so they could fight at night) and stealth aircraft design, used on the experimental flying wing jet aircraft called the Horton (Ho 229). This latter craft was designed in Göttingen and test-flown in the skies over that town in 1944. The design was intended in part to thwart radar detection. This was a precursor to the American stealth technology.

Because of the German shortage of raw materials and resources, they pioneered many synthetic substitutes. For example, synthetic oil, now commonly used, was invented and experiments undertaken to produce a synthetic gasoline and even synthetic human blood! As they had run out of gasoline to run their tanks at the end of the war, they had invented ways of running their engines on a lump of coal.

The Nazis were the first to use amphetamine (first synthesized in Germany in 1887) and methamphetamine as an aid to combat solders during extended military campaigns. This helped fuel the famous Blitzkrieg campaign that overran France, Belgium, and the Netherlands in 1940 in a matter of forty-six days. (The French made the mistake of issuing their soldiers *wine*!) Methamphetamine was available in tablet form under the brand name Pervitin. Despite early success, by 1941 clear negative side effects became obvious and usage was restricted. It is not unlikely that many Nazi atrocities were fueled by the use of this drug.

The occult dimension of advanced German technology was two-fold. First, it was highly secret within the Reich itself for obvious security reasons. In many ways, the Allies continued to keep these secrets for their own purposes after the war, as this technology became a prize fought over by both American and Soviet interests. Both sides of the Cold War tried various tricks to keep the other side from being sure about who knew what, and where their knowledge came from. Importantly, the Americans brought in the German aerospace experts and Americanized them, whereas the Soviets brought what Germans they could round up, had them further educate Soviet space-technicians, and then the Germans were sent back home (to East Germany). Besides this angle, the technologies on display seemed to belong to the realm of science fiction when observed by the West. (This was less the case for the Soviets, who had already dreamed of advanced space travel.) Such craft as the V-1, V-2, and the Me 262 seemed to come off the screen of a Buck Rogers serial during a Saturday matinee rather than the battlefield. These technologies were examples of things imagined and made real under the pressure of war. I will return to the topic of miraculous weaponry and technology in chapter 11, when we consider the mythologizing of German technology.

EUGENICS AND THE CREATION OF
THE ARYAN SUPERMAN

A wide-ranging and matter-of-fact summary of the development of the idea of genetics and racial hygiene is provided by Cornwell (2003, 71–84).

One area an investigator might think would be very rich with regard to evidence during the Nazi regime would be science related to the much-discussed "breeding of the Aryan superman," or the generation of a new type of human being beyond the limits of the present species. This all seems to have been more important to anti-German propaganda than it was to actual scientific pursuits in the Third Reich.* It is certainly true that "pure Aryan blood" was of supreme interest to the National Socialists and that they implemented many policies and laws designed to purify the gene pool of the German nation, but the manner in which they did so was not as fantastical as many have made it appear.

The down-to-earth yet far more sinister programs actually undertaken by the Nazis were envisioned by Fritz Lenz (1887–1976), who had founded a journal called the *Archiv für Rassen- und*

---

*This concept was first mentioned in the West by Rauschning in his propagandistic fantasies, once taken for fact but now rejected for historical purposes. This sort of mystical breeding of godlike beings is ultimately rooted in the ideology of Lanz von Liebenfels, which, as we have seen, had no tangible influence on actual National Socialist programs of racial hygiene.

Gesellschafts-Biologie (Archives for Racial and Social Biology) in 1913. In collaboration with Eugen Fischer and Erwin Baur he published his magnum opus, the two-volume textbook *Grundriss der menschlichen Erblichkeitslehre und Rassenhygiene* (An Outline of Human Heredity Theory and Racial Hygiene; 1921). In 1923 he became the first professor of eugenics in Munich, and in 1933 he set up the department of eugenics at the Kaiser Wilhelm Institute of Anthropology, Human Heredity, and Eugenics. Lenz joined the NSDAP the next year, and he and his colleagues became the leading authorities on matters of racial theory and racial hygiene in the Third Reich. Whatever mystical or esoteric ideas individual members of the Party might have held on their own were private matters. After the war, Lenz continued in his position at the University of Göttingen.

Although Lenz and his colleagues seemed to be focused on the definition of race by external appearance and objective markers (e.g., hair color, skin tone, eye color, skull shape, etc.), they were entirely willing to disregard these factors for the sake of general categorization of people, such as whether a person could be considered a "Slav" racially, and most of all if one could be determined to be a Jew by familial descent regardless of their apparent Nordic characteristics (Lenz 1941, 397).

Eugen Fischer (1874–1967) was an important collaborator with Lenz. Fischer was a professor of medicine, anthropology, and eugenics in Berlin. He served as the first director of the Kaiser Wilhelm Institute from 1927 to 1942. His works were used as sources for Hitler's ideas, but he would not actually join the NSDAP himself until 1940. He had become an acknowledged "expert" on race and the concept of miscegenation in the years of the early twentieth century. He devised tests for racial purity, such as the so-called Fischer-Saller Scale. He subjected many people to various experiments and forced sterilization even before the advent of the Third Reich in Germany's pre-Nazi eugenics programs, which functioned in cooperation with those found in America. Although he retired from academia before the end of WWII, he, too, was untouched by questions of any sort of criminality in the pursuit of his "studies."

Otmar Freiherr von Verschuer (1896–1969) was a biologist and eugenicist, and the second director of the Kaiser Wilhelm Institute from 1942 to 1948. It certainly comes as a shock to many that Nazi eugenics was not recognized for the "cosmic evil" it later became as postwar philosophical readjustments took place in the late 1940s and early 1950s. Verschuer was an important professor and teacher in the field and among his students was the now infamous Dr. Josef Mengele, SS-man and "physician" at the Auschwitz concentration camp. Verschuer carried out experiments with data collected by Mengele. He continued in his academic life after the war as before, and remained a powerful and influential academic in West Germany. During the war itself, he was accepted into the American Eugenics Society and remained in that organization the rest of his life. He was a pioneer in the field of twin methodology research in genetics and the understanding of the genetic inheritance of disease processes and various anomalies. With regard to his religion and politics, Verschuer remained active in the church and only joined the NSDAP in 1940, where he was not involved in political affairs.

The scientific work of men such as Lenz, Fischer, and Verschuer was used as a backing for the legitimacy of legislation in the Third Reich, most conspicuously the Nuremberg Laws of 1935, which stripped Jews of their citizenship, for example.

The main and most marked targets for the Nazi program of negative eugenics were the severely mentally ill or handicapped patients in hospitals and mental institutions. But swept up in this could also be persons who were deaf, blind, epileptic, and so on—especially if they were also poor. These people were labeled as "degenerates" and identified with the term "life unworthy of life" (*Lebensunwertes Leben*). Their conditions were thought by eugenicists to be *Erbkrankeiten*—"hereditary diseases." Statistics show that 400,000 such persons were sterilized and approximately 300,000 of them were killed (by various means, but occasionally by using gas). This latter program was called the Aktion T4. The purpose of Aktion T4 was to break the chain of hereditary disease in society.

NAZI PHYSICS AND ITS OCCULT DIMENSIONS

To Nazi physics can be ascribed the eccentric scientific theories of Hanns Hörbiger, which have already been introduced in chapter 5. In the halls of academia, controversy raged over the differences between what was called "German Physics" and "Jewish Physics." This story is summarized by Cornwell (2003, 178–90). Hörbiger's theories clearly belong to the same realm of occult science as the ideology of Theosophy. The concepts may have meaning mythically or even spiritually, but they do not stand the test of current scientific inquiry.

With the advent of the NS regime, all aspects of society were to be reformed under the guidance of National Socialist principles. This even included ideas about the constitution of the physical universe itself. Here, as elsewhere in the German society, there were usually individuals who were enthusiastic for Nazi ideas and also motivated to make use of them for their own advantage. This is the consistent nature of life in authoritarian and ideologically driven systems. Two academic physicists, Philipp Lenart and Johannes Stark, undertook the control of the science of physics in the Reich. Lenard wrote a four-volume study titled *Deutsche Physik* (German Physics), completed in 1936. And what was "German Physics," exactly? A main hallmark of what was meant by this term was opposition to the Einsteinian Theory of Relativity, because it was thought to somehow represent "Jewish Physics." Beyond this, however, German Physics was an idea that preferred experiment and practical application over pure intellectual theorizing, which they said exemplified "Jewish Physics."

Following an entirely different path from Lenard's "German Physics," but one that seems to exude certain occult ideas, we find the dedicated Nazi named Pascual Jordan (1902–1980). Jordan was a great theoretician of quantum mechanics in Göttingen—and was so dedicated as a Nazi he even joined an SA unit. Cornwell writes this about Jordan's ideas:

Quantum physics . . . revealed an underlying all-embracing vision of reality, in which conventional cause and effect are overturned and old distinctions between object and subject, the individual and society, are eliminated. Nazism, understood in terms of the new physics, would deliver a death blow to the morally bankrupt influence of the Enlightenment, with its emphasis on the individual and its tendency to objectify nature in terms of mere mechanistic determinism. In quantum physics he saw a direct relationship, and an exemplar, between the behaviour of molecules and sub-atomic particles, and the *Führerprinzip* in National Socialism. . . .

Biology, psychology, consciousness, telepathy, clairvoyance, spirituality, all could now be explained, described and controlled in light of the new quantum insights. (Cornwell 2003, 188)

Jordan was initially prevented from continuing his academic career after the war due to his membership in the NSDAP but was later declared "rehabilitated" to such a degree that he was able to resume academic work after two years.

HIMMLER'S PSEUDOSCIENCES

It would be a grave error to ascribe Himmler's interests in scientific research as benign eccentricity, as John Cornwell begins his discussion of the topic with the words:

In the lethal mix of power, cruelty, and dilettantism, pseudoscience began to flourish virtually unchallenged under the auspices of the SS in Hitler's Germany. An autodidact, lacking in judgment or even the basics of scientific research, Himmler found time to get involved in all manner of research schemes, starting early in the regime with bogus programs linked with the origins of Aryanism, leading ultimately to the murderous "medical research" in the death camps. While such activities were marginal to the enormous volume of scientific and technological work being conducted in the Third Reich as a whole, the direction of the SS-sponsored "researches" in time brought appalling suffering and death to their victims and degradation upon all those associated with their conduct and data. (Cornwell 2003, 191)

Of course, the pseudoscience was not limited to things border-ing on physics, biology, or medicine but rather extended well into the humanities and archaeology. His obsessions were behind Ernst Schäfer's expedition to Tibet* and willful misrepresentations of the contents of the text known as *Germania* by the Roman historian Tacitus.

Himmler continued to have scientists pursue Hörbiger's theories of the *Welteislehre* (World Ice Theory) even after most moderately edu-cated observers saw how untenable it was.

The Reichsführer-SS was also a fanatic about the removal of artifi-cial ingredients from food products, remarking that "[the food indus-tries] attack the countryside with their refined flour, sugar, and white bread" (Cornwell 2003, 196).

One of the most ironic examples of Himmler's obsessions was the fact that he had the prisoners at Dachau plant and maintain a garden of medicinal herbs to attempt to cure them of the maladies that the condi-tions and officials at the camp itself were inflicting upon them.

✳ ✳ ✳

Unusual scientific developments, especially in the field of aeronautics and in the area of supposed eugenics, dominated the Allies' anxieties regarding the Third Reich. These areas of inquiry had quite differ-ent postwar fates. The Allies very much coveted the German scientific developments in rocketry and other weapons systems. On the other hand, the whole program with regard to eugenics, which had been originally greatly inspired by American models and even funded by American interests, was ultimately rejected as an idea or aim.

The *mythology* that arose surrounding Nazi eugenics places it clearly in the occult realm: supposed belief in the breeding of the Aryan superman and the Master Race—the strongest, most beautiful human specimens possible—either as a new type or as a restoration of the pure god-man of a past Atlantean golden age. Ideas such as the reactiva-tion of vestigial organs (the "Third Eye," etc.) obviously belong to this

---

*This SS expedition to Tibet is chronicled in Christopher Hale's *Himmler's Crusade* (2003). See A Chronological Annotated Bibliography in this book.

mythology. However, the truth is that such things did not ever belong in any way to the National Socialist program of eugenics, which was a fairly down-to-earth endeavor enacted by established scientists. So, it must be said that there was virtually no occult dimension to the actual Nazi eugenics program. In fact, eugenics had open and widespread support in the halls of the academic and social establishment in the West generally. The original aims of eugenics did become taboo, and hence driven underground, when the myth of the Master Race was discredited.

CHAPTER 11

OCCULTISM AND THE THIRD REICH
The Anti-occult Reich as a Step toward Political Spellcasting

The story of occultism during the period of the Third Reich is double-edged: on the one hand, the National Socialists did utilize certain types of magic and occultism on different levels (most of it in rather unexpected forms, as this book shows), but on the other hand, there was a widespread and progressive suppression of occultism, occultists, occult practices, and occult organizations. Over time, any philosophy or new religious expression that challenged the authority and ideological hegemony of the Nazi Party, or even subtly competed with it or offered slightly different alternatives, was generally forbidden and banned.

As mentioned in chapter 6, astrology, for example, had become very popular among the general populace, but it was something that was extremely un-Nazi on many counts. It was seen to have a foreign origin, it was seen as mechanistic and deterministic (thus diminishing the power of effort and will), and most of all it was seen as universalistic— that is, the stars would affect all people equally and indiscriminately, without regard for the race of the subject. There were, of course, certain individuals among the Nazis (Rudolf Hess, for example) who might have taken astrology seriously. For the most part, however, astrology was only seen as a tool for potential propaganda.

What is conspicuous about the attitude of the National Socialists toward occultism in general was their negative policies toward it publically. What do the anti-occult policies of the Third Reich tell us about

365

the involvement of the Party with occult ideas? In all likelihood, they tell us quite a bit. If such practices and beliefs were thought to be harmless nonsense, no government would think to pass laws against them or prohibit organizations dedicated to them. These laws tell us not only that such ideas were present and popular (otherwise they would not have to be prohibited) but also that they were thought to be powerful enough to disrupt the agenda of the Party as far as its power to govern and control the population was concerned.

The suppression of occult organizations and individual practitioners came in four phases. This was a preplanned process, but the timing of official actions was often precipitated by certain events. The first phase came during the first years of Hitler's rise to power in 1933 when he became chancellor. Many occultists and alternative thinkers of all sorts who had any knowledge of what the NSDAP meant either went underground or left the country. Those who had a good place to go never returned. The Nazi hold on power was complete by 1935 and at that time organizations, some of which were even sympathetic to the cause of National Socialism, were given the opportunity to disband on a voluntary basis by August 1935. Many did. With Himmler's more complete command of the domestic police force under the SS organization called the Sicherheitsdienst (Security Service), he began to make the final move on occult organizations that had not voluntarily dissolved themselves two years earlier. The exact timing for this (July 1937) may have been triggered by the issuance of the papal encyclical by Pius XI called *Mit brennender Sorge* (With Burning Care) around Easter of 1937. This document was not written in the usual Latin, but was composed in German and intended to be a message to Catholic Germans. It was an attack on (or criticism of) National Socialist ideology with its perceived tendency toward neopaganism. Already in 1933, it was requested that all Freemasonic organizations disband voluntarily. Membership in the Nazi Party was forbidden to all who had not resigned from Masonry prior to January 30, 1933. Occult and quasi-Masonic lodges, such as the Fraternitas Saturni, OTO, and so on, were all outlawed by a Regulation by Himmler of July 20, 1937 (see Glowka 1981, 6). Much of the investigative work on these Freemasonic groups had been undertaken by

Adolf Eichmann. Eichmann afterward turned his attention to the Jews.* This Regulation of 1937 focused on organized orders and groups. But there were apparently still many astrologers, seers, and faith healers who continued working in Germany after that. Their demise came later, in the aftermath of the 1941 flight of Rudolf Hess to Scotland to try to negotiate a peace treaty with England. As we have seen, Hess was publically vilified in Germany and the whole affair was blamed on his occult ideas and the mental disease they caused. This was used as an excuse to crack down on the remaining occult practitioners in what was called *Aktion Hess*. This was a project mainly promoted by Martin Bormann and overseen by Reinhard Heydrich, Himmler's second in command in the SS. The fact that there was indeed an occult dimension to the Third Reich is proven as much by their fanatical interest in ridding the country of "occult" influence as anything else.

There is a need in any population for a religious dimension—that is to say, a true accounting for the numinous aspects of life. This need will be met in one form or another. The Nazis took special care to infuse their own image and ideology with characteristics of this dimension and then progressively eliminated other options for the population in an effort to funnel all of that collective energy into the cause of National Socialism. By contrast, one can note that this dimension was largely (but not entirely) ignored in the Soviet Union, and this was a major factor in its demise.

---

*Adolf Eichmann (1906–1962) is most famous for having been captured by the Israeli Mossad in Argentina and brought to Israel for trial and execution. He had been a high-ranking SS officer (Obersturmbannführer) assigned with the task of coordinating the transport of Jews from various part of Nazi-occupied Europe to ghettos and concentration camps, most notably Auschwitz. He had also drawn up plans to create a homeland region for the Jews (in a section of Poland or even Madagascar!), but the policy changed after the Wannsee Conference in January 1942. Auschwitz became an extermination camp where 75 percent of the arrivals were killed immediately. Eichmann was captured right after the war but escaped and lived in hiding in Germany until 1950. A Catholic organization headed by Bishop Alois Hudal arranged for his emigration to Argentina with false papers. At his trial he did not deny the reality of the Holocaust, nor his role in it, but claimed, as every bureaucratic criminal before or since has, that he was just "following orders."

As the occultist and stage magician Hanussen was murdered very soon after the National Socialists came to power, he did not personally play any significant role in the years of the actual Third Reich. However, his great popularity and the propaganda that he had generated in favor of the National Socialist cause, for whatever reason he undertook it, had a continuing effect in the public perception of Hitler and his Party. This astrologer and mentalist spread many ideas about Hitler's future success, which must have had a lasting effect during the first few years of the Third Reich, as well as affecting the image of Hitler in the foreign press.

Joseph Goebbels expressed continuing interest in the investigation of the works of Nostradamus for predictions that might be of use in pro-German propaganda. At first, he tried to round up genuine experts in the field to do research on this topic, but when the verses he was interested in exploiting simply could not be found or usefully interpreted, he demanded that they be altered to fit the propagandistic narrative. In the end, very little actually came of the effort to use the quatrains of Nostradamus by the Nazis, although rumors of their use became grist for the mill of the early view of the Nazis being enmeshed in the occult (Howe 1984, 182–91).

Howe also provides insight into how the Nazis tried to exploit the possibilities of using astrology, handwriting analysis, and other occult means to gain intelligence on enemy leaders and determine their tendencies or weaknesses. Howe was actually himself an operative on disinformation campaigns mounted against the Germans using faked documents, such as German editions of Nostradamus and issues of the German astrological journal (*Der*) *Zenit,* all of which predicted defeat for the Germans (Howe 1984, 204–234). Howe remained firmly skeptical about Hitler's supposed reliance on astrologers.

In chapter 8, I presented a substantial discussion of the ritual format used by the NSDAP and its construction of a festival calendar designed to establish a sort of sacralization of time in accordance with the aims and goals of the Party. Both the general effort and the specifics of each of these ceremonies or ritual observations had a decidedly *magical* function. In the postwar mythologizing of the Nazis, we see many fantastic speculations about their alleged secret use of ritual or ceremonial magic. It was, however, the *public* rituals, such as those discussed in chapter 8, which were the actual vehicles for this kind of magical manipulation.*

An important summary of the magical aspects of the real political mission of National Socialism is offered by Klaus Vondung in the epilogue to his book *Magie und Manipulation* (1971) titled "Magie statt Revolution" (Magic instead of Revolution). There he notes that although Hitler repeatedly and consistently referred to the NS movement as representing a revolution, it does not accord with past definitions of that word. Hitler acquired power legally and by means of established democratic norms of the day, and Germany for the most part remained stable with respect to class and economic concerns. (Working-class Germans were, however, given greater advantage than before.) Hitler and the Nazis used their legally acquired power and through various means (e.g., political maneuvering, terror campaigns, and—most importantly—*symbolic* manipulations) turned that power into an absolute possession.

The key to the working of NS magic was found in the personality of Hitler and his beliefs about himself and in the fact that he was able to extend that belief system in an institutionalized manner through the personalities of various other leaders: Goebbels, Himmler, Göring, and so on. Chief among his beliefs, as we have seen elsewhere, were his invincibility, immortality (he escaped over forty assassination attempts), and infallibility. He had developed a subjective model of the universe from which he operated (i.e., effected changes) in the environment. As long as the (magical) operation succeeded (1933–1942), it inspired only more belief in his mystique and made him all the more effective in his operation, or art. However, success was entirely dependent upon the existence a certain scale of magnitude of the environment in which he operated. When the level of cosmic opposition became too great to

---

*Logically and technically, when attempting to motivate the masses by means of magical ritual, formats for such rituals must be at least to some degree familiar and infused with meaning with respect to the potential target, or the ritual will appear merely bizarre and be rejected by the unconscious mind of the target. The Nazis knew this well and made use of ritual formats and appearances that would be appreciated by the masses.

resist, his world began to crumble. His will no longer had command over it. (By the way, similar stories might be told concerning Napoleon, Lenin, or Mao.) His contemporaries observed this. General Heinz Gudarian remarked:

> [Hitler] had a particular image of the world, and every fact had to fit into this imaginary image. The world had to be just as he conceived of it: but in reality, the image was another world. (Quoted in Vondung 1971, 211)

From a magical perspective, this imaginary world can be seen as the operating model of the National Socialists. As long as such a model of positive thinking works, its results can appear truly miraculous. The problem with the practitioners of such systems is often that they come to enchant themselves so much with the spell that they themselves become *objects*—not *subjects*—of the magic. That is, they are acted upon, rather than maintaining themselves as operators. All flexibility and objectivity are lost, and so the spell collapses.

As our review of occult ideas found in the text of *Mein Kampf* showed,* Hitler definitely seems to have made use of magical or occult concepts in many of his approaches to propaganda and operative communication with the masses. Among the most interesting of these are his ideas about the symbolism or operative effect of colors—and especially the color *red*—on the unconscious mind, as well as the use of timing in staging mass rallies at night in the belief that the mind is more susceptible to suggestion in these hours. His discussion of the concepts of psychology and the psychology of the masses is remarkable for its openness. It should also be noted that these discussions of psychology come barely twenty years after Freud's publication of *The Interpretation of Dreams* and at a time when the very term *psychology* was still tinged with ideas of the *occult*, especially in Germany. Hitler's overt references to the effects of symbols on the mind would have been the equivalent of Franklin Roosevelt openly discussing the hoped-for effects of the

---

*See chapter 7.

Masonic and mystical symbols on the Great Seal of the United States on the minds of Americans.*

Certainly, Hitler was obsessed with power gained through the manipulation of the masses of humanity in accordance with his will and direction, but most of the way in which he presented such things remained firmly within a modernistic framework that he could justify as being scientific. His methodology was, however, in many respects well beyond the consensus reality of his own day, and so can easily qualify as a kind of occult thinking.

There seems little doubt that once his power was complete, and the war he had planned was won, the antiquarian dimension of National Socialism would have been eradicated, just as the Bolsheviks encouraged avant-garde art and social experimentation in the very early years of the USSR, only to suppress it utterly under the oppressive weight of Stalinism once Soviet power had been absolutely established. It is unclear as to how much NS leadership was informed about the background and character of Soviet political culture and its deep connections with occult thinking,† but the degree to which the history of NS mirrors that of Bolshevism in this regard is uncanny. The great historical difference between the two movements in this context is that NS lasted only twenty-five years, whereas Bolshevism (if we count the beginning with the 1905 Revolution) lasted approximately eighty-five years—and continues to have a more active afterlife than NS. The NSDAP had only one leader, whereas Bolshevism went through several historical phases with a number of different leaders. In both cases the leaders were sometimes steeped in occult thinking, and naturally tried to restrict uncontrolled occultism in the public sphere.

Clearly, the National Socialist efforts to suppress the occult—its organized forms, publications, beliefs, and practices—were not done in the spirit of reason or because the Nazis did not believe in the power of the occult to affect the minds of the people, rather it was done precisely

---

*The possible involvement of Roosevelt with occult ideas will be discussed in chapter 12.
†Generally speaking, however, Hitler was an attentive student of Bolshevism as expressed both under Lenin and Stalin.

because they did acknowledge the power of such ideas to shape perceptions of reality. The free expression of occult ideas had to be controlled and directed. Occult techniques, analogous to the ability of stage magic to astound and move audiences, depends largely on the viewers' ignorance of its techniques. Nazi suppression of the occult therefore had two aims: (1) restriction of free public access to such ideas; and (2) the reservation of such practices to the personal use of NSDAP leadership and the official employment of such ideas by the Party itself.

As we have seen elsewhere, despite the fact that certain things might have been restricted or forbidden to the general public in Nazi Germany, this did not keep certain members of the Party from indulging in them. The NSDAP was a highly competitive syndicate, full of internecine conspiracies and intrigues. Anyone trying to navigate this political territory would have been often very insecure and anxious about their own position and even survival. In such environments, the need for reliance on the occult arts often surfaces. The memoir of the Nazi astrologer Wilhelm Wulff, *Zodiac and the Swastika* (1973), details some of this activity. As is often the case, psychic information, such as astrology might provide, serves the purpose of bolstering the confidence of the subject who may be undertaking highly dangerous or risky ventures.

ERNST SCHERTEL AND ADOLF HITLER

The case of Hitler's interest in the theories and practices of Ernst Schertel, as expressed in his book *Magie* (1923), was touched upon in chapter 6. This demonstrates that the Führer harbored many interests and obsessions that were private and even secret but found direct application in his practical activities. Such interests appear to have been often at odds with official positions or outward appearances.

One of the most curious connections that recently came to light through Timothy W. Ryback's research for his book *Hitler's Private Library* (2008) is this firm and irrefutable connection between the ideas of Schertel, sometimes referred to as the "Philosopher King of Weimar," and Adolf Hitler. This is especially curious because Schertel can in no way be considered a Nazi or even a Nazi sympathizer. Schertel did send an inscribed copy of his book *Magie* to Hitler upon its publication in 1923, just three years after the founding of the NSDAP. This was during the time of hyperinflation in the German economy, and Hitler and the Nazis were increasingly coming to the public's attention. They held their first *Parteitage* (Party Days) at the end of January of that year, and on November 9 the Beer Hall Putsch occurred in Munich. Hitler's image, fueled by the "Hitler Myth" conjured by Eckhart and promoted in the pages of the *Völkischer Beobachter,* probably led Schertel to believe that Hitler was some sort of force of nature.

The exact circumstances concerning the arrival of the book around 1923 are unknown. It is possible that the publisher had the book sent, and Schertel had no personal involvement in the process. As time went on, it could be seen that he would never have had any political or broader philosophical sympathies for the Nazis in general. Hitler, however, remained an ardent student of this text. This is known not only from the numerous passages in the book that are highlighted in Hitler's hand but also by the fact that this volume, which he received in 1923, would be one of the books actually recovered from the Führerbunker, where Hitler committed suicide twenty-two years later. It seems to have been a continuing source and reference book for him.

Hitler apparently much treasured his copy of Schertel's work *Magie,* as at some point he had highlighted numerous passages throughout the text. (The otherwise poor-quality 2009 English translation of the book does have a historically added feature of indicating those passages in boldface type to recommend it.) Among the highlighted passages is this:

> Every demonic-magical world is centered upon great individuals, from whom fundamental generative concepts are projected. Every magician is surrounded by a force field of para-cosmic energies; he functions . . . in the highest sense "ectropically" upon the cosmic dynamic. Those individuals who have been infected by him form his "congregation" or his *"Volk,"* and bring about a life-complex of very specific, imaginatively rooted constructs, which we call *culture.* In that moment when the imaginative-magical connective forces are

exhausted, the *Volk* will disintegrate and with it the culture as well. (Schertel 1923, 75–76; translation mine)

This and many other emphasized sections of the text indicate that Hitler was most interested in matters of transformation of the individual self into an effective magician who could work his will upon the environment, and matters that related to the modification of whole cultures in accordance with the magical-imaginative will of the magician. Here we do have a true connection between Hitler and the world of the occult in a positive, verifiable sense. These highlighted passages in Schertel's book, coupled with the noted passages in the text of *Mein Kampf,** are the best indicators of Hitler's connections to operative magical thinking.

There can be little doubt that Hitler was highly motivated to absorb techniques and practices that would give his personality great power— power to persuade and command not only the body politic of Germany as a whole but also the corporation of men who made up the NSDAP. By instilling quasi-divine qualities in his image and personality, he would ensure his command and influence over these bodies. Rightly or wrongly, it appears that he did ascribe some extraordinary dimensions to this process, which would have only bolstered his beliefs in the fate (*Schicksal*) and Providence (*Vorsehung*) that preordained his position in history. Most would count these beliefs as something akin to the occult and it is in the words of Schertel, and in Hitler's reading of them, that we get some deeper insight into this particular train of thought.

One passage from Schertel's book is fraught with irony and portents of things to come, but Hitler only highlighted the portions underlined here:

The only "law" to which the magician is subject is the will of his "god" or "demon," that is, the ectropic effect resulting from the cosmic forces condensed within him. . . . <u>Around that one basic law</u> <u>are layered the manifold prescriptions and rules to which the magi-</u> <u>cian voluntarily subjects himself in order to shape the *communio*</u>

---

*See the section "Some Magical Notes on *Mein Kampf*" in chapter 7.

with his demon in an ever more intimate way and to saturate himself in forever new ways with the para-cosmic forces. But whether he then wants to place the power acquired in this way in the service of the multitude, or uses it for his own aims, remains entirely left up to him. The *"Volk"* that he in any case gathers around himself, has nothing to do with an abstract *multitude,* whose "well-being" he would have to "serve," rather it represents only an expansion of his own ego-sphere. It has also, however, happened in the past that a magician has shattered, abandoned, or severely disciplined his own *Volk,* when it no longer appears to be capable of responding. Christ is the historical example for this, who originally came to the Jews and then turned to the gentiles. Moses, as Jehovah incarnate, likewise also often disciplined his people even as he was uplifting them.

Also, the *"Volk"* belonging to the magician is always set off against abstract "humanity" and the indiscriminate *multitude,* and will therefore at first be perceived as being "evil" just as the magician himself will be. Only once a magical world has been established and has succeeded does the Satanic root become "latent," that is, imperceptible, and everything that occurs in the context of this world then appears to the most harmless mind as something "good." In the same way, too, the most violent movement appears to be calm when the whole environment moves within the same direction.

At one time or another, however, every magical folk-group, that is, every "culture" falls victim to the forces opposing it, even if these have spared the magician himself. This end appears as the specter of the "Antichrist," about whom every magical founder of peoples was aware and whose breach into his world he wishes to put off as long as possible (until the "end of times").

The magician is the really heroic man, who is aware of his tragic life-line, which he nevertheless follows—for the sake of the demon who drives him. The magician is the peak of humanity, is a germ-cell of the highest ectropic energy, and therefore appears as an incarnation of the ultimate cosmic intelligence, as an ambassador of that deity. (Schertel 1923, 79–80; translation mine)

This passage also corroborates my general assessment of the Hitler phenomenon in the context of the Left-Hand Path regarding the central aspect of the personality of the Führer (Flowers 2012, 229–31).

∗ ∗ ∗

This third part of our study is the core of the work. By applying the current definitions and understandings of the terms *occult* and *esoteric* and *magic,* as well as employing them as a lens for understanding the historical data pertaining to various activities and ideas of the NSDAP and its leaders, a more precise discussion of the whole idea of Nazi occultism has become possible.

Throughout this study, and especially in part 4, it can be seen just how much fantasy, propaganda, and just plain yarn-spinning has surrounded this topic over the past seventy-five years. By separating fact from fiction, we may also gain a new understanding of just how amazing some of the facts actually are, without indulging in outlandish mythologizing.

During the quarter-century the NSDAP existed, and over the twelve-year period in which the Third Reich lasted, we can recognize certain elements that can be classed, according to our definitions, as occult or esoteric. These are to be found in the symbolic realm, in that of science (or better said, pseudoscience), and in the area of the more traditional occult practices and phenomena.

In the symbolic realm, it can be recognized that the whole thrust of the NSDAP program proceeded along a path to power that was cleared by the use of symbols and signs, which instilled in the defeated and downtrodden German population a sense of power, renewal, and invincibility. This was not just expressed in the words of NSDAP leaders or in propaganda but rather along every possible channel of communication between Hitler, the Party, and the general population: the logo of the swastika, the uniformed appearance of NSDAP members, and the symbolic appeal to the great German past all worked on the unconscious minds of the populace. And this did not only occur in the years leading up to the seizure of political power by the NSDAP, for such symbolic effectiveness further increased after 1933 once the full power of the message could be conveyed through even great lines of communication: the media, the education system, and the entire apparatus of the state.

Although the leaders of the NSDAP were certainly to a great extent the sons of the Life-Reform movement, it cannot be neglected that they were also first and foremost the sons of the nineteenth century with its unbridled belief and confidence in the methods and aims of science. The key then, as it is now, is that most nonscientists (and many so-called scientists today) do not so much practice the methods of science, as they are faithful acolytes of the *image* of science. Science regularly had been delivering on miracle after miracle in the fields of energy, weaponry, and gadgetry of every kind. Among the Nazis there was always the idea that the quest was toward the development of a scientific, modern method for the achievement of their goals. The apparent places where National Socialism worshipped the images of the past (e.g., with Himmler) have been overemphasized at the cost of a true image of what was occurring. Hitler was dedicated to a futuristic image. (He even tried to outlaw the use of the archaic and peculiar form of German writing and printing called *Fraktur*.)*

With regard to the actual use of occult or magical practices by the Nazis, it is clear that such was not very prevalent in the concrete history of the movement as compared to the use of what we can more aptly call symbolic or operative communication. There is certainly magic in what the Nazis did, but it was not typically understood as such by the rank and file, nor was it ever overtly expressed as magical or occult practices on a wide scale. Rather, such practices and beliefs were suppressed in the general population. All irrational or suprarational expressions, and general religious and pseudoreligious motivations and urges, were funneled directly into the program of the NSDAP under the guise of

---

*From the beginning, Hitler and the National Socialists were theoretically opposed to both Fraktur and the so-called Deutsche Schrift (the peculiar style of German cursive script that was in use through the early twentieth century). On the one hand, this script was a testimony to German influence stemming back to the time of the invention of the printing press, but it was "old-fashioned" and did not project the modernistic image the NSDAP wanted to foster. Fraktur became officially forbidden through a Schrifterlass (script edict) issued by Hitler in 1941 and signed by Martin Bormann.

something that was far more mainstream in the transformed National Socialist culture. But we can see, and must recognize, the presence of a more overt form of occultism in certain enclaves of the NS movement, most notably in the private obsessions of certain of its leaders, including Hitler himself and Heinrich Himmler.

As a part of my final assessment of the role of hidden roots of Nazism, I must reiterate another important fact. Although postwar academic careers have been built on the idea that the völkisch mystics Guido von List or Lanz von Liebenfels were behind it all, or that the great scientist Ernst Haeckel was the mastermind, or that magical spells cast by men such as Erik Jan Hanussen or Ernst Schertel lie at the heart of Hitler's power—the truth of the matter is that all of these men and/or their ideas were expressly rejected, pointedly ignored, and in most cases eventually forbidden by the regime of the NSDAP. In some cases, the men were put in concentration camps; in others, they were executed (if still living), or at minimum stripped of their honors and degrees and relegated to the dustbin of history. And indeed, some of them did have considerable indirect influence, and the reason why they were rejected was because the Nazis wanted to revisionistically obscure their own sources and origins. But those hidden origins are not as clear or straightforward as some would you believe. To a great extent the key to all this lies in the fact that certain of the individuals involved in shaping the ideology of the NSDAP were imaginative and creative thinkers, eager to enforce their own visions as they had come to understand them. (The same can be said of parallel movements; for example, Lenin did not simply accept and try to implement the ideas of Marx.)*

---

*Major figures of the Russian Revolution are known to have had personal associations with the occult. Lenin's family had a tradition that his great-grandmother was executed as a witch by the authority of the Russian Orthodox Church. His connection to her instilled an irrational belief in him that miracles are possible, that anything is feasible, no matter how unlikely it might seem to others. Stalin had his own "witch." Her name was Natalia Lvova. She was said to be his secret adviser in matters of the supernatural. She was apparently a practitioner of Russian folk-magic and healing practices. For example, she advised him never to allow himself to be photographed. It is thought that most of the photos of Stalin are actually of his double (of which he supposedly had several). More about all of this appears in the pages of my book *The Occult Roots of Bolshevism* (2022).

The great pivot-point in the story of applied occultism, or *magic,* in the Third Reich is that such features of culture, which had been building up to a fever pitch from the late nineteenth through the early twentieth centuries, were effectively rechanneled and directed with a singular focus on the policies, programs, and personalities of the NSDAP. This was done through a combination of restricting all forms of occultism that were not already oriented toward National Socialism and translating those energies and enthusiasm into partisan directions. The NSDSP made it so that those frenetic energies of the time simply had no other channel through which to find expression. The quasi-cultic form of National Socialism, with its attention to every detail of ideology, aesthetics, and inspiration, was tailor-made for total cultural transformation. The raw energy for this mechanism was provided by the significant grassroots desire for radical change on all fronts, combined with the desperate situation imposed on Germany at the conclusion of WWI. Again, it should be emphasized that these cultural mechanisms are not unique to the German-speaking world of the early twentieth century. What perhaps makes them appear unique is the very skill and sense of artistry with which the Nazis applied their sorcerous spell of politics and psychology.

What I have presented here is not simply an attempt to debunk the whole idea that the Nazis were steeped in occult ideas as it is an endeavor to bring the question of Nazi occultism into sharper focus with a more refined lens of understanding, free of the passions of love or hate.

The Mythology of Nazi Occultism

INTRODUCTION TO PART IV

The study of Nazi occultism is best divided into two separate categories. The first has been the major topic of the first three parts of this book: its real roots, immediate prelude, and actual existence in Germany during the time of the Third Reich itself. The second aspect of the study will be the topic of the last two chapters of this book—the myth and mythologizing of Nazi occultism. Clearly, the two aspects are related, but what is remarkable is the extent to which they are independent of one another. The myths of Nazi occultism are often born of anti-Nazi and anti-German propaganda, or of wild sectarian speculation and fantasizing, or of fanatic yarn-spinning worthy of some West Texas teller of tall tales with a sci-fi twist.

The actual history of the Third Reich and the events of the Second World War were so astounding, blood-drenched, and traumatic on a worldwide scale that it is no wonder they would inspire writers with wild imaginations and axes to grind to produce some masterpieces of myth and fantasy. And the further away from the events we have gotten chronologically, the more extreme the tales have become. As actual sources of information fade, the imagination can expand to new heights. This is just one more aspect of the bigger story, which lends itself to the interpretation that we are swimming in an ocean of myth as that term is to be understood accurately. It is the Nazis—not the Bolsheviks, not the Red Chinese, not the minions of Pol Pot—who are the focus of all cosmic evil on a transcendent scale. It is the Nazis who have departed from the realm of history and entered into an empire of pure mythology. It is the purpose of this book to re-historicize these mythic elements and at the same time not ignore the power of the mythology itself. The myths may be fabrications from a historical perspective, yet they should also be recognized as reflections of the cultural values and needs of the contemporary world. They are, after all, *myths*.

Part 4 is divided into two distinct chapters: one on the wartime propaganda and mythologizing of Third Reich (which often served as the roots for the postwar expansions of these ideas), and the other on the postwar canon of myth and imagination that has become its own self-perpetuating source of "fantastic realism."

An extremely important dimension to understanding the development of the mythology of Nazi occultism is the drive toward paganizing and even Satanizing Nazism in the minds of both pro- and anti-Nazi writers and propagandists. If Germany was so pagan and Satanic (as a wartime propagandist such as Lewis Spence would have it), why then did political parties with the word *Christian* in their names proliferate in Germany immediately after the war—and continue their dominant role to this day? The Christlich Demokratische Union (CDU) and the Christlich Soziale Union (CSU) have dominated postwar politics in Germany. The use of the code word *Christian* was surely an effort to reassert Germany's Christian identity and to imply its supposed loss of that identity during the Nazi era. In many ways, these successful efforts at rebranding reflected a strategy taken straight from the program of Nazi methodology itself.

The falsification of history represented by the mythology of Nazi occultism as it developed in the years after the end of WWII—the attempt to characterize the nature of the NSDAP and its leaders as pagans or even Satanists—will be seen to emerge from multiple sources. There were Christians (especially Catholics in an organized way) interested in deflecting guilt for Nazi war crimes away from themselves after *centuries* of the systematic preaching of anti-Judaic policies. There were also Allied apologists endeavoring to recast the war as a "crusade against cosmic evil." Such an agenda is nothing new; it is the usual pattern found throughout history when wars, almost always fought for concrete economic and strategic reasons, are recast as *moral* imperatives. Of course, these attempts at demonization of the Nazis worked and continue to work so famously well simply because there was a *grain* of truth to them. There were pagan (but not Satanic) elements in German culture in the early twentieth century, and some of the Nazis were adherents of this movement to one degree or another. It is fairly easy for writers to transform a mere element of something into a general truth about it—to imply that a part of something is definitive of the whole. The revision of history worked so well because it is what people *wanted* to believe. (This is how all such reenvisionings of the past tend to work.) A corollary of this is the Romantic revision of Nazism by the postwar generations of actual pagans and Satanists. Those who continued, or sought to continue, the ideological strain connected to the revival of indigenous, pre-Christian culture in Germanic nations (from Europe to America) were often brought under the *spell* of the Nazi use of imagery and symbolism. Similarly, Satanists (such as Anton LaVey)—contrarians by nature—were drawn to the allure of the antinomian character of using the "forbidden" and "evil" symbolism of the Nazis in their campaigns against conventional or consensus thinking.

In general, it is my belief that the first three parts of this book clearly outline a balanced and rational view of the underlying questions related to our topic. In this fourth part of the book, we will look squarely at the mythology of postwar Nazi occultism.

CHAPTER 12

THE ROOTS OF THE MYTH OF NAZI OCCULTISM IN WARTIME PROPAGANDA

Imaginative Propaganda Lays the Foundation of Postwar Tabloid Scholarship

The story of Nazi occultism begins during the time of WWII itself and even in the years leading up to that war. This was the cauldron in which the later elements of the postwar mythology of Nazi occultism were first brewed. Without an understanding of the wartime propaganda, the later features of the mythology of Nazi occultism will be less well understood.

The word *propaganda* originally was a technical term used by the Roman Catholic Church to indicate information about the religion and establishing the church in non-Christian areas. Even there, of course, it was tinged with the operative imperative of success over truth. In propaganda, the ends always justify the means. Political movements of the early twentieth century were especially adept at the practice of propaganda, the Soviets as well as the Nazis, of course, but the Allies engaged in this political art form as well. Those interested in focusing on the dangers of Germany and Hitler in England, and those interested in involving America in the European conflict, were so convinced of the righteousness of their cause that the telling of wild stories and narratives meant to demonize and/or ridicule the potential enemy were seen as virtuous. Any means necessary were seen as good, if the end result was a good one. This is an old practice, but by the end of the nineteenth century it was being openly studied and more consciously developed.

Awareness of its nature and effects have in no way diminished its use or effectiveness. We have seen it in recent years on every level and in many instances in both foreign and domestic conflicts. Here we are focused on the use of propaganda to demonize the National Socialists of Germany. Some might say that this effort did not require too much energy, as the Nazis made such good villains when viewed from the conventional Western perspective.

Propaganda comes in two types: black propaganda, which vilifies the enemy, and white propaganda, which urges one's own side to fight the good fight. Propaganda is a narrative with the characteristics of a story. The same is also true of history. For this reason, good storytellers make for good propagandists and compelling historians. Historical narratives can in many respects be seen as ex post facto propaganda. The past is reshaped to fit the present narrative and set the stage for future developments. If the history is driven by an agenda, it clearly falls into this category; if the history is influenced by reason, the narrative is far more nuanced.

For the most part anti-German, or more specifically anti-Nazi, propaganda in the USA was focused on ridiculing Hitler and the Nazi leadership, not in demonizing the German people. The fact that such a large part of the American population is of German descent and that many of these were involved with the military made this untenable. On the other hand, propaganda leveled against the Japanese tended to be extremely racist. There was actually *relatively* little in the way of building up ideas that the Nazis were somehow involved in sinister cults, paganism, and so on. In those days, our ministries were astute enough to realize that such propaganda could easily backfire and glamorize the Nazis in a counterproductive way. The postwar mythologizers demonstrate an ambiguous approach. The focus on the occult and demonic in postwar anti-Nazi propaganda may reveal the true source of this effort: the church and Soviet intelligence. Wartime propaganda was generally aimed at the average Joe. Telling him that "Hitler is a devil worshipper," or "the Nazis are all pagans," would have just flown over his head.

How propaganda might move along a chain between the positive and negative is interestingly addressed by Orrin Klapp in his landmark book *Heroes, Villains, and Fools* (1962). These three archetypal images can be seen historically to flow from one category to the other, and they can be manipulated by things such as propaganda. Today's hero can be turned into a villain tomorrow, but he is often first made into a fool. By the same token, villains of today can be made harmless fools and then transformed into the heroes of tomorrow. History is full of examples, and the process is ongoing.

An occult edge was found in some wartime propaganda. MGM Studios produced several documentaries that purported to deal with the predictions of the French prophet Nostradamus (1506–1566). One of these is *More about Nostradamus* (1941), which gives a short biography of Nostradamus, pointing out predictions of his that have come true, and then his prophecies are connected to the events of WWII. (Joseph Goebbels had tried to do a similar thing in Germany, as we have seen.) These films would predict victory for the Allies and early deaths for Hitler and Mussolini, for example.

The famous quatrain of Nostradamus (century 2, quatrain 24) that is supposed to refer to Hitler reads:

> *Bestes farouches de faim fleuves tranner:*
> *Plus part du camp encontre Hister sera:*
> *En caige de fer le grand fera treisner,*
> *Quand Rin enfant Germain observera.*

This has been translated in many various ways. The word *Hister* is said to be a misunderstanding of "Hitler." The only problem with the latter interpretation is that *Hister* is used elsewhere in the quatrains to mean the river Danube.* A straightforward translation of the verse is:

> Beasts ferocious with hunger will swim across rivers.
> The greater part of the region will be against the Hister,
> The great one will cause it to be dragged in an iron cage,
> When the German child will observe nothing.

---

*Hister/Ister is a Latinized form of the ancient Greek name for this river: Ἴστρος.

The poetry of Nostradamus, often written with words from Occitan, Latin, and Greek mixed in with anagrams and unconventional spellings of early modern French, is notoriously difficult to interpret. In this respect, it follows in the tradition of ancient oracles whose utterances were almost always enigmatic. The works of Nostradamus still often seem to defy logical and scholarly treatment.*

The remarkable thing about the anti-Nazi wartime propaganda that was aimed at building the case for there being something extraordinarily sinister about Hitler and the Nazis is that the message did not die with the end of the war. Usually, the aims of propaganda are forgotten after a war has been concluded. It must be said that much of it was: both the Japanese and Germans went from being the epitome of evil to being among America's best friends after the war. This was because the USA and the West needed them as bulwarks against the new "evil empire," the Soviet Union.

LEWIS SPENCE

In reading many of the books that deal with the idea of Nazi occultism, one will sometimes find a reference to a book by the Scottish occultist Lewis Spence titled *The Occult Causes of the Present War* and published by Rider in London. The first edition appeared in 1940 and several further editions appeared over the next few years. As it was written and published during the Second World War, it is one of the earliest sources of the mythos of Nazi occultism. It might be expected that Spence could shed some light on the subject, since he had intimate knowledge of the German occult-magical milieu in the early part of the century, and was in fact an initiate of the German Druiden-Orden (Druidic Order). He had also earlier written a book on Germanic mythology. However, the book in question actually turns out to be entirely anti-German propaganda of the most jingoistic sort, informed by very few facts.

---

*The best resource for the material in English is Nostradamus, *The Prophecies,* translated and edited by Richard Sieburth and Stéphane Gerson.

The chapter titles of the book seem promising and intriguing enough:

>　I.　The Satanic Element in Nazism
>　II.　The Satanic Power
>　III.　The Satanic Power in Old Germany
>　IV.　Witchcraft, Satanism, and the Vehmgerichte
>　V.　The Satanic Power in Modern Germany
>　VI.　The Nazi Pagan Doctrine
>　VII.　The Nazi Pagan Church
>　VIII.　Nazism and Satanism

But when one realizes that the sole purpose of this little 144-page book was to function as wartime propaganda, it quickly becomes apparent that not much real information will be forthcoming. The book propagandizes against everything German or Germanic. It must have been read and consulted by later writers who produced the mythology of Nazi occultism, even if they did not cite Spence's work directly. Many of the themes of later works on the occult and the Nazis were obviously first laid out in this book.

What is interesting, or at least amusing, from the standpoint of the history of ideas, is Spence's regular use of circular logic. For example, the fact that so many witches were burned in Germany is proof positive of the Satanic character of the German people. In this Spence casts the churchmen who burned the witches as heroes, preserving law and order. The degree to which Spence himself indulges in what the popular liberal mindset of our contemporary society would fashionably condemn as Nazi thinking is also striking; for example, his disbelief that any white men could act as savagely as the Germans, or his analysis of Hitler's moral character from the shape of his head and face—Spence dismisses him as a "low-grade savage." Moreover, Spence condemns the entire German race in terms an actual Nazi might use to condemn Jews or members of supposed inferior races.

In reading this book, one realizes that Spence is not so much opposed to the structures of Nazi thinking as he is outraged by the

Germans applying it favorably to themselves. The book is full of statements of British ethnic superiority (especially that of the Celtic Scots—Spence's own ethnos, of course). Another amusing aspect of this is his insistence that the whole Continent of Europe is infected with Satanism—it is common knowledge that the British are too decent and fair-minded to harbor such an infamy! It is easy to see also why this book was never reprinted after the war. Its title suitably relegates it to the curiosity cabinet of history—and today, in any case, the author's own racially based logic would discredit the book among its intended audience. However, it can be seen as an important starting point for the flood of books about Nazi occultism that would come later.

AN ALLIANCE OF OCCULTISTS

In contrast to more authoritarian governments such as the Third Reich or the Soviet Union, the Western Allies did not have extensive propaganda machines broadcasting and publishing a steady stream of uniform and approved party-line messages from the state. That does not mean the West did not have sophisticated levels of both white and black propaganda on its side. In those days, Hollywood was supportive of the governmental war effort and the War Department itself even produced several propaganda films in tandem with famous Hollywood producers and directors, so information flowed relatively freely and what the people saw, heard, or read, they tended to believe. (This is in stark contrast to most people's attitudes today.)

Many people do not realize the degree to which WWII-era American and British leaders and advisers were steeped in occult ideas. Both Franklin Roosevelt and Winston Churchill were high-degree Freemasons. Churchill is known to have been involved with a neo-Druidic order as well, although this was probably not serious.

These occult, or quasi-occult, connections are only indicative of the fact that these men were susceptible to belief in things which others might find strange or unusual. They therefore might have been on the lookout for the same among the Nazis, and of course they found a good deal of it. They were likely to think of such things as meaningful and dangerous, not merely misguided or frivolous.

It cannot be said that Churchill was very deeply involved in actual occult thinking. It is possible that the vehemence of his opposition to the Nazis was rooted in the fact that he was, however, deeply in debt to London bankers and Hitler's greatest affront to the establishment was not his anti-Semitism or militarism but rather his aim to eliminate the practice of lending money for interest. This was a direct attack on the heart and soul of the financial infrastructure of the West. The occult dimension of finance will be discussed further when we get to the topic of Walter Johannes Stein. Based on Trevor Ravenscroft's *The Spear of Destiny,* Stein was supposed to have been an adviser to Churchill on occult matters pertaining to Hitler. This has not been proved or shown, and at this point actually appears unlikely.

Mitch Horowitz paints a vivid picture of the occult dimensions of the administration of Franklin D. Roosevelt in his *Occult America* (2010, 164–91). Roosevelt was himself a 33rd-degree Freemason and had as his vice president Henry Wallace between 1941 and 1945. Wallace was a known mystic and student of various occult schools from Theosophy to the thoughts of his acknowledged guru, the Russian painter and mystical philosopher Nicholas Roehrich. The Roosevelt White House was unusually open to extraordinary ideas, which the president apparently found stimulating. Famously, Roosevelt, with the encouragement of Wallace, had the Great Seal of the United States placed on the one-dollar bill in 1935. This was intended to have some sort of salutary and beneficial effect on the nation.*

An important adviser to British intelligence was the famous writer of thrillers on Satanic themes, Dennis Wheatley (1897–1977). He was a WWI veteran who had been gassed by chlorine at Passchendaele. After managing his family's wine business, he sold the company and set off on a successful career in writing fiction. One of his most famous and

---

*Apparently, the intention was to help to boost the country out of the throes of the Great Depression. In that case, the magic did not work—and only war with Hitler and Tojo could provide the needed lift.

successful works was the novel *The Devil Rides Out* (1934). For this he consulted occultists such as Aleister Crowley, Montague Summers, and Rollo Ahmed. This and other novels written in the early 1930s earned him the title "The Prince of Thriller Writers."

During WWII, Wheatley was a member of the London Controlling Section, a unit which secretly coordinated strategic military deception and propaganda efforts. One of his most well-known reports was on the concept of Total War, which detailed plans on military, economic, and media-based approaches to international conflict. It is known that he believed Nazism and Communism to be under the control of Satanic powers.

Wheatley continued to make his reputation as an expert on Satanism and black magic after the war. In his stories he demonstrated vehement hostility to such concepts, although he was a member of the Ghost Club. Wheatley was himself a staunch conservative and supporter of the monarchy and the British class system. It can only be assumed that Wheatley's attitudes and beliefs played some part in the nature of his advice to the Allied forces during the war.

Walther Johannes Stein (1891–1957) was an anthroposophist and writer who served as an artillery officer in WWI. After the war, he fin-

Fig. 12.1. Walter Johannes Stein

ished his studies in Vienna and received a Ph.D. with a 1918 dissertation titled *Historisch-kritische Beiträge zur Entwicklung der neueren Philosophie* (Historical-Critical Contributions to the Development of Modern Philosophy). This work was undertaken with the help of Rudolf Steiner. He then undertook a carreer in conjunction with Anthroposophy, at first lecturing on Steiner's theory of Social Threefolding (*Dreigliederung*), and then as a teacher at the Waldorf School in Stuttgart.

In 1932, Stein moved to London at the invitation of the industrialist Daniel Nicol Dunlop. Dunlop was an avid theosophist, and then anthroposophist, and author of books on magic and occultism. But he was also a businessman who had worked for the Westinghouse Electric Company in the USA in the 1890s. On his return to England, he helped found the British Electrical and Allied Manufacturers' Association in 1911. After the end of WWI, Dunlop undertook the organization of the World Power Conference (now called the World Energy Council). Dunlop died suddenly in 1935, but Stein continued privately and independently with work that was based on their collaboration, which included publishing a new journal called *The Present Age*. Stein released an essential economic platform in the journal in an article titled "The Earth as a Basis of World Economy." Curiously, the journal ceased to publish after the beginning of WWII.

Although it is a common misunderstanding that Stein was brought to England to advise Churchill, it is clear that he did run in influential circles within the British government and was friendly with the royal families of Belgium and Holland during the war. He was consulted about Hitler and the occult, but Churchill was apparently adamant about keeping any such ideas secret and did not want them used in official propaganda, as he thought it would be counterproductive.

STEIN-RAVENSCROFT AND THE QUESTION OF EVIL

By now it is well known that much of what has been written in such books as Trevor Ravenscroft's *The Spear of Destiny* is a combination of sectarian propaganda and pure idiosyncratic fantasy. I will discuss

Ravenscroft's work in more detail in the next chapter. But the questions remain: How did a political and cultural force of the character of National Socialism arise in the midst of a highly educated modern society? What was the nature and history of the groups and individuals involved in this dramatic historical episode? Too much credit should not be ascribed to the creative writings of authors such as Ravenscroft, since the human mind—especially one full of vague fears, anyway—is quite capable of conjuring all sorts of cosmic evils, as the media-driven witch hunts of the late 1980s showed. Satan was already being invoked to explain Nazism during the Second World War itself, as Lewis Spence's previously mentioned book *The Occult Causes of the Present War* (1940) illustrates. But what is the exact nature of this devil, of this evil—of this black magic?

To begin to attempt to answer these questions with any accuracy, we can dispense with paying much attention to the wilder claims of occult Nazi theories from Spence to Ravenscroft—at least until we have gotten some reasonable perspective on the whole. That was the purpose of the first three parts of this book. Anyone who has seriously read any National Socialist writings or propaganda of any kind will know that no overt appeal to evil or black magical powers was ever made. On the contrary, their enemies were usually charged with such epithets. Most sensationalistic writers are unable or unwilling to define exactly what characterizes good and evil in their tales. They simply assume who the bad guys are, and assume that we will go right along with their somnambulistic game.

If the degree of Nazi evil is to be measured by its level of cruelty, then certainly it can be adjudged no more evil than dozens of other political and religious systems of the past two centuries alone. Although in our *quantified* society we may be impressed by the magnitude of numbers, on a moral basis it really matters little whether one million, six million, or ten million innocents were put to death. Why, then, do the Nazis make such damn good villains? There is actually a score of reasons why this is so, not the least of which is their own sense of style, which we have already observed. The most diabolical of them were even fashion-conscious enough to wear black uniforms, with silver skulls and crossbones, and sinister-looking runes. But their level of evil seems to go beyond all this styling and profiling. It ascends to a level beyond conventional evil that most critics dare not penetrate—a very dangerous realm of moral or even theological evil. In our present-day world, many find this dangerous because confrontation with it is fraught with the possibility that, like Luke Skywalker, they may find some essential aspect of themselves lurking deep within it. (And, of course, historical investigation would confirm this.)

Psychologically, it is not uncommon for modern audiences to identify, consciously or unconsciously (and almost *always* aesthetically), with the black-clad, ruthless, empire-building villain. This ranges from Captain Nemo to the Wicked Witch of the West, to Dracula, to Maleficent, to Luke's father—Lord Vader. The underlying reason for all this is that we sympathize—even though some may feel that they shouldn't—with that Faustian Seeker of Knowledge and Power. This seeker is someone with a sense of a unique and individual grand purpose and meaning in life, and who possesses the will and ability to carry out these plans. The good guy is often boring, because he just wants to maintain the status quo, serve the king, be a "team player," and perhaps restore order where it has been disturbed by the evil machinations of the villain.

True, these examples are all drawn from fiction, but history is also a kind of rational fiction, subjectively reconstructed by historians from the often meager facts at their disposal. Sometimes this process can even become quite irrational, as we all know. In any event, we have the tendency to understand history and even contemporary events in terms of archetypal paradigms, or myths, which are then shared with—and in turn reflected by—the literary and cinematic worlds.

It might be said that actual black magic sets out not to do the will of God or of Nature (often understood as one in the same) but to do its *own* will—a will forged independent of God's laws or against the grain of nature. In this, magicians seek to set themselves apart from the limits of Nature, apart from the conventional notions of God: to set themselves up as self-directed, independent deities—or at least to *evolve* in that direction. The quest and practice of such a path is, from both a historical and a contemporary perspective, the only viable theoretical definition of so-called black magic in a philosophical or theological sense.

What becomes frightening for many persons contemplating this is the degree to which modern (or postmodern) humanity derives its motivations and values from the Faustian model. A so-called white magician, or religious individual, supposedly seeks only to do the will of some universal (international), transpersonal deity or even a collective group will—to harmonize and ultimately become one with it. But the Faustian type rebels against this and seeks to do his or her own will—a will peculiar to him or her. The structural implications of National Socialism are a curious and powerful mix of these two extremes. Its ability to blend them is based in the principle of elitism. To the Nazi, the concept of "God" is replaced by that of the Volk—the "people" or, more pointedly, the "race." The common man was to become one with the will of the Volk. The leadership, and most especially *the* leader (Führer), exercised his personal will to power in the extreme. This Volk, the collective organic body of the Germanic ethnic stock, aided by its priests (the leadership of National Socialism) became the center of the deity—focused, as with the unique initiatory magician, in the individual vehicle. The Nazis were to separate this new "God" from all others, economically and biologically, and develop it to a new level of being. If there is a crux to the issue of the nature of evil with regard to the Nazis, or to the question of whether they practiced any sort of black magic, surely this is near the center of it. National Socialism may be seen to represent a race-based, nationalistic rebellion against the natural cosmic order (or perhaps conventional order), just as the Faustian magician represents an analogous rebellion in the individual ego.

The individual or collective practice of what has been defined as black magic* always seems to focus on the model of an internally directed and willed process leading to higher, more powerful, or godlike states of being. In this regard, National Socialism could perhaps be

---

*A considered and nonsensational treatment of black magic and its attendant "left-hand path" can be found in my book *Lords of the Left-Hand Path*. There, too, I treat the National Socialist movement and the philosophy of Hitler from this perspective (2012).

called a form of black magic in that it set about—against the grain of Nature and prevailing consensus reality—to evolve itself, as an exponent of the distinct German Volk, into a higher, more powerful, godlike race of supermen based on *particular* national characteristics.

Most critics of Nazism who throw around terms such as *Satanic* or *black magical* do so with little understanding of this, however. They seem to be charging the Nazis with little more than excessive cruelty, or for having sided against those whom their psychic scriptwriter has provided with white hats, or good guy badges. But with deeper understanding, the problem of the relationship of Nazism to our concepts of evil becomes enormously more interesting and far more awesome in its implications for anyone who contemplates it beyond its mere historical importance.

Many younger people today, when asked why the Americans fought in the Second World War, will often answer that it was to help the Jews escape persecution. Of course, history shows that the plight of the Jews was hardly ever mentioned either before, or particularly during, the War. As Roosevelt would have had a significant interest in diabolizing the German Nazis as much as possible in his effort to mobilize America for the difficult war effort, it might seem rather surprising that the persecution of the Jews, which was well known as a general fact, was not much used in American anti-German propaganda. The liberation of the concentration camps was treated as a surprise discovery in the media. The reason for this approach was that America herself was still a general practitioner of anti-Semitism on many levels: neighborhoods (especially in the North) often excluded Jews and quotas were placed on Jews entering Ivy League schools. After all, it was the all-American industrial hero Henry Ford who was a powerful influence on Hitler's anti-Semitism with his collected work *The International Jew* (four small volumes published between 1920 and 1922). Hitler had a portrait of Ford hanging in his office.

Today it is generally considered shameful the degree to which the American government ignored efforts to help Jews fleeing Nazi persecution. The usual explanation for this is that it would have been politically *unpopular* for the government to be seen to help this apparently still widely despised population. After the war, and in the aftermath of the full realization of the genocidal nature of National Socialist policies, American postwar propaganda quickly caught up to the idea of rewriting history to indicate that America had some interest in coming to the aid of the Jews in Europe. In history, and the writing of history, the victors always seek the moral high ground, both to justify their (sometimes criminal) past actions by recasting them in a noble and selfless image, and to help prepare them for future battles ahead. (For example, the oppression of Jewish dissidents was a significant part of anti-Soviet propaganda during the Cold War.) In American domestic history, the War between the States (1861–1865) is almost always today understood as a war to free the slaves,* when in fact it was a war to preserve the Union at the expense of the South and prevent the economic development of those same Southern states to the benefit of the more economically well-placed Northern ones.

Hermann Rauschning (1887–1982) made a name for himself among the Allies by trading on his supposed close relationship with Adolf Hitler and writing two books: *Conversations with Hitler,* the American title of which was *Voice of Destruction* (1940), and *Revolution of Nihilism* (1939). His homeland was in the Danzig region. He held a Ph.D. from the University of Berlin and was a wounded WWI veteran. Politically, he was a lifelong conservative who supported the monarchy. Rauschning was originally a member of the German National People's Party, but joined the NSDAP in 1932, as it seemed the most viable alternative to restore the German lands that had been ceded to Poland after the Treaty of Versailles. In 1933, Rauschning became President of the Senate of Danzig as a representative of the NSDAP. He was a strong proponent for conquering Poland and turning it into a vassal state. On the other hand, he was not an enthusiastic anti-Semite, and

---

*Although I say that the American Civil War might be thus understood, this is a hopelessly optimistic assertion, since the average student probably knows little about the history of the war, as their educational system has generally failed them. This systematic failure of *general* education is seen as a fundamental factor in the ever-increasing possibilities for insinuating agenda-driven versions of history into the popular imagination. In America, this process has already occurred.

Fig. 12.2. Hermann
Rauschning in 1933

could generally be characterized as a Christian, conservative, nationalist, and monarchist. This set of stances was not uncommon at the
time in Germany and Austria, but it was a position that had no effective leadership or organized voice. In 1936 he resigned from politics,
and from the NSDAP and fled the country. He initially settled in the
United Kingdom for a period until moving on to the United States in
1941. The next year he became a citizen of the USA, and lived the rest
of his life as a farmer in Oregon.

As soon as Rauschning arrived in the United Kingdom, he began to
write about the Nazis as a way of warning the world of Hitler's intentions and character. However, his own motives for writing appears to
have been directed toward others like himself in Germany who belonged
to the conservative resistance to Hitler, for example, among those who
were involved with what was loosely called *Geheimes Deutschland,*
"Secret Germany." At the time the governments of the UK and the
USA had little interest in Rauschning, officially. His books on Hitler
and the Nazis did become bestsellers, so they were widely read by the
general public in the English-speaking world.

Clearly, Rauschning was opposed to Hitler as someone who had
betrayed the nationalist cause and become what Rauschning called a

revolutionary, having more in common with the Bolsheviks than with German nationalism. In his first book, *The Revolution of Nihilism*, Rauschning writes, "[T]he National Socialism that came to power in 1933 was no longer a nationalist but a revolutionary movement" (1939, 16).

His second book, published in 1940 and titled *The Voice of Destruction* in the US, is a virtual textbook and treasure trove for later Nazi occult writers. It contains chapter headings such as "Antichrist," "Yes! We are Barbarians!" "Is Hitler a Dictator?" "Magic, Black and White," "The Human Solstice," and "Hitler Himself."

In the chapter called "Antichrist," Rauschning tries to outline how anti-Christian Hitler is by writing about his supposed plans to create a pagan movement.

"You see," Hitler returned triumphantly; "that is what I'm building on. Our peasants have not forgotten their true religion. It still lives. It is merely covered over. The Christian mythology has simply coated it like a layer of tallow. It has preserved the true contents of the pot. I have said this to Darré, and told him that we must start the great reformation. He has suggested means to me, magnificent means! I have approved them. The old beliefs will be brought back to honor again. In our 'Green Week' and in the 'Traveling Agricultural Exhibition' he will allude to our inherited religion in picturesque and expressive language that even the simplest peasant can understand.

"It will not be done in the old way, running riot in colorful costumes and dreaming of a departed, romantic age. The peasant will be told what the Church has destroyed for him: the whole of the secret knowledge of nature, of the divine, the shapeless, the daemonic. The peasant shall learn to hate the Church on that basis. Gradually he will be taught by what wiles the soul of the German has been raped. We shall wash off the Christian veneer and bring out a religion peculiar to our race. And this is where we must begin. Not in the great cities, Goebbels! There we shall only lose ourselves in the stupid godlessness propaganda of the Marxists: free sex in nature and that sort of bad taste. The urban masses are empty. Where all is extinguished, nothing can be aroused. But our peasantry still lives in heathen beliefs and values." (Rauschning 1940, 55)

Rauschning demonstrates something of the counterfeit nature of his quote when he includes the Slavs as being part of a similar plan and movement in the next paragraph. Hitler would have never included the Slavs in a positive plan, but Rauschning himself was interested in softening the stance of the Nazis against the Poles and other Slavic peoples.

In a chapter called "Is Hitler a Dictator?" (pp. 194–214), Rauschning claims to show how Hitler did not operate autocratically, but that he is an instrument of something else, for example "the Party." As I mentioned earlier (in chapter 7), Hitler strategically worked through the Gauleiter (local district administrators of the NSDAP)—he would choose them carefully, then get their opinions through backchannels on various topics, present those opinions as his own (or ideas close to them) and "magically" they would follow him. In another telling passage, Rauschning reports that Hitler said, "Mastery always means the transmission of a stronger will to a weaker one. How shall I press my will upon my opponent? By first splitting and paralyzing his will, putting him at loggerheads with himself, throwing him into confusion" (1940, 213).

Rauschning seems to have read—or perhaps only heard of—the contents of work by Lanz von Liebenfels. For example, he becomes the conduit for some of the most fantastic ideas about the breeding of the Aryan superman. In *The Voice of Destruction,* we read: "There was the eye of Cyclops or median eye, the organ of magic perception of the Infinite, now reduced to a rudimentary pineal gland" and, Rauschning continues, "[Hitler] saw himself . . . as the prophet of the rebirth of man in a new form" (1940, 244).

Rauschning's agenda makes him pick his material and present it in ways that serve his own propagandistic purpose. Once his true motives are understood, and his actual audience identified, the nature of the work becomes clearer. By claiming to have been privy to secret talks and contact with Hitler, Rauschning could put any and all ideas or statements into either Hitler's mouth or into other "anonymous informants." The key to decoding what Rauschning has to say is to be aware of his own aims and prejudices. As a Christian, conservative monarchist, he is ready to believe and fear all sorts of strange ideas. Once Rauschning had decided that Adolf Hitler was bad for Germany and resigned from the NSDAP, Hitler became the opposite of what Rauschning thought of as good. Thus, Hitler was attacked as being a pagan and a revolutionary.

Earlier generations of historians used Rauschning's writings as genuine sources, and tended to defend this assessment over the years, but that is no longer the case. These texts are now considered by mainstream historians and Hitler biographers as highly dubious and without value. Ian Kershaw found Rauschning's accounts so unreliable as to dismiss them altogether, while Steigmann-Gall deems the works of Rauschning "fraudulent" (2003, 29). Rauschning's books have also been criticized by revisionist historians and so-called Holocaust deniers motivated by their own agendas.

It would be incorrect to dismiss every word of Rauschning's account as a total fabrication, however. He was a German and had been involved in the NSDAP (with some access, albeit limited, to Hitler) as well as other related political factions, and as such he probably does give us a picture of certain thoughts and ideas that had informal currency in those circles. It is the fantastic components that spice Rauschning's narrative which are most questionable—and which provide grist for the mill of even more fanciful postwar authors like Pauwels and Bergier, whose work we will consider in the next chapter. So while Rauschning's passages on strange and occult behaviors of the Führer might be unbelievable, his reports on how the Party operated offer some worthwhile insights.

Nowadays we are quite used to former insiders coming out with tell-all books to be read by a gullible public already eager to believe the most lurid details. Rauschning's works fall somewhat into that category, except that they were also used as valuable wartime anti-Nazi and anti-German propaganda on a popular level—which was their real value.

EXPOSÉS OF THE AMERICAN NAZI UNDERGROUND

Whether actual reports of activities of the NSDAP in America or of the German-American Bund in whatever guises it might have had, or the fantasies of wartime Americans looking for the "fifth column" under every bush and behind every tree, there was a good deal of anti-Nazi propaganda produced in the popular media during the war years in the USA. It was in major motion pictures, documentaries, and cartoons. Even Moe, Larry, and Curly did their part in the effort.

Little of this mass-market propaganda appears to have been based on any occult ideas or fantasies. A work typical of the time is John Roy Carlson's *Under Cover: My Four Years in the Nazi Underworld of America—The Amazing Revelation of How Axis Agents and Our Enemies Within Are Now Plotting to Destroy the United States* (1943). It went through eight printings in its first year. For the most part this book reflects the idea that agents of Japan and Germany were trying to infiltrate American organizations, first to keep America out of the war, and then to undermine democracy in America. Carlson chronicles the pro-Christian, anti-Semitic groups such as the Christian

Fig. 12.3. The flag of the German-American Bund

Front, National Workers League, and a dozen other active organizations. There were even the Black Nazis of Harlem—Black Nationalists who admired Hitler and sometimes used the "Heil Hitler!" greeting and looked to Hirohito as a liberator (Carlson 1943, 154–63). These groups and their aims were all identified under the term *un-American*. The US Congress first established the House Committee on Un-American Activities immediately after the Bolshevik Revolution in Russia, but in 1938 they turned their attention to the Nazis and Japanese.

WUNDERWAFFEN TO THE RESCUE!

As wartime losses became more obvious to the German populace during WWII, the Third Reich began to use white propaganda to instill faith in the Volk that their superior technology would, in the end, win the day for them. The terms *Geheimwaffen* (secret weapons) and *Vergeltungswaffen* (vengeance weapons) were often heard. German belief in the technological solution to military problems went back to the

Fig. 12.4. A V-1 flying bomb being rolled out for launch in 1944
(German Federal Archive)

time of WWI and beyond. During the Great War, weapons like the M-Gerät howitzer, known as the "Big Bertha" (*Dicke Bertha*), and the Paris Gun were examples. Such beliefs and attitudes are a natural result of the general cultural picture described in chapter 2 concerning the advanced state of German technology in the late nineteenth and early twentieth centuries. Clear German technical superiority in the Franco-Prussian War, especially in the field of artillery, gave greater credence to the later attitudes. In the initial stages of the Second World War, the Germans also demonstrated their technical superiority in all sorts of armaments. This superiority partly stemmed from the situation in which the older generation of German armaments had been destroyed under terms of the Treaty of Versailles. Therefore, the weapons manufactured after 1933 represented a whole new generation of armaments, making use of more recent technological advances.

The German use of the term *Wunderwaffe* itself is an example of both occult thinking and propaganda. Its best translation is "miracle weapon" even with the implication of intervention from a supernatural source of knowledge. The choice and use of this word in German has to be seen as reflective of the virtually mystical or occult aspect of thinking that is evident in theories like Hörbiger's Glacial Cosmology and many of the Nazi leaders' proclivity for mystical ideas. The hard and fast technical advances in evidence on the German side in the fields of rocket engineering, avionics, and submarine technology all gave a background or context for the idea of the *Wunderwaffen*. On the Allied side, there was some trepidation about the actual possibility of the sudden development of weapons that could turn the tide of the war at the last minute. The observation of the phenomenon that became known among the American bomber crews as the "foo fighters"—balls of light moving at high speeds—excited such concerns.

In the closing months of the war, white propaganda was spread in Germany that the Führer would unleash some Wunderwaffe in the nick of time to win the war at the last minute, when all seemed lost. Although this was probably more of an act of psychological encouragement to the people, intended just to prolong the inevitable and make the policy of "victory or annihilation" more certain, Allied intelligence did pick up on these signals and must have wondered. This wonder turned to myth after the war.

Immediately after the end of the war, both American and Soviet interests were on an all-out search for the German scientists and technicians responsible for the considerable German military advances in theory and practice. The Americans called their effort Operation Overcast. The most famous part of this operation was the rounding up of the scientists who worked with Wernher von Braun on rocket technologies, bringing them to the US, and organizing them to develop the American space program for NASA.

An intriguing glimpse into the vision of the German rocket scientists going back into pre-Nazi times is provided by the first serious film about the possibilities of space travel, Fritz Lang's *Frau im Mond* (Woman in the Moon; 1929). The film showed features such as the rocket named *Friede* (Peace) being built in a tall building and moved to the launch pad; the rocket blasts off after a countdown from ten to zero; in flight, the rocket ejects a first and second stage, the crew

Fig. 12.5. *Frau im Mond*
logo on a V-2 rocket
(Wikimedia Commons)

rests in horizontal chairs to minimize g-force effects; and foot straps are used to hold the crew down in zero gravity. Obviously, much of this would become a part of space exploration as engineered by German scientists in both America and the Soviet Union. German rocket scientists Hermann Oberth and Willy Ley are known to have acted as advisers for this film, and the Wernher von Braun circle at the Verein für Raumschiffahrt (Society for Space Travel) were enthusiastic about the film. They even painted the logo from the film on the tail of one of the V-2 rockets.

The often heard idea that the so-called miracle weapons were brought into the fray too late to make any difference and that if they had implemented them sooner the Germans could have somehow won the war, is generally held today to be a misinterpretation of the possibilities. Of all the Nazis, it was perhaps "crazy" Rudolf Hess who knew best: Germany simply could never have won a war on two fronts. The Germans made the same mistake as the Spanish had done with their Armada, trying to rely on larger weapons, when many smaller, simpler, more reliable, and faster weapons would win the day. While Hitler was trying to build ever bigger tanks that could carry guns of the same caliber as were on the Bismarck battleship, the Russians built thousands of the T-34 and IS-series tanks, which proved to be a superior strategy.

Propaganda is comfortable with lies. Its value is only measured by its effectiveness. Once the conflict for which it was created has past, it should be forgotten. But often in history a sort of Frankenstein's monster of propaganda is shaped that proves itself to be immortal and to fulfill a purpose for which it was not originally intended. It takes on a life of its own. Such is the case with much of the anti-Nazi propaganda.

Propaganda may be useless in discovering the truth about anything, but it does reveal the attitudes of the creators of the propaganda toward their object. Also in the case of Nazi propaganda—both pro-Nazi and anti-Nazi—the scope and power of the tales it tells only grows as the years go by.

As Steigmann-Gall intimates, the Nazis have assumed an archetypal place in the collective consciousness of the West. They have ascended to a kind of transcendental world where their images have become immortal and eternally meaningful—even if often *fictional*.

> It is apparent that certain presumptions about Nazism will never fully disappear. If for no other reason, Nazism serves as a useful foil, a way of gauging good and evil in the world. We are given to presuming that the things we tend to dislike in modern society must have reigned triumphant in Nazism. In fact, what we suppose Nazism must surely have been about usually tells us as much about contemporary societies as about the past purportedly under review. (Steigmann-Gall 2003, 266)

What we discover is that wartime propaganda material is a hastily planted garden sown with the seeds of the fantastic, its fruit only intended for consumption during the season of war. But these seeds have grown like perennial weeds to clutter and choke the garden of the reasonable mind for all eternity.

The only tool that can be applied to this weed-bound garden is the sharp hoe of a critical mind motivated by a search for hidden truths. Much can be learned in this critical process, and the lessons learned are not limited to the particular historical period being studied. The process of turning historical events into mythic realities is an eternally recurring process.

CHAPTER 13

AFTERMATH:
ESOTERIC NAZISM SINCE 1945

The Generation of a New-Age Mythology

As soon as the Second World War was over in May 1945, the world began to struggle with questions about how it all could have happened. As traumatic as the events of 1914 to 1918 had been, the level of destruction and death visited upon the world as a result of this second phase of the larger war were astounding to anyone who chose to contemplate it—whole cities destroyed, as many as *sixty million* dead on both sides (counting both civilian and military losses). The world had never witnessed such an orgy of death and destruction, and for many people it seemed to require some cosmic explanation.

In the circumstances of relative intellectual luxury that the postwar world provided, people who had been on either side of the war began to think and, after thinking (or emoting), they began to write. Some of what they wrote was based on earlier—wartime—concepts, fantasies (nightmares), or propaganda. On the Allied as well as the Axis side, some of it was written in the spirit of self-justification. The winners of wars often rewrite history to turn their struggles for the preservation and expansion of their powers into self-righteous and holy crusades of good versus evil. Certainly, no war in history ever fit the bill better for such a mythology than "The Big One." On the other side, some Germans indulged in fantasies about what could have been, and how miracles could have saved their cause. Most Germans, just like almost all Japanese, simply returned to the work of building good lives

409

for themselves—and with the magnanimous help of the victors, they accomplished just that in relatively short order.

Upon closer analysis, a complex of motivations can be discerned in these postwar texts. Most are anti-Nazi in their sentiments and pick up on themes set out during the war. These include that the Nazis were Satanists, pagans, heretics, mad scientists, mass-hypnotists, and so on. The motivations behind the anti-Nazi school of Nazi occult literature span a spectrum ranging from strange sectarian beliefs on the part of individual authors, to efforts to misdirect the public as to the actual nature of National Socialism and to obfuscate the deeper causes of the crimes of the Nazis. Some of the writers actually appear to be pro-Nazi in their sentiments. These may not be sympathetic to political or cultural features of actual National Socialist ideology but are certainly examples of the allure of Nazi aesthetics and branding, which continued to exert its effectiveness over time and space. In this model, the idea of being anti-Nazi merely means that the writer is motivated to portray Nazi ideology, or individuals active within that ideology historically, as intrinsically evil or metaphysically criminal. A good number of the authors, especially in the 1970s, seem to have been motivated mainly by profit. Those who might be characterized as pro-Nazi are either proponents of what they *think* Nazism was, or they seek to emulate some part of that movement for their own purposes.

And then there are those "doubting angels" who have taken neither side in this polarized battle of good and evil, and who seek to discover the objective truth and utilize the techniques and methods pioneered by the Nazis for the sake of individual initiation. Such is the academic and practical approach to the seeking of the *Gral* exemplified by the Order of the Trapezoid within the Temple of Set, for example.

After this discussion of motivations ranging from the political to the sectarian, and also taking into account the neutral parties, I cannot conclude without mentioning what is probably the greatest motivator for those writing the kind of material we see in the body of post-1945 books of Nazi occultism: it is hard to resist telling a tall tale, a lurid and intriguing account about the most fascinating topic of the mid-twentieth century and one with enduring appeal. Stories about Nazis sell books. Once the genii of occult Nazism were fully out of the bottle by the late 1960s with *The Morning of the Magicians,* there was no interest in putting them back in for the sake of rationality or truth. It was all just too lucrative, too exiting, and too far out, man.

THE ANTI-NAZI SCHOOL OF OCCULT LITERATURE

The anti-Nazi mythologizing of the post-1945 period was obviously not motivated by the same factors that spurred Lewis Spence to write *The Occult Causes of the Present War.* There was no longer a war to win. Rather, it was a more nebulous motivation to demonize the National Socialists further, in an attempt to discourage any postwar romanticizing of them, and to rewrite the history of the Nazis to make them *primarily* into proponents of such things as paganism or even Satanism.

Just as WWII came to an end, a Catholic professor of religion named Andrew Krzesinski came out with a short booklet, obviously meant for mass distribution (it cost fifty cents) titled *Religion of Nazi Germany* (1945). This was the first salvo in the postwar campaign to show the world how Nazi Germany had been guided in its criminal behavior by dark and sinister forces—atheistic, pagan, and even *Satanic.*

It must be said that Krzesinski's assessment of the "Satanic character" of Nazism is far more sophisticated than the occult ramblings of Lewis Spence, whose jargon seemed to conjure images of black-robed Nazis chanting hymns to Satan in darkened subterranean chambers. Rather, Krzesinski, with some sense of accuracy, writes:

We are using the expression Satanism to indicate a system, adopted by the Nazis, in which the place of God is taken by man or by a nation, virtues are regarded as crimes, and crimes as virtues, love of neighbour is condemned and hatred extolled, religious life is disorganized and rendered impossible, churches are closed or desecrated, priests are humiliated and killed. . . .

In this system there is no place for God. In spite of that, the Nazis speak of God, but this God who receives a pantheistic feature is limited to activity in the life of the German nation. . . . This theory means, practically, that the only God is the German nation. . . . [W]e learn that all other nations should obey Germany on account of her divine character, and help her in her attempt at world domination. (Krzesinski 1945, 37)

The same sort of definition could be given from a Christian perspective regarding the Satanic character of Bolshevism. To the church, anything that thwarts its own centuries-long attempts at world domination can be characterized as Satanic for *opposing* its aims.

There were two primary aims behind postwar anti-Nazi mythologizing and propaganda: first, to cover the tracks of the more accurate causes of Nazi crimes against humanity (i.e., centuries of official anti-Semitism promulgated by the churches on all levels) and second, to help eliminate any possibility of the re-emergence of National Socialism in Germany or elsewhere. The label "National Socialist" or "Nazi" had to be made so distasteful that no sane person would want to ever identify with it again. In occupied postwar Germany there was, of course, an actual far-reaching program called *Entnazifizierung* (denazification) under the Befreiungsgesetz, the "Law for Liberation from National Socialism and Militarism." The first aim was almost entirely achieved, whereas the second can be said to have been generally accomplished.

As we have seen, in 1958 the Swiss political psychologist Wilfried Daim came out with a scholarly study of the ideas of Lanz von Liebenfels titled *Der Mann, der Hitler die Ideen gab* (The Man Who Gave Hitler his Ideas). Daim did excellent work analyzing the works of Liebenfels and explaining his ideology, but he did very little in the way of clarifying in any specific way the linkage between National Socialist concepts and the obsessions of the head of the ONT. For this reason, despite all the erudition displayed by Daim, we have to count this work as belonging to the traditions of mythologizing the Nazis. As the substantial section on Liebenfels in chapter 4 of this book shows, the fantastic concepts of the ONT in little to no way line up with the much more pragmatic and scientific Nazi ideas of eugenics and breeding of the Herrenvolk, or "Master Race." Liebenfels was a mystic of the flesh, whereas the Nazis generally saw the breeding of humans as analogous to that of any other animal, which could be reared for its ideal physical and other traits. Lanz supported eugenics and idolized the Aryan archetype of humanity—but so did countless other groups in many countries at the time. Most significantly, the early works of Liebenfels did *not* focus on anti-Semitism. For Lanz, it was simply a matter of blond hair and blue eyes. If a Jew was endowed with these traits, he or she was seen by him as belonging to the noble race. Daim's book did forge a link between Lanz and Hitler in the popular imagination, and it must be said that it was a link that Lanz himself had liked to suggest on occasion—until after the war when he imagined that this fantastic connection might get him in trouble with the occupying forces. That all of this was merely a figment of his own imagination and that of his followers is demonstrated by the fact that the Allied authorities in charge of rounding up proto-Nazi ideologues did not give him a second look. He was never interviewed or seriously investigated at all.

LOUIS PAUWELS AND JACQUES BERGIER AND *THE MORNING OF THE MAGICIANS*

The writing team of Louis Pauwels and Jacques Bergier was apparently a bit of an odd couple. Pauwels was a conservative ally of the French New Right who eventually returned to his Catholic faith, and Bergier was a Russian Jew who spent time in a Nazi concentration camp.

Louis Pauwels (1920–1997) was a native of Belgium who began his writing and editing career just after WWII. He spent more than a year as a student of G. I. Gurdjieff and later wrote a book about him. He met Jacques Bergier in 1954 and formed a partnership with him, which resulted in *Le Matin des Magiciens* in 1960. His interests and connections in society were broad. Philosophically, perhaps the best presentations of his own ideas are found in the book titled *The Eternal Man* (1972), also coauthored with Bergier. Pauwels was a mentor to Alain de Benoist, who dedicated the original French version of his book later translated as *On Being a Pagan* (2018) to him. After Pauwels's conversion to Catholicism in 1982, he renounced many of his past interests and works.

Although *The Morning of the Magicians* became a sort of inspirational textbook for Nazi occultists and magicians in the years following its publication, the original motive for writing the book (besides selling a lot of copies) was not to promote Nazism but rather to convince the reader of the depth of the strangeness in which the Nazis were entangled and thus act as a warning against people of the present generation entertaining such ideas themselves. For this reason, this book belongs to the anti-Nazi camp.

Jacques Bergier (= Yakov Mikhailovich Berger [1912–1978]) was by his own account* and that of those who knew him, a prodigious intellect. There were reputedly scientists and miraculous rabbis in this family tree. The upheavals of the Russian Civil War after the Revolution forced the Jewish Berger family first to a small town in northwestern Ukraine, and then to emigrate to France in 1925. In France, where he Gallicized his name to Jacques Bergier, he studied atomic physics at the Sorbonne. He worked with the French Resistance to the Nazi occupation and was eventually arrested and spent over a year in the Mauthausen-Gusen concentration camp—a place where the jet fighter Me 262 was assembled. After the war, he met Louis Pauwels, and they formed a longtime collaboration in publishing, the apex of which was the French edition of *Le Matin des Magiciens,* which was followed by an English translation (*The Dawn of Magic*) in the UK in 1963 and the American paperback edition in 1968, now more faithfully titled as *The Morning of the Magicians.* This work became a staple of the occult revival in the West. Bergier was enamored with science, technology, science fiction, and extraterrestrial life and visitations. This blend certainly makes itself felt in the contents of *The Morning of the Magicians.*

Following their tremendous success with *Le Matin des Magiciens,* the authors founded a magazine dedicated to the same brand of fantastic realism called *Planète* (The Planet), which was published continuously between 1961 and 1972. This instrument greatly extended the reach of their ideas in the French-speaking world and informed a generation in

---

*He wrote an autobiography in 1978 titled *Je ne suis pas une légende* (I Am Not a Legend).

the field of the fantastic (= imaginary) configured in realistic form. The style has also been referred to as "neo-surrealistic." Influenced by science fiction, and perhaps by the teaching methods of G. I. Gurdjieff, these authors spun yarns and populated them with symbols, characters, and events inspired by the incredible events that occurred during their lives. Clearly, their methods were to loosen the bonds of conventional thinking and infuse fantastic possibilities in order (they hoped) to unleash new creative potentials on a mass scale.

Pauwels and Bergier greatly played up the role of Karl Haushofer (see chapter 10) as a secret mastermind behind all sorts of fantastic Nazi projects. But the bare facts of Haushofer's life tend to cast a huge amount of doubt on all of these stories—that he was a close confidant of Hitler, a member of the Thule Society, a student of Zen Buddhism, or an "initiate of Tibetan lamas."

Pauwels and Bergier did not invent the Haushofer story out of whole cloth. The role of this professorial figure in Nazi policies had been publicized during the war itself, for example in the dramatized short documentary film called *Plan for Destruction* (1943), which was even nominated for an Academy Award. Immediately after the war, articles appeared that ascribed a sinister tone to Haushofer's role, such as Edmund Walsh's 1946 piece in *Life* magazine and Willy Ley's 1947 article in *Astounding Science Fiction*.

The Myth of the Vril Society

In Willy Ley's article "Pseudoscience in Naziland" (*Astounding Science Fiction;* 1947), he writes dismissively about an esoteric group that was

> literally founded upon a novel. That group which I think called itself *Wahrheitsgesellschaft*—Society for Truth—and which was more or less localized in Berlin, devoted its spare time looking for *Vril*. Yes, their convictions were founded on Bulwer-Lytton's "The Coming Race." They knew that the book was fiction, Bulwer-Lytton had used that device in order to be able to tell the truth about this "power." The subterranean humanity was nonsense, *Vril* was not. Possibly it had enabled the British, who kept it as a State secret, to

amass their colonial empire. . . . For reasons which I failed to penetrate, the secret of *Vril* could be found by contemplating the structure of an apple, sliced in halves. (Ley 1946, 92)

Based more or less on these and a few other meager "facts," Bergier and Pauwels let their imaginations run wild and spun the yarn that the Vril Society was a group of Berlin-based occult scientists, characterized as an inner circle of the Thule Society. They also speculate that this group was in contact with the English Golden Dawn order—another fanciful tale that few ever follow up on.

In his book *Monsieur Gurdjieff* (published in France in 1954, in English translation as *Gurdjieff* in 1971), Louis Pauwels had already begun to spin or transmit remarkable tales about Haushofer, the Nazis, and the Vril. Pauwels (1971, 62–65) claims he is merely "transcribing" these reports (which he admits sound "strange" and "fantastic") without judgment as to their validity (1971, 62–65). This report tells of Gurdjieff's link with Karl Haushofer in Tibet, and how Haushofer founded the "Thule Groups" into which Hitler and Himmler were initiated. This group, according to the report, made a link with the Tibetan "King of Fear," who ruled the "city of violence," Shampullah (*sic*). All of the leaders of the Nazi Party were members of this group, according to the report. It is said that Haushofer advised Hitler to make the swastika his sign and had him use an inverted form of it (in 1928). For whatever reason, it is said that the Tibetan authorities demanded of the Nazis that they make a special effort to exterminate the people known as "Gypsies."* Here, too, is mentioned the idea that many Tibetan and Hindu soldiers were sent to Berlin to defend it in the last

---

*Of course, the name "Gypsies" is an absolute misnomer; the actual designation of these people is Romani. They are a people from Central or South Asia who migrated into Europe beginning in the twelfth century. They are speakers of an Indo-European language related to Hindi. The medieval moniker "Gypsy" intimated that this exotic people were from "Egypt," as the Christians of the period had little awareness of world history beyond what they read in the Bible. Any strange or exotic people (especially those one might, for whatever reason, distrust or dislike) were thought perhaps to be from that land of cosmic evil, Egypt.

days of WWII. All of this material would be worked up even further in the text of *The Morning of the Magicians.* Almost none of it could be factually proved to be true.

It is widely thought that these and other similar stories were actually taken from secret talks or lectures given by Gurdjieff to his pupils in occupied France, where he was able to continue his work despite German occupation. He, like certain Buddhist teachers, was known for weaving historical fact with fantastic tales to teach certain lessons in thinking. One might have hoped the book *Voices in the Dark* (2000), which contains talks given by Gurdjieff during the Nazi occupation of France, would have thrown some light on this, but only darkness prevailed. This book does intersperse various discussions of occult Nazi topics, but mostly without any insight or Gurdjieffian wisdom.

As we saw in chapter 5, there was an obscure group in Berlin during the 1920s called the Reichsarbeitsgemeinschaft "Das kommende Deutschland" (Imperial Working Group: "The Coming Germany"). However, Pauwels and Bergier appear to have been totally unaware of its existence.

In the previous chapter, the wartime works of the ex-Nazi Hermann Rauschning were discussed. The French translations of these books, especially *The Voice of Destruction* (1940), were heavily used as sources by Pauwels and Bergier. At the outset of the chapter titled "Hitler Himself" in *The Voice of Destruction,* the question is posed: *Is Hitler mad?* Pauwels and Bergier include a passage from this chapter. The text comes from what Rauschning refers to as a reliable informant. Following is a perhaps more accurate translation of the same passage.

> Hitler wakes at night with convulsive shrieks. He shouts for help. He sits on the edge of the bed, as if unable to stir. He shakes with fear, making the whole bed vibrate. He shouts confused, totally unintelligible phrases. He gasps, as if imagining himself to be suffocating.
>
> . . . Hitler stood swaying in his room, looking wildly about him. "He! He! He's been here!" he gasped. His lips were blue. Sweat streamed down his face. Suddenly he began to reel off figures, and

odd words and broken phrases, entirely devoid of sense. It sounded horrible. He used strangely composed and entirely un-German word formations. Then he stood quite still, only his lips moving. He was massaged and offered something to drink. Then he suddenly broke out—"There, there! In the corner! Who's that?" (Rauschning 1940, 256)

Pauwels and Bergier try to give this questionable and hearsay account a context that suggests some sort of a visitation from a mysterious entity from beyond this realm of reality. The "Secret Chiefs" of the Golden Dawn are mentioned suggestively. But the overall context of this account in the text by Rauschning makes one think, if genuine, these are reports of an episode of PTSD. Rauschning mentions them more in the spirit of merely trying to intimate that Hitler is in some way unbalanced and out-of-control mentally.

One could spend a great deal of time tracking down the mystifications and falsifications present in *The Morning of the Magicians.* Such a search only bears fruit if the endeavor is focused within one area of study. Taken as a whole, the work is a reality-based form of pure fiction or fantasy and serves the purposes of imaginative literature—which is no small thing.

TREVOR RAVENSCROFT AND *THE SPEAR OF DESTINY*

When an investigator begins a descent into the treacherous subterranean fields of occult connections in the world of political phenomena, matters can quickly become so confused and so obscure that the rational mind is soon pushed over what has aptly been called the "boggle threshold."* This usually has as much to do with the way in which phenomena are interpreted as with the character of the events themselves.

---

*The "boggle threshold" is a phrase coined by the writer Renée Haynes, and means "the level at which the mind 'boggles' or is thwarted by the degree of improbability of a phenomenon."

Although we can count *The Morning of the Magicians* as the first in the wave of Nazi occult literature, the second masterpiece of this kind of material has to be counted as Trevor Ravenscroft's *The Spear of Destiny* (1973). In his now (in)famous work, Ravenscroft posited a sectarian and esoteric viewpoint that Adolf Hitler was in fact the reincarnation of a certain evil genius, Landulf II. Landulf II was supposedly used as the model for Clinschor in Wolfram von Eschenbach's thirteenth-century epic poem *Parzivâl,* and subsequently for Klingsor in Richard Wagner's *Parsifal.* Landulf reached out over the centuries, so the story goes, to exert his evil black magic in the modern world.

It has been convincingly demonstrated that most of the facts in Ravenscroft's story are actually fabrications, and that is being charitable. If true on any level, Ravenscroft's yarn could only be considered some-how "mystically factual." Nicholas Goodrick-Clarke in his *The Occult Roots of Nazism* devotes a whole section to the basic level of fabrication involved in Ravenscroft's book. In appendix E of his work, Goodrick-Clarke shows that Ravenscroft went so far as to make up names, places (including addresses), dates, and so forth.

But how did *this* particular version of the modern mythos of Nazi occultism originate? The key may perhaps be found in the person of Ravenscroft's supposed mentor, Walter Johannes Stein. Stein was an anthroposophist who wrote the book *Weltgeschichte im Lichte des heiligen Gral* (World History in the Light of the Holy Grail) in 1928. In turn, the key to unlock Stein's conceptual world is most logically found in the Anthroposophical doctrines of Rudolf Steiner (1861–1925).

Facts show that Ravenscroft's yarn was largely a fictional concoction. In fact, he never even met Stein at all! But he perhaps had some access to Stein's papers after his death. Ravenscroft was also involved in Anthroposophy in England. But the largely fictional character of the story told in *The Spear of Destiny* came out in a court case in 1980, when Ravenscroft sued the novelist James Herbert for copyright infringement in the latter's novel titled *The Spear* (1978). Ravenscroft asserted that the contents of his own book were fictional creations, and not historical material. Herbert had wrongly assumed that the material was actually a matter of history, and so not subject to copyright. The court ruled in Ravenscroft's favor: the contents of *The Spear of Destiny* are indeed *fictional*. Evidence shows that Ravenscroft originally offered the book as a work of fiction, but the initial publisher preferred that it be cast as a historical reality.

Himmler's planned *Mittelpunkt der Welt,* the Wewelsburg, also became the focal point of a 1978 novel by Kyle Duncan called *Black Camelot,* which played some role in the history of mythologizing esoteric Nazism. The book is a novel of spy-intrigue in which Himmler and his band of demonic Grail knights attempt to sow discord among the Allies during WWII.

In Ravenscroft's (or Stein's) historical mythos, a special role of wickedness is reserved for the infamous Guido von List (1848–1919). Ravenscroft invented a Viennese book dealer named Ernst Pretzsche, who served as a fictional link between Hitler and occult figures in Vienna. At one point Ravenscroft writes:

> A group photograph on the office desk showed Pretzsche beside a man whom Stein recognised as the infamous Guido von List, the founder member and leading figure of an Occult Lodge whose activities, when uncovered by the Press, had profoundly shocked the people of Vienna. Up to the time he was unmasked, Guido von List had enjoyed a very large following as a political writer whose books were widely praised for their themes of Pan-Germanic mysticism. When it was revealed that he was the leader of a blood brotherhood which had substituted the Swastika for the Cross in rituals involving sexual perversion and the practice of medieval black magic, List had fled from Vienna in fear of being lynched by an incensed populace with strong Roman Catholic sentiments. (Ravenscroft 1973, 59)

All of this is entirely fictional.

Curiously enough, Stein's mentor and the founder of Anthroposophy, Rudolf Steiner, was certainly a personal acquaintance of List, the Armanist founder of early twentieth-century runic occultism. They were both part of the same literary circles in Vienna in the late 1880s and early 1890s. My study of Guido von List presented in

The Secret of the Runes outlines this and other phases of List's career. However, despite the fact that both List and Steiner were open to many of the same influences, such as nascent Theosophy, they developed their ideologies in radically different directions.

As we know, Guido von List went on to be one of the founding fathers, along with Jörg Lanz von Liebenfels, of a general Pan-Germanic mystical school now known collectively as "Ariosophy" (Aryan wisdom). Its major tenets are that the root of wisdom and of occult power is housed within the particular racial stock of the "Aryans" (i.e., Indo-European or "Indo-Germanic" peoples) and that the aim of the movement is the evolution (or re-evolution) of the Aryans into a Master Race of supermen. This school of (originally) occult thought was not represented by any single organization, but was used as a generic term encompassing dozens of groups and orders. Chief among these were the Guido von List Society and the Ordo Novi Templi headed by Liebenfels. Steiner's development took another direction, but one which explains well why Guido von List and the Ariosophists would become a perfect model of "evil" from the Anthroposophical perspective.

Writing in his study entitled *The Occult Movement in the Nineteenth Century*, Steiner says that "right occultism" is that which seeks a spiritual goal for its own sake, identifiable with the universal-human, while "left occultism" is that which seeks "its own special aims" (1915, 29–30). Here Steiner is speaking of "right" and "left" more in the sense of the right- and left-hand spiritual paths rather than in political jargon, although this may have had some relevance as well. Steiner, of course, sees himself in the "right," working for the benefit and evolution of the universal-human in Anthropo-sophy (Human-wisdom). It is clear that Steiner would have seen heinous "leftward"-leaning tendencies first in Theosophy itself (from which Steiner broke in 1913) and most especially in the widespread and multifaceted Ariosophical movement. The latter he would have seen to be using occult means to promote the particular interests of a single faction of humanity over all others. This originally occult Ariosophical doctrine certainly had its effects in politics and helped shape some of the founding principles of what evolved into National Socialism.

It is fairly obvious that the roots of the sectarian mythology codified in Ravenscroft's book are to be found in the esoteric doctrines of Rudolf Steiner, as interpreted and transmitted by Walter Johannes Stein indirectly to Trevor Ravenscroft. Moreover, it is clear that the notion of the particular form of Nazi evil has, for this esoteric school, more to do with the fact that they belong to the spiritual "left"—pursuing their "own particular aims"—rather than to the universal-human "occult right" as envisioned by Steiner.

Research clearly shows that the esoteric right/left dichotomy posited by Steiner was carried forth by Walter Johannes Stein in the form of certain universalistic *socioeconomic* theories. Stein esoterically held that the blood of Christ entered the Earth at Golgotha, making the whole Earth the physical body of Christ, and this "esoteric fact" is to be realized through the development of a "world-embracing economy." This economy "directed from a universal point of view" is predicated on the dissolution of national frontiers. This world economy was to be directed by a nebulous body called by him the "Order of Christ"—presumably a dedicated band of friendly, hard-working government bureaucrats (cf. the IRS, UN, etc.). Stein held that "the creation of a system of World Economy is the real mission of the Anglo-Saxon/Germanic people" (Lawrie 1990, 130). Stein had, after all, been brought to England in 1933 by British business magnate Daniel Nicol Dunlap to aid in the operations of the World Power Conference (later known as the World Energy Conference). In England, he continued to work—this included acting as an adviser to Winston Churchill (who some say became a patient of Stein, who was a homeopathic practitioner).

In stark contrast to Stein's universalistic theories of global economy based upon the presence of the transubstantiated blood of Christ in the body of the Earth, are the National Socialist economic theories based upon the existence of discreet individual nations (*Völker*)—who, linked to their own part of the Earth, compete with each other for the world's resources. The NS aim was to establish an autarky with its own economic space (*Lebensraum*) commensurate with its economic power. This economic system would then become fully independent and self-sufficient—remaining apart from the rest of the world economy. The esoteric basis for NS economics is rooted in the idea of blood and soil (*Blut und Boden*). The autarky would be free of usury, or the earning of money based on interest paid on loans. Stein, on the other hand, saw the international financial network based on interest as the manifestation of the Holy Grail itself—an inexhaustible source of wealth.

Each of these economic theories talks about "blood and soil," of course. The esoteric right sees a one-world economy with no national borders, the esoteric left sees individuated national economies functioning in relative isolation. The "blood" of the right is a collective entity—embodied in the notion of a universal Christ—and the "soil" is the whole Earth, while the left sees the "blood" as a metaphor signifying the nation (Volk) and the "soil" is the physical land or space occupied by that nation.

These issues—exoteric though their manifestations may appear as they flicker across the television screen on the evening news—are clear and present esoteric realities facing us today. But the essential philosophical question remains here as elsewhere: Where, if anywhere, does the true *evil* lie in any this?

With regard to the object popularly now known as "the spear of destiny," the truth is not what legend would have you believe. But history and archaeology do tell a remarkable story nevertheless. The contents of this section have been largely abridged from a more extensive treatment of the topic in my book *The Mysteries of the Goths* (2011). The phrase "spear of destiny" was actually first given to the relic otherwise known as the *Heilige Lanze,* the "holy lance," an object found in the imperial regalia of the Holy Roman Empire and the Austrian Empire now housed in the Hofburg in Vienna, in an article that appeared in the *Sunday Dispatch* (Nov. 6, 1960) by Max Caulfield many years before the publication of Trevor Ravenscroft's scurrilous book on the subject.

When the Germanic peoples were first Christianized, their kings and chieftains typically carried *spears* as symbols of their sovereign power—a power ultimately derived from their own "divine blood." This divine blood stemmed from their godlike or semi-divine ancestors. With Christianization, apologists cast about in scripture to find a notable spear in biblical mythology, and found reference to the one used by the Roman soldier, identified in later Christian tradition as Longinus, to pierce the side of Jesus as he hung on the cross. Due to obscure passages in the Old Testament that were later interpreted as dealing with the signs of the true Messiah, which imply "not a bone of him shall be broken" (John 19:36; erroneously ascribed to Isaiah by Ravenscroft), it was essential in this mythology for Longinus to prove that Jesus was dead by thrusting the spear into him—otherwise his legs would have been broken to hasten his death so that the body could be taken down before the beginning of the Jewish Sabbath. It was therefore said that the spear of Longinus proved that Jesus was the Messiah; that at that moment Longinus held the destiny of the world in his hands—and that subsequently, he who possesses the spear similarly holds the destiny of the world in his hands. All this makes for a fine medieval Christian myth to syncretize the use of a spear by the kings with Christian symbolism—but it, like the Shroud of Turin, cannot have had anything to do with the life and death of the historical Jesus. The spear of destiny is a spear blade of Germanic manufacture dating from the eighth to tenth centuries. In other words, it was forged some six hundred to eight hundred years after the death of the historical Jesus.

If the *sancta lancea* could not have belonged to a Roman soldier, what can we learn about its origins from its art-historical and other physical characteristics? It could have been forged among the Alamanni, Franks, or Langobards as early as the eighth century, but no later than the tenth century—most probably it comes from around 800 CE (Paulsen 1969, 301). As a symbol, the spear clearly has its origins in Germanic pre-Christian usage.*

The spear in question is most likely of Langobardic manufacture. The transference of a spear is known to have taken place as a part of the Langobardic coronation ceremony for kings. According to Howard Adelson's 1966 article "The Holy Lance and the Heredity of the German Monarchy," this transference was more important than the actual reception of the crown by Langobardic rulers.

---

*Brackmann (1943, 407–9) clearly outlines the development of the symbolism of the spear of Wodan into a spear of supposed Christian significance.

Over several centuries of the first millennium, the Langobards migrated from Scandinavia to the northern part of the Italian peninsula along the River Po around 558. The region of Lombardy still bears their name. They dominated northern Italy for two hundred years until they were defeated by the Franks of Karl the Great (Charlemagne) in 773–774. Perhaps Karl took a certain royal spearhead as a sign of his conquest of the Langobards and that it was this very spearhead that became the sancta lancea. It is recorded that Charlemagne carried a spear, or even simply a spearhead, with him everywhere. This functioned for him as a talisman of royal power. He never let it leave his possession, it is said that he slept with it, that it was the source of clairvoyant visions, and that when he fell from his horse one day shortly before his death the fact that the lance flew away from him some twenty feet was seen as an ill omen.

Another account of the sancta lancea says that a certain Langobardic Count Samson bequeathed such a symbolic spear to King Rudolf I of Burgundy (888–912), who subsequently lost it in battle to the German monarch Heinrich (Henry) I (the Fowler), whom we met in connection with the personal beliefs of Heinrich Himmler. It seems unlikely that the spear of Charlemagne and that of Heinrich I were one and the same object, due to their variant origins. However, it is possible that both have symbolic origins as Langobardic royal scepters, which had retained the Germanic significance of being signs of royal power derived from an ancestral bloodline. Over time, the original pagan rationale behind the symbol was forgotten. But for this pagan mythic basis to be lost entirely, it had to be replaced by a Christian one. This underlying necessity for ersatz myths for established practices and customs or symbolic objects, times, or places is the driving force behind the syncretizing of pagan and Christian traditions.

The deepest possible secret borne by the spear of destiny has nothing to do with the later superficial Christian overlay but rather with the essential original meaning of the spear as a sign of the direct bloodline relationship between the gods and the tribal aristocracy who bore such spears as signs of their nobility, leadership, and freedom. The mythology exploited in books such as *Holy Blood, Holy Grail* and

The Da Vinci Code—the notion that Jesus did not die on the cross but escaped to the south of France, where he sired a bloodline of secret kings—is itself actually a syncretic Christianization of Germanic tribal traditions about the gods' engendering of noble bloodlines. It is therefore most likely that if there is any validity to this tradition at all, it was originally a Germanic one that was progressively Christianized over the centuries as its original message and purpose became lost even to those who originally bore the tradition.

ESOTERIC NATIONAL SOCIALISM

As we have seen, most writers follow the approved metanarrative with regard to the immorality and cosmic evil represented by the Nazi regime. But as time wore on and the generations changed, Nazi myth and imagery began to take on new dimensions. On the one hand, the Nazis became even more cosmically evil than they had ever been before, while on the other hand, certain rebellious and antinomian types began to embrace Nazi imagery for their own sense of empowerment. In a sense, the extreme estimation of Nazi *evil* created a Frankenstein's monster in some people's minds. Even if we cannot call what has been produced recently *pro*-Nazi, it is something less absolute than the anti-Nazi propaganda of both wartime and postwar propaganda.

In this section, we are concerned with occult or esoteric groups or individuals producing works linked to Nazi mythology in ways that do not categorically condemn the Nazis as the paragons of evil. Purely political groups such as the American Nazi Party (later National Socialist White People's Party) founded by George Lincoln Rockwell (1918–1967) fall outside our scope. It must be said, however, that even such movements as the modern Ku Klux Klan or the American Nazis are touched by the aura of the occult, because they deal with utterly rejected symbols and attempt to conjure personal or collective power through the use and manipulation of such symbols. Not all of the individuals and groups discussed here actually espouse the core of National Socialist ideology. That is, they are not necessarily anti-Semitic or even nationalistic or racist in any way. Some simply make use of the imagery of Nazism to get attention, while others seek to study the supposed use of occult technologies by the Nazis in order to be able to use some of the techniques themselves on a smaller scale, or simply wish to understand such techniques.

HITLERIAN ESOTERICISM

The worship of Hitler as a demi-god in an esoteric and occult religious fashion by certain groups, but also by some isolated individuals, has been a continuing phenomenon since the end of WWII. The production of National Socialist propaganda images focused on Hitler were, after all, designed to encourage the development of such ideas in the German public during the time of the Third Reich itself. These images survived the war and were viewed by people in film, but more widely in television images, especially in the 1950s and continuing through the following decades. Such images could still exert powerful effects—so much so that a cult grew in the minds of some people who were ready to believe in the power of Hitler's image. This led to the growth of what is best described as Hitlerian Esotericism: the belief that Hitler was an individual of special power and nature who transcends the normal bounds of humanity.

To many, this formulation may sound insane—and it might well be—but it is not something that has to be characterized as all that unusual. Most founders of the world's major revealed religions belong to this category. If one happens to believe in a certain religion, then the investment of special qualities in the founder of that religion seems perfectly understandable, and entirely obvious. To those outside that religion, however, the special status of the founder's image may seem absurd.

In the twentieth century, we saw the development of the cult of personality in the political realm raised to a science by the Marxist-Leninist stream of thought: Marx, Lenin, Stalin, Mao. Folkloristic manifestations of ideas about popular figures from John F. Kennedy to Elvis Presley having survived their supposed deaths are a common feature of tabloid journalism. It is no wonder that a figure as iconic as Hitler would be the subject of similar mythologizing.

Esoteric Hitlerism can be divided into three major mythic schools:

1. The Avatar Myth
2. The Survival Myth
3. The Return Myth

These three mythologies are not mutually exclusive, as some people believe in one of these mythic possibilities, some in two, and others perhaps in all three. Like so much else that is strange and unusual about certain beliefs connected with Nazi Germany, these myths are rooted in Cold War propaganda. Myths of Hitler's survival, or of his assumption of a godlike or demonlike status post mortem, might have naturally been expected, given his godlike status among the Nazis and his complete demonization among the Allies. However, in this instance the first and strongest piece of lore was insinuated into the rumor mill by none other than Joseph Stalin, who used Marshal Georgy Zhukov as his instrument in a press conference on June 9, 1945, just a month after the end of the war. When asked about Hitler's death at the Potsdam Conference in July 1945, Stalin replied that Hitler was living in Spain or Argentina! This disinformation was part of a plan to disorient and confuse the Western Allies. Few realize today the extent to which Stalin himself was involved with what can be termed occult practices according to our definitions. Hard and detailed information about the discovery of Hitler's body and its disposal by the Soviets would not come to light for another twenty years after the war.

In the Avatar Myth, Hitler is seen as an incarnation of a divine being on the model of the Avatar in the Hindu religion. Avatars are seen as human or quasi-human incarnations of one of the Hindu gods. The main exponents of the Avatar Myth as it relates to Hitler are Savitri Devi (= Maximiani Julia Portas) and Miguel Serrano. The theory behind this is that Adolf Hitler was a divine being, an incarnation of a god, sent to issue a new message to the world. Another myth is that Hitler did not die in the Bunker at all, but was transported to a secret location (Antarctica, South America, or even a spacecraft orbiting the Earth, from which he is directing, or will direct, the development of the Fourth Reich). Finally, there is the Arthurian- or Barbarossa-type myth that Hitler did die as reported, but he awaits an hour of need and opportunity to return (in a new incarnation) as a Savior when the time is right.

Perhaps the best general introduction to this world of esoteric neo-Nazism is that contained in Nicholas Goodrick-Clarke's 2002 work titled *Black Sun: Aryan Cults, Esoteric Nazism and the Politics of Identity*. Here I will review a few of the groups and names attached to these movements.

SAVITRI DEVI—AND HITLER AS AVATAR

Maximiani Portas (1905–1982) was born in Lyon, France, to an English mother and a Greek father of French citizenship. Details of this woman's life and her involvement in the creation of a form of Hitler worship are outlined in Nicholas Goodrick-Clarke's book *Hitler's Priestess* (1998).

Despite her French citizenship, from an early age she identified as a Greek. She studied chemistry and philosophy at the University of Lyon, eventually earning a Ph.D. in 1935. Leading up to this she renounced her French citizenship in 1928 and in 1929 decided that she was a National Socialist. Instead of going to Germany, she went to India in 1932 in search of the continuing Aryan tradition. She became a Hindu, taking the name Savitri Devi ("Savitri" is the name of a female deity who is the daughter of the solar god Savitr, and *devī* is the old Sanskrit word for "goddess"). In India, she worked against the spread of both Christianity and Islam there. She also worked for the interests of Germany and Japan.

During WWII itself, Savitri Devi married a Bengali Brahmin named Asit Krishna Mukherji who also held National Socialist views and sympathies and edited a pro-German newspaper called *New Mercury*. The married couple entertained Allied military men and passed on what they learned to Axis intelligence.

Shortly after the end of the war, Savitri Devi traveled in Europe and attempted to bolster postwar German resistance to the Allied victors and was arrested, tried, and convicted in 1949 of distributing literature that promoted Nazism in the occupied zones. She was sentenced to

Fig. 13.1. Savitri Devi circa 1937

two years but served only eight months. During her time of incarceration, she was able to meet many fellow NS activists.

In 1953, Savitri Devi made what she referred to as a pilgrimage to the surviving monuments of Nazi Germany and the historically and mythically potent sites in the country. Her reflections on this journey were the substance of her 1958 book aptly titled *Pilgrimage*.

The 1950s would be her period of greatest writing activity in the field of the Hitler cult: *Defiance* (1950), *Gold in the Furnace* (1953), *Pilgrimage* (1958), and *The Lightning and the Sun* (1958). These were originally published in India to avoid censorship. She was aided and supported by a network of friends she made in the postwar NS resistance network. These included Hans-Ulrich Rudel, Johann von Leers, and Otto Skorzeny.*

---

*All of these men were important in one way or another to the Nazi regime and continued their activities in the wider world after the war. Hans-Ulrich Rudel (1916–1962) was a fighter pilot and the most decorated member of the Wehrmacht. He became active in right-wing politics in Germany after the war in connection with the Deutsche Rechtspartei. Johann von Leers (1902–1965) was a writer, professor, and follower of Ernst Bergmann and J. W. Hauer during the war. After the war he went to Egypt, converted to Islam (afterward known as Omar Amin von Leers), and helped organize Arab resistance to Israel. Otto Skorzeny (1908–1975) was the legendary SS-commando who escaped postwar justice and went underground until 1950, when he resurfaced under the protection of Franco in Spain and Perón in Argentina.

Savitri Devi was a radical animal-rights activist and philosopher. As early as 1959 she went on record with a major book titled *The Impeachment of Man*. This stance was fueled by her own animal-loving sentiments, the Hindu attitude toward animals, and even the great anti-vivisectionist and vegetarian dimension of the German Lebensreform movement, which had attracted so many that also became National Socialists. *The Impeachment of Man* recounts the history of man's cruelty to animals through the ages. This aspect of her life is culminated in her eccentric 1965 work titled *Long-Whiskers and the Two-Legged Goddess, or The True Story of a "Most Objectionable Nazi" and . . . Half-a-Dozen Cats*. In general, her philosophical stance is one of pantheistic monism, which accords man no special place or status in the cosmos.

In the 1960s Savitri Devi became more involved in the organizations of neo-Nazi groups throughout the world. She participated in the foundation of the World Union of National Socialists in 1962 and forged a relationship with the American Nazi leader George Lincoln Rockwell, whose organization heavily publicized her works and led to her increased prestige in Nazi circles. Subsequently, she became close to the notorious Holocaust denier and promoter of the idea of Nazi UFOs, Ernst Zündel. It is said that she was the first to suggest to Zündel that the Nazi genocide of the Jews was a hoax. With Zündel's help, her works were brought to an ever-wider readership from the 1970s forward. She retired to an apartment in New Delhi in 1971 and lived there with her cats and a cobra.

Savitri Devi died in 1982 of heart failure while traveling in England after years of deteriorating health. She remained active in NS causes to the very end, however. Her ashes are reportedly in a Nazi hall of honor beside those of George Lincoln Rockwell.

The Esoteric Hitlerism of Savitri Devi

Savitri Devi created a system of esoteric Hitlerism through a synthesis of Nazi ideology and Hindu cosmology, theology, and myth. Her creation was also full of her own imaginative elements. This ideology is most clearly laid out in the book *The Lightning and the Sun,* first published in 1958. She theorizes that there are different types of world-historical men, who are indeed avatars (incarnations) of divine principles as recognized in Hinduism. Some are "Men in Time," some are "Men above Time," while others are "Men against Time." Time itself is divided into great cycles, called *yugas* in Sanskrit. Avatars have it as their mission to bring such cycles to and end and fulfill their development. Some such men exemplify lightning and are violent and forceful, such as Genghis Khan, while others who exemplify the sun are full of light and truth, which she sees first exemplified in the Egyptian king Akhenaton. The awaited avatar of the future will be one who combines both the lightning and the sun.

Savitri Devi's assessment of the esoteric role of Hitler is summarized:

Adolf Hitler: the One-before-the-last and most tragic of all that series of men "against Time" that stretches from the beginning of the far-gone legendary "Silver Age" [*Treta Yuga*] to the end of the one in which we are living. He would have been, in our Time-cycle, *the last* Embodiment of Him Who comes back, age after age "to establish on earth the reign of righteousness"; the last, and fully successful One, Whom Sanskrit Tradition names *Kalki*. For He alone will possess, mathematically balanced, and all to the supreme degree, the virtues which seem incompatible. He alone will be not merely "both 'Sun' and 'Lightning,'" but equally "Sun" and "Lightning."

Considered in the light of cosmic truth, the hatred of the advanced Dark Age world for Heinrich Himmler is but an unconscious expression of its fear of the invincible divine Destroyer,—Kalki—Who is to come. The East and West—Marxists and Anti-Marxists or so-called such—vaguely felt (and feel) that, had it been but for a little more "Lightning" power—a little more "cold-blooded inhumanity" such as Himmler possessed—Adolf Hitler *would have been He, ... and have put an end to this Time-cycle.* (Devi 1958, 396)

In the end, she sees Hitler as a sacrifice for the future of humanity, a sacrifice that would soon lead to the end of the Kali Yuga. Savitri Devi laments the defeat of Nazi Germany as a thwarting of cosmic evolution and at the same time holds out the hope of—and faith in—a future return of the avenger, Kalki, who will lead the Aryan world to a final victory. This view partakes of enough of a mythology with which the average Western reader could have been expected to be familiar (a Christian ideology of a coming savior), which it then links to the history of Nazi Germany, that it became a powerful new mythology to inspire a new wave of National Socialist esotericism.

MIGUEL SERRANO

Another chief proponent of what can be called Hitlerian Esotericism is Miguel Joaquín Diego del Carmen Serrano Fernández (1917–2009). In his later extremely esoteric ideology he was obviously greatly influenced by the ideas of Savitri Devi. Before that, however, he was actually already a political proponent of National Socialism in his native Chile as a young man during the Second World War. Chile remained neutral during the war, which made his stance possible. According to Serrano, he was initiated into a völkisch esoteric current by a "mysterious" German immigrant to Chile during these years. Later in life he entered the diplomatic service of his country. This career would last from 1953 to 1970 and was brought to an end when the Marxist regime of Salvador Allende took power in Chile. With the overthrow of Allende, Serrano returned to Chile and seriously began to articulate the idea of Esoteric Hitlerism. It is clear that he had been interested in esoteric matters his whole life, he was versed in German culture, and he had been an adherent of National Socialist ideology since the 1930s. Clearly, the published work of Savitri Devi was formative on Serrano's ideas about Hitler being an "avatar." However, it is also quite apparent that his esoteric Nazism stemmed from his own subjective universe and creative imagination, and was, moreover, to a great extent a product of the times in which he began to write the works that supported these ideas—that is, from the late 1970s onward. He was an energetic synthesizer of ideas from various sources, all refocused on the role of Adolf Hitler in world history and the place of the symbols of National Socialism in the future of the world. Over time his works gained great influence and prestige (at least by reputation) in the circles of current Esoteric Hitlerism. It seems that Serrano made use of the wave of esoteric enthusiasm that was in Western culture in the late 1960s and early 1970s. With his unusual links to establishment figures, such as Carl Jung and Hermann Hesse, his writings have gained a certain prestige, but they failed to be very widely disseminated beyond the Spanish-speaking world due to some shady dealings regarding translation rights to his later books, which greatly delayed their appearance in English.

Serrano published the best-known work in his series of works on Esoteric Hitlerism, *Adolf Hitler, el Último Avatāra* (Adolf Hitler: The Last Avatar) in 1984. In the final analysis, Serrano's writings can be seen as poetic, mystical, inspired perhaps, but ultimately a tour de force synthesis of various pieces of the features of Hitlerian Esotericism that had come before him.

The back-cover material for the translation of *Adolf Hitler, el Último Avatāra* reads as a summary of Serrano's ideology concerning the personage of Adolf Hitler.

The title of this book has its origins in the Hindu conception of a god or deity, especially Vishnu, the Preserver in the Trilogy of Hinduism: Brahma being the Creator and Shiva the Destroyer. Vishnu is an ancient Vedic God, Aryan, white and blond whose residence is in the North Pole. Avatar is a Sanskrit word. So far there have been nine incarnations within the three great divisions of time made by Hinduism. The last three known incarnations are heroic-religious, corresponding to Rama, Krishna and Buddha. The tenth, that of Kalki, riding a white horse, will close the Kali-Yuga, the Iron Age of the Greeks, the Darkest Age, which is to say, the present time. He will appear within the vortex of the final catastrophe and will come to judge. The author of this book argues this incarnation of the divinity Vishnu-Wotan is announced by Adolf Hitler ("The Man to Come") who has already made his glowing appearance and must return with his Ultimate Battalion (the *Wildes Heer*, Furious Order of Wotan-Odin) on the edge of catastrophe, to save his Folk and judge their enemies.

So, clearly, Serrano was greatly influenced by the philosophy of Savitri Devi, which had preceded his writings on the subject by several decades. Serrano's Hitlerian ideology lies in conceptions embedded in Hinduism, welded together with messianic concepts, which had also been at the root of the system laid out by Savitri Devi. Serrano brought more of the ideas of the messianic myth that were at home in Germany well before the advent of the National Socialists (e.g., the Kyffhäuser movement).

Serrano fully indulged in the speculations about Hitler's survival of the war and had him living in a secret UFO base at the South Pole under the ice of Antarctica—planning and awaiting his triumphant return as the avenging Kalki. In the musings of Serrano, we see all of the myths of esoteric Hitlerianism—the avatar, the survivor, and the returning avenger—synthesized and expressed in one ideology.

THE LANDIG CIRCLE

Wilhelm Landig (1909–1997) was a former SS-man from Vienna who began to organize a sort of neo-Nazi esoteric circle in his home city in 1950. Important members of his circle were Erich Halik (Claude Schweighardt) and Rudolf J. Mund (1920–1985). This Landig Circle appears to have revived a number of aspects of National Socialist esoterica, invented a few more, and assimilated whatever came along during the era when NS-esoterica was being generated at a rapid pace after the original appearance of *The Morning of the Magicians*. Prominent themes in the literature of the Landig Circle included Polar mythology (Thule, Hyperborea), Atlantis, the Black Sun, Vril, the World Ice Theory, connections with Tibet (Agartha), and Nazi UFOs. This group embraced elements of the philosophies of Julius Evola and Herman Wirth.

The Landig Circle, often through works published by the Volkstum Verlag, popularized these ideas in neo-Nazi subcultures and helped to create a new mythology. Key to this program was Landig's own Thule Trilogy of fiction works: *Götzen gegen Thule* (Idols against Thule; 1971), *Wolfszeit um Thule* (Wolf-Age around Thule; 1980), and *Rebellen für Thule – Das Erbe von Atlantis* (Rebels for Thule—The Legacy of

Atlantis; 1991). To this body of fictional works can be added the 1991 thriller titled *Die Schwarze Sonne von Tashi Lhunpo* (The Black Sun of Tashi Lhunpo) by Russell McCloud, which was probably the pen name for a team of ghostwriters including Stephan Mögle-Stadel. It was in this last book that the emblem of the solar wheel from the Wewelsburg north tower floor was first attached to the name "Black Sun," and it became a sort of ersatz swastika in the neo-Nazi scene.

The Landig Circle in Vienna became a place where the older and younger generations were able to exchange ideas and feed off of one another for a period. From the early 1980s within the Landig Circle there had been an active belief in the existence of surviving Nazi flying saucers. These are thought to have secret bases beneath the polar ice caps, especially in Antarctica. By the early 1990s this all became welded together with a neo-Templar ideology organized in the Tempelhofgesellschaft (Templar Court Society) formed by Ralf Ettl. This was envisioned as a renewal of the Templar organization as a dualistic Marcionite sect.* The Tempelhofgesellschaft propagated the belief that the National Socialists were in league with a group of extraterrestrials based in the planetary system around Aldebaran, who were locked in a cosmic battle against the forces and people of El Shaddai (Jahweh)—the Jews. The innovated mythology of Ettl and Jürgen-Ratthofer, well documented by Goodrick-Clarke (2002, 157–72) and Strube (2012, 223–68), mixes Gnosticism, Nazism, flying saucers, the Vril force or free energy, and fictionalized connections with leading personalities in the pantheon of Nazi occult figures, such as Rudolf von Sebottendorf and Karl Haushofer. New and spectacular figures were also introduced to the mythology. Chief among these is the beautiful and mysterious Maria Orsic. She was supposedly a Croatian-born medium who deciphered medieval Templar texts pur-

---

*Marcion was a Christian heretic who flourished around 144 CE and taught that Jesus was not a man and Jewish Messiah at all but rather a spiritual entity sent by the Monad to reveal the truth about the God of Righteousness, as opposed to the God of Wrathfulness, also called the Alien God. This Alien God is the Demiurge who created the world and is told about in the Old Testament. The Marcionite sect was similar to Gnosticism but not entirely a part of that movement.

ported to relate to an Aryan-Sumerian tradition (!) of a connection between the Aldebaran system and the Earth, and the efforts of the Aldebaranian race to aid the National Socialists. It is thought that some Nazis escaped to Aldebaran in the interdimensional technology represented by the vehicle known as Die Glocke (the Bell). Clearly, such contemporary mythologizing and Internet-based folklore belongs to a realm caught somewhere between the worlds of private religion-building, science fiction, and psychological desperation: it is a middle ground between light and shadow, between fact and fiction, and exists between the pit of man's hate and the summit of his insight. We have fully entered the dimension of imagination.

In the context of the history of religions or the study of so-called New Religious movements, the Landig Circle and Tempelhofgesellschaft constitute the sort of cult that awaits an external savior or messiah from beyond this Earth to come save or empower a group that perceives itself to be weak or oppressed. This is also the essence of the Judeo-Christian cult. The subjective power derived from holding such irrational beliefs, however, has its own reward in psychologically bolstering its adherents. These imaginative constructs are not only popular in neo-Nazi circles but have also descended into popular culture and entertainment via films and even computer games.

CHRISTIAN IDENTITY

The Christian Identity movement harbors some old ideas in new packages. It is mainly an Anglo-American phenomenon with respect to the obsession with identifying Caucasian Europeans with the Jews of the Old Testament. In the latter half of the twentieth century Christian Identity has become a significant part of what Matthias Gardell identified as a "smorgasbord" of eleven components that float around in the minds of members of a certain subcultural group, which most would call right wing or alt right today. These components are:

1. Klandom
2. National Socialism

3. White-Power music and skinhead culture
4. Warrior ideals
5. Conspiracy theories
6. Anti-Semitism
7. Populism
8. Separatism
9. Christian Identity
10. Race as religion
11. Ásatrú/Odinism

Gardell (2003, 67–136) aptly points out that not all of these elements may find a home in the minds of all adherents to this often-amorphous ideology, but some go together very seamlessly, while others are virtually incompatible (e.g., Ásatrú and Christian Identity). For our purposes, it should be noted that National Socialism is just one part of this mixture. The place of NS in this constellation is usually one of image and style, rather than real philosophy or substance.

Perhaps in part because the anti-Nazi propagandists of various kinds tend to focus their mythologizing on a connection between National Socialism and paganism or even Satanism, the connection between Hitlerian Esotericism and Christian mythology and sentiment is usually virtually ignored. This does not mean that such a connection is not vital to the ideology. It was an element present in the Third Reich itself, and such a link has also reared its head in the current scene as well. It must be recognized, however, that because labels like "pagan" and "heathen," as well as even "Satanism," no longer carry the same stigma they did fifty years ago, contemporary Hitlerists have become much more open to embracing these ideas than they ever were in the past. Individuals who deviate from the standard, consensus values, morality, and norms of their culture in one area of life (e.g., religion, politics, sexual orientation) will be more likely to deviate from those patterns in other areas of life as well. For them, the spell of consensus reality has been broken and the Hounds of Tindalos have broken the Barrier.

The two basic ideas that might be seen as being fundamental to what is called Christian Identity are:

1. The Jews of the Old Testament are not the same as those who call themselves Jews today and that the true identity of the Old Testament Jews is to be found among an Aryan elite in Europe. In other words, the Old Testament Hebrews are Aryans, not Semites.

2. The personage of Jesus Christ is not to be identified as a Jew but rather that he was himself an Aryan (perhaps even part German), which then allows the modern Aryan to identify with Jesus on a bloodline basis.

Such beliefs may appear much more radical to a modern mind, schooled in matters of history, than they would have to the medieval mind-set, for which such concepts came far more naturally. It seems that when an alien, "revealed" religion is imposed upon a people (as Christianity often was in early medieval northern Europe) many elements of the population will be reluctant to give up certain feelings of identity between themselves and their gods and goddesses. The acceptance of a foreign history (i.e., that of the Hebrews of the Old Testament) as their own, or the acknowledgment of an exotic individual (Jesus) as their Savior and hero, comes only with difficulty to a traditional people. For this reason, we have examples such as the ninth-century *Hêliand* in Old Saxon literature, which depicts Jesus as a Germanic warrior-chieftain with his retinue of bodyguards (disciples), and the whole story is even re-situated in familiar German landscapes. Such sentiments are actually only natural and expected with the forceful introduction of ideas from the outside. It should be noted how the image of Jesus was modified in northern Europe until he came to look like the ideal of a Germanic (Frankish) king with long blond hair and a beard—the sort of standard folk image that persists to this day. (The earliest known images of Jesus depicted him as a beardless youth.) Such an enculturation process should not be seen as anything unusual when it comes to the Germanic peoples. Today we see that certain Black Nationalists have their "Black Jesus" theories, which find some acceptance among African Americans. There is simply a natural yearning to envision the appearance of God as a reflection of one's own self.

The idea that Nordic (Anglo-Saxon and Norse) people represent the lost tribes of Israel and are the actual heroes of the Old Testament begins as early as the sixteenth century but became more systematic with the British Israelite theories of John Wilson (1799–1870) and Edward Hine (1825–1891). This was imported into North America at the end of the nineteenth century and became a more fixed, racial, and anti-Semitic school of thought by the 1930s. Of course, the idea that Jesus was an Aryan goes back to German and French biblical critics of the nineteenth century, whom we met in chapter 2.

The origins of the American brand of Christian Identity, which is closely connected to the symbols and ideology of National Socialism, can be traced to the organization of Howard B. Rand (1889–1991) called the Anglo-Saxon Federation of America. William J. Cameron, Henry Ford's press secretary and a writer for Ford's newspaper, the *Dearborn Independent,* became involved with Rand in 1930. Cameron had been the editor of the newspaper since 1921. He wrote and published articles on *The Protocols of the Elders of Zion* and ran Ford's essays, which were later published as *The International Jew.*

In the middle of the twentieth century, Christian Identity took a hard turn into ever deeper forms of occult history through sectarian interpretations of biblical texts in the Old Testament. This is one more example, of which there have been many in this book, where alternative interpretations of myths and histories have been used to create a new metanarrative through which individuals might reorient their viewpoints on life. In this technique there is a powerful form of sorcery, which remains a part of our lives today. Understanding how it works and viewing examples of it in history may lead to a more rational future. This often amorphous ideology developed an elaborate racial myth that almost rivals that of Lanz von Liebenfels. The agenda of the Identity mythology was to demonize the Jews. It did this by concocting a new mythology in which the present-day Jews are identified as the spawn of the Serpent (Satan) and Eve through their son Cain. This engendered a race of subhuman creatures that oppose the good race of Aryans descended from the legitimate offspring of Abel. Wesley Swift became the most active synthesizer and organizer of Christian Identity ideology in the US. Based in southern California, Swift organized for the KKK and established his own congregation of Identity Christians.

This is the kind of ideology to which Richard Butler (1918–2004) found himself attracted in the years after the end of WWII. Butler was a dedicated anti-communist and racialist. In the 1950s he became involved in anti-communist causes and in 1961 he was formally introduced to Christian Identity at the Anglo-Saxon Christian Congregation in Lancaster, California, which was led by Wesley Swift. Swift and Butler tried to forge a relationship with George Lincoln Rockwell's American Nazi Party, and Rockwell felt that such a move might help him recruit more members.

Butler inherited the congregation at the Lancaster church, but moved his base of operations to a compound near Coeur d'Alene, Idaho, in the 1970s. What was now also known as Aryan Nations continued to embrace the imagery of National Socialism more and more, and in the 1980s the organization began to garner increased media attention. In the end, Aryan Nations succumbed to its own irrationalism. It was infiltrated by law enforcement and subjected to lawsuits, which virtually destroyed the organization. Similar associations met comparable fates in the 1980s and 1990s in the US.

Although such groups are often heavily publicized and pursued by the media, perhaps because they offer the raw material for narratives the media love to pursue, such organizations generally are abysmal failures in the US. For the most part they ignore the negative historical lessons of German National Socialism by ignoring the actual zeitgeist in which they live, chasing instead a romantic and unrealistic vision of the past. Masses of Americans are simply not going to be motivated by images of swastikas and theories about the Jews being the Satanic spawn of the Serpent and Eve.

IN THE SIGN OF THE BLACK SUN

The symbol and concept of the Black Sun has taken on ever greater importance in the history of postwar Esoteric Nazism. The term had virtually no place in pre-1945 National Socialist myth and ideology. It is

Fig. 13.2. Black Sun

likely to have later been associated with the SS due to its being called the Black Order in some circles.* Blackness itself was a conventional sign of the sinister and evil, and the self-contradictory poetry of the term *black sun* was certainly seen to be pregnant with mystery and power.

A very comprehensive presentation of data on this topic and its history has been collected and published by James Pontolillo in his almost 800-page study: *The Black Sun Unveiled* (2013). The symbol and phrase "black sun" is known to us from alchemy (*sol niger*) and is also identified with the concept of a Central Sun, the center of the galaxy, hidden and invisible to us.

Pontolillo traces the development of the concept of the Black or Central Sun through time and notes how it was first attached in a general way to the location of the SS-castle Wewelsburg, first through the attention drawn to this location by the "Wewelsburg Working" of Michael A. Aquino (October 19, 1982), then through other writers picking up on this and embellishing it for their own purposes (e.g., Serrano). Finally, the direct association was made between the concept of the Black Sun and the twelve-spoked solar disk from the north tower of the Wewelsburg castle in the 1991 book *Die Schwarze Sonne von Tashi Lhunpo,* written under the corporate author name Russell McCloud.

---

*As we noted in chapter 7, the original use of black for the SS uniforms was based on a traditional association of that color with the peasantry or farmers. Once the symbolism was cut loose from any traditional associations and allowed to play on the imaginations of late twentieth-century New Agers, however, the color associations went in a more sinister direction.

The concept of the Black Sun has been signified by a variety of symbols or graphic signs over the years: a black disk, a disk with a black point in the center, and more recently (post-1991) it has been firmly attached to that solar symbol motif from the floor design of the north tower in Himmler's Wewelsburg castle shown at the head of this section. That symbol was, as we have seen, based on a solar-wheel motif used by Alemannic jewelers from the Migration Age. Hundreds of blanks for the construction of brooches have been found with designs very similar to this one.

Pontolillo's survey of data related to the concept and symbol of the Black Sun reveals its ambiguity and flexibility as far as meaning is concerned. In the final analysis, as a symbol, it has become a new form of the old NS-swastika and has taken on the unambiguously *religious* qualities of what present-day believers think is an essential part of the National Socialist message. That message has been transformed from the one that Hitler insisted upon in *Mein Kampf*—that results must be obtained quickly and completely—to one that is decidedly millenarian in character. The Black Sun is a sign for those who have retreated to solitude to await the coming of the once and future Führer to emerge one way or another when the time is right to establish a New Reich. In this way, the adherents of the Black Sun find familiar company in the West: as the Christians and Jews await their Messiah, the religious National Socialists of today wait under the sign of the Black Sun for the return of the Wolf.* What the swastika was to the old Nazis, the Black Sun symbol is to the religious millenarian believers of the present and future.

The personality of Otto Rahn, whom we met in chapter 7, became greatly enhanced in importance in the postwar mythologizing of Nazi

---

*As the original National Socialists actually felt themselves to be a dispossessed, defeated, and misunderstood people, both as Germans and as adherents to their philosophy, current folk in Europe, America, and elsewhere who identify with the symbols of the Nazis and their philosophy have much more reason to have these thoughts and feelings—which only intensifies the mystical and quasi-religious fervor concerning the return of the once and future Führer. "Wolf" was Hitler's code name and nickname, as we know.

esoterica. Rahn was one of Himmler's pet projects, who, like several others, ran afoul of the National Socialist apparatus. His main contributions were the two books he wrote, *Kreuzzug gegen den Gral* (Crusade Against the Grail; 1933) and *Luzifers Hofgesind* (Lucifer's Court; 1937). But in the mill of Nazi occult literature that sprang up in the wake of *Morning of the Magicians,* Rahn took on greater importance. Because of the often open-ended nature of Rahn's works, his words were susceptible to interpretation and reinterpretation by later mystics and speculative writers. One of the main writers who used Rahn's work toward explaining his own mythology was the Chilean mystic Miguel Serrano. In his book *Adolf Hitler, el Último Avatāra* he discusses the "Castle of the Order" (487–503) and the "Mystery of the *Gral*" (504–516), where the ideas first put forward by Otto Rahn are brought to bear in a new interpretation of Esoteric Hitlerism.

POSTWAR RENEWAL OF THE LEAGUE FOR KNOWLEDGE OF GOD: MATHILDE LUDENDORFF

The organization of the Bund für Gotterkenntnis (League for Knowledge of God) was, of course, shattered by the events of WWII. But shortly after the end of the war, in 1947, Mathilde Ludendorff received permission from Allied authorities to renew the religious organization she had headed earlier. However, in 1950 a tribunal named her as a principal offender in conjunction with the denazification program. Nevertheless, the next year she succeeded in registering the group. By 1963 it was determined by federal German authorities that the organization was hostile to the constitution and it was banned. Ludendorff herself died in 1966. The ban on the BfG was lifted in 1973 on a technicality, but the group remains on a watch list.

The ideology of the present-day BfG remains the same as it was originally. To join the BfG, prospective members as of 1951 had to show formal proof that they had resigned from any and all Christian churches to which they might have belonged. The group promotes ideas of racial purity and consciousness on a family level and hold fast to the idea that only if a people remains racially aware can it survive as a nation or folk group.

In a Ludendorff pamphlet that was republished by the BfG in 1975, she writes:

> Among the deadly dangers to which peoples are subject, I have identified miscegenation as the greatest one and have proven in detail how much the individual human is robbed by this of the true guidance of all of his abilities of consciousness provided by racial inheritance housed in the unconscious. The mongrel [*Rassenmischling*] is not as instinctually secure as is the person of pure race, who is quite often the beneficiary of the assistance of the folk-soul. (Ludendorff 1975, 16)

Current literature of the BfG tries to portray the organization as one that was actually persecuted by the Nazis and counts itself as a force of resistance against National Socialism historically.

SATANIC NAZI ESOTERICISM

For many in both the anti-Nazi and pro-Nazi camps of the Satanic sphere of esotericism, the same general fallacy of thought rules: Nazis = Evil, Satanists = Evil, therefore Nazis = Satanists! There was, of course, no sympathy for the devil among actual National Socialists. The closest thing one can find in this regard is expressed by the followers of Otto Rahn who expressed their compassion for the fallen angel "Lucifer, who suffered injustice!" This was a reference to the gnostic interpretation of the myth of the Garden of Eden (reflected in the Hebrew Bible), in which the Serpent is seen as Lucifer, the God of Light who was unjustly punished by the Demiurge (Jehovah) for facilitating the initiation of Adam and Eve into the Light of Consciousness. In this Cathar interpretation, however, Lucifer is seen as categorically the Good God, whereas Jehovah is cast as the Dark Demiurge. In general, any use by the paleo-Nazis of demonic or vampiric imagery was employed in an entirely negative way and directed toward the Jews or other "parasitic" populations.

Anton LaVey

There is no more unusual exponent of pro-Nazi occult mythologizing than the infamous Black Pope and founder of the Church of Satan (1966), Anton Szandor LaVey (1930–1997).* This involvement is a bundle of contradictions. LaVey was himself apparently at least part Jewish. His original name was Howard Stanton Levey. In no way was he ever a proponent of actual National Socialist ideology; his libertarian philosophy is more rooted in the thoughts of Ayn Rand and Ragnar Redbeard.† LaVey was an ingenious and creative artist who cast a spell of fascination over a whole generation. Many of the sources for the shape of his interest in Nazi occultism most likely stem from *The Morning of the Magicians,* like so many others. But LaVey put his own spin on things and forged a specific brand of Nazi mythology in just a few words. He also creatively linked the artificial mythos surrounding the works of the American writer of weird tales, Howard Phillips Lovecraft (1890–1937), to that of the Nazis. The result is his intriguing ritual text called *Die elektrischen Vorspiele* (The Electrical Prelude[s]). This was first published in his book titled

---

*No objective, comprehensive, well-researched biography exists for this figure of modern American folklore. Legendary biographies include Burton Wolfe, *The Devil's Avenger* (1973) and Blanche Barton, *The Secret Life of a Satanist* (1990). Michael Aquino (1989) provides an inside look at life in his *Church of Satan* between 1968 and 1975. The respected writer Lawrence Wright wrote an exposé-type article, "Anton LaVey: Sympathy for the Devil," which appears in his book *Saints and Sinners* (1993), 121–56.

†In fact, LaVey's philosophy is more than just rooted in the works of these authors. It has been shown that the bedrock of LaVey's principles were first founded on the works of Ayn Rand, which was demonstrated in the article "The Hidden Source of the Satanic Philosophy" by George C. Smith, which first appeared in *The Scroll of Set* XIII:3 (June 1987): 4–6. This is reprinted by Aquino (1989, A-45–47). Whole sections of LaVey's *Satanic Bible* were lifted directly from Ragnar Redbeard's book *Might is Right* (1896). This is something that LaVey later freely acknowledged, and he even wrote an introduction to an edition of this now virtually banned book.

The Satanic Rituals (1972, 106–130). It is also not unlikely that LaVey was familiar with Lewis Spence's *The Occult Causes of the Present War,* which, as we have seen, attempts to link Nazism directly to every sort of imaginable Satanic influence.

LaVey came of age during the Second World War. He was an imaginative young man who read voraciously (especially in the areas of horror, science fiction, and the occult) and was musically very talented. For the most part, he supported himself as a live keyboard musician at nightclubs in the San Francisco Bay area. His interest in the occult led him to begin giving lectures and demonstrations around 1961 in his home at 6114 California Street in San Francisco, California.* These gatherings, dubbed "The Magic Circle," were frequented by many interesting and often influential people. The 1960s were in full swing and people were ready to explore the weird and way-out. LaVey provided them with these experiences. At one point a publicist suggested that LaVey expand his operation and make a business entity out of what he was doing—thus was born the Church of Satan in 1966. LaVey received a good deal of media attention and became a minor celebrity. His 1969 book titled *The Satanic Bible* was a big hit. This was followed by *The Satanic Rituals* (1972), wherein LaVey makes his greatest contribution to the mythology of Nazi occultism. In 1975 one of LaVey's chief officers in the church, Michael A. Aquino, split with the organization over certain doctrinal matters and a portion of the church membership followed him. This led to a somewhat inactive phase for LaVey, who reemerged from relative obscurity in the mid-1980s and enjoyed a renaissance of notoriety until his death in 1997.

There are frequent references to Germanic or Norse symbolism in LaVey's work. Some of this stems from Wagnerian sources. A book that he used as a source for some of the content in *The Satanic Bible* was

---

*This house became a landmark in San Francisco folklore for at least three decades. LaVey spun many a myth around the structure. Shortly after the Black Pope's death, the structure was condemned by the city and it was demolished in 2001 and a condo built on the site. Here is another example of a unique cultural element being homogenized. Such is the fate of much that is unique and mythic in our world today.

Might is Right by Ragnar Redbeard (Arthur Desmond),* written in 1896, which expressed a Nietzschean philosophy in Viking imagery. On a more political note, LaVey also flirted with the National Renaissance Party, as outlined in some detail in chapter 31 of Michael Aquino's *The Church of Satan* titled "Satan and Swastika." LaVey rejected the racialist component and was only interested in such things with regard to their history as techniques for the control of others or of the masses. He referred to *Mein Kampf* as a "political Satanic Bible," a phrase that appears in Konrad Heiden's introduction to the Manheim translation of Hitler's *Mein Kampf* (p. xix).

LaVey toyed with the symbolism of Nazism and probably had a fascination with this imagery like all boys of his generation and the next. But in his imagination, the swastika was entwined with the decadent world of Weimar Germany. In fact, this imagination has a stroke of genius, because just such an unlikely synthesis did occur in the real lives of many Germans between the two World Wars. LaVey conjured the following story about traveling to Berlin in 1945 immediately after the Second World War with his "uncle Bill."

One day at the command post in Berlin where his uncle was stationed, Tony attended the showing of some German films confiscated from the Nazis' motion picture production office. The movies that interested Tony most were the *schauerfilme* (horror films) such as *The Testament of Dr. Mabuse,* about a mad hypnotist and depravity in high and low places in pre-Hitler Germany; and *Metropolis,* about a wizard-scientist named Rotwang who confounds a revolt of slave like workers by sending a humanoid to double for the Joan of Arc type of woman serving as the workers' leader. One of the *schauerfilme* told the story of an effete young man, the scion of a

---

*The identity of Redbeard has been convincingly demonstrated through recent research by Trevor Blake and Kevin Slaughter, who have also produced a definitive edition of *Might is Right* (2019). However, the contents of Desmond's Victorian-era book have apparently been deemed so dangerous for the human mind that it was necessary to ban (i.e., erase) all editions of this particular work from mainstream bookselling platforms (Amazon, etc.) in 2020.

multi-millionaire family of munitions-makers, who entertained his friends with Black Masses. The particular Black Mass favored by this wealthy young German made use of a trapezoid suspended from the ceiling, a revolving pentagon of mirrors, creepy electronic organ music, and electric lights buzzing through his black chapel. A German interpreting the films for the viewing Army brass explained that what they were seeing was not merely fiction, but an authentic representation of a ceremony preferred by the Black Order, a secret society of Satan worshipers. Did such people really exist? (Wolfe 1974, 28)

It is unlikely that "uncle Bill" existed, and it is just as improbable that fifteen-year-old Anton traveled to barely pacified Berlin and watched movies. The film with the trapezoidal Black Mass has not been identified. But it was this line of imagination through which he evoked the ritual he called "Die elektrischen Vorspiele."

The published text of this ritual is retrofitted with a parallel German-language text. The effect of this is supposed to be that LaVey had an original German liturgy from which to work. In fact, as any speaker of German can immediately see, the German is a (bad) translation of the English original. The "author" of the German version is likely to have been a member of LaVey's early Magic Circle with some ability in German.

The introductory remarks about the ritual feed the reader with more fascinating imagery derived from the wartime imaginations of the Allies, who often seemed to hold the belief that Hitler and the Nazis must have somehow been in league with the devil. Only for LaVey, this diabolical connection was a positive thing. He maintains the following in the historical preface to the text of the ritual:

The principle of utilizing electrical and magnetic energy to effect magical ends is sorely neglected by most occult scholars, yet it employed with almost maniacal gusto by the contemporary German school of Satanic magic. . . .

The German societies *Vril, Thule, Freunden von Lucifer,*

Germania, and *Ahnenerbe,* while maintaining the basic magic repertoire of the earlier Illuminati, became what has been loosely defined as the *Schwartze Orden* [*sic*]—the *Black Order*—which flourished between the two World Wars. . . .

When *Die elektrischen Vorspiele* was performed in Nazi Germany (circa 1932–35) by the intellectual element of the budding *Sicherheitsdienst RFSS,* the banners and symbols of the time were used as an integral part of the decor. Participants were garbed in full dress, whether uniformed or not. Topical music was added—usually *Morgenrot* at the beginning and *Unsere Fahne Flattert uns Voran* as a closing anthem. (LaVey 1972, 106–110)

When it comes to the text of the ritual itself, the general theme is hammered home.

PROCLAMATION

CELEBRANT:

See the red sunrise in the East!
We desire Power!

ALL:

We shall have Power!

CELEBRANT:

We desire Wealth!

ALL:

We shall have Wealth!

CELEBRANT:

We desire Wisdom!

ALL:

We shall have Wisdom!

CELEBRANT:

We desire Recognition!

ALL:

We shall have Recognition!

CELEBRANT:

We desire Followers!

ALL:

We shall have Followers!

CELEBRANT:

Was wir wollen, werden wir haben!
*Wir werden haben, was wir wollen!**
The Twilight is come—
The Twilight of the Gods—
The dawn breaks in the east!
It is the morning of magic!†
The world is afire!
Loki lives upon the earth!

Clearly, LaVey wishes to imply that it was through these type of Satanic ceremonies that the Nazis seized and held power in Germany. This was the occult answer to the question that seemed to plague and torment the twentieth century: How did the Nazis come to power? The question is answered in just the sort of way the imaginations of men like Lewis Spence had envisioned it, and as boys like LaVey had wished it was.

As a side note, it must be mentioned that the body of LaVey's Nazi ritual was directly based on a section of the text known as *The Emerald Tablets of Thoth the Atlantean* by an eccentric American writer named Maurice Doreal (= Claude D. Dodgin [1898–1963]). LaVey mentions that the text is supposedly based on the Emerald Tablet, and most assumed that by this he meant the late antique text known as the "Emerald Tablet of Hermes." However, he was actually

---

*These two lines translate to "That which we desire, we shall have! We shall have, that which we desire!" This is the operative crux of the working.

†This line is undoubtedly a not-so-subtle nod to the work of Pauwels and Bergier.

referring to the section of Doreal's text called "Emerald Tablet VIII: Key of Mysteries." This is a rare bit of source indication in the works of the Black Pope.

The gist of the meaning and context of LaVey's ritual clearly falls within the well-known early twentieth-century German obsession with the idea of the will of some sort of Svengali-type figure manipulating events, or more usually human beings (either individually or in some sort of mass hypnosis), to carry out the orders of the manipulator. As we have noted, this theme was well developed in early German cinema with films like *The Cabinet of Dr. Caligari, The Golem, Dr. Mabuse, der Spieler,* and *Metropolis.* LaVey was influenced by the imagery of these and similar films, and was persuaded to believe that the theme was somehow linked to the much-vaunted ability of the National Socialists in general, and Hitler in particular, to control the masses. In this general conclusion, we can see that he was not far off.

LaVey's work of imaginative liturgy and mythology, coupled with all of the Nazi mythologizing that had appeared by 1972, acted as a match applied to the kindling of everything that had gone before it. This work inspired a new generation and began to give rise to a wide range of splinter groups and ideas much more obsessively and totally dedicated to Nazi imagery than LaVey ever would have been.

The Order of the Black Ram

One such group was the Order of the Black Ram (OBR), which was established by members of the Babylon Grotto of the Church of Satan who were also involved with the National Renaissance Party. It existed from 1973 to about 1976. During much of that time it published a newsletter called *Liber Venificia,* later combined with the *Grimorium Verum* of the Ordo Templi Satanas, both of which provide obvious insight into the ideologies of these groups.

Chief philosophical or ideological influences on the founders of the OBR are Anton LaVey and Robert Heinlein—with important crosscurrents provided by Friedrich Nietzsche and Adolf Hitler. Jane Roberts and the "Seth material" find a happy home among the members of the OBR, as do the writings of Carlos Castaneda*—things for which LaVey would probably have had little tolerance.

The OBR took the natural and organic component of LaVey's philosophy very much to heart. They wanted to create a neo-tribal form of Aryan Satanism. In this regard members of the group made, or continued to maintain, close ties with racialist and National Socialist groups in the United States as well as with certain branches of the then fledgling Odinist movement.

In the pages of *Liber Venificia* there occasionally appeared articles of a truly taboo nature: ones that promoted the idea of the Aryans as the Satanic Race—a race with its roots in the stars, that created Atlantis and founded the great civilizations of Man, and is not without its enemies in the present world.

In many ways the OBR was a trendsetter for the kind of organizations that would become active in the following decades.

The Order of the Nine Angles

A supposed group that called itself the Order of the Nine Angles (ONA) produced a great deal of written material in the 1980s. It is unclear as to what extent the ONA existed as an actual organization beyond the writings it produced and distributed, but it certainly used Nazi imagery as a central part of its appeal.

Whatever other explanations are given for the name "Order of the Nine Angles," all evidence points to it having been inspired by the name of a ritual written by Michael Aquino for Anton LaVey's book *The Satanic Rituals*—"The Ceremony of the Nine Angles."

This organization was discussed in some detail in Nicholas

---

*The works of Carlos Castaneda became essential reading for some New Agers in the 1970s. He claimed to have been initiated into the ways of southwestern American Indian shamanism by a mysterious figure known as Don Juan. It turns out that "Don Juan" was a code name for the Gurdjieffian teacher Lord John (Pentland); on this backgroud, see William Patrick Patterson's *The Life and Teaching of Carlos Castaneda* (2008). Castaneda rightly thought he could sell the ideas better if they were wrapped in a new package: an old ruse practiced by skilled tricksters.

Goodrick-Clarke's *Black Sun* (2002, 215–26) and Mathias Gardell's *Gods of the Blood* (2003, 292–95).

The leader of the group called himself Anton Long (= David Myatt). He developed a synthesis of various ideas drawn from National Socialism, neo-Nazism, and Satanism. The ONA had a theory of history based on the works of Arnold Toynbee and Oswald Spengler, whereby world history is divided into various epochs governed by the organic rising and falling of dominant civilizations. In this there are clear references to Anton LaVey's theory of the alternating dominance between Ages of Fire and Ice expressed in *The Satanic Rituals* (1972, 219–20). The ONA literature refers to this as "sinister dialectics," which govern cosmic evolution.

The ONA occasionally ascribes to a form of esoteric Hitlerism, espouses Aryan racial superiority, denies the occurrence of the Holocaust, and holds that National Socialists are today an oppressed class.

The heroic Aryan heritage of Western man has been infected by the spirit of Judeo-Christian doctrines, which must be eliminated in the individual and in society before the new Aeon of Fire can emerge. This distortion of Aryan values stemming from Christianity, and in some way connected to the Jews, is an idea that in the case of the ONA seems to derive directly from the works of Oswald Spengler and Francis Parker Yockey. The new Aeon will be one in which the Aryans will be able to establish a Galactic civilization to colonize planets in outer space. (In this there is some reflection of Russian Cosmism.)

As a demonstration of the LaVeyan ideology of using bad guy imagery for psychological and manipulative effects, over time the ONA tended to replace the images of Hitler and the Nazis with those of Osama bin Laden and Islam—as more up-to-date bogeymen. In general, the ONA appears to be a chaotic or anarchistic impulse that lacks any of the values which motivated historical National Socialism. It was under Myatt's direction that the ideology of the group moved progressively more and more into an Islamic direction.

The legacy of the ONA has been sparse except for occasional outcroppings of aberrant behavior on the parts of individuals who might have been inspired by its writings and ideas. In this its operating model can be seen to owe much to the more recent internet-based radicalization model for the generation of lone wolves.

The Werewolf Order

Another supposed Left-Hand Path organization with direct links to the Church of Satan and to Nazi imagery was the Werewolf Order (WO), once headed by Nikolas and Zeena Schreck. The WO did not characterize itself as a church or organization in the usual sense. External manifestations of it included the musical/performance-art group called Radio Werewolf, in which Schreck, Zeena, and for a time her son Stanton, among others, performed. Zeena is the daughter of Anton LaVey.

In the summer of 1988, Radio Werewolf organized youth rallies designed to inaugurate a counter-force to the 1967 "Summer of Love"—1988 was to be the "Summer of Hate." For a period, the Schrecks cozied up to the neo-Nazi leader Tom Metzger of W.A.R. (White Aryan Resistance) and appeared on his cable-television program.

The material produced and distributed by Radio Werewolf was bombastic, elitist, and ferocious in its tenor. Connections to National Socialism seem more a matter of aesthetics and the general idea of superior and inferior races, although these do not appear to be ethnically determined as much as they are psychological. The WO ideology indicated that "Werewolves" are another type of humanity living in the midst of "sheep," who naturally fear and loathe the superior Werewolf race.

Ultimately, the WO might best be characterized as a private order or, perhaps more accurately, as an experiment in the marketing of the recordings of the Schrecks under the name Radio Werewolf.

Michael Aquino and the Order of the Trapezoid

Besides these minor offshoots, certainly the most important exponent of esotericism related to the symbols of National Socialism among the schools of the Left-Hand Path is the Order of the Trapezoid within the Temple of Set. The Temple of Set was founded in 1975 by Michael Aquino (1946–2019) and other ex–Church of Satan members. Aquino was a Lieutenant Colonel in the United States Army, who saw action in

Vietnam and was an expert in psychological operations (PSYOP). He also had a Ph.D. from the University of California at Santa Barbara in Political Science (1980).

Interest in the symbolism and technologies of National Socialist ideology and ceremonial, as well as the mythology surrounding it, tends to be rather objective in the Order of the Trapezoid, which was formally established as an order within the organizational structure of the Temple of Set in 1983. Aquino wrote the following by way of introduction of the Temple of Set to the idea of the Order of the Trapezoid.

"The uncanny attraction of the Third Reich—Nazi Germany— lies in the fact that it endorsed and practiced both dynamism and life-worship without restraint and to a world-shaking degree of success. In The Revolution of Nihilism *(1939), Hermann Rauschning said:*

"This irrational element in National Socialism is the actual source of its strength. It is the reliance on it that accounts for its 'sleepwalker's immunity' in the face of one practical problem after another. It explains why it was possible for National Socialism to attain power almost without the slightest tangible idea of what it was going to do. The movement was without even vague general ideas on the subject; all it had was boundless confidence: things would smooth themselves out one way or another. . . . Its strength lay in incessant activity and in embarking on anything as long as it kept things moving. . . . National Socialism is action pure and simple, dynamics in vacuo, revolution at a variable tempo, ready to be changed at any moment."

Similarly, the life-worship of the Third Reich was not what the "Mediterranean" mind understands by this term. The "life" is the life of the state, or more properly the Volk *(perhaps best translated as the "soul of the people"). The individual achieves self-realization as, through his efforts, he contributes to the strengthening of this "soul."*

Just as the Third Reich's dynamism got out of hand, leading it to embark on irrational and destructive conquests abroad, so its life-worship—which could have been a truly evolutionary synthesis of the most sublime ideas of Hegel and Nietzsche—became perverted into crude xenophobia, hatreds built upon superficial notions of "race," and ultimately a maddened stampede towards a Wagnerian *Götterdämmerung* in defiance of a return to rationalism. Said Heinrich Himmler on April 21, 1945:

"We have made serious mistakes. If I could have a fresh start, I would do many things differently now. But it is too late. We wanted greatness and security for Germany, and we are leaving behind us a pile of ruins, a fallen world . . ."

The Order of the Trapezoid proposes to extract the positive, the constructive, and the exalted from the Germanic magical tradition—and to just as carefully avoid and reject those excesses and distortions which have made this tradition an object of the most of the most extraordinary fear, condemnation, and suppression in the postwar period. . . .

Nevertheless the care required in any investigation into this tradition cannot be overemphasized. Magical and research ability is not enough; ethical sensitivity and social discretion are just as important. (From the Charter of the Order of the Trapezoid, January 30, [1983])

The basis of this order is reported to be a magical working conducted by Michael Aquino in the crypt of the tower in the Wewelsburg castle near Paderborn, Germany, on October 19, 1982. As we have seen (chapter 7), this castle was used by Himmler as a training center for SS-men and was supposed to have been developed into the headquarters of the SS "state within a state"—the so-called Mittelpunkt der Welt. The whole SS mystique is seen by Aquino to be an exponent of these men's nobler and more heroic aspirations cast in the Romantic idealism of the Grail, quite separate from the nastiness into which the SS fell during the course of the war.

One may accuse Aquino and his Knights of the Trapezoid of being hopeless Romantics or naive revisionists, but they are certainly motivated by idealism and intellectual curiosity, and not hate or violence.

So, it must be emphasized that the Temple of Set's Order of the Trapezoid has nothing whatsoever to do with the political or racial aims of National Socialism. There are former Jews who have been members of the order and one past Grand Master of the order is an African American. Another significant difference between LaVey's presentation of Nazi occultism and that of the Temple of Set's Order of the Trapezoid is that LaVey's approach was that of a spell-caster who was putting this "esoteric knowledge" out to the general public in the form of mass-market paperbacks, whereas the communications of the Order of the Trapezoid were for many years reserved to certain members within the Temple of Set, usually as private publications.

The Nazis and the devil had been connected in the imaginations of writers since the war itself. But it would only be after the war was over, and the devil himself had undergone some rehabilitation in the popular imagination, that this originally propagandistic flourish could be seen in any sort of positive light. In the rebellious countercultures of the 1960s, those who wanted to shock the public could have had no better combination than the Nazis and the devil. Clearly, it was Anton LaVey who first made this linkage in any sort of active way. Once this door was open, others entered it—and not all with the same knowledge base, skills, or agendas.

In all cases in which NS imagery and lore is used by Left-Hand Path thinkers, one of the main motives seems to be the use of the idea of conventional evil as a springboard into initiatory development. The practitioner of the Left-Hand Path explores his society's notion of evil in a critical manner on the theory that the morality of the masses must lead in a misguided direction. This is in itself contrary to Nazi logic, which typically embraced the morality and tastes of the masses and utilized it to mobilize a political power base.

So far, our focus of interest with respect to the postwar mythologizing of occult aspects of the Third Reich has remained on the symbolic or magical in the usual sense of the word. There is, however, another dimension of occult thinking in connection with the world of Nazi Germany, which takes us into the field of technology and "forbidden science."

TECHNO-NAZI OCCULTISM

Postwar speculation about Nazi secret science and Nazi Wunderwaffen has proved to be a popular genre of literature and documentary film-making.* As with so much else in this field of study, there is a factual basis to something that then, over time, becomes a grander myth in the repeated retellings. Sometimes the grander myth has an ulterior motive as well. What makes the subject of Nazi secret sciences and miracle weapons a matter of occultism is that the science involved was often perhaps on the edge of a not-yet-established kind and, more importantly, the *beliefs* about these developments in postwar times land us in the middle of a mystical approach. This subject becomes a pseudoscientific version of the same kind of motive that fuels the belief in the use of magical, demonic, or other kinds of more traditional occultism. In this field, as well as the others, the aspect that makes the myth so compelling to some is that there is always a grain of truth to all of it.

In the final analysis, this is what appears to be the truth about Nazi secret weaponry and military technologies: there was an enormous program to create miracle weapons to save the Nazis from losing the war. Unfortunately for them, Hitler held off pushing ahead on these programs until it was too late for them to make any difference in the final outcome of the war. After the war, plans and prototypes of these technologies were captured by the Allies. The vast majority of these resources—documents, prototypes, and scientists—went to the United States. Wernher von Braun and his crew of rocket scientists were the best-known exponents of this phenomenon, but by no means the only ones. The Soviets captured a few of these men and prototypes as well, but a small number by comparison. Experiments with these technologies began very shortly after the war, fueled by the atmosphere of the emerging Cold War between America and the Soviets. Nazi scientists and materials were shipped over to the western United States and

---

*There are probably as many or more books and DVDs about the subject of the Wunderwaffen, real and imagined, than there are on more usual topics of Nazi occultism. Interest comes from conspiracy theorists, weapons enthusiasts and experts, occultists, and neo-Nazis.

Wright-Patterson Air Force Base in Ohio. When the results of these experiments and the flights of some of the experimental prototypes began being observed by the public, the government, through covert channels, quickly began to ascribe these sightings and discoveries to assumed extraterrestrial sources. The reason for this makes sense in only one context: as a way to *misdirect* Soviet intelligence about American development of German technologies. A cursory review of many of the German munitions packages reveals just how much of the current American arsenal of jet aircraft, intercontinental ballistic missiles, cruise missiles, smart bombs, and stealth aircraft have their direct sources in German models: the Me 262, V-2, V-1 "buzz bomb," Fritz I, and Horton, respectively. What future developments will come from other Nazi prototypes and designs? This program of misdirection toward the Soviets is most understandable given the general atmosphere of the immediate postwar world of US intelligence. The Americans were aware that their technological secrets were being passed to the Soviets via spies, such as Julius and Ethel Rosenberg. So by making people believe that other technologies were not the result of German/American military science but rather extraterrestrial visitations, it was thought that the Soviets might be thrown off the track.*

It is probably not without good reason that many of the UFO sightings of the late 1940s and early 1950s were in areas around the laboratories, test sites, and proving grounds of the American military and aircraft manufacturers—for example, in the states of Washington (Boeing) and New Mexico (White Sands, Los Alamos). It is likely that the origin of extraterrestrial UFO explanations for unusual phenomena that were observed in the late 1940s can be traced to US government disinformation campaigns to explain the testing of captured German technologies. The rationale for these disinformation campaigns is, again, best explained in terms of counterintelligence meant to confuse the Russians and hide any advances in technology being explored or exploited from this captured technology.

---

*The fact that the Soviets had a strong predilection for actually believing in extraterrestrial possibilities is discussed in my monograph *The Occult Roots of Bolshevism*.

Mythology of Nazi UFOs

The myth of Nazi Ufology falls into the same patterns as we see with modern UFO mythology stemming from nineteenth- and twentieth-century sources. By the same token, the UFO myth—understanding the word *myth* as discussed in the introduction to this book—falls into the mythic paradigms familiar since the beginning of time concerning the intrusion into our cosmic order by beings or forces "from the outside"—from above or from below. Such beings can be understood as gods or angels that have come to aid or save mankind (or an individual) or, conversely, they can be seen as monsters or demons bent on destruction and death. This mythology is clearly on display in science-fiction films of the mid-twentieth century, where we see wise and benevolent visitors (*The Day the Earth Stood Still* [1951] or *E.T.* [1982]) or monstrous and demonic destroyers (*The Thing* [1953] or *Independence Day* [1996]). All the same myths pertain to the Nazi UFOs—neo-Nazis see them as a future mode of gaining ultimate victory and salvation, while most people see them as a menace recurring from the past. It must be said that most people who read or watch films dedicated to the idea of Nazi UFOs are consuming this material as a sort of historical pornography—sci-fi with a sinister edge. As a myth, or fairy tale, the paradigms remain the same as do the functions of these patterns in human consciousness.

Graham M. Simmons, in his down-to-earth study of advanced German aviation technology captured by the Allies in Operation

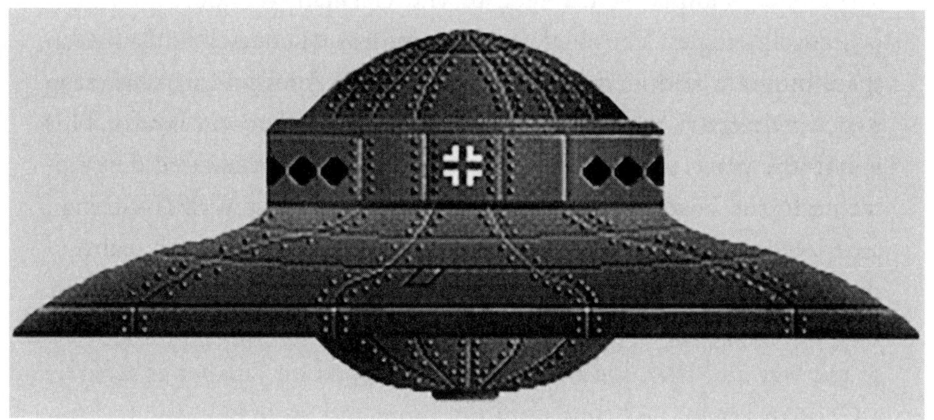

Fig. 13.3. A fanciful depiction of the alleged Nazi flying disc Haunebu II

LUSTY (LUftwaffe-Secret-TechnologY) and Operation Big, offers a chapter called "Flights of Fancy" (pp. 255–58), in which he tries to put the Nazi UFO-mythology into some rational perspective. These mythical miracle weapons are known by many names: Rundflugzeug (Round Aircraft), Feuerball (Fireball), Diskus, Haunebu(rg-Gerät) (Hauneburg Device), V-7, Vril, Kugelblitz (Ball Lightning), Andromeda-Gerät (Andromeda Device), Flugkreisel (Flying Spinner), Kugelwaffe (Ball Weapon), and Reichsflugscheibe (Reich Flying Disc).

Certain actual data used to support this mythology include the fact that the Nazis did explore and claim territory in Antarctica in 1938, they did develop several sorts of alternative propulsion devices (they tested many and perfected some), and there were repeated sightings by Allied airmen of what came to be called the "foo fighters" (which appeared to be fast-moving balls of light, tailing and harassing American and British bombers over Germany).

Simmons traces the mythology of such machines back to statements made in an Italian daily newspaper, *Il Giornale d'Italia,* in March 1950 by a professor named Giuseppe Belluzzo. Here Belluzzo claims to have worked with the Germans on a flying disc-fan vehicle called the Flugkreisel in 1942. Such a disc is said to have been test-flown, attaining an altitude of 12,400 meters in three minutes and a speed of 2,200 kilometers per hour.

Certain events and developments after the war led to the widespread believability of the idea of the German Wunderwaffen and other technologies. The chief development was, of course, the American space program leading to a lunar landing with Apollo 11 in 1969, atop a rocket designed by the Nazi rocket expert Wernher von Braun. This is not the place to enumerate the confirmed or speculative developments in the East or West stemming from advanced WWII German technologies. Here we want to limit ourselves to the fantastic realm of the imagination—fueled now and then by actual events. Some believe that the Nazis did develop and test an atomic bomb just before the end of the war and that one of the bombs dropped on Japan was actually a German version. As time went on, more and more fantastic technological wonders were "discovered," including anti-gravitational devices and ones that could travel between dimensions of time and space. More often than not, these ideas are also attached to the idea of the special form of energy called Vril and devices for harnessing free energy. Such extreme ideas not only find a home among neo-Nazis but also among Ufologists and general conspiracy theorists.

Nazi "miracle weapons" and advanced technologies also find an ever-increasing place in the entertainment industry. They are seen in science-fiction literature, films and even computer games. Robert Heinlein wrote a juvenile novel set in post-WWII 1947 about kids participating in a moon mission who discover that the Nazis already have a base on the moon! Such a Nazi lunar station is also the subject of the 2012 science-fiction film *Iron Sky*. The line between historical investigation and science-fiction fantasy is often a thin one when it comes to Nazi UFOs.

Operation Highjump

A historical event that took place in 1947 led to a widespread complex of postwar Nazi mythology. This was the Antarctic expedition of Admiral Richard E. Byrd dubbed "Operation Highjump." The fact that this expedition took place at all was fuel for myth-makers and fantasists of all kinds. That same year an Argentine émigré from Hungary named Szabó Ladislao wrote a book titled *Hitler está vivo* (Hitler Is Alive). This placed Hitler in a secret Nazi base beneath the Antarctic ice cap. This book was soon translated into French and information from it began to spread into the English-speaking world.

The facts surrounding Byrd's expedition appear to be that Byrd's Operation Highjump began in August 1946 and ended in February of the next year. It had as its main objectives the training and testing of troops in frigid conditions, the determination of possibilities for establishing military bases in the region, and scientific research regarding electromagnetic, geological, hydrographic, and meteorological conditions. Another part of the mission was abandoned and even officially denied before the expedition ended, which was the extension of US sovereignty over a certain area of the continent. After the expedition, Byrd expressed his concern that the poles could in the future be militarized and that they no longer could be considered to act as a barrier to enemy attack, as had been the case in the past.

There had been three Antarctic expeditions mounted by the Germans in the early twentieth century: one in 1901 to 1903, another in 1911 to 1912, and the infamous Deutsche Antarktische Expedition in 1938 to 1939. The last of these was undertaken during the time of the Third Reich and had as part of its purpose the establishment of some sovereign territory on the continent to be called "Neu Schwabenland" (New Swabia).

In the 1970s an uncopyrighted document called *The Flight to the Land Beyond the North Pole: A Copy of Admiral Richard B. [sic] Byrd's Diary,* with a foreword by Dr. William Bernard, began to circulate among the UFO and conspiracy-theorist subculture. It purported to give an account of Byrd's alleged encounter with surviving Nazis under the ice at the North Pole, where they had a vast complex and were equipped with flying saucer–type craft. This account quickly gave rise to a whole cottage industry of books about Nazi UFOs emerging from the poles and the hidden truth behind Admiral Byrd's mission. Secret American nuclear tests in the Antarctic region in the last 1950s or early 1960s were rumored to have the intention of destroying these Nazi bases but were actually experimental atmospheric tests.

Fig. 13.4. Expedition insignia

This, like so much else about the postwar mythologizing of the Third Reich and its aftermath, can perhaps best be explained by the phenomena of overactive imaginations stimulated by the imagery and allure of Nazi symbols, coupled with the mass psychology of an under-educated populace—an increasing number of whom can no longer discriminate between fantasy and reality.

Ernst Zündel

The first great popularizer of the vast array of Nazi secret weaponry was a German immigrant to Canada named Ernst Zündel (1939–2017). He was a graphic artist by trade, which made his role in the production of literature relating to the Wunderwaffen of the Third Reich an easy path. Zündel is best known as a holocaust denier. His Samisdat Publishers put out works such as *The Hitler We Loved* and *Did Six Million Really Die? The Truth at Last*. In Canada, such writings are considered criminal. He also became the target of direct action by a group calling itself the "Jewish Armed Resistance Movement," which firebombed his house and sent him an explosive device. (No criminal indictments came of this.) Zündel was tried for "inciting hatred against an identifiable group" in Canada, convicted, and deported to Germany, where he was also tried in 2007 and imprisoned on similar charges. He was released in 2010 and died in his native hometown in 2017.

This background history shows that Zündel had clear propagandistic motives for his works involving the WWII German miracle weaponry. His point was to show the technical superiority of the Germans. But his real underlying motive appears to have been to produce a more lucrative published product by taking advantage of the UFO craze. He later directly or indirectly acknowledged this.

Zündel's main contributions to the mythology of Nazi UFOs are his books *UFOs: Nazi Secret Weapon?* (1974), *Secret Nazi Polar Expeditions* (1978), and *Hitler at the South Pole* (1979). His general mythology was that the Germans possessed advanced technologies and developed flying saucers with which they flew to Antarctica, called Neuschwabenland in this mythology, and set up secret underground bases from which they will reemerge to conquer the world at some

Fig. 13.5. Samisdat Nazi UFO ad

future point. These bases were at the entrance into the "hollow earth." This mythology takes advantage of the actual German expedition to Antarctica (1938–1939), where a portion of the continent was explored and was called "Neuschwabenland" (New Swabia).

A Samisdat newsletter of 1978 advertised an expedition to Antarctica to find the bases and the entrance to the hollow earth. This adventure obviously never happened.

Although Zündel did not invent the mythology of Nazi UFOs, he is probably more responsible than anyone else for popularizing them, which led to a second wave of literature on the subject, and a second wave of mythologizing. The idea entered comic books, role-playing games, video games, and spawned a cottage industry of books about the subject.

One of the more amusing and ironic chapters of the myth of Nazi UFOs comes from the world of advertising. Most remarkably, it also comes from the company that Hitler was instrumental in founding: Volkswagen. Most history enthusiasts are aware that Hitler's code name was "Wolf." This stems from the etymology of the name Adolf, which means "Noble wolf." When the Volkswagen factory was built, the city that formed around it was named Wolfsburg in Hitler's honor. The logo that appeared on the steering wheel of my 1973 Volkswagen Beetle showed a wolf atop a castle (= Wolfsburg = wolf's castle). The UFOs? At various times on television Volkswagen advertised the Beetle (VW Type 1) with an image of the car spinning and turning into a flying saucer, with the tagline "Reverse-engineered from UFOs" (!) This indicates that the company was aware of the mythic connection between Nazis and UFOs and was actually bold enough to exploit it as advertising. I miss my Beetle—her name was Heidi.

* * *

The story of Nazi occultism is clearly divided into two almost separate categories: first, what was actually present in the time of the Third Reich and leading up to it; and second, what outsiders made of the spiritual trauma that National Socialism seems to have inflicted upon history—the mythologizing and the attempt to understand in a meaningful way the events, symbols, and ideas inherent in this ideology.

The are two possible motivating forces behind the generation of mythology depicting the Nazis as Satanists or, more commonly, as pagans. It is fueled either by Satanists or pagans who have become interested for one reason or another in the symbolism of National Socialism, or by adherents of religious (Christian), political, or mystical interests who wish to demonize the Nazis for their own advantage. The main dimension to the latter motive is the desire on the parts of the orthodox churches (Catholic and Protestant) to deflect their own guilt for the Holocaust, which had its real roots in their centuries-long theory and practice of anti-Semitism.

With a motive similar to that of the churches, the scientific community of the West, and especially in America, has wished to deflect its own guilt in the construction of the eugenic theories and practices that were put into place by the Nazis. Just as the church had written the script for centuries on the question of the Jews, which led to the attempt to implement the Final Solution, the eugenics establishment of the US had worked for some decades to establish their ideas. These were put into practice by the Nazis on a grand and nationwide scale as never before possible. As the moral tide turned decisively against this idea in the years after the war, the scientific community tried to ascribe these ideas to the Nazis alone so that when one thinks of such ideas they think of the Nazis, and mainly only them. In this effort, the scientific community has been largely successful. All of the other efforts at mythologically demonizing the Nazis fold into the interests of all parties that are concerned with alleviating themselves of suspicion and guilt.

The world of the occult in all its classical forms was very much a part of German and Central European culture in the early part of the twentieth century. The leaders of what became the Nazi Party all grew up and came of age in that cultural milieu, and so the world of the occult was important to them on different levels. They were shaped by it. They often feared and rejected it as evil, foreign, Jewish-based, or illogical and unscientific. But on some level, they recognized its power within the masses. This is why the Nazis spent so much time attempting to control occult impulses in the culture.

The NSDAP designed itself to become the all and everything in the lives of the individuals making up the masses of the German population. It was to become their religion, their philosophy, and their sole rationale for living and for dying. As such it was steeped in the mystical, the magical, and the mythic on all levels. But rarely was it what outsiders tried to make it into—a Satanic or pagan movement. It was the National Socialist movement—self-defined and self-obsessed, and centered first and foremost on one man: the Führer.

A SUMMARY AND FINAL ASSESSMENT

This book has presented a great number of ideas in a compact explication. Its composition has been complex with three themes—symbolic culture, scientific culture, and occult culture—presented in four distinct historical frameworks: the deep roots in the nineteenth century, the pre- and early NS era, the NS era itself, and the Allied wartime propaganda and global postwar media production of analysis and mythologizing, with the mythologizing seen as belonging to camps that are either pro-Nazi (or at least having a neutral treatment) or anti-Nazi, with sensationalistic or agenda-driven motives.

In any final assessment on the true nature of the NS regime in Germany, we have to view it as a gangster state. This is not to say that movements such as National Socialism and even Bolshevism do not start out with, and are not originally fueled by, what are thought to be high ideas—as barbarous or misguided as they might be—but that the endowment of such movements with sudden and absolute power tends, as the saying goes, to corrupt, suddenly and absolutely. A review of how the various Nazi leaders and their close followers enriched themselves personally and indulged in their assorted vices under the cover of their own brand of political correctness will quickly convince the observer of the actual story. But some still are subject to the idealistic spell cast by movements such as the NSDAP or even the Bolsheviks. Their actual histories should remain as a warning from history. It is too bad history is not widely taught anymore.

One of the indicators of the attitudes of Nazi Party members toward the racketeering involved in politics is shown in the chapter titled

"Enrich Yourselves" in Hermann Rauschning's *Voice of Destruction* (1940, 91–103). Rauschning is, of course, often unreliable, but his outlines of the gangster approach to government and finances as taught by Hitler are generally corroborated elsewhere.

This book was constructed with a certain lens of observation. Three areas were discussed separately—the world of symbols (comprising the Geisteswissenschaften, or humanities and social sciences), the world of science (comprising the Naturwissenschaften and their offshoots), and the secret sciences (Geheimwissenschaften) or the occult as such. In each area of investigation, the esoteric or hidden dimensions of meaning were emphasized as they relate to the Third Rich. The Nazi era itself is viewed not in a synchronic manner, strictly within its own defined limits of 1933 to 1945, but rather I look to the deep roots of each of the areas in question in the nineteenth century, and to the years immediately preceding the advent of the Third Reich, the time of the regime of the NSDAP itself, and finally we have two additional chapters on the wartime and postwar mythologizing of the Third Reich in all of its dimensions. After years of reading books on occult Nazism in whatever guise, I was always left with the feeling that something is missing. The missing elements are not simple or easy to clarify, but the instrument of topical analysis and diachronic examination seemed to me to be the best way of getting at the problems. The final aim is a *rational demystification of a modern myth*—that is, a reasonable analysis leading to the clarification of ideas along rational lines, rather than any further sensationalizing and mythologizing of the subject in question. So often books like *The Spear of Destiny,* ostensibly written as a warning against evil, have the unintended (?) result of further romanticizing the Nazis and encouraging the very ideas being attacked. This is because the new myths were just as irrational as the original data. Unreason was used to attack unreason, and the effect was merely the expansion of unreason. The very topic of Nazi Germany excites many people to intellectual acts of unreason, enflames passions, and ignites both fear and unbridled admiration. In my case, I largely approach the subject as a historian and as a Germanist, a student of German and Germanic culture and languages for many decades.

So many past forays into the field of Nazi occultism focus almost entirely on the völkisch aspect, with a dash of Satanic verbiage to spice things up. As I hope this book has shown, that aspect, as important as it was, is not the whole story of the occult roots of Nazism. Neither is the idea of "volkism" limited to the Germanic world! The concept of a certain people or tribe (usually one's own) being exceptional or superior and possessing a special destiny in history is as old as the Stone Age, and it is a well-known biblical trope. However, what the Germans seem to have added to the age-old picture is a modern theoretical basis, which nevertheless reaches back to an ancient mythic source. German volkism, either directly or indirectly, gave rise to a number of other contemporary movements among many peoples, using similar theories and myths. The Zionism of Theodor Herzl arose in the same Viennese environment as many German-speaking völkisch groups with similar ideology. The great Black Nationalist W. E. Burghardt Du Bois absorbed many of these ideas as a student in Berlin in the 1890s. The Nation of Islam has an ideology similar to German *Volkstum*. Mexican Americans (Chicanos) of the American Southwest have formed various allied political/religious organizations (M.E.Ch.A., La Raza Unida) that dream of the reconquest of parts of the United States and the establishment of a homeland called Aztlán—a mythical name of the old Aztec homeland. They operate under the motto *Por La Raza todo, fuera de La Raza nada:* "For the Race everything, outside the Race nothing." All of this is just to say the kind of ideology represented by the Nazis is not limited to them.

One of the aspects that is emphasized repeatedly in this study is the actual practice by the Nazis of magic on a mass scale. Much was made over the years about Hitler's ability to mesmerize the masses. Here we have delved into the methods of this form of magic. The actual effectiveness of the use of *operative* (magical) methods of communication on the German people from 1920 to 1945 can, to a certain extent, be gauged by the continuing effectiveness of its relics and legacy. The spells cast by Hitler and the National Socialists in the form of symbols, signs, rituals, and ideas continue to work—in one way or another, either by attraction or repulsion—on most people who are exposed to them today.

An example of this effectiveness is illustrated by the logo design known as the swastika. The swastika is a captivating visual symbol. When I was in elementary school in Dallas, Texas, in the early 1960s I cannot begin to tell you how many desks had swastikas carved into them. None of this was driven by hate or anti-Semitism—most of the kids did not even know any actual Jewish people. The reasons behind it are at least twofold: the symbol has an intrinsic compelling quality due to its shape and proportions, and most boys of the day (who loved to "play army") had fallen under the spell of Nazi *style*—as seen in numerous media representations ranging from documentaries to *Hogan's Heroes*. It just seemed that everything about the Nazis was "neater" (midsixties boy talk for "double-plus-good")—their symbols, uniforms, and even their tanks just looked better. Yes, the old spells cast on the Germans—recorded in the media and projected through television screens—still *worked,* apart from any politics or ideology.

An example of the poor methodology typically used in the composition of questionable books (or segments of books) on the subject of Nazi occultism is found in Alan Baker's *Invisible Eagle* (2000), in a chapter where he discusses the idea of the hollow earth. This chapter is more than forty pages long. At the beginning of the chapter, Baker (2000, 160) simply counts the belief in a hollow earth as one of the "strange and irrational beliefs held by the Nazis." But the bulk of the chapter has nothing to do with Nazi or even German theories at all. He can only really come up with one example (previously reported in *The Morning of the Magicians*) of Germans using this theory. This is the experiment whereby German radars on the island of Rügen were aimed forty-five degrees into the sky to try to locate British naval vessels in the sea, assuming a hollow earth model in which the sea is on the *inside* of the globe. There is brief mention of one German theorist, Peter Bender, who developed his own *Hohlweltlehre* (Hollow World Theory) in 1918. Bender only gets a half a page of discussion here, however. Bender is not linked to the Nazis, and when all is said and done the only documented evidence for Nazi belief in a hollow earth is the one experiment on Rügen. Ninety percent of the chapter is made up of a discussion of hollow earth theories in general, accounts of UFOs from the interior of the Earth, and so on—all of which remains unlinked to the topic of National Socialist Germany. It is writing such as this which has led to the current crop of Nazi esotericists who, based on such literature, also make the same sorts of associations between Nazism and other unusual theories. To be able to say this or that belief was once held by the Nazis, one needs to document that the idea was at least represented by one of the leading National Socialist ideologues or was part of a German program during the Nazi period. Merely finding one or two random German fellows who lived at the time and who believed in a given theory does not meet the criterion. This pattern is by no means isolated but rather is a repeated pattern in myriad books whereby any unusual idea or practice is first linked to Germany in some tenuous way, and if the link can be brought into the early twentieth century, all the better. That alone may suffice to call it a Nazi idea. And if one historical Nazi can be found who ever read a book on the subject, then it seems to be fair game to be promoted to a widespread and general Nazi doctrine. Throughout the course of this book, I have tried to keep all this in perspective. It is well known that Hitler thoroughly disapproved of Himmler's neo-Germanic passions and most of Rosenberg's ideas. It should therefore be kept in mind that even leading ideologues could write and enact ideas which, although tolerated for political or personal reasons within the National Socialist regime, were not necessarily in harmony with the mainstream of actual National Socialist ideology. Curiously, Baker totally ignores an actual connection between the Nazi era and the hollow earth in the work of Johannes Lang (*Hohlwelttheorie;* 1938) and others!

In an insightful and useful study titled "The Hielscher Legend," which appears in the second volume of the journal *Tyr,* Peter Bahn delves into the mistreatment of the subject of Friedrich Hielscher in the pages of *The Morning of the Magicians.* Bahn (2003–2004, 251–56) demonstrates throughout his research the misinformation spread about Hielscher and his organization. It is an illustrative example of how Nazi occult yarns were spun.

I have seen from my own personal experience how writers, some even purporting to be scholars, often happily twist the facts and realities of something to fit their own "templates of thought." These can be driven by personal obsessions or religious loyalties and fears, but most often by ideological mandates and orthodoxies. Such writers are sometimes compelled by actual National Socialist sympathies but far more often by the politically correct camp of cultural Marxists. In all cases the meaning of what is written has been predetermined; the facts (either actual or imagined) are then merely arranged to fit the conclusion—or merely to suggest it in lurid ways.

An additional question might be posed: Is Nazi Germany unique in its occult roots? The answer to this question is resoundingly negative. The best and closest example is found in the development and history of Bolshevik Russia. The roots of Leninist thought are decidedly occult. Lenin and many of his friends—such as V. D. Bonch-Bruevich, A. V. Lunacharsky, and Maxim Gorky—were deeply imbued with occult beliefs, practices, and theories. Had Theosophy itself not been the invention of a Russian émigré H. P. Blavatsky? This idea of the occult roots of Bolshevism is today much under-studied and little understood in popular culture in the West. Lenin and his cohorts constructed an esoteric form of Marxism informed by gnostic and theosophical ideas, folded it into a form of cosmic materialism, and once they had gained power in the state, they suppressed outward forms of organized occultism, just as the National Socialists did. In general, the development and developmental trajectory of what we have termed ideas in history are very similar.

THE POWER OF STRANGE BELIEFS

There is a kind of occultism that consists not of arcane practices but rather is more of an occult religion—a system of faith in what is considered secret information. Two examples of such systems are Theosophy and Anthroposophy. This is not a new phenomenon, nor is it all that unusual. Occult systems of this sort typically consist of secret teachings about hidden realities of history, society, and nature. There is a kind of psychological energy that can be conveyed to the individual through fanatic belief in such ideas. Many major religions such as Christianity and Islam work on a similar level. The Christian, for example, believes that the Hebrew storm-god begat an (apparently) human son on a virgin girl, and this son was killed as a sacrifice to alleviate any and all who believe in him of all their sins and transgressions and attain eternal life. This drawn from a mythology and spiritual rationale that was far removed from the people who came to believe in this idea (e.g., Greeks, Romans, Celts, Germans). It often appears that the more outré the belief, the greater the energy generated seems to be. As old as these patterns are, they do seem to have spread faster and perhaps deeper with the advent of forms of communications such as the internet and social media. The rush to throw one's mind into the most extreme levels of unreason becomes a race to see who can hold the weirder views—until a person's mind becomes nothing but a puddle of fanatic goo in which Nazis, flying saucers, and extraterrestrial races of Greys and Reptilians are vying for the last vestiges of sanity. The resulting cultural environment is one in which any masterful manipulators of the human mind, such as the National Socialists represented, would have a very easy time of plying their craft. The only thing that seems to be saving us is the fact that the degenerative effects of this cultural environment seem to have infected almost all of the would-be manipulators as well. For this reason alone, they are often rendered ineffective. The world is ripe to dominated by that one-eyed man in the country of the blind.

Much of the way in which Nazi occultism or Nazi magic *actually* worked was by manipulating the hopes and fears of a proud and desperate people. We see even today how people vote for candidates for president who appear as blank slates upon which the electorate can project their hopes. He (or she) is what the individual voter hopes—facts and actual positions are irrelevant to the appearance that is projected and the sense of identity or recognition the individual voter feels. Hitler was a master of this process long before it had become common. The National Socialists hated democracy, identified its weaknesses, and exploited them. Hitler and National Socialism were seen as representing a scientific futurity, a messianic fulfillment of prophecy (whether biblical or that of Barbarossa returning from the Kyffhäuser), a healthy alternative, a natural response to problems, a relief to economic woes and oppression—and yes, to some, an avenue for the return to the Germanic past and the practice of an authentic national culture and religion. The key to the practical application of this form of magic was in the control of Hitler's image. Nothing could be allowed to distract the citizen from his or her fantasies. Hitler remained officially unmarried to encourage the romantic fantasies of the female electorate. Positive and powerful symbols and signals had to be projected in the form of myths, ideas, signs and logos that could then become a screen upon which the will of the Volk could be blended and melded with that of the Party.

It is clear that the appeal and allure of National Socialism existed in its call to *biological* solidarity, as opposed to the *class* solidarity theoretically demanded by Marxist socialism. The deep roots of this idea go back to the tribal past of the Germanic peoples. National Socialism is untenable in the modern world simply because the "nation" (i.e., the state) can no longer in any way be identified with the "race." A modern nation-state is far too large, diverse, and complex to be reduced to a single *biological* ethnos—if such a thing can even be said to exist. Mass murder is the only way to solve this theoretical problem. (Similar tactics are also used widely by every Marxist-based form of socialism.) The Romantic longing of the Germans of the Reform era for a more organic and holistic state, rooted in ideas about their own tribal pasts, inspired by stories of exotic tribal societies (American Indians, Polynesians, etc.), is understandable. But the sheer size of the modern nation-state simply precludes such a solution. National Socialism was attempted on far too large a scale to be successful. The yearnings of the Reform-minded people of the early twentieth century could only be satisfied on a smaller scale, with something akin to *tribal socialism*. One of the main reasons socialism never works on a mass level is because it requires an authority to coercively take the fruits of one man's labor and redistribute it to others who are favored by that authority, while at the same time there is no trust or affection between the giver and taker of the benefit. Socialism works in *families,* but not in *states.*

It is hoped that readers will be able to make use of this book on several levels. Certainly it defines and discusses the history of the topic in ways far better than any of its predecessors, but it is also designed to be a tool for dispelling the clouds of unreason that surround the current world phase of human history. Once one grasps the methods and structure of the presentation, a tool can be developed for analyzing numerous historical phenomena that appear to be similar in nature to the National Socialist movement in Germany. Fundamental to the approach is the precise definition of terms such that readers are discouraged (at least in theory) from applying their own misunderstandings to the terminology. By demystifying the topic, the real mysteries, the real unknowns, and the profound mythic constructs, in which the human spirit moves and with which it struggles, can be isolated and laid bare to be explored free of superstition and coercion. The fanaticism represented by Nazism cannot be combated by merely opposing it with another form of unreasonable fanaticism. At the same time, if the contents of this book have demonstrated nothing else, it should be obvious that what motivated the members of the NSDAP movement were profound urges and needs, which slumber in the heart of every human—to belong to something greater than yourself; to live with a sense of holistic bonding with your neighbors; and to be safe, prosperous, and healthy, with a sense of greater transcendent purpose or duty. One would hope that such goals could be reached without war and the murder of innocent men, women, and children.

A mystery as vast, complex, and often confusing as the present one cannot be wrapped up and definitively solved between the covers of a single book. Many volumes have been written on the subject, and most of them have only added to the confusion rather than clarifying the topic. In many ways, what is presented here could best be characterized as an *outline* of the subject of Nazi occultism. Each part of this outline could be expanded upon with more extensive books of its own, using some of the same methods and theories—utilizing the same lens of understanding. It is my hope that the book will act as just such a catalyst.

In the final analysis, after accessing and studying the original sources in the German language for more than forty years of research, it is my conclusion that the occult, esoteric, and even pagan elements present in National Socialism are almost entirely a matter of something that was present in the individual Party leaders and the rank and file of the membership, not something that was official or overtly promoted by the regime. There was a struggle between the pagan and Christian wings of the Party on a deep ideological basis; Hitler gave the victory to the Christian faction. The pagan faction of the country, almost all of whom did sympathize to some degree with the NSDAP program (in the beginning, at least), accounted for 15 to 20 percent of the population. This was a significant minority, but not numerous enough to constitute "the masses" Hitler was so interested in manipulating. To have sided with that minority, toward which he had no personal ideological sympathy in any event, would have been ideological suicide. The Nazis, and Hitler in particular, were masters of the magic of propaganda aimed as acquiring power and maintaining it. The secrets and ritual of this form of magic are on display in *Mein Kampf* and in the ceremonial programs of the NSDAP. These methods were not, however, aimed at a revival of paganism or at some worship of anything or anyone other than Hitler, the apparatus of the NSDAP, and the idealized (Nazified) image of the German Volk and state. Hitler's models were largely taken from those of his rivals, the Bolsheviks of Russia. The Nazis imitated the game of the Sozis, they just looked much better doing it.

What then, a reader may ask, is responsible for the overwhelming amount of material, books and widespread opinion that the Nazis were a pagan thing or were devil worshippers in league with the dark lord? By tracing the actual evidence for this, it is clear that such ideas stem from wartime propaganda, which told a story too good to give up, and postwar mythologizing that was lucrative to sell, exciting to tell and read, but only based on the most elusive facts. The bulk of it all was constructed of outright lies, or "stories" as my parents would have said. To lie is a crime. If it is a crime, what is the opportunity, the method, and the motive of the liars? Their methods are clear and the evidence is in the great mill of Nazi occult literature. Their opportunity is provided by the hunger the general public has to read potboilers based on fact (tabloid news syndrome), but the *motive* is more interesting. The motives of the various participants are several: many of the writers are essentially journalists or (would-be) writers of fiction who are just wanting to make a buck doing an interesting project. Then there are the fellow travelers who actually believe the propaganda and identify with the lurid tales and wish to emulate them. They have been taken in by the Hitlerian spell. All of these are the useful idiots in the story. Finally, there are those who actually have something to gain (*cui bono?*) on a deeper level if the masses believe that the Nazis were essentially pagans or Satanists. These are the orthodox churches who had promoted anti-Semitism for centuries and whose efforts finally bore their ultimate fruit at Auschwitz. After the war, they, like so many others, searched for a scapegoat and the only likely candidate was found in the pagan faction and—ludicrously enough—the Satanic myth. (Satan had been used before in church propaganda, why not again?) The crimes of the NSDAP were real and should not be denied. But they have to be looked at from a criminological perspective with some sophistication.

In the late 1980s, when visiting a local psychic fair, I noticed a woman in her booth, before which was displayed a watercolor portrait of a Nazi officer. As it turned out, the picture was of her boss imagined as wearing a Nazi uniform. She had developed the theory that all of the mean men in people's lives today are actually reincarnated Nazis! This shows the degree to which the Nazi archetype, as mythologized in the postwar era, has assumed a New Age form of demonology. I suppose she could liberate the oppressed for a fee. This was just one more piece of hard evidence for the level of unreason to which the Nazi mythology has risen.

Finally, I would like to conclude the main text of this book with an explanation as to what motivated me to write it at all. The motives are several. First, it is a perennially fascinating topic of enduring interest to a wide readership. Everyone would like to write a book on an interesting topic. But secondly I would like to bring some reason and clarity to a subject fraught with unreason and obscurity, both of the kind that comes to the topic naturally and of the type that is due to the throngs of obsessed fanatics on all sides who are bent on clouding our minds with their dark hopes and misguided fears. The occult-oriented writers stoke fear, and the academic ones use the demonization of National Socialism as a cover to be able to write about the subject while remaining above reproach, or simply as an elaborate "virtue signal" to ensure job security. It would appear that, as Steigmann-Gall points out, the Nazis have assumed a place of cultural myth in which all of our ideas of absolute evil are enshrined. But would we be wiser to challenge this assumption so that we might more clearly see the dangers of the present, rather than focusing on a mythologized vision of the past?

APPENDIX A

A SIMPLIFIED VERSION OF THE ORGANIZATIONAL STRUCTURE OF THE AHNENERBE

ORGANIZATION OF THE AHNENERBE

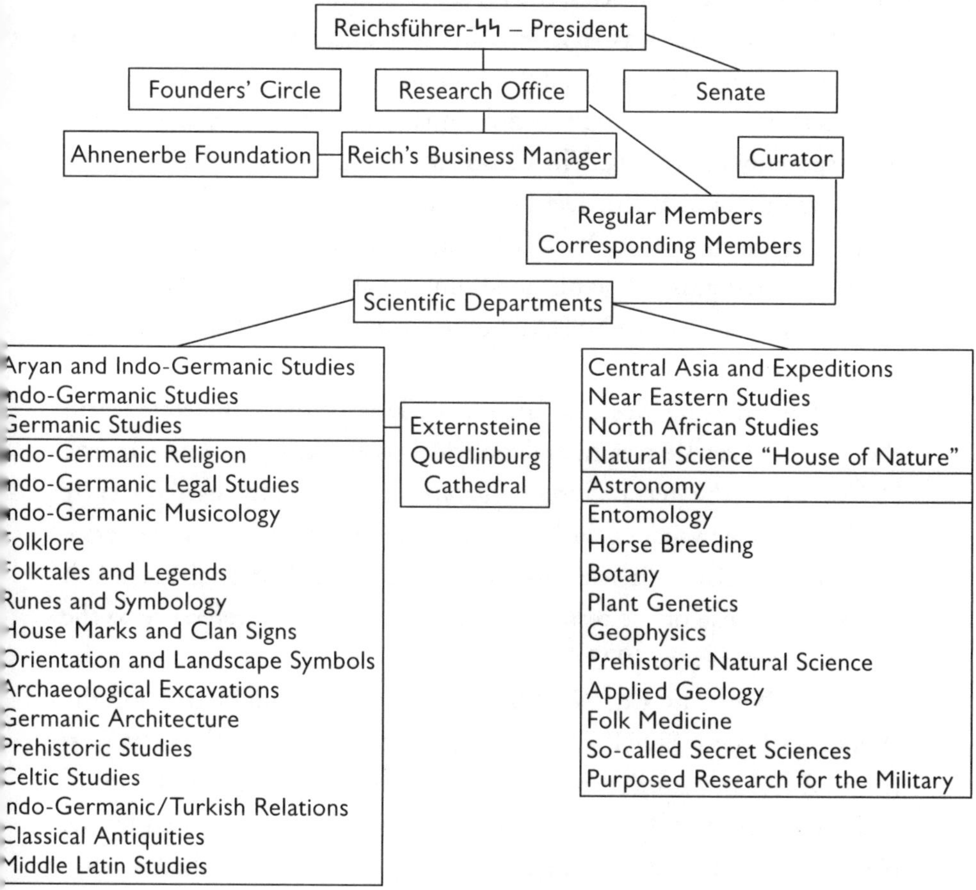

APPENDIX B

THE WORD *NAZI*

Today those with sympathies for the National Socialist movement in Germany (and its current offspring) often find the use of the term *Nazi* offensive. I am not concerned with being politically correct, even here, and it behooves us to discuss the actual history of this little word.

The word *Nazi* was first seen in German as a nickname for the given name Ignaz (pron. ig-natz), common in Bavaria and Austria. The word was used disparagingly as a designation for a simple, foolish person, especially in Austria. The decadent German author Hanns Heinz Ewers wrote a piece titled "Der Nazi," which can be found in his archive of works written in New York between 1914 and 1918. The title character was distinguished by his hoodlum-like characteristics. Ewers later became a member of the NSDAP but was ostracized for his earlier decadent works and lifestyle.

The word *Nazi* was also used as early as 1903 with reference to the Nationalsozialen, a liberal political association founded in the 1890s, while the term *Nationalsozialist* was actually used as early as 1887 in a newspaper with the headline "Fürst Bismarck der erste Nationalsozialist" (Prince Bismarck, the First National-Socialist). However, the use of the term in the present sense, as a reference to the NSDAP, comes from 1923.

From 1930 onward, Nazi became a common nickname for the members of the NSDAP and was used in contrast with the term *Sozi* [pron. ZOH-tzee] for members of the Sozialdemokratische Partei of both Germany and Austria. Although the word *Nazi* was used by the National Socialists as a self-designation (Goebbels published a book in 1927 titled *Der Nazi-Sozi: Fragen und Antworten* [The Nazi-Sozi: Questions and Answers]), the term was later prohibited in official publications.

After the war the term *Nazi* became more common. The term *Naso* (pron. nah-zoh) for "National Socialist" was also common before the end of the war. Many have heard recordings of radio broadcasts by Churchill in which he regularly (intentionally?) mispronounces the word as "NAH-zee." The term *Nazi* gained ascendency in Allied usage following the lead of the anti-Nazi German American journalist Konrad Heiden, who was well aware of the negative connotations of the word in Bavarian-Austrian dialect well before the advent of the NSDAP.

A CHRONOLOGICAL ANNOTATED BIBLIOGRAPHY

Titles were selected for this annotated bibliography because they contain either the key concepts of the occult or a related idea in the title or overall conception of the book, or they contain major sections dealing with the topic of Nazi occultism.

1940. Lewis Spence, *The Occult Causes of the Present War.* London: Rider.

This book is discussed in some detail in chapter 10. It was really an instrument of British wartime propaganda, with the assignment to demonize the Germans (not merely the Nazi Party and Hitler, but the whole people). It was not a sincere effort, as Spence had had many prewar contacts with German occult orders (e.g., the Druidic Order). This book did set the stage for much of what would later appear in the post–*Morning of the Magicians* literature touching on themes of the Nazis and the occult. Interestingly, Spence did not emphasize paganism as much as he did Satanism—a connection that is extremely flimsy, as the actual evidence shows. However, if it is one's assignment to demonize a people, what better way to do so than state that they are a Satanic race? Spence seems to have used "Nazi thinking" in the effort to defeat Nazism.

1940. Hermann Rauschning. *The Voice of Destruction.* **New York: Putnam.**

> Rauschning's writings during the war had a marginal propagandistic value because they, like the words of *Mein Kampf* itself, went over the heads of the masses in America. However, for the postwar mythologizing of the Third Reich, his works were a goldmine. It took many years of research to show that Rauschning's more lurid accounts were likely fictional or merely contemporary rumors of one kind or another. It is conceivable that some of his words could have been ascribed to low-level Nazis with no connection to the official ideology. In any event, it is a key work to the understanding of the development of the Nazi occult mythology.

1958. Wilfried Daim, *Der Mann, der Hitler die Ideen gab.* **Munich: Isar.**

> This book is a serious work of scholarship and an excellent and well-documented introduction to the ideas of Lanz von Liebenfels. However, in the final analysis, the thesis that Hitler was somehow seriously influenced by the actual ideas of Liebenfels must be abandoned. This is simply because Lanz's ideas have too little in common with those of Hitler. Lanz was not a dedicated anti-Semite, and his tracts cannot be characterized as anti-Semitic (except insofar as the majority of Jews might happen to be brunettes). A cursory reading of Lanz's seminal work, *Theozoology,* will convince the reader objectively of these facts. Most of the similarities between Hitler's ideas and those held by Lanz can be accounted for in their common breeding ground in turn-of-the-century völkisch ideology and their common root in the Judeo-Christian myth of the Fall of Man and the advent of a Savior leading to the perfection of the world. Notes, bibliography.

1959. Dr. Johannes von Müllern-Schönhausen. *Die Lösung des Rätsels Adolf Hitler: Der Versuch einer Deutung der geheimnisvollsten Erscheinung der*

Weltgeschichte. Vienna: Verlag zur Förderung wissenschaftlicher Forschung.

The author emphasizes a legendary episode between Hitler and the hypnotist and showman Erik Jan Hanussen, in which Hanussen is said to have provided Hitler with a mandrake root (Ger. *Alraune*) that gave Hitler his uncanny power to succeed against all odds. This legend is partially a reflection of the popular cultural influence of a novel by Hanns Heinz Ewers entitled *Alraune* (1911). Müllern-Schönhausen's book is notable for being a pre–Pauwels/Bergier foray into Nazi occultism. The author is a well-known collector and forger of Nazi memorabilia. No notes, bibliography, or index.

1960. Louis Pauwels and Jacques Bergier, *The Morning of the Magicians.*

Originally this book was published in French in 1960 under the title *Le Matin des Magiciens* (Paris: Gallimard), and translated into English as *The Dawn of Magic* in England (1963) and *The Morning of the Magicians* for the American edition (1968). In many ways, this is the book that started the current and sustained industry of Nazi occultism in earnest. The book is not primarily about this topic, but contains a lengthy 100-page section titled "A Few Years in the Absolute Elsewhere," which speculates on all sorts of Nazi occult connections—especially with regard to alternative science, Hans Hörbiger, etc. It has been speculated that the ostensible purpose of the authors was to present a text that was the verbal equivalent of an acid trip, in the sense that it would open the readers' minds to radical alternative explanations of reality. This alternative history would then allow for the development of an alternative future. Pauwels was active in what became known as the "French New Right." No notes, bibliography, or index.

1967. Ellic Howe, *Astrology and the Third Reich*. Wellingborough: Aquarian.

Originally titled *Urania's Children* in England, this is a scholarly book on the history of the use of astrology by and within National Socialist Germany. The author is a leading academic expert in the field of secret societies and the occult. Admirably, the author surveys the history of astrology in Europe leading up to the time of the Third Reich. The second part of the book is mainly a study of the activities and role of the Swiss astrologer Karl Ernst Kraft in the Nazi culture of propaganda and astrology. The tone is objective and the book is well referenced with an extensive index. There is no bibliography.

1968. Wilhelm Wulff, *Zodiac and Swastika*. New York Coward, McCann & Geoghegan.

This book was first published in German under the title *Tierkreis und Hakenkreuz* in 1968. The American edition appeared in 1973. This is a memoir of the author, who was an astrologer associated with high-level officers of the SS, including Walter Schellenberg and Heinrich Himmler himself. No notes, bibliography, or sources.

1971. Jean-Michel Angebert [= Michel Bertrand and Jean-Victor Angelini], *The Occult and the Third Reich*. [English translation 1974.]

This is a translation of a 1971 French book. Taking the evidence for interest by the Nazis in the Holy Grail, this corporate author spins a yarn as inventive and fantastic as that of Stein-Ravenscroft. This time the Nazis are somehow identified as being heirs to the medieval heretical sect called the Cathars, who had a basically Manichean view of the world. The subject of the Cathars had been the obsession of the SS-man Otto Rahn, and it is this connection that allows for the interpretation to seem at all plausible. (Of course, Rahn was a peripheral and minor figure in the history of National Socialism, and one of Himmler's esoteric pets, much like Karl Maria Wiligut. However, in the case of Wiligut, actual lore and ritual was generated in the official sphere of SS ceremonies. Notes, bibliography, index.

1972. Anton Szandor LaVey, *The Satanic Rituals*. New York: Avon.

On pages 106–130 of this book there is a ritual called "Die elektrischen Vorspiele" (The Electrical Preludes). The introduction to this ritual reads in part: "When Die elektrischen Vorspiele was performed in Nazi Germany (circa 1932–35) by the intellectual element of the budding Sicherheitsdienst RFSS, the banners and symbols of the time were used as an integral part of the decor." Here LaVey is placing into a (fictionalized) secret Satanic ritual context what was actually taking place in the public arena using much more reliable— if, at the time, unconventional and even occult—means. However, LaVey's further legitimizing the mythic idea of Satanic Nazism historically certainly had a profound effect on the subsequent development of some Left-Hand Path adherents of a type of esoteric Nazism. In fact, the ritual in question was first written by LaVey in English and then "translated" (badly) "back" into German. Obviously, the tone is bombastic, and there are, of course, no references, notes or bibliography!

1973. Trevor Ravenscroft, *The Spear of Destiny*. New York: G. P. Putnam's Sons.

Ravenscroft's tour de force is perhaps the single greatest example of the semi-fictional genre of Nazi occultism. The author supposedly relied heavily on the theories and guidance of Walter Johannes Stein, and posits the theory that Hitler wanted to obtain and wield the spear of Longinus, which according to myth had pierced the side of Jesus as he was crucified. Almost everything about this book is a hoax or out-and-out disinformation. But because it spins a compelling yarn, à la the later *Da Vinci Code,* it was influential on a generation of amateur investigators of Nazi occultism and spawned a number of spinoffs. The style is erudite, but the tone is breathless, associative, and panicked. The book is unreferenced, of course, with a rudimentary bibliography and index.

1974. J. H. Brennan, *The Occult Reich*. New York: New American Library.

This is a mass-market paperback designed to capitalize on the occult Nazi craze of the early 1970s. Brennan's central interest seems to be the explanation of Hitler's power over the masses of the German people in terms of a theory somehow connected with the animal magnetism of Mesmer. Otherwise Brennan proceeds through the usual list of suspects, including Sebottendorf, Haushofer, and even Gurdjieff. Largely, this is a rehash of *The Morning of the Magicians*. The conflagration of Germany at the end of the war and the mass murder of the Jews is seen as a Satanic sacrifice. No notes, bibliography, or index.

1976. Francis King, *Satan and Swastika*. Frogmore, UK: Mayflower.

Sadly, this writer seems to have just jumped (or been pushed) onto the occult Nazi bandwagon in the wake of Ravenscroft's sensational success. The book is another rundown of the tried and true subjects and themes. Notably, the text became a conduit for the entry of the lore of Anton LaVey's Nazi ritual published in his *Satanic Rituals* (1972) into more general occult literature. King's book also contains two interesting background chapters on "The Nature of the Occult" and "Racist Elements in the Occult Revival." Unreferenced, with an index.

1976. James Webb, *The Occult Establishment*. La Salle, Ill.: Open Court.

This book is not entirely dedicated to the topic of the Nazis and the occult, but it contains an important chapter titled "The Magi of the North" (pp. 275–344), which discusses the topic of völkisch occultism and its connections with the Nazis, as well as the cosmological theories of Hörbiger and the economic ideas of Gottfried Feder. Webb's works are generally well above the average of studies of this subject matter. Underlying his presentation is a theory that the occult in general represents a flight from reason reflected in modernism and that occultism further expresses kinds of rejected knowledge in a given culture. Notes, bibliography, index.

1977. Dusty Sklar, *The Nazis and the Occult*. New York: Dorset.

This book was originally published under the title of *Gods and Beasts*. Ms. Sklar treats the usual group of suspected proto-Nazis, but to this list she also adds the name of the Swiss psychotherapist Carl Jung—a thread that would be further exploited on a higher scholarly level and for greater gain by Richard Noll. She seems to accept Rauschning's fabrications and the revelations of J. Stein to Trevor Ravenscroft as unquestionable facts. The final chapter, "The Dangers of Occult Thinking," reveals the apparent motive for writing the book: a warning to America about the dangers of the Rev. Sun Myung Moon's Unification Church and other supposed occultists. Basically unreferenced, but has a brief list of "Sources Quoted" and a "Selected Bibliography," as well as an index.

1977. Robert G. L. Waite. *The Psychopathic God: Adolf Hitler*. New York: New American Library.

It is, of course, a popular idea that Hitler must have been *insane*. This book proceeds from that assumption and explains in virtually Freudian terms, using material from his "family of origin," and so on, how this man could have become who he was. The book is well researched and if taken as a psychological profile is useful. However, the larger question of why all men with a similar set (or an even more extreme set) of personal stimuli do not, or cannot, become what Hitler was, remains eternally unanswered. Notes, indexed, but lacking a separate bibliography.

1981. Nigel Pennick, *Hitler's Secret Sciences: His Quest for the Hidden Knowledge of the Ancients*. Suffolk, UK: Neville Spearman.

Pennick, who is a well-respected expert on occult geomancy, has a good deal of interesting things to report about the supposed occult landscape of Germany as seen by the Nazis. The book contains the usual lineup of characters, often handled in a somewhat superficial way. There are also some noticeable misinterpretations of source material. For example, Lanz von Liebenfels in his *Theozoologie* is said to merge "Darwinist evolution with a divine origin of society as expounded in Norse mythology" (p. 25). This is what we perhaps expect given the abundance of propaganda in this direction, but in fact, as a reading of the text of *Theozoology* shows, Lanz's theories are hardly Darwinian and almost all of his discussions take place within the mythic framework of the Bible and Middle Eastern or Greek culture. The style is somewhat superficial, unreferenced, with a basic bibliography and no index.

1981. Gerald Suster, *Hitler and the Age of Horus* (later retitled as *Hitler: Black Magician*). London: Sphere, 1981. Published in the USA as *Hitler: The Occult Messiah,* 1981.

In the undisciplined mind of the 1960s and 1970s, it was enough to suggest that since Hitler lived in the early twentieth century, and so did Aleister Crowley, and both were candidates for being called the "most evil man in the world," there *must* be some connection, man! The deeper roots of the Crowley-Hitler linkage in the popular imagination certainly go back to the actual common denominator: Friedrich Nietzsche. Nietzsche had brought the human will to the forefront of thinking in the late nineteenth century, and the concept of the will was central to the philosophies of both Crowley and Hitler. Crowley had been a pro-German operative at the time of the First World War, which was due to his affected pro-Irish sympathies. He vigorously disavowed his work for the Germans toward the end of his life, due to the taint of the Nazi-German equation in the late 1940s. Notes, bibliography, index.

1985. Nicholas Goodrick-Clarke, *The Occult Roots of Nazism.* Wellingborough: Aquarian.

This is by far the best book of its kind. It is well researched and documented. Its contents are fundamental to the understanding of the völkisch movement. However, its theoretical foundations are skewed on two counts: (1) the author focuses entirely on just the *völkisch* element of Nazi *occultism* and ignores the other occult roots entirely; and (2) he views the revival of Germanic ideas as entirely reactionary, in what appears to be the Marxist sense. This theoretical foundation is more obvious in the author's 1981 Oxford dissertation titled *The Ariosophists of Austria and Germany 1890–1935: Reactionary Political Fantasy in Relation to Social Anxiety,* upon which the book is based. Occult volkism, such as that represented by Guido von List, is seen as a reaction to the German loss of the First World War, when, in fact, the movement was already strong well before the war started. In any event, this book is one that should be thoroughly studied by anyone who is interested in the topic at hand. Goodrick-Clarke does a great service by focusing on the idea of the mythology of Nazi occultism. His access to primary sources and archives is an essential component in the quality of his work. Heavily referenced, with extensive bibliography and index.

1985. E. R. Carmin, *"Guru" Hitler: Die Geburt des Nationalsozialismus aus dem Geiste von Mystik und Magie.* Zurich: SV International, 1985.

The pseudonymous Carmin is an author who is more interested in the workings of actual politics than the average writer on our topic. One of his main underlying interests seems to be the role of socialism in the story of National Socialism. In general, the book is a catalog of the usual suspects, with accounts such as that of Rauschning playing an important role, but often with his own story to tell about them, which is usually unsubstantiated by documentation. Bibliography and index.

1993. Joscelyn Godwin. *Arktos: The Polar Myth in Science, Symbolism and Nazi Survival.* Grand Rapids, Mich.: Phanes Press.

Godwin's fascinating and insightful book is not entirely focused on Nazi mythology but puts some of its contents into a larger perspective in connection with the idea of the Arctic pole. He discusses the Aryan myth, the legend of the Arctic homeland of the Aryans, the Thule Society, and the SS. The author's viewpoint remains objective and scholarly throughout. Although many of the same themes are covered as in other books, Godwin brings a new perspective and analytical lens to the table. The tone is scholarly but accessible, referenced, with an extensive bibliography, and indexed.

1994. E. R. Carmin. *Das schwarze Reich: Okkultismus und Politik im 20. Jahrhundert.* **[n.p.]: Tegtmeier.**

This is an expanded version of the 1985 work that was published in different formats. Carmin's identity remains unknown. This version contains an enormous amount of material on financial and governmental conspiracies, which does not always appear in all formats. Extensive notes, no bibliography or index.

1995. Ken Anderson. *Hitler and the Occult.* **Amherst, N.Y.: Prometheus.**

Anderson's book purports to be a rational investigation of claims of Nazi occultism; however, the author (or more probably, his editor) appears to be ambivalent toward a rational approach. Several occult myths, most prominently that of the "Spear of Destiny," are featured and doubted in many ways, but not dismissed as being irrelevant to the study of Hitler and his links to the occult. The author also erroneously seems to believe that Hitler was simply incapable of understanding occult ideas. The tone is journalistic and slightly sensationalistic, lightly referenced, no bibliography, basic index.

1995. Peter Levenda, *Unholy Alliance.* **New York: Avon.**

This book is filled with a wide range of fantasy content, which is expected in most books on the topic of Nazi occultism. In many ways it is reminiscent of the scope of Lewis Spence's wartime propaganda. Levenda generally follows the narrative formula used by Pauwels/Bergier and Ravenscroft in that he weaves historical fact with imagination in a measure that lends to the fantasy an air of reality, aided by the appearance of scholarly apparatus. Levenda is also a skillful storyteller and novelist, and a much better researcher than most in the field. The last fourth of the book is devoted to post-1945 Nazi occultists. I would characterize Levenda's effort as one of the best of the genre. Referenced, with bibliography and index.

2000. Alan Baker, *Invisible Eagle*. London: Virgin.

Baker's interests in Nazi occultism are decidedly weighted in the direction of pseudoscience. For example, chapter headings include "A Hideous Strength—The Vril Society (pseudophysics)," "Fantastic Prehistory—The Lost Aryan Homeland," "The Phantom Kingdom—The Nazi-Tibet Connection," and "The Secret at the Heart of the World—Nazi Cosmology and Belief in the Hollow Earth" (all having to do with alternative theories of geology and geography). The usual suspects are also discussed, and a chapter is devoted to the perennial "Spear of Destiny" myth. Additionally, and in keeping with the general pseudoscientific bent of the book, chapters are given over to the ideas of Nazi flying saucers and the fantastic ideas of Nazi survival. Baker does address the fact that there is a great deal of fantasy involved in the whole field of Nazi occultism in his final chapter, but does not treat this topic in any systematic way. Notes, bibliography, index.

2001. Hans Thomas Hakl, *Unknown Sources: National Socialism and the Occult*. Translated by Nicholas Goodrick-Clarke. Edmonds, Wash.: Holmes.

Hakl's brief cataloging of the personalities and organizations said to have had an occult influence on the origins and development of National Socialism is a sobering and valuable exercise. Hakl is a healthy skeptic when it comes to the whole question of Nazi occultism but does not discount the mythic and symbolic aspects of the movement. Perhaps the most important section of the book is that headed "Possible Sources of the Nazi Occult Mythology." Notes with bibliographic references.

2003. Christopher Hale, *Himmler's Crusade: The Nazi Expedition to Find the Origins of the Aryan Race.* Hoboken, N.J.: Wiley & Sons.

Although SS expeditions to Tibet to seek the secret source of the Aryan race appear to be a fantastical topic, Hale approaches the subject with a sober eye. The book is a down-to-earth history of the expeditions, the personalities involved, and the trials and tribulations of the journeys themselves. This is not an occult-type book at all. Notes, bibliography, index.

2007. Paul Roland. *The Nazis and the Occult: The Dark Forces Unleashed by the Third Reich.* Edison, N.J.: Chartwell.

This is a poorly documented but highly illustrated coffee table–type book generally dedicated to the sensationalistic presentation of the idea that dark forces were unleashed by the Nazis. On the surface, Roland covers most of the occult bases: the dark gurus who influenced Hitler (Wagner, Nietzsche, List, Liebenfels, Hörbiger, et al.) are all trotted out. The "Spear of Destiny" myth is given a full chapter. Hitler is discussed as a medium and a magician. Astrology is also given a full chapter, as is the idea of Nazi forms of occultism—some plausible (e.g., runes, the Grail) and others fairly spurious (e.g., the hollow earth and Vril power). The SS is discussed vaguely in terms of a "Black Knighthood" and finally there is a thin chapter on "Satan and the Swastika," which relies heavily on the wartime propaganda of Lewis Spence. The most disconcerting aspect of Roland's book is that it appears to be sensationalistic, but when he gets the chance he often debunks the very ideas he is trying to build up with the overall appearance of the book. Additionally, he just as often returns to the fantasy world himself in the text. It seems that Roland started out to write (probably on commission) a text to illustrate some dramatic photos and graphics but in the process learned that many of the works he was drawing from are often fantasies or hoaxes, such as the works of Rauschning (which he both exposes and quotes as a source at the same time). Unreferenced, with limited bibliography and index.

2017. Eric Kurlander. *Hitler's Monsters: A Supernatural History of the Third Reich.* **New Haven: Yale University Press.**

Kurlander makes use of an impressive array of source material. His overriding theme of tracing Nazi crimes back to the German obsession with horror, the uncanny, and monsters, especially during the Weimar Era, is intriguing and tempting (as well as fun) to believe. However, this theme also does border on the supernatural, as the title suggests, rather than being rooted in the historically verifiable facts of the National Socialist regime and its leaders. As a study of the relations of ideas such as those of Hanns Heinz Ewers to Nazism this book is an intriguing addition to the corpus. But Kurlander fails to take Reformbewegungen and their influences into account but seems to take such historically discredited sources such as Rauschning as reliable and credible. Kurlander's book has been harshly criticized by some German historians for its errors in translation and interpretation of source materials. Notes, bibliography, index.

REFERENCES

(See also A Chronological Annotated Bibliography)

Ach, Manfred, and Clemens Pentrop. 1977. *Hitlers "Religion": Pseudoreligiöse Elemente im nationalsozialistischen Sprachgebrauch.* Munich: Arbeitsgemeinschaft für Religions- und Weltanschauungsfragen.

Adelson, Howard. 1966. "The Holy Lance and the Heredity of the German Monarchy." *The Art Bulletin* 48: 177–91.

Anderson, Ken. 1995. *Hitler and the Occult.* Amherst, N.Y.: Prometheus.

Angebert, Jean-Michel. 1974. *The Occult and the Third Reich.* New York: McGraw-Hill. [Original French title: *Hitler et la tradition cathare.*]

Aquino, Michael A. 1989. *The Church of Satan.* Second edition. San Francisco: Temple of Set.

Bahn, Peter. 1996. "Das Geheimnis der Vril-Energie: Berichte und Erfahrungen zu einer mächtigen Naturkraft." In *Neue Horizonte in Technik und Bewusstsein,* edited by Adolf Schneider and Inge Schneider. Bern: Jupiter.

———. 2003–2004. "The Friedrich Hielscher Legend: The Founding of a Twentieth-Century Panentheistic 'Church' and Its Subsequent Misinterpretations." *Tyr* 2: 243–62.

———. 2004. *Friedrich Hielscher 1902–1990: Einführung in Leben und Werk.* Schnellbach: Bublies.

Baker, Alan. 2000. *The Invisible Eagle.* London: Virgin.

Balzli, Johannes. 1917. *Guido v. List: Der Wiederentdecker uralter Arischer Weisheit—Sein Leben und sein Schaffen.* Vienna: Guido-von-List–Gesellschaft.

Barger, Charles. 1998. *The SS Family: Procedure for Conducting Family Celebrations.* (Translation of Fritz Weitzl, *Die Gestaltung der Fest im Jahres- und Lebenslauf in der SS-Familie* [1939].) Surrey, UK: Ulric of England.

Bashford, Alison, and Philippa Levine, eds. 2012. *Oxford Handbook of the History of Eugenics.* Oxford: Oxford University Press.

Benz, Wolfgang, et al., eds. 1997. *Enzyklopädie des Nationalsoziialismus.* Munich: Deutsche Taschenbuch.

Bergen, Doris L. 1994. "Catholics, Protestants, and Christian Antisemitism in Nazi Germany." *Central European History* 27:3: 329–48.

———. 1996. *Twisted Cross: The German Christian Movement in the Third Reich.* Chapel Hill: University of North Carolina Press.

Bergmann, Ernst. 1934. *Die 25 Thesen der Deutschreligion: Ein Katechismus.* Second edition. Breslau: Hirt.

Bernard, Raymond. 1969. *The Hollow Earth: The Greatest Geographical Discovery in History.* New York: University Books.

Birken, Lawrence. 1995. *Hitler as Philosophe: Remnants of the Enlightenment in National Socialism.* Westport, Conn.: Praeger.

Blachetta, Walther. 1941. *Das Buch der deutschen Sinnzeichen.* Berlin-Lichterfelde: Widukind/Boss.

Blavatsky, Helene P. 1970 (1888). *The Secret Doctrine.* Pasadena, Calif.: Theosophical University Press.

Brackmann, Albert. 1943. "Zur Geschichte der heiligen Lanze Heinrichs I." *Deutsches Archiv für Geschichte des Mittelalters* 6: 401–411.

Bramwell, Anna. 1985. *Blood and Soil: Richard Walther Darré and Hitler's 'Green Party'.* Bourne End, UK: Kensal.

Brennan, J. H. 1974. *The Occult Reich.* New York: Signet.

Bronder, Dietrich. 1975. *Bevor Hitler kam: Eine historische Studie.* Second edition. Geneva: Marva.

Brüggemeier, Franz-Joseph, et al., eds. 2005. *How Green Were the Nazis? Nature, Environment, and Nation in the Third Reich.* Athens: Ohio University Press.

Buechner, Howard. 1991. *Emerald Cup—Ark of Gold: The Quest of SS Lt. Otto Rahn of the Third Reich.* Metairie, La.: Thunderbird.

Buechner, Howard, and Wilhelm Bernhart. 1989. *Adolf Hitler and the Secrets of the Holy Lance.* Revised edition. Metairie, La.: Thunderbird.

———. 1989. *Hitler's Ashes: Seeds of a New Reich.* Metairie, La.: Thunderbird.

Campbell, Bruce. 1980. *Ancient Wisdom Revived.* Berkeley: University of California Press.

Carlson, John Roy. 1943. *Under Cover: My Four Years in the Nazi Underworld of America—The Amazing Revelation of How Axis Agents and Our Enemies Within Are Now Plotting to Destroy the United States.* New York: Dutton.

Carmin, E. R. 1985. *"Guru" Hitler: Die Geburt des Nationalsozialismus aus dem Geiste von Mystik und Magie.* Zürich: SV International.

———. 1994. *Das schwarze Reich: Okkultismus und Politik im 20. Jahrhundert.* [N.p.]: Tegtmeier.

Chamberlain, Houston Stewart. 1899. *Die Grundlagen des Neunzehnten Jahrhunderts.* Third edition. 2 vols. Munich: Bruckmann.

———. 1907. *Richard Wagner.* 4th edition. Munich: Bruckmann.

Chiltoff, Dr. A. 1886. "Fernwirkung des Willens." *Die Sphinx* 1:3 (March): 211.

Cornwell, John. 2003. *Hitler's Scientists: Science, War, and the Devil's Pact.* New York: Penguin.

Cumbey, Constance. 1983. *The Hidden Dangers of the Rainbow: The New Age Movement and the Coming Age of Barbarism.* Shreveport, La.: Huntington House.

Cyranka, Daniel. 2016. "Religious Revolution and Spiritualism in Germany around 1848." *Aries* 16:1: 13–48.

Daim, Wilfried. 1958. *Der Mann, der Hitler die Ideen gab.* Munich: Isar.

Davies, Peter. 2007. "'Männerbund' and 'Mutterrecht': Herman Wirth, Sophie Rogge-Börner and the *Ura-Linda-Chronik.*" *German Life and Letters* 60:1 (January): 98–115.

Devi, Savitri [= Maximiani Julia Portas]. 1958. *The Lightning and the Sun.* Calcutta: Mukherjee.

Dierks, Margarete. 1986. *Jakob Wilhelm Hauer: Leben—Werk—Wirkung.* Heidelberg: Schneider.

Dow, James R., and Hannjost Lixfeld, eds. 1994. *The Nazification of an Academic Discipline: Folklore in the Third Reich.* Bloomington: University of Indiana Press.

Duncan, Kyle. 1978. *Black Camelot.* New York: St. Martin's.

Edwardes, Michael. 1977. *The Dark Side of History: Magic in the Making of Man.* New York: Stein and Day.

Eliade, Mircea. 1963. *Myth and Reality.* Translated by Willard R. Trask. New York: Harper and Row.

Fabricius, D. Cajus. 1937. *Positive Christianity in the Third Reich.* Dresden: Püschel.

Fahrenkrog, Ludwig, ed. 1923. Das Deutsche Buch. Third revised and expanded edition. Leipzig: Hartung.

Faivre, Antoine. 1994. *Access to Western Esotericism.* New York: State University of New York.

Farin, Michael, ed. 2003. *Phantom Schmerz: Quellentexte zur Begriffsgeschichte des Masochismus.* Munich: Belleville/Neue Gallerie Graz.

Farrell, Joseph P. 2004. *Reich of the Black Sun: Nazi Secret Weapons and the Cold War Allied Legend.* Kempton, Ill.: Adventures Unlimited.

———. 2006. *The SS Brotherhood of the Bell: The Nazis' Incredible Secret Technology.* Kempton, Ill.: Adventures Unlimited.

Feldman, Burton, and Robert D. Richardson Jr. 1972. *The Raise of Modern Mythology 1680–1860.* Bloomington: University of Indiana Press.

Ferdinand, Maximilian. 1897. *D.I.S. Die arische "Sexual-Religion" als Volks-Veredelung in Zeugen, Leben und Sterben.* Leipzig: Friedrich.

Flowers, Stephen E. 2022. *Dancing with the Demon: The Magical and Erotic World of Dr. Ernst Schertel, the Philosopher King of Weimar.* [Includes a new translation of Schertel's *Magie.*] North Augusta, S.C.: Arcana Europa.

———. 2018. *The Fraternitas Saturni: History, Doctrine, and Rituals of the Magical Order of the Brotherhood of Saturn.* Rochester, Vt.: Inner Traditions.

———. 2012. *Lords of the Left-Hand Path: Forbidden Practices and Spiritual Heresies from the Cult of Set to the Church of Satan.* Rochester, Vt.: Inner Traditions.

———. 2022. *The Occult Roots of Bolshevism: From Cosmist Philosophy to Magical Marxism.* Bastrop, Tex.: Lodestar.

———. 2021. *The Revival of the Runes: The Modern Rediscovery and Reinvention of the Germanic Runes.* Rochester, Vt.: Inner Traditions.

———. 2022. *Runes and Runology.* Bastrop, Tex.: Lodestar.

Flowers, Stephen E. and Michael Moynihan, eds. and trans. 2007. *The Secret King: The Myth and Reality of Nazi Occultism.* Los Angeles and Waterbury Center, Vt.: Feral House/Dominion.

Foitzik, Doris. 1997. *Rote Sterne, braune Runen: Politische Weihnachten zwischen 1870 und 1970.* Münster: Waxmann.

Friedrich, Christof. 1976. *Secret Nazi Polar Expeditions.* Toronto: Samisdat.

Frischauer, Willi. 1962. *Himmler: The Evil Genius of the Third Reich.* New York: Belmont.

Fritsch, Theodor. 1933. *Handbuch der Judenfrage.* 34th edition. Leipzig: Hammer.

Gardell, Matthias. 2003. *The Gods of the Blood: The Pagan Revival and White Separatism.* Durham, N.C.: Duke University Press.

Gasman, Daniel. 1998. *Haeckel's Monism and the Birth of Fascist Ideology.* New York: Lang.

———. 1971. *The Scientific Origins of National Socialism: Social Darwinism in Ernst Haeckel and the German Monist League*. New York: American Elsevier.

Gay, Peter. 1968. *Weimar Culture: The Outsider as Insider*. New York: Harper.

Gilbhard, Hermann. 1994. *Die Thule-Gesellschaft: Vom okkulten Mummenschanz zum Hakenkreuz*. Munich: Kiessling.

Glaser, Hermann. 1978. *The Cultural Roots of National Socialism*. Translated by E. A. Menze. Austin: University of Texas Press.

Glowka, Hans-Jürgen. 1981. *Deutsche Okkultgruppen 1875–1937*. Munich: Arbeitsgemeinschaft für Religions- und Weltanschauungsfragen.

Godwin, Joscelyn. 1993. *Arktos: The Polar Myth in Science, Symbolism and Nazi Survival*. Grand Rapids, Mich.: Phanes.

Goebbels, Joseph. 1987. *Michael: A Novel*. Translated by Joachim Neugroschel. New York: Amok.

Goodrick-Clarke, Nicholas. 2002. *Black Sun: Aryan Cults, Esoteric Nazism, and the Politics of Identity*. New York: New York University Press.

———. 2004. *Helena Blavatsky*. Berkeley, Calif.: North Atlantic.

———. 1998. *Hitler's Priestess: Savitri Devi, the Hindu-Aryan Myth, and Neo-Nazism*. New York: New York University Press.

———. 1985. *The Occult Roots of Nazism: The Ariosophists of Austria and Germany 1890–1935*. Wellingborough, UK: Aquarian.

Gordon, Mel. 2001. *Erik Jan Hanussen: Hitler's Jewish Clairvoyant*. Los Angeles: Feral House.

———. 2006. *Voluptuous Panic: The Erotic World of Weimar Berlin*. Second edition. Los Angeles: Feral House.

Gottlieb, Craig. *The SS Totenkopf Ring*. Atglen: Schiffer, 2008.

Gregorius, Gregor A. 1958. "Die Geheimlehre des Adonis-Kultes." *Blätter für angewandte okkulte Lebenskunst* 95 (February): 1–12.

Grimm, Jacob. 1966 (1882–1888). *Teutonic Mythology*. Translated by James S. Stallybrass. Fourth edition. 4 vols. New York: Dover.

Grimm, Jacob, and Wilhelm Grimm. 1994. *Deutsche Sagen*. Frankfurt: Deutscher Klassiker Verlag.

Grisko, Michael, ed. 1999. *Freikörperkultur und Lebenswelt: Studien zur Vor- und Frühgeschichte der Freikörperkultur in Deutschland*. Kassel: Kassel University Press.

Haeckel, Ernst. 1914. *Gott-Natur (Theophysis) Studien über monistische Religion*. Leipzig: Kröner.

———. 1992 (1900). *The Riddle of the Universe*. Buffalo, N.Y.: Prometheus.

Haehl, Richard. 1922. *Samuel Hahnemann: His Life and Work*. London: Homeopathic Publishing.

Hakl, Hans Thomas. 2000. *Unknown Sources: National Socialism and the Occult*. Edmonds, Wash.: Holmes.

Hale, Christopher. 2003. *Himmler's Crusade: The Nazi Expedition to Find the Origins of the Aryan Race*. Hoboken: Wiley & Sons.

Hau, Michael. 2003. *The Cult of Health and Beauty in Germany: A Social History 1890–1930*. Chicago: University of Chicago Press.

Hein, Bastian. 2015. *Die SS: Geschichte und Verbrechen*. Munich: Beck.

Heller, Friedrich Paul, and Anton Maegerle. 1998. *Thule: Vom völkischen Okkultismus bis zur Neuen Rechten*. Second edition. Stuttgart: Schmetterling.

Hemberger, Adolf. 1971. *Organisationsformen, Rituale, Lehren, und magische Thematik der freimauerischen und freimauerartigen Bünde im deutschen Sprachraum Mitteleuropas. Teil 1. Der mystisch-magische Orden Fraternitas Saturni*. Frankfurt/Main: Hemberger.

Hermand, Jost. 1969. *Von Mainz nach Weimar (1793–1919): Studien zur deutschen Literatur*. Stuttgart: Metzler.

———. 1971. "The Distorted Vision: Pre-Fascist Mythology at the Turn of the Century." Translated by H. G. Huettich and G. Mason. In *Myth and Reason: A Symposium,* edited by Walter D. Wetzels. Austin: University of Texas Press, 101–26.

———. 1992. *Old Dreams of a New Reich: Volkish Utopias and National Socialism*. Translated by Paul Levesque and Stefan Soldovieri. Bloomington: Indiana University Press.

Herzl, Theodor. 1904. *A Jewish State: An Attempt at a Modern Solution of the Jewish Question*. Translated by Sylvie D'Avigdor; revised by J. De Haas. New York: Maccabæan.

Hielscher, Friedrich. 2015 (1930). *The Real Powers*. Translated with an Afterword by Michael Moynihan. Waterbury Center, Vt.: Dominion.

Himmler, Heinrich. 1937. *Die Schutzstaffel als antibolschewistische Kampforganisation*. Third edition. Munich: Zentralverlag der NSDAP.

Hinz, Berthold. 1979. *Art in the Third Reich*. Translated by R. and R. Kimber. New York: Pantheon.

Hitler, Adolf. 1971. *Mein Kampf.* Translated by Ralph Manheim, with an Introduction by Konrad Heiden. Boston: Houghton Mifflin.

Horowitz, Mitch. 2010. *Occult America*. New York: Bantam.

Howe, Ellic. 1984. *Astrology and the Third Reich*. Wellingborough, UK: Aquarian.

———. 1970. "Germanen Order." In Richard Cavendish, ed. *Man, Myth and Magic*. London: BPC Publishing, vol 6, 1081–1082.

———. 1978. *The Magicians of the Golden Dawn: A Documentary History of a Magical Order 1887–1923*. York Beach, Me.: Weiser.

Howe, Ellic, and Helmut Mölller. 1978. "Theodor Reuss: Winkelmauerei in Deutschland 1900–1923." *Quatuor Coronati* 15 : 28–47.

Hunger, Ulrich. 1984. *Die Runenkunde im Dritten Reich*. Frankfurt: Lang.

Hüser, Karl. 1982. *Wewelsburg 1933–1945: Kult und Terrorstätte der SS*. Paderborn: Bonifatius.

Infield, Glenn B. 1979. *Hitler's Secret Life: The Mysteries of the Eagle's Nest*. New York: Stein and Day.

Isenberg, Nancy. 2016. *White Trash*. New York: Viking.

Jahn, Friedrich Ludwig. 1810. *Deutsches Volkstum*. Frankfurt am Main: Naumann.

Jones, J. Sidney. 1983. *Hitler in Vienna 1907–1913*. New York: Stein and Day.

Kater, Michael. 1974. *Das "Ahnenerbe" der SS 1935–1945: Ein Beitrag zur Kulturpolitik des Dritten Reiches*. Stuttgart: Deutsche Verlags Anstalt.

———. 1971. "Die Artamanen—Völkische Jugend in der Weimarer Republik." *Historische Zeitschrift* 213: 577–638.

Kennedy, Gordon. 1998. *Children of the Sun: A Pictorial Anthology from Germany to California 1883–1949*. Ojai, Calif.: Nivaria.

Kerbs, Diethart, and Jürgen Reulecke, eds. 1998. *Handbuch der deutschen Reformbewegungen*. Wuppertal: Hammer.

Kertzer, David I. 2001. *The Popes Against the Jews: The Vatican's Role in the Rise of Modern Anti-Semitism*. New York: Knopf.

King, Francis. 1976. *Satan and Swastika: The Occult and the Nazi Party*. Frogmore, UK: Mayflower.

Kiss, Edmund. 1930. *Das gläserne Meer*. Leipzig: Hase & Koehler.

———. 1933. *Welt-Eis-Lehre*. Leipzig: Koehler & Amelang.

Kohn, Hans. 1960. *The Mind of Germany: The Education of a Nation*. New York: Harper and Row.

Krzesinski, Andrew J. 1945. *Religion of Nazi Germany*. Boston: Humphries.

Kubizek, August. 2006. *The Young Hitler I Knew*. Translated by G. Brooks. London: Greenhill.

Kugel, Wilfried. 1998. *Hanussen: Die wahre Geschichte des Hermann Steinschneider*. Düsseldorf: Grupello.

Kummer, Siegfried Adolf. 1932. *Heilige Runenmacht*. Hamburg: Uranus.

———. 1993. *Rune-Magic*. Translated by Stephen E. Flowers. Smithville, Tex.: Rûna-Raven.

———. 1933–1934. *Runen-Magie*. Dresden: Gartmann.

———. 1934. *Runen-Raunen: Eine Sammlung eingesandter Berichte nach den Runenkunden von S. A. Kummer*. Dresden: Self-published.

———. 1934. *Walhall: Hand- und Bilderschrift für Runenkunde, Mystik und Vorgeschichte. Briefe an Runenfreunde zum persönlichen Gebrauch*. Dresden: Self-published.

Kurlander, Eric. 2017. *Hitler's Monsters: A Supernatural History of the Third Reich*. New Haven: Yale University Press.

Kurtzahn, E. Tristan. 1924. *Die Runen als Heilszeichen und Schicksalslose*. Bad Oldesloe: Uranus.

Ladislao, Szabó. 1947. *Hitler está vivo*. Buenos Aires: El Tábano.

Landig, Wilhelm. 1981. *Götzen gegen Thule*. Hannover: Pfeiffer.

———. 1991. *Rebellen für Thule—Das Erbe von Atlantis*. Vienna: Volkstum.

———. 1971. *Wolfszeit um Thule*. Vienna: Volkstum.

Lane, Barbara Miller, and Leila J. Rupp. 1978. *Nazi Ideology before 1933*. Austin: University of Texas Press.

Lang, Johannes. 1938. *Hohlwelttheorie*. Second edition. Frankfurt/Main: Schirmer & Mahlau.

Lange, Hans-Jürgen, ed. 1995. *Otto Rahn: Leben und Werk*. [Includes the texts of both *Kreuzzug gegen den Gral* and *Luzifers Hofgesind*.] Engerda: Arun.

———. 1998. *Weisthor: Karl Maria Wiligut, Himmlers Rasputin und seine Erben*. Engerda: Arun.

Langer, Walter C. 1972. *The Mind of Adolf Hitler: The Secret Wartime Report*. New York: New American Library.

Lanz von Liebenfels, Jörg. 1905. *Theozoologie oder Die Kunde von den Sodoms-Äfflingen und dem Götter-Elektron: Eine Einführung in die älteste und neueste Weltanschauung und eine Rechtfertigung des Fürstentums und des Adels*. Vienna: Moderner Verlag.

LaVey, Anton Szandor. 1969. *The Satanic Bible*. New York: Avon.

———. 1972. *The Satanic Rituals*. New York: Avon.

Lawrie, Charles. 1990. "'Doctor Stone': Walter Stein and the Holy Grail." In

The Household of the Grail, edited by John Matthews. Wellingborough, UK: Aquarian, 120–36.

Lechler, Jörg. 1934. *Vom Hakenkreuz: Die Geschichte eines Symbols.* Leipzig: Kabitzsch.

Lehner, Kurt M. 2015. *Friedrich Hielscher: Nationalrevolutionär, Widerständler, Heidenpriester.* Paderborn: Schöningh.

Lenthe, Eckehard. 2018. *Wotan's Awakening: The Life and Times of Guido von List 1848–1919.* Translated by Annabel Moynihan; edited by Michael Moynihan. Waterbury Center, Vt.: Dominion.

Lenz, Fritz. 1941. "Über Wege und Irrwege rassenkundlicher Untersuchungen." *Zeitschrift für Morphologie und Anthropologie* 39:3: 385–413.

Leschnitzer, Adolf. 1956. *The Magic Background of Modern Anti-Semitism: An Analysis of the German-Jewish Relationship.* New York: International Universities Press.

Levenda, Peter. 1995. *Unholy Alliance.* New York: Avon.

Ley, Robert, ed. 1937. *Organisationsbuch der NSDAP.* Third edition. Munich: Zentralverlag der NSDAP.

Ley, Willy. 1947. "Pseudoscience in Naziland." *Astounding Science Fiction,* vol. 39, no. 3 (May): 90–98.

Linse, Ulrich. 1996. *Geisterseher und Wunderwirker: Heilssuche im Industriezeitalter.* Frankfurt am Main: Fischer.

List, Guido von. 1910. *Die Bilderschrift der Ario-Germanen.* Guido-von-List-Bücherei 5. Vienna: Guido-von-List-Gesellschaft.

———. 1891. *Deutsch-mythologische Landschaftsbilder.* 2 vols. Berlin: Lustenoder.

———. 1908. *Das Geheimnis der Runen.* Guido-von-List Bücherei 1. Gross-Lichterfelde: Zillmann.

———. 1996. *The Invincible: An Outline of Germanic Philosophy.* Translated and edited by Edred Thorsson. Smithville, Tex.: Rûna-Raven.

———. 2014. *The Religion of the Aryo-Germanic Folk.* Translated by Stephen E. Flowers. Smithville, Tex.: Lodestar.

———. 1988. *The Secret of the Runes.* Translated by Stephen E. Flowers. Rochester, Vt.: Destiny.

———. 1911. *Der Übergang von Wuotanismus zum Christentum.* Berlin-Lichterfelde: Guido-von-List-Verlag.

———. 1914. *Die Ursprache der Ario-Germanen und ihre Mysteriensprache.* Guido-von-List-Bücherei 6. Vienna: Guido-von-List-Gesellschaft.

Lixfeld, Hannjost, ed. 1994. *Folklore and Fascism: The Reich Institute for German Volkskunde*. Bloomington: University of Indiana Press.

Lorenz, Horst, ed. 2004. *Rosen aus Germaniens Bergen: Eine Denkschrift zum 50. Todestag des Begründers des Neutemplerordens Jörg Lanz von Liebenfels*. Ilvesheim: Weltswende.

Lost, Frank. 2013. *Nazi Secrets: An Occult Breach in the Fabric of History*. [N.p.]: Lost.

Lother, Helmut. 1934. *Neugermanische Religion und Christentum: Eine kirchengeschichtliche Vorlesung*. Gütersloh: Bartelsmann.

Ludendorff, Mathilde. 1975. *Ist Gotterkenntnis möglich?* Pähl: Weltanschauungsgemeinschaft Gotterkenntnis Mathilde Ludendorff.

Mackinder, Halford J. 1996. *Democratic Ideals and Reality: A Study in the Politics of Reconstruction*. Washington, D.C.: National Defense University Press.

Maclellen, Alec. 1988. *The Secret of the Spear: The Mystery of the Spear of Longinus*. London: Souvenir.

Marby, Friedrich Bernhard. 1932. *Marby-Runen-Gymnastik*. Marby-Runen-Bücherei 3/4. Stuttgart: Marby.

———. 1935. *Rassische Gymnastik als Aufrassungsweg*. Marby-Runen-Bücherei 5/6. Stuttgart: Marby.

———. 1935. *Die Rosengärten und das ewige Land der Rasse*. Marby-Runen-Bücherei 7/8. Stuttgart: Marby.

———. 1931. *Runenschrift, Runenwort, Runengymnastik*. Marby-Runen-Bücherei 1/2. Stuttgart: Marby.

Mees, Bernard. 2008. *The Science of the Swastika*. Budapest: Central European University Press.

Michell, John. 1977. *Secrets of the Stones: The Story of Astro-Archaeology*. Harmondsworth, UK: Penguin

Moon, Peter. 1997. *The Black Sun: Montauk's Nazi-Tibetan Connection*. New York: Sky.

Mosse, George L. 1981. *The Crisis of German Ideology: Intellectual Origins of the Third Reich*. New York: Schocken.

———. 1961. "The Mystical Origins of National Socialism." *Journal of the History of Ideas* 22: 81–96.

———. 1975. *The Nationalization of the Masses: Political Symbolism and Mass Movements in Germany from the Napoleonic Wars through the Third Reich*. New York: New American Library.

———. 1981. *Nazi Culture*. New York: Schocken.

Mund, Rudolf. 1976. *J. Jörg Lanz v. Liebenfels und der Neue Templer Orden: Die Esoterik des Christentums*. Stuttgart: Spieth.

———. 1982. *Der Rasputin Himmlers: Die Wiligut-Saga*. Vienna: Volkstum.

Müllern-Schönhausen, Dr. Johannes von. 1959. *Die Lösung des Rätsels Adolf Hitler: Der Versuch einer Deutung der geheimnisvollsten Erscheinung der Weltgeschichte*. Vienna: Verlag zur Förderung wissenschaftlicher Forschung.

Nanko, Ulrich. 1993. *Die Deutsche Glabuensbewegung: Eine historische und soziologische Untersuchung*. Marburg: Diagonal.

Noll, Richard. 1997. *The Aryan Christ: The Secret Life of Carl Jung*. New York: Random House.

———. 1994. *The Jung Cult: Origins of a Charismatic Movement*. Princeton: Princeton University Press.

Nolte, Ernest. 1965. *Three Faces of Fascism: Action Française, Italian Fascism, National Socialism*. Translated by Leila Vennewitz. New York: Mentor.

Nostradamus. 2013. *The Prophecies*. Translated and edited by Richard Sieburth and Stéphane Gerson. New York: Penguin.

Nova, Fritz. 1986. *Alfred Rosenberg: Philosopher of the Third Reich*. New York: Hippocrene.

Ohler, Norman. 2017. *Blitzed: Drugs in Nazi Germany*. New York: Penguin.

Overy, Richard. 2009. *The Bombing War: Europe 1939–1945*. London: Allen Lane.

Padfield, Peter. 1990. *Himmler*. New York: MJF.

Patterson, William Patrick. 2008. *The Life and Teaching of Carlos Castaneda*. Fairfax: Arete.

———. 2000. *Voices in the Dark: Esoteric, Occult & Secular Voices in Nazi-Occupied Paris 1940–44*. Fairfax: Arete.

Paulsen, Peter. 1969. "Flügellanzen: Zum archälogischen Horizont der Wiener 'sancta lancea.'" *Frühmittelalterlichen Studien* 3: 289–312.

Pauwels, Louis. 1971. *Gurdjieff*. New York: Weiser.

Pauwels, Louis, and Jacques Bergier. 1972. *The Eternal Man*. Translated by Michael Heron. New York: Avon.

———. 1968. *The Morning of the Magicians*. New York: Avon. [Original French title: *Le Matin des Magiciens*. Published in England as *The Dawn of Magic*.]

Pennick, Nigel. 1981. *Hitler's Secret Sciences: His Quest for the Hidden Knowledge of the Ancients*. Suffolk, UK: Spearman.

Phelps, Reginald H. 1968. "'Before Hitler Came': Thule Society and Germanen Orden." *Journal of Modern History* 35: 245–61.

Poewe, Karla. 2006. *New Religions and the Nazis*. London: Routledge.

Poliakov, Leon. 1974. *The Aryan Myth: A History of Racist and Nationalist Ideas in Europe*. New York: New American Library.

Pontolillo, James. 2013. *The Black Sun Unveiled*. Kingsport: Morryster and Sons.

Pringle, Heather. 2006. *The Master Plan: Himmler's Scholars and the Holocaust*. New York: Hyperion.

Puschner, Uwe, and Clemens Vollnals, eds. 2012. *Die völkisch-religiöse Bewegung im Nationalsozialismus: Eine Beziehungs- und Konfliktgeschichte*. Göttingen: Vandenhoeck & Ruprecht.

Quinn, Malcolm. 1994. *The Swastika: Constructing the Symbol*. London: Routledge.

Rahn, Otto. 2006. *Crusade Against the Grail: The Struggle between the Cathars, the Templars, and the Church of Rome*. Translated and annotated by Christopher Jones. Rochester, Vt.: Inner Traditions.

———. 1995. *Leben & Werk: Kreuzzug gegen den Gral & Luzifers Hofgesind*. Edited by Hans-Jürgen Lange. Engerda: Arun.

———. 2008. *Lucifer's Court: A Heretic's Journey in Search of the Light Bringers*. Translated and annotated by Christopher Jones. Rochester, Vt.: Inner Traditions.

Rauschning, Hermann. 1939. *The Revolution of Nihilism: Warning to the West*. Translated by E. W. Dickes. New York: Longmans, Green & Co.

———. 1940. *The Voice of Destruction*. New York: G. P. Putnam's Sons.

Ravenscroft, Trevor. 1973. *The Spear of Destiny*. New York: G. P. Putnam's Sons.

Ravenscroft, Trevor, and T. Wallace Murphy. 1992. *The Mark of the Beast*. New York: Citadel.

Redbeard, Ragnar [Arthur Desmond]. 2019. *Might is Right: The Authoritative Edition*. Edited by Trevor Blake; introduction by Peter H. Gilmore. Baltimore, Md.: Underworld Amusements.

Reichenbach, Karl von. 1968. *The Odic Force: Letters on Od and Magnetism*. Translated by F. D. O'Byrne. Secaucus, N.J.: University.

Reinhardt, Kurt F. 1961. *Germany: 2000 Years*. Second edition. 2 vols. New York: Unger.

Reuter, Otto Sigfrid. 1934. *Germanische Himmelskunde: Untersuchungen zur Geschichte des Geistes*. Munich: Lehmann.

———. 2009. *Der Himmel über den Germanen*. Munich: Zentral Verlag der NSDAP, n.d.

Richards, Robert J. "Myth 19: That Darwin and Haeckel Were Complicit in Nazi Biology." In *Galileo Goes to Jail and Other Myths About Science and Religion*, edited by Ronald Numbers. Cambridge: Harvard University Press, 170–77.

Roland, Paul. 2007. *The Nazis and the Occult: The Dark Forces Unleashed by the Third Reich*. Edison, N.J.: Chartwell.

Rose, Detlev. 1994. *Die Thule-Gesellschaft: Legende und Wirklichkeit*. Tübingen: Graebert.

Rosenberg, Alfred. 1982. *The Myth of the Twentieth Century*. Translated by Vivian Bird. Torrance, Calif.: Noontide.

Rosenthal, Bernice Glatzer, ed. 1997. *The Occult in Russian and Soviet Culture*. Ithaca, N.Y.: Cornell University Press.

Rüsten, Rudolf. 1914. *Was tut not? Ein Führer durch die gesamte Literatur der Deutschbewegung*. Leipzig: Hedeler.

Ryback, Timothy W. 2008. *Hitler's Private Library*. New York: Knopf.

Scheible, Johann, ed. 1845–1849. *Das Kloster*. 12 vols. Stuttgart: Scheible.

Schertel, Ernst. 1978 (1923). *Magie: Geschichte, Theorie, Praxis*. Berlin: Schikowski.

———. 2009. *Magic: History—Theory—Practice*. Translated by Cotum Research. Boise: Cotum.

Schlund, Erhard P. 1981 (1924, 2nd ed.). *Neugermanisches Heidentum im heutigen Deutschland*. Munich: Arbeitsgemeinschaft für Religions- und Weltanschauungsfragen.

Schmidt, Ina, and Stefan Breuer, eds. 2005. *Ernst Jünger–Friedrich Hielscher Briefwechsel*. Stuttgart: Klett-Cotta.

Schwarzwäller, Wulf. 1990. *The Unknown Hitler: Behind the Image of History's Darkest Name*. Translated by Aurelius von Kappau. New York: Berkley.

Sebottendorf, Rudolf von. 1933. *Bevor Hitler kam: Urkundliches aus der Frühzeit der nationalsozialistischen Bewegung*. Munich: Deukula.

———. 2013. *Secret Practices of the Sufi Freemasons*. Translated, edited, and introduced by Stephen E. Flowers. Rochester, Vt.: Inner Traditions.

Serrano, Miguel. 1984. *Adolf Hitler, el Último Avatára*. Bogota: Editorial Solar.

Shore, Bradd. 1996. *Culture in Mind*. Oxford: Oxford University Press.

Simons, Graham M. 2016. *Operation Lusty: The Race for Hitler's Secret Technology*. Barnsley, UK: Pen and Sword.

Sklar, Dusty. 1977. *The Nazis and the Occult*. New York: Dorset.

Smith, Morton. 1978. *Jesus the Magician*. New York: Harper and Row.

Speer, Albert. 1970. *Inside the Third Reich: Memoirs*. New York: Simon & Schuster.

Spence, Lewis. 1940. *The Occult Causes of the Present War*. London: Rider.

Spotts, Frederic. 2009. *Hitler and the Power of Aesthetics*. Woodstock, N.Y.: Overlook.

Stackelberg, Roderick. 1981. *Idealism Debased: From Völkisch Ideology to National Socialism*. Kent: Kent University Press.

Steigmann-Gall, Richard. 2003. *The Holy Reich: Nazi Conceptions of Christianity, 1919–1945*. Cambridge: Cambridge University Press.

Stein, Walter J. 1990 (1958). *The British: Their Psychology and Destiny*. London: Temple Lodge.

Steiner, Rudolf. 1915. *The Occult Movement in the Nineteenth Century and Its Relation to Modern Culture*. London: Steiner.

Stevens, Henry. 2007. *Hitler's Suppressed and Still-Secret Weapons, Science and Technology*. Kempton, Ill.: Adventures Unlimited.

Stranges, Frank E. 1982. *Nazi UFO Secrets and Bases Exposed*. Van Nuys, Calif.: I.E.C.

Strube, Julian. 2012. "Die Erfindung des esoterischen Nationalsozialismus im Zeichen der Schwarzen Sonne." *Zeitschrift für Religionswissenschaft* 20:2: 223–68.

Sünner, Rüdiger. 1999. *Schwarze Sonne: Entfesselung und Mißbrauch der Mythen in Nationalsozialismus und rechter Esoterik*. Freiburg: Herder.

Suster, Gerald. 1981. *Hitler: The Occult Messiah*. New York: St. Martin's. [Later republished as *Hitler: Black Magician*.]

Sweet, Henry. 1911. "Grimm, Jacob Ludwig Carl." *Encyclopædia Brittanica*. Eleventh edition. 29 vols. Cambridge: Cambridge University Press, Vol. 12, pp. 600–602.

Tacitus, Cornelius. 1975. *The Histories*. Translated by Kenneth Wellesley. Harmondsworth, UK: Penguin.

Thomas, Donald E. 1971. "Esoteric Religion and Racism in the Thought of Houston Chamberlain." *Journal of Popular Culture* 5:3 (Winter): 69–81.

Thorsson, Edred. 2018. *Rune Might: Secret Practices of the German Rune Magicians*. Third revised and expanded edition. Rochester, Vt.: Inner Traditions.

Toepfer, Karl. 1997. *Empire of Ecstasy: Nudity and Movement in German Body Culture 1910–1935.* Berkeley: University of California Press.

Treitel, Corinna. 2004. *A Science for the Soul: Occultism and the Genesis of the German Modern.* Baltimore: Johns Hopkins University Press.

Trevor-Roper, Hugh, ed. 2000. *Hitler's Table Talk 1941–1944.* Translated by Norman Cameron and R. H. Stevens. New York: Enigma.

Viereck, Peter. 1961. *Metapolitics: The Roots of the Nazi Mind.* Second edition. New York: Capricorn.

Vondung, Klaus. 1971. *Magie und Manipulation: Ideologischer Kult und politische Religion des Nationalsozialismus.* Göttingen: Vandenhoeck & Ruprecht.

Vries, Jan de. 1942. "Rood–Wit–Zwart." *Volkskunde* 43: 53–62.

Waite, Robert G. L. 1977. *The Psychopathic God: Adolf Hitler.* New York: New American Library.

Walsh, Edmund A. 1946. "The Mystery of Haushofer." *Life* (September 16): 107–20.

Webb, James. 1980. *The Harmonious Circle.* New York: Putnam.

———. 1976. *The Occult Establishment.* La Salle, Ill.: Open Court.

Wedemeyer-Kolwe, Bernd. 2009. "Runengymnastik: Von völkischer Körperkultur zu alternativen Selbsterfahrungspraktik." In *Völkisch und National: Zur Aktualität alter Denkmuster im 21. Jahrhundert,* edited by G. Ulrich Grossmann and Uwe Puschner. Darmstadt: Wissenschaftliche Buchgesellschaft, 329–40.

Weigel, Karl Theodor. 1943. *Beiträge zur Sinnbildforschung.* Berlin: Metzner.

———. 1937. Weigel, Karl Theodor. *Runen und Sinnbilder.* Berlin: Metzner.

———. 1936. "Unsere Stellung zu den Runen." *SS-Leitheft* 2: 56–58.

Wiedemann, Felix. 2012. "'Altes Wissen' oder 'Fremdkörper im deutschen Volksglauben'?: Hexendeutungen im Nationalsozialismus zwischen Neuheidentum, Antiklerikalismus und Antisemitismus." In *Die völkisch-religiöse Bewegung im Nationalsozialismus,* edited by Uwe Puschner and Clemens Vollnals. Göttingen: Vandenhoeck & Ruprecht, 437–58.

Wilson, Thomas. 1894. *Swastika: The Earliest Known Symbol and its Migrations.* Washington, D.C.: Smithsonian.

Wirth, Herman. 1928. *Der Aufgang der Menschheit.* Jena: Diederichs.

———. 1931–1936. *Die heilige Urschrift der Menschheit: Symbolgeschichtliche Untersuchungen diesseits und jenseits des Nordatlantik.* Leipzig: Koehler & Amelang.

Wistrich, Robert. 1982. *Who's Who in Nazi Germany*. New York: Macmillan.

Wulff, Wilhelm. 1973. *Zodiac and Swastika: How Astrology Guided Hitler's Germany*. New York: Coward, McCann & Geoghegan. [Original German title: *Tierkreis und Hakenkreuz*.]

PERIODICALS

Germanien, 1929–1943.

Runen: Zeitschrift für germanische Geistesoffenbarungen und Wissenschaften (Merkblatt für den Freundschaftsgrad des Germanen-Ordens Walvater).

Der Schulungsbrief.

Das Schwarze Korps: Zeitung der Schutzstaffelnder NSDAP. Berlin, 1935–1944.

INDEX

BOOKS OF RELATED INTEREST

Revival of the Runes
The Modern Rediscovery and Reinvention of the Germanic Runes
by Stephen E. Flowers, Ph.D.

The Fraternitas Saturni
History, Doctrine, and Rituals of the Magical Order
of the Brotherhood of Saturn
by Stephen E. Flowers, Ph.D.

Original Magic
The Rituals and Initiations of the Persian Magi
by Stephen E. Flowers, Ph.D.

Icelandic Magic
Practical Secrets of the Northern Grimoires
by Stephen E. Flowers, Ph.D.

Lords of the Left-Hand Path
Forbidden Practices and Spiritual Heresies
by Stephen E. Flowers, Ph.D.

The Secret of the Runes
Translated by Guido von List
Edited by Stephen E. Flowers, Ph.D.

The Magian Tarok
The Origins of the Tarot in the Mithraic and Hermetic Traditions
by Stephen E. Flowers, Ph.D.

Secret Practices of the Sufi Freemasons
The Islamic Teachings at the Heart of Alchemy
by Baron Rudolf von Sebottendorff
Translated by Stephen E. Flowers, Ph.D.

INNER TRADITIONS • BEAR & COMPANY
P.O. Box 388
Rochester, VT 05767
1-800-246-8648
www.InnerTraditions.com
Or contact your local bookseller